"It is propitious to have readily available single-session therapy for those who often desperately seek the relief that psychiatry and psychotropic medications have not and are not able to provide. This book illustrates incisive and immediate interventions for such patients."

—Nicholas A. Cummings, Ph.D., Sc.D., former President, American Psychological Association; President, Cummings Foundation for Behavioral Health; author of *The Collected Papers of Nicholas A. Cummings* and *Understanding the Behavioral Healthcare Crisis*

"All the most important authors, the most recent results, and the most important applications are in *Single-Session Therapy by Walk-In or Appointment.* It is the best resource for anyone who wants to know how to help people in each single — and often unique —session."

—Dr. Flavio Cannistrá, Director of the Italian Institute for Single-Session Therapy, Rome; and co-editor of *The Italian Handbook of Single-Session Therapy*

"This informative and engaging book features detailed accounts of single-session therapy and highlights ways to implement walk-in clinics in a culturally sensitive fashion. Kudos to these pioneers for providing innovative ways to offer mental-health services."

—Donald H. Meichenbaum, Ph.D., Distinguished Professor Emeritus, University of Waterloo, Ontario, Canada; and Research Director of the Melissa Institute for Violence Prevention and Treatment, Miami, Florida; author of *Roadmap to Resilience* and *The Evolution of Cognitive Behavioral Therapy*

"*Single-Session Therapy by Walk-In or Appointment* opens our eyes to the power of the single session as a service delivery model that crosses theoretical orientations, cultures, and contexts. This collection offers an outstanding guide for practice."

—Shelley Green, Ph.D., Professor of Family Therapy, Nova Southeastern University, Fort Lauderdale, Florida; co-editor, *Quickies: The Handbook of Brief Sex Therapy*

Single-Session Therapy by Walk-In or Appointment

Single-Session Therapy by Walk-In or Appointment is based on the finding that one session is often all a client will need and choose to attend. The option of a single-session responds to the growing need for greater accessibility and responsiveness of mental-health services. With considerable data supporting both the demand for and the effectiveness of walk-in and by-appointment single sessions, the field is expanding rapidly. This book includes many clinical examples and cultural nuances, as well as discussions of recent research, training and supervision, and implementation and administrative arrangements. This is an essential title for clinicians, program developers, and policy makers interested in providing the effective, client-responsive, economic option of one-at-a-time single-session therapy on a walk-in or by-appointment basis.

Michael F. Hoyt, Ph.D., is a psychologist based in Mill Valley, California. One of the originators (with M. Talmon and R. Rosenbaum) of the Single-Session Therapy approach, he is the author of *Brief Therapy and Beyond* and numerous other publications.

Monte Bobele, Ph.D., is Professor Emeritus at Our Lady of the Lake University in San Antonio, Texas. He coedited (with A. Slive) *When One Hour is All You Have: Effective Therapy for Walk-In Clients.*

Arnold Slive, Ph.D., is an adjunct professor at Our Lady of the Lake University in San Antonio, Texas. He coedited (with M. Bobele) *When One Hour is All You Have: Effective Therapy for Walk-In Clients.*

Jeff Young, Ph.D., is the Director at the Bouverie Centre at La Trobe University in Melbourne, Australia, where he and his team have trained thousands of professionals in the use of single-session therapy and helped many agencies implement SST services.

Moshe Talmon, Ph.D., is a clinical psychologist based in Israel. He is a lecturer at Tel Aviv University. One of the originators (with M. Hoyt and R. Rosenbaum) of the SST approach, he is the author of *Single Session Therapy: Maximizing the Effect of the First (and Often Only) Therapeutic Encounter.*

Single-Session Therapy by Walk-In or Appointment

Administrative, Clinical, and Supervisory Aspects of One-at-a-Time Services

Edited by

Michael F. Hoyt
Monte Bobele
Arnold Slive
Jeff Young
Moshe Talmon

Routledge
Taylor & Francis Group
NEW YORK AND LONDON

First published 2018
by Routledge
711 Third Avenue, New York, NY 10017

and by Routledge
2 Park Square, Milton Park, Abingdon, Oxon, OX14 4RN

Routledge is an imprint of the Taylor & Francis Group, an informa business

Library of Congress Cataloging-in-Publication Data
A catalog record for this title has been requested

ISBN: 978-0-8153-6237-1 (hbk)
ISBN: 978-0-8153-6238-8 (pbk)
ISBN: 978-1-351-11243-7 (ebk)

Typeset in Galliard
by Keystroke, Neville Lodge, Tettenhall, Wolverhampton

"A journey of a thousand miles begins with a single step."
—Lao Tzu (6th century BCE)

Contents

List of Illustrations

Figures

Tables

About the Contributors

Editors

Michael F. Hoyt, Ph.D. is a psychologist based in Mill Valley, California. One of the originators (with Moshe Talmon and Bob Rosenbaum) of the SST approach, he was a staff member at Kaiser Permanente for more than 30 years. He is a recipient of the APF Cummings Psyche Prize for lifetime contributions to the role of psychologists in organized healthcare, and has been honored as a Continuing Education Distinguished Speaker by both the American Psychological Association and the International Association of Marriage and Family Counselors. He has authored and edited numerous books, including *Brief Therapy and Managed Care*; *Some Stories Are Better than Others*; *The Handbook of Constructive Therapies*; *Brief Psychotherapies: Principles and Practices*; *Therapist Stories of Inspiration, Passion, and Renewal: What's Love Got to Do with It?*; *Capturing the Moment: Single Session Therapy and Walk-In Services* (with Talmon); and *Brief Therapy and Beyond: Stories, Language, Love, Hope, and Time.*

Monte Bobele, Ph.D., ABPP is Professor Emeritus of Psychology at Our Lady of the Lake University (OLLU) in San Antonio, Texas. He coedited *When One Hour is All You Have: Effective Therapy for Walk-In Clients.* He introduced the walk-in/single-session model to OLLU's Community Counseling Service over 20 years ago. He received the Texas Psychological Association's 2012 Outstanding Contribution to Education Award, and OLLU's 2013 Fleming Award for Teaching Excellence. In 2011, he was awarded a Fulbright Specialist Grant to help develop a walk-in service in a university clinic in Mexico City. He has since consulted on the opening of several other walk-in services in Mexico. He has taught graduate courses and trainings in single-session therapy in the U.S., Mexico, Australia, and Canada. He has also been involved in OLLU's program designed to train culturally and linguistically competent psychologists to work with Spanish-speaking populations and has co-led several immersion programs in Mexico.

Arnold Slive, Ph.D. is a licensed psychologist (Texas). He is an AAMFT Clinical Fellow as well as an Approved Supervisor for more than 25 years.

He is a visiting professor at Our Lady of the Lake University in San Antonio, Texas. He formerly lived in Calgary, Alberta, Canada, where he was a founder of Eastside Family Centre, and had a 20-year relationship with Wood's Homes as Clinical Director and consultant. He is a past president of the Alberta Association of Marriage and Family Therapy. He is the recipient of the Divisional Contribution Award (AAMFT) and the Innovative Services to Family Award. He is a Fulbright Specialist and coeditor of *When One Hour is All You Have: Effective Counseling for Walk-In Clients* (2011). Arnie now lives in Austin, Texas, where he consults to family agencies, operates a small private practice, teaches, and has assisted in the development of two walk-in single-session counseling services.

Jeff Young, Ph.D. is the Director of The Bouverie Centre, Victoria's Family Institute, La Trobe University in Melbourne, Australia. He is a clinical psychologist and family therapist who has worked, published, and presented in the area of mental health for over 30 years. Jeff and his team have trained thousands of professionals in the use of single-session therapy and helped many services implement SST as an efficient and accessible service delivery model. He is also developing a book describing an approach to therapy for working with people who don't like counseling or counselors. Jeff has been the President of the Victorian Association of Family Therapists, the President of the *Australian & New Zealand Journal of Family Therapy*, and a member of the editorial committee for the *Dulwich Centre Newsletter*. In 2017 he received the *Australian and New Zealand Journal of Family Therapy* award for distinguished contributions to family therapy.

Moshe Talmon, Ph.D. is a clinical psychologist based in Israel. He received his doctorate at the University of Pennsylvania and interned at the Philadelphia Child Guidance Clinic. He is a senior lecturer at the Academic College of Tel Aviv-Yaffo and the international program at Tel Aviv University. During his tenure at Kaiser Permanente (1985-1991) he initiated a series of studies on single-session therapy (with Michael Hoyt and Robert Rosenbaum). He is the author of the bestselling *Single Session Therapy: Maximizing the Effect of the First (and Often Only) Therapeutic Encounter* and of *Single Session Solutions: A Guide to Practical, Effective, and Affordable Therapy*; he is also the coeditor (with Hoyt) of *Capturing the Moment: Single Session Therapy and Walk-In Services.* He provides consultation, training, and supervision worldwide.

Additional Authors

"Ariane" is a young caregiver, high school graduate, and visitor to a walk-in therapy clinic.

Rachel Barbara-May, M.S.W., is the Chief Social Worker at Alfred Child and Youth Mental Health Service, Melbourne, Australia. She is also the workforce development coordinator at Headspace South East in Melbourne.

Monica Barnes, R.N., M.N., is a therapist with the Adult Mental Health Program and Single Session Walk-In Clinic at the South Calgary Health Centre in Calgary, Alberta, Canada.

Joanna Bedggood, M.S.W., R.S.W., is Manager of Student Wellness, Student Support Services, King's University College at Western University, Ontario, Canada. Formerly, she was the Director of the Walk-In Counselling Clinic at KW Counselling Services in Kitchener, Ontario, Canada.

Cheryl-Anne Cait, M.S.W., Ph.D., is an associate professor at the Faculty of Social Work at Wilfrid Laurier University and has worked at Laurier since 2002. She has over 25 years' experience working as a clinical social worker in community mental health and in inpatient and outpatient psychiatry with children, adolescents and their families.

Patricia Carruthers, R.P.N., Ph.D., is a Clinical Nurse Specialist in the Adult Mental Health and Single Session Walk-In Clinic at the South Calgary Health Centre in Calgary, Alberta, Canada.

Kevin M. Conroy, Ph.D., is a Catholic priest and the Director of Maryknoll Mental Health Program (Cambodia), which develops mental health services with the poor. He has worked in Cambodia for 12 years assisting to develop the graduate program in Clinical Psychology at Royal University of Phnom Penh (RUPP).

Scot Cooper, B.A., R.P., is a Registered Psychotherapist, international trainer and consultant in brief narrative therapy. He is a supervisor of the Child Clinical/Brief Services at HN REACH, a children's mental-health center in Caledonia, Ontario, Canada where he practices, supervises students, and oversees the Walk-In Clinic. He is also the lead for Brief Narrative Practices, a portal to personalized post-graduate specialty training and consultation in brief therapy.

Paul Denborough, M.D., is a child and youth psychiatrist and the Clinical Director of Alfred Child and Youth Mental Health Service and Headspace South East, Melbourne, Australia.

Cindy Jing Fang, M.S.W., R.S.W., is a Research Assistant at the Research Department of Wood's Homes in Calgary, Canada.

Chrystal Fullen, M.S. is a 4th year doctoral candidate at Our Lady of the Lake University. She works in the community providing psychotherapy and assessment services to children and adults at multiple training clinics. She supervises graduate students in OLLU's Community Counseling Service and is completing her dissertation on SST.

Maja Gigovic, M.Sc., R. Psych., is a psychologist at the Adult Mental Health Program and Single Session Walk-In Clinic at the South Calgary Health Centre in Calgary, Alberta, Canada.

Brian Guthrie, Ph.D., R.S.W., is Associate Professor, Department of Child Studies and Social Work, Mount Royal University, Calgary, Alberta, Canada.

Adriana Gil-Wilkerson, M.S., is a faculty member at the Houston Galveston Institute and is the Walk-In Counseling Program Coordinator. She is also a doctoral candidate at Sam Houston State University.

Sandy Harper-Jaques, R.N., M.N., R.M.F.T., is a marriage and family therapist and a registered nurse. She is the owner of Resonance Counseling and Consulting in Calgary, Alberta, Canada; and also works at the Mental Health Walk-In service at the South Calgary Health Centre.

Brittany Houston, M.S. is a 4th year psychology doctoral student at Our Lady of the Lake University. She has provided therapeutic and assessment services to adults and children in a variety of settings, including private practice, veteran hospitals, university counseling centers, non-profits, and schools.

Leslie Josling, B.Sc., M.Sc., G.Dipl., R.S.W., is the Executive Director of KW Counselling Services in Kitchener, Ontario. She has been developing and managing innovative psychotherapeutic services for children and adults for over 25 years.

Susan B. Levin, Ph.D., is the Executive Director of the Houston Galveston Institute; she is also on the faculty of Our Lady of the Lake University Master's psychology program, and is an Associate of the Taos Institute.

Bruce MacLaurin, M.S.W., is an Assistant Professor at the Faculty of Social Work, University of Calgary; and a Senior Researcher at Wood's Homes. His research and publishing is focused primarily on child maltreatment, youth at risk, child welfare service delivery, and outcome measurement. He has 15 years of front-line and management experience in non-profit child and family services in Alberta and Ontario.

Ashlee M. Martinez, M.S., is a Doctoral Candidate at Our Lady of the Lake University, and the General Mental Health Psychology Doctoral Intern at South Texas Veterans Health Care System in San Antonio, Texas. She also serves as an Adjunct Instructor at OLLU and Research Area Specialist for the Department of Family and Community Medicine at University of Texas Health, San Antonio.

Nancy McElheran, A.N., M.N., A.A.M.F.T., is a Licensed Clinical Nurse Specialist and an AAMFT Clinical Fellow and Approved Supervisor. She was the Director and Clinical Coordinator of the Eastside Family Centre in Calgary, Canada and was involved in its development and operation for 17 years. She maintains her consultation, supervisory and teaching role at the Eastside Family Centre.

Tess McGrane, M.S., M.Clin.Fam.Th., is leading the single session family therapy service at Headspace Elsternwick in Melbourne, Australia. She is also a senior nurse in the workforce development team at Alfred Psychiatry.

John K. Miller, Ph.D., L.M.F.T., is a Full Professor in the School of Social Development and Public Policy in the Department of Social Work at Fudan University in Shanghai, and an Adjunct Professor in the Department of Psychology at the Royal University of Phnom Penh (RUPP) in Cambodia. He is also the Director of the Sino-American Family Therapy Institute (SAFTI) and has been leading scholarly, academic, and humanitarian exchanges to Cambodia for the past 12 years.

Lacey Moffat, M.S., is a Doctoral Candidate at Our Lady of the Lake. She is currently a Doctoral Psychology Intern at the Southern Louisiana Internship Consortium in Baton Rouge, Louisiana. Her internship placement includes working with students at the Louisiana State University's Counseling Center as well as at East Louisiana Mental Health System in Jackson, Louisiana providing therapy and assessment to the adult forensic population.

Margaret Oakander, B.Sc. (Hons), M.D., F.R.C.P. (C), is an Associate Clinical Professor in the Department of Psychiatry, University of Calgary. She is the Clinical Medical Director of Sunridge Primary Mental Health Clinic and the Southern Alberta Shared Mental Health Care Program. She is also the Senior Medical Advisor for the Eastside Family Centre in Calgary and has consulted there since the Centre's inception in 1990.

Harry Park, M.S.W., R.S.W., is an accredited Clinical Social Worker and Supervisor with the Alberta College of Social Work. Harry was involved in the creation of the Eastside Family Centre in 1990 and with the development of its clinical approach and continues to provide consultation and supervision at the Centre.

Jason J. Platt, Ph.D., is a Professor at Alliant International University and the Director of the International Center for Therapy and Dialogue in Mexico City, Mexico.

Sylvia Rapini De Yatim, M.S., is a licensed professional counselor working with the bilingual team at the Houston Galveston Institute's Walk-In Counseling Center. She is also a doctoral student in the Counseling Psychology program at Our Lady of the Lake University.

Alexandra Robinson, M.Sc., is a previous student and clinician at Eastside Family Centre and is now a predoctoral clinical psychology intern at the International Multicultural Counseling and Education Center in Los Angeles. Alexandra is particularly interested in effective ways to use single-session therapy to serve the most vulnerable and underserved populations.

Irma J. Rodriguez, M.A., is the Director of Centro Atención a la Comunidad (CAC) in Mexico City; Faculty and Supervisor at Grupo Campos Elíseos (GCE, Mexico) and the Houston Galveston Institute (HGI), where she is the organizer of the International Summer Institute and a member of the International Certification of Collaborative Practices. She is a family therapist and also maintains a private practice.

Robert Rosenbaum, Ph.D., is a psychotherapist, neuropsychologist, and international teacher of Dayan (Wild Goose) qigong and Zen meditation. He is based in Sacramento, California. He was a co-originator (with Talmon and Hoyt) of the Single-Session Therapy approach.

Pam Rycroft, M. Psych, is a psychologist and family therapist who works at the Bouverie Centre in Melbourne, Victoria. Currently her work has a focus on supervising and training workers in various health and welfare roles.

Jeanette Santos, M.A., is a bilingual (Spanish-English) Psychology Doctoral Candidate at Our Lady of the Lake University. She is currently an active duty psychology resident at Lackland Air Force Base in San Antonio, Texas.

Martin Söderquist, Ph.D., is a licensed psychologist and family therapist. He is currently working as a couples counselor in Malmö, Sweden.

Terry Soo-Hoo, Ph.D., is Professor of Educational Psychology, California State University East Bay, Hayward, California. He is also the Clinical Director of the Mental Research Institute (MRI). He provides culturally sensitive therapy and conducts training and consultation for organizations and mental-health agencies.

Janet Stewart, R. Psych., is the manager of the Eastside Family Centre in Calgary, Canada. She has been with Wood's Homes as a crisis counselor and an intensive treatment and walk-in therapy clinician for 14 years. She has played a critical role in the implementation of the outcome measurement approach at the Eastside Family Centre.

Karen Story, B.A., M.C.P.P., M.C.F.T., is a social worker, child and adolescent psychotherapist, and family therapist. She currently works as a member of the Acquired Brain Injury team at the Bouverie Centre in Melbourne, Australia; she also maintains a private practice.

Mary Weeks, M.S.W., L.I.S.W., is Executive Director of Walk-In Counseling Center, in Minneapolis, Minnesota, started in 1969 as one of the first free, anonymous, no-appointment counseling centers with all clinical services provided by volunteers.

Karen Young, M.S.W., R.S.W., is the Director of Windz Institute, a brief and narrative therapy training center in Ontario operated by Reach Out Centre for Kids. Karen trains therapists and counselors at organizations across

Canada and internationally in single-session, walk-in, and brief therapies informed by narrative practices.

Lori Zook-Stanley, M.S.W., L.I.C.S.W., has a private psychotherapy practice in Minneapolis, Minnesota. She is a former Clinical Director of Walk-In Counseling Center in Minneapolis.

Acknowledgments

Many heads, hearts, and hands collaborated in the making of this book. We express our deep appreciation:

- to the clients/patients whose stories are contained herein, to the authors who wrote the chapters, and to the agencies and other settings that provided the clinical services described;
- to Wood's Homes and the Eastside Family Centre for their generous support of the *Capturing the Moment 2: Scaling New Heights in Single Session Therapy and Walk-In Services* symposium held in Banff, Canada (September 28–30, 2015) where earlier versions of many of the papers contained herein were first presented; and to United Way, the University of Calgary, and PlyGem for additional sponsorship of the conference;
- to Lillian Rand and the editorial board at Routledge Publishing for embracing this project, and to Keystroke for its excellent production;
- to the writers, illustrators, and publishers who permitted use of copyrighted materials;
- to our respective academic and clinical institutions: for Hoyt, Kaiser Permanente, the Stanley Garfield Memorial Award for Clinical Innovation and the APF Cummings Psyche Prize; for Bobele and Slive, Our Lady of the Lake University, San Antonio; for Young, the Bouverie Centre at La Trobe University, Melbourne; and for Talmon, Kaiser Permanente and the Stanley Garfield Memorial Award for Clinical Innovation, Tel-Aviv University and the Academic College of Tel Aviv-Yaffo;
- to our colleagues, teachers, and students, for expanding the conversation about health and hope;
- to one another, for the pleasures of teamwork and mutual learning; and
- to our families and friends for their love and support.

Michael F. Hoyt, Mill Valley, California
Monte Bobele, San Antonio, Texas
Arnold Slive, Austin, Texas
Jeff Young, Melbourne, Victoria, Australia
Moshe Talmon, Herzeliya, Israel

Section 1

Editors' Introduction

1 Single-Session/One-at-a-Time Walk-In Therapy

Michael F. Hoyt, Monte Bobele, Arnold Slive, Jeff Young, and Moshe Talmon

The town of Banff, perched in the beautiful Canadian Rockies, was the site for the appropriately named Capturing the Moment 2: Scaling New Heights in Single Session Therapy and Walk-In Services symposium held September 28–30, 2015.[1] Building on the first Capturing the Moment conference, which was held near Melbourne, Australia during March 2012, an international group of presenters and a keenly attentive audience came together in Banff from Canada, the U.S., Israel, Australia, Haiti, China, Finland, Mexico, and Sweden to exchange the latest information about developments in the rapidly growing field of single-session, walk-in, and one-at-a-time therapy. Therapy models and techniques, cultural nuances, implementation of service delivery systems, issues of training and supervision, and research findings were discussed and explored.

While many of the contributions contained herein were inspired by those presentations, they are much amplified. The papers are carefully curated around the theme of single-session/one-at-a-time therapy (SST/OAAT), and there are papers in this book that were not presented at the conference and conference papers that were not included in this book. As will be discussed later, the book is distinguished by its clear focus on the practice of SST/OAAT, by its attention to the walk-in (and by-appointment) delivery model, by its range of contexts and applications, by a broad array of clinical case examples, and by its assortment of contributing expert practitioners.

The field of Single-Session Therapy (SST) is expanding rapidly, as more consumers use one-at-a-time (OAAT) services in clinics, health maintenance organizations, and walk-in (and call-in and online) counseling centers. The growing need for accessible services that are responsive to client need is increasingly being recognized by practicing professionals and by graduate students preparing for careers in healthcare, as well as by funders, program planners, and policymakers interested in cost-effective service delivery systems.

Intentional SST/OAAT

Although therapists have sometimes seen clients for one visit of successful therapy since the time of Freud (see Sproel, 1975; Bloom, 1981/1992), the concept of intentional (or planned) Single-Session Therapy was most clearly articulated by Talmon (1990, p. xv; see Chapter 10 this volume) in his eponymous book, *Single Session Therapy: Maximizing the Effect of the First (and Often Only) Therapeutic Encounter*: "Single-session therapy is defined here as one face-to-face meeting between a therapist and patient with no previous or subsequent sessions within one year. As such, SST is the most frequently used length of therapy."[2]

Along with colleagues Bob Rosenbaum and Michael Hoyt, in the late 1980s, Talmon conducted studies of SST at a large health maintenance organization (Kaiser Permanente) based in Northern California. After examining the existing clinical and research literature, they retrospectively reviewed the charts of 200 patients who had *de facto* attended therapy for only one visit and found that many of the patients had been very satisfied with their one-session experience and did not feel the need for continuing therapy. Talmon and his colleagues then prospectively treated a series of 58 outpatients, ages 8 to 80, with a wide range of diagnoses. They presented statistical data and clinical examples in a series of publications (Talmon, 1990, 1993; Hoyt, et. al., 1992; Rosenbaum, et al., 1990). Their basic quantitative findings were that:

- over half of the patients (58.6%) elected to complete their therapy in one session even when more sessions were available
- more than 88% reported significant improvement in their original "presenting complaint" and more than 65% also reported "ripple" improvements in related areas of functioning, and
- while not experimentally assigned to one session or longer, on follow-up there was no difference in satisfaction and outcome scores between those who chose to stop after one visit (SST) versus those who continued for more sessions.

It is important to recognize that in the Kaiser study, clients were advised that although more sessions would be available if desired, the therapist's intention was to work with them to see if one session could be adequate to meet their needs. Although earlier there had been reports of incidental one-off sessions where the therapists' expectations were for on-going therapy, this "SST" approach was different. *SST is therapy that the therapist expects, from the beginning, to potentially comprise a single visit. The therapist acts as if the first session will be the last.* It is a planned, deliberate approach to make the most of the first encounter, informed by the research that shows many clients will not return for future planned sessions. As Hymmen, Stalker, and Cait (2013, p. 61) have written:

> SST refers to a conscious approach to make the most of the first session knowing it may be the only session the client decides to attend—not to the situation where there is an expectation that the client will attend multiple sessions but chooses to attend just one. Service delivery methodologies that make the most of the first session, whilst providing options for further

support should clients decide they want further support can be scheduled or provided in a "walk-in counseling clinic."

As we will see in the following chapters, there are many ways in which SST thinking can influence a range of practice situations. Single-session therapists employ a variety of theoretical models and work in diverse settings: clinics, private-practice offices, hospital consultation-liaisons, "second-opinion" interviews, and clinical demonstrations.[3] What these practices all have in common is the idea that *all we really have is now and this one meeting may be enough—or may be all that the client will decide to attend.* Contact data suggests that when therapy is organized with a planned and deliberate attitude that one session may be sufficient, clients frequently decide one session is adequate and choose to attend only that one session; although perhaps 50% will decide they require further work and will return for at least another visit (Young & Rycroft, 2012; Young, Rycroft, & Weir, 2014—see Chapter 3 this volume).[4]

In his Foreword to Slive and Bobele's (2011) book, Hoyt (p. xii) referred to SST as being "one at a time." Bobele and Slive (2014) elaborated this idea in their chapter, "One Session at a Time: When You Have a Whole Hour." We chose the title of the present volume, *Single-Session Therapy by Walk-In or Appointment: Administrative, Clinical, and Supervisory Aspects of One-at-a-Time Services*, to emphasize just that: *therapy takes place one contact at a time, and one contact may be all the time that is needed.*[5] Rosenbaum (2008, p. 8), one of the co-originators of the SST approach, put it this way: "Psychotherapy is not long or short; to view it this way sets up a false dichotomy. Psychotherapy depends instead on 'good moments' where something profound shifts for a client. All the rest is preparation and consolidation."

SST/OAAT addresses the dilemma of how to provide the opportunity for a single session to be sufficient while providing options for on-going care and support. This has led to innovative walk-in services. Developed in response to community consultation, walk-in services are beginning to have a considerable impact on health service provision in parts of Canada and the United States—and are expanding worldwide.

Walk Right In and Sit Right Down: A Brief History of Walk-In Services

Recognizing that, if it were accessible and affordable, many clients would come for psychological (and medical) help just at their moment of need, in 1967 both the Los Angeles Free Clinic (now called the Saban Clinic) and the Haight-Ashbury (San Francisco) Free Clinic were established to provide such services. Two years later, in 1969 the Minneapolis Walk-In Counseling Clinic (see Chapter 9, this volume) opened its doors. In Calgary, Canada, the Wood's Homes Eastside Family Centre began in 1990 to provide walk-in/single-session community-based mental-health services (Clements, McElheran, Hackney, & Park, 2011; McElheran, et al., 2014; Slive, Maclaurin, Oakander, & Amundson, 1995; Slive, McElheran, & Lawson. 2008; see Chapter 5). In the early 1990s, while on an American Association for Marriage and Family Therapy (AAMFT) site visit to Calgary, Monte Bobele met Arnie Slive and saw the innovative work being done; he subsequently brought the idea back to San Antonio, Texas, and began to incorporate WI/SST training and services into the graduate counseling psychology programs at Our Lady of the Lake University.

Slive, et al. (2008, p. 6) succinctly described the essentials of a WI/SST service:

> Developed . . . as a result of community demands for greater accessibility to mental health services, walk-in therapy enables clients to meet with a mental health professional at their moment of choosing. There is no red tape, no triage, no intake process, no waiting list, and no wait. There is no formal assessment, no formal diagnostic process, just one hour of therapy focused on clients' stated wants. As well as meeting client needs, walk-in therapy is highly rewarding to professionals due to the simple fact that the clients' ability to access the service at their chosen moments of need without having to jump over multiple hurdles means that a large percentage are highly motivated. Also, with walk-in therapy there are no missed appointments or cancellations, thereby increasing efficiency.

Bobele and Slive (2014, p. 98) also noted that a walk-in session can be both a discrete event and part of a larger process:

> We prefer to think of walk-in therapy as a solitary pearl. Pearls begin as a solution to an oyster's problem. The formation of a pearl has a beginning, a middle, and a point where it is complete. If a jeweler anticipates making a long string of pearls, then each one is understood as related to, connected to, the one before and the one to come. Therapy is a lot like this process. If therapists view each session as connected to the one before and a precursor to the ones to come, then no session truly stands on its own. Instead, it is always contextualized by what came before and the anticipation of what is coming after.

Many of the chapters in this book describe ways, both administratively and clinically, that such services can be organized to provide timely access. Clients[6] who walk in often come expecting a single session—and some may intermittently return again for another single session, or for more continuous services.

The Emerging Empirical Basis for SST/OAAT Practice

Case studies and aggregate statistics are both empirical (from the Greek *empeirokos*, meaning "experienced" or "based on observation"). The idiographic-nomothetic debate has a long history in psychology and counseling (Cone, 1986; McLeod, 2007). *Idiographic* (from the Greek *idios*) means "own" or "private" and refers to what is individual or unique; *nomothetic* (from the Greek *nomos*) means "law" and refers to what is common or general. Idiographic studies are usually qualitative (e.g., case reports), whereas nomothetic studies are usually quantitative and based on comparisons of numerical data across groups. Both can be valuable although, as May (1958) recognized, qualitative case studies actually can be ***more*** empirical because they are more experience-close and convey more of what actually happens in a therapeutic encounter.

Hurn (2005, p. 35) observed that "it seems that Single-Session Therapy may be very hard to define. In addition, the bespoke nature of the session produces many differences that can impede a sound methodology when researching this form of therapy." Moreover, as Jerome Frank commented in his foreword to Talmon's (1990, p. xi) *Single Session Therapy*, the brevity of effective SST may be problematic for researchers who assume that successful psychotherapy requires considerable time because "improvement after a single session must occur before the postulated therapeutic mechanisms [e.g., gradual working through of unconscious patterns] have had time to work" (p. xi).

SST is essentially a delivery system (not a specific "school" or theoretical approach – see Chapter 3). The most significant evidence supporting the adoption of a SST approach is client contact data that all schools of counseling and theoretical approaches need to address: ***that a large number of clients will attend only one session, whether this is planned or not.*** This simple finding has a profound implication for all approaches to counseling. SST is a contextual model, a socially situated healing practice that endeavors to activate clients' own resources (see Bohart & Tallman, 1999; Duncan, et al., 2010; Wampold & Imel, 2015).

Most practicing clinicians learn from immersion in the study of their own cases (reflection and supervision) as well as those of others. Toward this goal, there is a considerable idiographic SST literature available (see Slive & Bobele, 2011; Hoyt & Talmon, 2014). However, nomothetic-quantitative research can also provide instruction and encouragement, demonstrating that all practitioners will have a significant number of clients attending for one session and that outcomes of this one session are often positive. Consider the following sampling, which was drawn from a broad range of service practitioners and contexts:

- Researchers have found that brief therapy reduces medical utilization, and this has been known for a long time (see Mumford, et al., 1984). Follette and Cummings (1967) reported a 60% reduction in medical utilization over a 5-year period after a single session of psychotherapy in a study at Kaiser Permanente. Cummings and Follette (1976) reported the benefits of SST to still be in effect after 8 years and attributed reduced medical utilization to decreases in emotional stress. Schade, Torres, and Beyerbach (2011) in a study in Santiago, Chile, reported a brief family intervention reduced medical costs for somataform patients.
- Malan, et al. (1968) in a study at the Tavistock Clinic in London found that 51% of "untreated" neurotic patients that had only an intake interview

showed less symptomatology; and in a follow-up, Malan, et al. (1975) reported that half of those patients, who were judged to have showed increased insight into a central conflict and to have expressed a sense of personal responsibility, were found to have made important and enduring psychodynamic modifications.

- Talmon (1990) found that, at Kaiser Permanente in Northern California, 34 of 58 (58.6%) outpatients with a variety of problems elected to complete therapy in one session and more than 88% reported continuing to benefit on 3- and 13-month follow-up.
- Kellner, et al. (1992), at the University of New Mexico-Albuquerque, reported two single-session treatments that significantly reduced recurring nightmares.
- Kaffman (1995) reported that of 211 patients in an Israeli kibbutz, one-third needed only one session of therapy to report continuous improvement.
- Boyan (1996) surveyed the first 50 families seen at the Bouverie Centre's SST pilot program. Of the 36 families who agreed to participate in the research, 53% elected to attend only one session, 78% reported that their presenting problems were much improved (56%) or a little better (22%) as a result of the one session and 100% said they would recommend the service to others. In another study (O'Neill, 2017) at the Bouverie Centre, 25 SST clients were interviewed by telephone and most reported that they were satisfied with the services they had received and those few who were concerned about the availability of services reported that their worries were alleviated once they met with the therapist.
- Campbell (1999) assessed the effectiveness of SST interventions on family coping. Results from 33 families who completed both the pre and post measures indicated significant reduction on the problem measures and significant increases on coping measures.
- Hampson, et al. (1999) at a child and adolescent mental health center in Canberra, Australia, found that 96% (N = 70) were satisfied with the scheduled SST and 88% reported the session helpful.
- Stacey, et al. (2001) reported that brief family therapy, including single session therapy, yielded enduring benefits for most children according to parents' questionnaire ratings and telephone interviews.
- Humfress, et al. (2002) found that a single session of motivational interviewing was more effective in helping psychiatric patients comply with and benefit from treatment than the counseling they would usually have received.
- McCambridge and Strang (2004), Daley and Zuckoff (1998), and Carroll, et al. (2001) found a single session of motivational interviewing to significantly reduce alcohol and drug abuse.
- Perkins (2006) and Perkins and Scarlett (2008) documented the effectiveness of single sessions with children and adolescents in Australia in comparison to a non-treatment control group.

- Lambrecht, et al. (2007) in Sheffield, England, reported reduced self-harm (overdoses and cutting) after one session of solution-focused brief therapy.
- Slive, et al. (1995), Miller and Slive (2004), and Miller (2008) reported high levels of client satisfaction for walk-in SSTs in several studies conducted at the Eastside Family Centre in Calgary, Canada.
- Weir, Wills, Young, and Perlesz (2008) reviewed community counseling services in Victoria, Australia, for more than 100,000 clients and found that 42% chose to have a single session even when more sessions were offered. Another study, by Carey, Tai, & Stiles (2013) in Alice Springs, Australia, also found that letting clients schedule appointments when they desired was effective and efficient.
- Gilboa-Shechtman and Shahar (2006), in an article aptly entitled "The Sooner, the Better," present evidence in their study of psychotherapy for depression that early positive responders were more likely to maintain gains.
- Kashdan, et al. (2012) found in a randomized clinical trial that one session of exposure therapy yielded superior results. Similar one-session positive results were reported by Ollendick, et al. (2009) with youth in the U.S. and in Sweden having spider phobias; and by Basoglu, Salcioglu, and Livanou (2007) for people experiencing PTSD after the 1999 Turkish earthquake. Nuthall and Townend (2007) also reported a CBT-based early intervention to be effective in preventing panic disorder.
- Church (2014; also see Church, 2016) reported that emotional freedom techniques (EFT) in one session yielded positive results in a variety of studies involving anxiety and PTSD.
- Harper-Jaques and Foucault (2014) assessed 98 clients who completed all questionnaires one month after being seen at the walk-in service at the South Calgary (Canada) Health Centre and found high satisfaction, lower distress, and increased hope; moreover, 44% reported that SST was adequate.
- Stalker, et al. (2015) compared outcomes for clients served in a walk-in service to clients served in a traditional by-appointment counseling agency. Walk-in clients improved faster and were less distressed than the clients who were served at a clinic where clients were seen multiple sessions by-appointment after being on a wait-list.
- Bartlett, et al. (2008) in a review that summarized the rate of stopping therapy after the first session as approximately 50%, appreciated that clients often achieved their original goals in a relatively brief period of time, but they still framed much of their discussion in terms of "dropping out," "early withdrawal," and "attrition." Westmacott and Hunsley (2010) found that the most frequently reported reason for stopping therapy was feeling better; a substantial minority of individuals also reported terminating because of treatment dissatisfaction or wanting to solve problems independently. In a meta-analysis of "premature discontinuation" in adult psychotherapy involving 669 studies and almost 84,000 clients, Swift and

Greenberg (2012) offered various definitions of "dropping out," including the client stopping the intervention without meeting "the therapeutic goals" or before "completing the full course of the intervention." They specified that "premature termination occurs unilaterally by the client, rather than through mutual agreement between the therapist and client to end treatment. Dropping out of therapy can be contrasted to both completing and rejecting therapy" (p. 547) and went on to note (p. 548) that "Therapist judgment has historically been considered the preferable classification . . . but this method depends on clinical judgment that can be biased and flawed . . ." They reported (p. 555) that "Dropout rates were highest when determined by therapist judgment (37.6%) and were lowest when determined by completion of a set of sessions (18.3%) or a treatment protocol (18.4%)" and acknowledged (p. 556) that, "In reality, some clients will recover from their distress and impairment in just a couple of sessions, and other clients may need 100+ sessions to recover . . . Research has found that therapist judgment is not always accurate . . . and clients and therapists sometimes disagree about how many sessions are needed." Similarly, a large-scale (N = 8482) multi-national World Health Organization survey reported 21.6% "dropping out" of mental-health treatment after the second visit and an overall 31.7% drop-out rate "defined [drop-out] as stopping treatment before the *provider* wanted" (Wells, et al., 2013, p. 42, emphasis added). Unfortunately, they did not ask the *patients* why they had stopped treatment, and there was no mention of the possibility of successful single session (or other brief) therapy.

- Rodda, et al. (2015) reported single-session web-based counseling to be beneficial for people seeking help for problem gambling.
- Binfet (2017), in a randomized controlled study of 163 university students in British Columbia, Canada, found that a single-session 20-minute exposure to a therapy dog resulted in significant decreases in perceived stress and homesickness and significant improvement in sense of school belonging. Other studies (see Green, 2014) have also reported the benefits of single-session equine-assisted therapy.
- Ryan and O'Connor (2017), reporting from Ireland, describe a feasibility study of a single-session psychology clinic for parents of children with autism spectrum disorder. Good attendance rates and a relatively high level of satisfaction suggest the single-session structure is an acceptable format; the authors call for more detailed investigation of the impact of sessions on both parental anxiety and child outcomes, as well as to help identify more clearly who may benefit most from this model. Earlier studies (some already cited, plus Fry, 2012 Gee, et al., 2015; Gibbons & Plath, 2012; Nieuwboer, Fukkink, & Hermanns, 2015; Sommers-Flanagan, 2007) also indicate value, both in terms of early access and clinical outcomes, of SST child-family programs.

After conducting a thorough review of relevant databases, Hymmen, et al. (2012, p. 1; also see Cameron, 2007) observed: "The findings suggest that the majority of clients attending either previously scheduled or walk-in SST find it sufficient and helpful." They also recommended (p. 11):

> This development provides a significant opportunity to begin a new chapter of SST research . . . While SST will likely continue to be adopted by resource-stretched community counseling and mental health programs, it remains vital that the field has evidence of the appropriateness and effectiveness of this approach.

The chapters in the present volume contain many additional reports, quantitative and qualitative, of successful SSTs.

Do People Really Benefit from One Session—and If So, How?

Extensive research and clinical experience (see Slive & Bobele, 2011; Hoyt & Talmon, 2014) have demonstrated that many people *do* benefit from one-at-a-time (single-session) therapy. A broad spectrum of theoretical approaches has been found to be helpful with many presenting problems (including anxiety and depression, grief, post-traumatic stress, self-harm, substance abuse, possible psychotic disorders, and intense interpersonal conflicts—not just "easy" cases). Our contributors provide additional important data about outcomes and processes later in this volume.

O'Hanlon and Weiner-Davis (1989, pp. 77–78) wrote: "We have observed enough 'one-session cures' to be utterly convinced that they are neither flukes, miracles, nor magic. Rather, something powerfully therapeutic occurs in the interaction between therapist and client during these sessions." How does a single session help? While there is no simple answer, in their review of the literature on SST and walk-in services, Talmon and Hoyt (2014) identified three interrelated important factors: mindset, time and client empowerment—each covered in more detail below.

Mindset

Each session is approached as a singular event, based on the belief that something good can come from one session and that the one session may be the last. Eric Berne (the originator of Transactional Analysis; quoted by Goulding & Goulding, 1979, p. 4, emphasis in original) would approach every group therapy session with the thought, "How can I cure everyone in this room *today*?" Wells and Phelps (1990, p. 16) noted the pressures for briefer, more efficient treatments and predicted "The Survival of the Shortest." In preparing a student for a first session with a new client, Jay Haley advised: "Maybe you don't have a case really, except for the first interview. That would be nice, I think. Every therapist should shoot for one session" (Haley & Richeport,

2003, p. 33). Toward that end, Hoyt, et al. (1992, p. 69) report that they would begin sessions with some variant of the following:

> Many people who come here and talk about their problems find that just one time can help a lot . . . I'm willing to work hard today to help you get a better handle on things. Does that sound like something you'd like to do?

Bobele, López, Scamardo, and Solórzano (2008, p. 87) highlighted the advantages of SST:

> Our single-session model normalizes the client's experience as much as possible. Change was promoted by emphasizing strengths, abilities, and skills . . . The therapist must be willing to approach clients from the stance, "Each session has the potential of being a single-session," to create an expectancy of change.

Bobele and Slive (2014, p. 98, emphasis in original; also see Chapter 2 this volume) amplify: "[O]ur belief [is] that any session could be the last session. We don't conduct any session as if there will be another session. In other words, we do *one session at a time*" and our clients (and therapists) do not expect any follow-up contact, in person or via phone or Internet. Young (Chapter 3) suggests that SST is everything that follows clinically and organizationally from accepting three findings: that the most common number of session is one; that these sessions are typically reported as sufficient by clients; and that it is not easy, if possible at all, to predict which clients will attend once and which clients will elect to return for further sessions. Young, et al. (2014) earlier had noted that a client may require and want further sessions and the service system should be able to provide both of these potentials. Walk-in/SST services provide this support by eschewing red tape, which allows clients to return as easily as they started. (SST by appointment also provides ways clients can access additional support.) The availability of options for a return single session (or longer) actually may encourage some clients (and therapists) to engage in a first session as if it may also be the last session.

The expectations that therapists (and clients) bring to the encounter do much to shape what happens (see Battino, 2006, 2014; Kirsch, 1990). Bobele and Slive (2014) listed a number of ideas that inform their one-at-a-time SST mindset:

- Clients know what works best for them.
- Clients are far less interested in psychotherapy than are therapists, and prefer brief therapeutic encounters.

- Clients frequently choose to attend only one session and overwhelmingly express satisfaction with that session.
- Research demonstrates that most change occurs early in therapy, followed by ever-decreasing improvements as sessions continue.
- Rapid change is not only possible, but also common in human experience. There is no established direct correlation between the severity and duration of a complaint and the duration of effective treatment.

Time

Single-Session Therapy is predicated on the therapist's belief and expectation that change can occur *in the moment.* Bobele and Slive (2014) remind us that we have "a WHOLE hour"; and Appelbaum (1975) observed "Parkinson's Law in Psychotherapy," the tendency for therapy to expand or contract to fit the time allotted.

When the American baseball player-cum-philosopher Yogi Berra was asked, "What time is it?" he reputedly replied, "Do you mean NOW?" Indeed, there is no time but the present. The idea that "this is it—we may only have this one meeting" helps to concentrate the mind and conveys the existential implication to "get on with it." The idea is that SST can help engender a pleasant urgency (rather than feeling frantic or pell-mell) for the client and the therapist. Sessions are necessarily "one-at-a-time" but not necessarily only one time. If the therapist or client decides that more sessions are needed, it does not denote an "SST failure" – rather, it simply means that more sessions are needed. Creating a no-failure context for client or therapist when only one session is required or when more sessions are required is a critical challenge.

Client empowerment

The fundamental assumption of all forms of deliberate brief therapy, including SST, is that clients have the capacity to alter their thoughts, emotions, and behaviors in order to bring about significant and beneficial changes (Hoyt, 2009). The single-session therapist endeavors to create a "context of competence" (Hoyt, 2014—see Chapter 11 this volume), helping the client to apply his or her skills to solve the problem that has brought them to therapy (see Figure 1.1).

There is also the related belief that once a person has made a change, there can be a positive cascade of "ripple effects." Thus, Haley (1982, p. 23) wrote: "The small change invariably led to the larger one. As [Milton] Erickson put it, if you want a large change you should ask for a small one."

Single-session (SST) and one-at-a-time (OAAT) therapy are *client-led* (or "client-driven") in four senses of the term:

"Basically, there's nothing wrong with you that what's right with you can't cure."

Figure 1.1 What's right with you (from *The New Yorker*, February 8, 1993. ©*The New Yorker*. Used with permission)

(1) *It is the client who elects and initiates therapy.* SST/OAAT "strikes while the iron is hot" and "captures the moment" to take advantage of the client's motivation.

(2) *It is the client who defines the goals of therapy.* This may entail both a description of reducing or eliminating a symptom, problem, or bothersome situation ("I'll not be so anxious and isolated") as well as, often with the assistance of the therapist, the articulation of what will be going on instead ("I'll be happy and more involved with people").[7] Taking a client's goals seriously and giving primacy to the client's views and values serves to engender hope and set a direction while creating a template for how therapist and client will work together.

(3) *It is the client whose existing skills, abilities, and competencies are seen as primary in making a difference.* "Our remedies often in ourselves do lie" said Shakespeare (in *All's Well that Ends Well*, Act I, Scene 1, line 216). As suggested by the cartoon in Figure 1.1, the strong focus is on whatever the client brings to the session that can be utilized to help the client achieve his/her/their goals. In this volume, various therapists—often identifying with a non-pathologizing solution-focused, collaborative, or narrative therapy approach—endeavor to identify and help clients apply

their own pre-existing (albeit sometimes overlooked) abilities. Consistent with the idea that it is clients' contributions and the therapeutic alliance that are most responsible for therapeutic change (Duncan, Miller, Wampold, & Hubble, 2010), in the following chapters readers will see how different therapists use their expertise primarily to help clients better use their own expertise.[8] Clients and therapists both "capture the moment" and "create the moment."

(4) *It is the client who decides whether one session has been enough (for now), or if more sessions (another one, or continuing) are in order.*

Therapy, Be It One Session or More, Is Not a Panacea

While many people do benefit from one-at-a-time (single-session) therapy, by walk-in or appointment, there remains a serious need for increased funding for all mental health and other social services. Researchers have demonstrated that very brief therapy may help some people, and thus may make additional services available for those who need longer-term work. We believe that greater attention to funding and supporting human needs is required if we are to move toward being a more humane and just world.

The Book in Hand[9]

One of the features of this volume is the range of approaches, clinical examples,[10] cultural nuances, research findings, and many insights offered by the various authors. As an old African saying has it, "One head cannot contain all knowledge" (Turle, 1992, p. 105).

The book is divided into five overlapping sections.

Section 1 contains this **Editors' Introduction**.

Section 2: Administrative comprises eight chapters. In Chapter 2, "The Three Top Reasons Why Walk-In/Single-Sessions Make Perfect Sense," Arnie Slive and Monte Bobele explain why practitioners and agencies should consider adding WI/SST to their service delivery models. The advantages of walk-in/SSTs are demonstrated with a case example.

In Chapter 3, "Single-Session Therapy: The Misunderstood Gift That Keeps On Giving," Jeff Young describes some of the single-session family therapy work being done at the Bouverie Centre (who sponsored the first Capturing the Moment symposium in 2012) in Melbourne, Australia. He notes that the potential growth of SST may be facilitated by seeing it as a service delivery model, rather than as a specific model of therapy, that is relevant across services, disciplines, and client presentations. He also offers some observations on ways to increase effectiveness when working with clients who are reluctant to attend therapy or counseling.

In Chapter 4, "Change in the Winds: The Growth of Walk-In Therapy Clinics in Ontario, Canada," Karen Young gives an excellent overview of the way narrative therapy practices can facilitate successful walk-in SSTs.

In Chapter 5, "Twenty-Five Years of Walk-In Single Sessions at the Eastside Family Centre: Clinical and Research Dimensions," Janet Stewart, Nancy McElheran, Harry Park, Margaret Oakander, Bruce MacLaurin, Cindy Fang, and Alexandra Robinson provide an overview of the extensive work done at the EFC in Calgary, Canada, along with several case examples of WI/SST and a summary of research findings.

In Chapter 6, "The Walk-In Counseling Model: Research and Advocacy," Leslie Josling and Cheryl-Anne Cait describe some of the work at KW Counselling Services, which is located in Kitchner-Waterloo in southern Ontario, Canada. They present both quantitative and qualitative data to show how researchers can document and investigate practices to advocate for additional needed resources.

In Chapter 7, "Development of a Single-Session Family Program at Child and Youth Mental-Health Services, South Melbourne," Rachel Barbara-May, Paul Denborough, and Tess McGrane provide statistical data about their clientele as well as accounts of clinical cases to illustrate ways that SST/OAAT services are used to address the needs of youth and families.

In Chapter 8, "Single-Session Therapy in the Majority World: Addressing the Challenge of Service Delivery in Cambodia and the Implications for Other Global Contexts," John Miller, Jason Platt, and Kevin Conroy remind us that the majority of the world does not operate from typical Western psychological assumptions about problems and their resolution, and then go on to describe and beautifully illustrate different ways one-session interventions can be used effectively even in dire circumstances such as those that exist in post-war Cambodia. They emphasize to beware of any single story explanations and to remain acutely sensitive to cultural context wherever we may be working.

In Chapter 9, "Walk-In Counseling Center of Minneapolis/St. Paul: The Magic of Our Model for Clients and Volunteers," Mary Weeks and Lori Zook-Stanley share the key elements of their model and the characteristics of "The Walk-In Way," including the power of an all-volunteer team working together.

Section 3: Clinical comprises twelve chapters. In Chapter 10, "The Eternal Now: On Becoming and Being a Single-Session Therapist," Moshe Talmon describes various elements of his evolution as a therapist, with a particular focus on issues like flexibility, versatility, humbleness, love and trust as alternatives to traditional views that favor therapists' knowledge, mastery, and power.

In Chapter 11, "SST: Stories, Structures, Themes, Cautions, and Prospects," Michael Hoyt offers observations on the history, methodologies, possible abuses, and future promises of Single-Session Therapy.

In Chapter 12, "One . . . Two . . . Three Ways to Help You Today: Therapeutic Models in a Single-Session Therapy Program," Monica Barnes, Patricia Carruthers, and Maja Gigovic at the South Calgary Health Centre present a case example to illustrate how multiple therapeutic approaches based on differing theories can all be used synergistically to help the same client.

In Chapter 13, "Working with Clients' Cultural Context in SST," Terry Soo-Hoo uses a case example involving an Asian-American client to show how essential it may be to understand and work within a client's values and belief system, especially when there are time constraints (as in SST) and rapidly forming a therapeutic alliance is important.

In Chapter 14, "'Coming In for Tune-Ups': A Family's Experience of Episodic Long-Term Single-Session Therapy at the Bouverie Centre, Melbourne," Karen Story presents a case example of the use of intermittent SST family therapy to illustrate the effective and efficient use of resources.

In Chapter 15, "Westside Stories: Walk-In and Single-Session Therapy in San Antonio," Monte Bobele, Chrystal Fullen, Brittany Houston, Ashlee Martinez, Lacey Moffat, and Jeanette Santos portray a range of interesting case examples.

In Chapter 16, "Single-Session Walk-Ins as a Collaborative Learning Community at the Houston Galveston Institute," Sue Levin, Adriana Gil-Wilkerson, and Sylvia Rapani De Yatim describe and illustrate the use of Collaborative Therapy principles and reflecting teams that are the basis of their work. They also present some research data supporting the effectiveness of their walk-in service.

In Chapter 17, "Co-Crafting Take-Home Documents at the Walk-In," Scot Cooper and "Ariane" (a young client) collaborate to describe how they developed some special documents to both help the client and to help others. There is also a discussion, considered from a narrative therapy framework, of other types of take-home documents and their possible use.

In Chapter 18, "Coincidence Favors the Prepared Mind: Single Sessions with Couples in Sweden," Martin Söderquist describes the evolution of his team's work with couples and illustrates several examples with verbatim excerpts from sessions.

In Chapter 19, "*Terapia Breve Sin Cita*: Collaboration with a Marginalized Community in Mexico City," Irma Rodriguez illustrates with several culturally sensitive examples how "brief therapy without appointment" can be used to help those who might otherwise not receive needed services.

In Chapter 20, "Reflections on Providing Single-Session Therapy in Post-Disaster Haiti," Brian Guthrie also emphasizes the importance of cultural sensitivity in his moving account of how he was able to apply some of the general principles of SST ("when one hour is all you have") when doing relief work in 2012, two years after the terrible earthquake that devastated that country. A case example is provided to illustrate both what can be accomplished as well as limitations when facing major disruptions and lack of social services.

In Chapter 21, "Some Ways to End an SST," Michael Hoyt and Robert Rosenbaum discuss the tasks and skills associated with finishing well to enhance the potential benefits of SST.

Section 4: Supervisory comprises three chapters. In Chapter 22, "The First Time: Teaching Skills that Prepare Interns and New Therapists for Walk-In Counseling," Joanna Bedggood describes training methods, key knowledge and competencies, and specific clinical skills that are taught at the KW Counseling Service in Kitchener-Waterloo, Ontario, Canada.

In Chapter 23, "Supervision and the Single-Session Therapist: Learnings from Ten Years of Practice," Sandy Harper-Jaques, a supervisor and researcher for many years at South Calgary Health Centre, provides a "road map" for supervising, including describing various exercises and case examples.

In Chapter 24, "Capturing the Moment in Supervision," Pam Rycroft, a senior supervisor at the Boverie Centre in Melbourne, describes and illustrates with an extended example how the principles of SST can be applied in a parallel process to the work of making a difference in one-session-at-a-time supervision.

Section 5: Conclusion contains Chapter 25, in which the editors review, glean lessons, and discuss implications and future directions (including more research, more cultural awareness, and more use of Internet resources, social media, and e-therapy).

One at a Time

Readers are encouraged to turn first to the chapters that most intrigue them, but then sometime to return to the others. Just like the therapies they describe, some will help solve problems immediately, while others will plant seeds that may yield benefits later.

Notes

1 Kudos to Wood's Homes for their generous support, and to the organizing committee (Jane Matheson, Dean Soenen, Janet Stewart, Nancy McElheran, Arnie Slive, and Sandy Harper-Jaques) for all their fine work. Additional thanks to the other major sponsors of the conference: United Way, University of Calgary, and PlyGem; and to Jane Matheson, CEO at Wood's Homes, to Karen Sorenson, the Mayor of Banff, and to Sandra Manyfeathers of the Blackfoot First Nation People, who extended warm welcomes to the meeting.

2 This SST definition of *no other sessions in the year before or after* is, of course, arbitrary and was used for research purposes. The work reported in Talmon (1990) was based on the finding that many people attend only one session and so the therapist and client should approach the first session as if it were going to be the last. In the chapters that follow, we report that SST clients may be seen more than once in a year (nowadays either face-to-face or via telephone or online); the basic SST desideratum is that a session be approached as though it could be the only (single) session, complete unto itself.

3 Other "single-session" contacts are also possible, such as one-time meetings in an emergency room when on-call. These encounters are usually forms of *crisis intervention*, emergency psychological care aimed at assisting individuals/families to restore equilibrium to their biopsychosocial functioning and to minimize the potential for psychological trauma. Crisis intervention is often ultra-brief, but SST is not necessarily aimed to be a crisis intervention unless this is what the client needs at the moment (Hoyt & Talmon, 2014, p. 13).

4 Battino (2014) has thus introduced the term *Sequential Single Session Therapy (SSST)*.

5 Readers may note that there has been a progression from *Single Session Therapy* (Talmon, 1990) and *Single Session Solutions* (Talmon, 1993) to *When All You*

Have Is One Hour (Slive & Bobele, 2011) to *Capturing the Moment* (Hoyt & Talmon, 2014) to the present title.

6 Throughout this volume the term *client* (rather than *patient*) will generally be used to emphasize the egalitarian and minimize the implication of pathology and hierarchy. According to Hoyt and Talmon (2014, p. 11): "What one calls the participants and the process (*therapy? counseling? treatment? intervention? consultation? facilitation? work? practice? meeting? encounter? conversation? coaching?*) helps to establish a meaning context (topics, roles, power relations, ideas about how change occurs), and thus, influences their work together."

7 de Shazer (1991, p. 112) specified that workable goals have the following general characteristics: (1) small rather than large; (2) salient to clients; (3) described in specific, behavioral terms; (4) achievable within the practical contexts of clients' lives; (5) perceived by the clients as involving their "hard work;" (6) described as the "start of something" and not as the "end of something;" (7) treated as involving new behavior(s) rather than the absence or cessation of existing behavior(s). Meichenbaum (2013, p. 201) similarly writes: "One of the best ways is to engage clients into collaborative goal setting that provides 'SMART' goals: Specific, Measurable, Achievable, Realistic and Time-Limited goals."

8 There are also other approaches to SST/OAAT not featured in this book—including REBT/CBT (Dryden, 2016, 2017), psychodynamic, redecision/Gestalt, and some forms of strategic therapy—in which change is primarily brought about by the therapist forming an opinion about what is wrong ("How is the client stuck?") and then proceeding to provide what the therapist discerns to be the needed remedy—be it insight, explanation and instruction, specific skill training, paradoxical behavioral directives to obviate interpersonal problems, etc.

9 Although contributions come from various countries, Americanized spelling and punctuation will be used throughout (unless involving a proper name or used in a published title); e.g. *center* rather than *centre*, *counseling* rather than *counselling*, *Single-Session Therapy* (hyphenated) rather than *Single Session Therapy*.

10 There are more than 40 case examples included, all appropriately disguised to protect patient confidentiality.

References

Appelbaum, S.A. (1975). Parkinson's Law in psychotherapy. *International Journal of Psychoanalytic Psychotherapy*, *4*, 426–436.

Barrett, M.S., Chua, W.-J., Crits-Christoph, P., Gibbons, M.B., & Thompson, D. (2008). Early withdrawal from mental health treatment: Implications for psychotherapy practice. *Psychotherapy: Theory, Research, Practice, Training*, *45*(2), 247–267.

Basoglu, M., Salgioglu, E., & Livanou, M. (2007). A randomized controlled study of single-session behavioral treatment of earthquake-related post-traumatic stress disorder using an earthquake simulator. *Psychological Medicine*, *37*(2), 203–213.

Battino, R. (2006). *Expectation: The very brief therapy book.* Norwalk, CT: Crown House Publishing.

Battino, R. (2014). Expectation: The essence of very brief therapy. In M.F. Hoyt & M. Talmon (Eds.), *Capturing the moment: Single session therapy and walk-in services* (pp. 393–406.) Bethel, CT: Crown House Publishing.

Binfet, J.-T. (2017). The effects of group-administered canine therapy on university students' wellbeing: A randomized controlled trial. *Anthrozoös*, *30*(3), doi.org/10.1080/08927936.2017.

Bloom, B.L. (1981). Focused single-session therapy: Initial development and evaluation. In S.H. Budman (Ed.), *Forms of brief therapy* (pp. 167–216). New York: Guilford Press. A revised and expanded version ("Bloom's focused single-session therapy") appeared in B.L. Bloom, *Planned short-term psychotherapy: A clinical handbook* (2nd ed., pp. 97–121). Boston: Allyn & Bacon, 1992.

Bobele, M., López, S. S.-G., Scamardo, M., & Solórzano, B. (2008). Single-session/walk-in therapy with Mexican-American clients. *Journal of Systemic Therapies*, *27*(4), 75–89.

Bobele, M. & Slive, A. (2014). One session at a time: When you have a whole hour. In M.F. Hoyt & M. Talmon (Eds.), *Capturing the moment: Single session therapy and walk-in services* (pp. 95–120). Bethel, CT: Crown House Publishing.

Bohart, A.C., & Tallman, K. (1999). *How clients make therapy work: The process of active self-healing*. Washington, DC: APA Books.

Boyan, P. (1996) Clients' perceptions of single session consultations as an option to waiting for family therapy. *Australian and New Zealand Journal of Family Therapy*, *20*(4), 195–200.

Cameron, C. (2007). Single session and walk-in psychotherapy: A descriptive account of the literature. *Counselling and Psychotherapy Research*, *7*(4), 245–249.

Campbell, A. (1999). Single session interventions: An example of clinical research in practice. *Australian and New Zealand Journal of Family Therapy*, *20*(4), 183-194.

Carey, T.A., Tai, S.J., & Stiles, W.B. (2013). Effective and efficient: Using patient-led appointment scheduling in routine mental health practice in remote Australia. *Professional Psychology: Research and Practice*, *44*(6), 405–414.

Carroll, K.M., Libby, B., Sheehan, J., & Hyland, N. (2001). Motivational interviewing to enhance treatment initiation in substance abusers: An effectiveness study. *American Journal on Addictions*, *10*, 335–339.

Church, D. (2014). Clinical EFT (Emotional Freedom Techniques) as single session therapy: Cases, research, indications, and cautions. In M.F. Hoyt & M. Talmon (Eds.), *Capturing the moment: Single session therapy and walk-in services* (pp. 299–324). Bethel, CT: Crown House Publishing.

Church, D. (2016). Sometimes just one session of therapy can be enough. *Huffington Post,* August 27.

Clements, R., McElheran, N., Hackney, L., & Park, H. (2011). The Eastside family Centre: 20 years of single-session walk-in therapy: Where we have been and where we are going. In A. Slive & M. Bobele (Eds.), *When one hour is all you have: Effective therapy for walk-in clients* (pp. 109–127). Phoenix, AZ: Zeig, Tucker, and Thesien.

Cone, J. D. (1986). Idiographic, nomothetic, and related perspectives in behavioral assessment. In R.O. Nelson & S.C. Hayes (Eds.), *Conceptual foundations of behavioral assessment* (pp. 111–128). New York: Guilford Press.

Cummings, N.A., & Follette, W.T. (1976). Brief psychotherapy and medical utilization. In H. Dorken, et al. (Eds.), *The professional psychologist today.* San Francisco: Jossey-Bass.

Daley, D.C., & Zuckoff, A. (1998). Improving compliance with the initial outpatient session among discharged inpatient dual diagnosis clients. *Social Work*, *43*, 470–473.

de Shazer, S. (1991). *Putting difference to work*. New York: Norton.
Dryden, W. (2016). *When time is at a premium: Cognitive-behavioural approaches to single-session therapy and very brief coaching*. London, England: Rationality Publications.
Dryden, W. (2017). *Single-session integrated cognitive behavior therapy (SSI-CBT): Distinctive features*. New York: Routledge.
Duncan, B.L. & Miller, S.D. (2000). *The heroic client: Doing client-directed, outcome-oriented therapy*. San Francisco: Jossey-Bass.
Duncan, B.L., Miller, S.D., Wampold, B.E., & Hubble, M.A. (Eds.) (2010). *The heart and soul of change: Delivering what works in therapy* (2nd ed.). Washington, DC: APA Books.
Feaster, D.J., Newman, F., & Rice, C. (2003). Longitudinal analysis when the experimenter does not determine when the treatment ends: What is dose-response? *Clinical Psychology and Psychotherapy*, *10*(6), 352–360.
Follette, W.T., & Cummings, N.A. (1967). Psychiatric services and medical utilization in a prepaid health plan setting. *Medical Care*, *5*, 25–35.
Fry, D. (2012), Implementing single session family consultation: A reflective team approach. *Australian and New Zealand Journal of Family Therapy*, *33*(1), 54–69.
Gee, D., Mildred, H., Brann, P., & Taylor, M. (2015). Brief intervention: A promising framework for child and youth mental health? *Administration and Policy in Mental Health and Mental Health Services Research*, *42*(2), 121–125.
Gibbons, J, & Plath, D. (2012). Single session social work in hospitals. *Australian and New Zealand Journal of Family Therapy*, *33*(1), 39–53.
Gilboa-Schechtman, E., & Shahar, G. (2006). The sooner, the better: Temporal patterns in brief treatment of depression and their role in long-term outcome. *Psychotherapy Research*, *16*(3), 374–384.
Green, S. (2014). Horse sense: Equine assisted single session consultations. In M.F. Hoyt & M. Talmon (Eds.), *Capturing the moment: Single session therapy and walk-in services* (pp. 425–440). Bethel, CT: Crown House Publishing.
Goulding, M.M. & Goulding, R.L. (1979). *Changing lives through redecision therapy*. New York: Grove Press.
Haley, J. (1982). The contribution to therapy of Milton H. Erickson, M.D. In J.K. Zeig (Ed.), *Ericksonian approaches to hypnosis and psychotherapy* (pp. 5–25). New York: Brunner/Mazel.
Haley, J. & Richeport-Haley, M. (2003). *The art of strategic therapy*. New York: Brunner-Routledge.
Hampson R., O'Hanlon, J., Franklin, A., Pentony, M., Fridgant, L., & Heins, T. (1999). The place of single-session family consultations: Five years' experience in Canberra. *Australian and New Zealand Journal of Family Therapy*, *20*(4), 195–200.
Harper-Jaques, S. & Foucault, D. (2014). Walk-in single session therapy: Client satisfaction and clinical outcomes. *Journal of Systemic Therapies*, *33*(3), 29–49.
Hoyt, M.F. (2009). *Brief psychotherapies: Principles and practices*. Phoenix, AZ: Zeig, Tucker, & Theisen.
Hoyt, M.F., Rosenbaum, R., & Talmon, M. (1992). Planned single-session psychotherapy. In S.H. Budman, M.F. Hoyt, & S. Friedman (Eds.), *The first session in brief therapy* (pp. 59–86). New York: Guilford Press.

Hoyt, M.F. & Talmon, M. (Eds.) (2014). *Capturing the moment: Single session therapy and walk-in services.* Bethel, CT: Crown House Publishing.

Humfress, H., Igel, V., Lamont, A., Tanner, M., Morgan, J., & Schmidt, U. (2002). The effect of a brief motivational intervention on community psychiatric patients' attitudes to their care, motivation to change, compliance, and outcome: A case contact study. *Journal of Mental Health, 11*, 155–166.

Hurn, R. (2005). Single-session therapy: Planned success or unplanned failure? *Counselling Psychology Review, 20*(4), 33–40.

Hymmen, P., Stalker, C., & Cait, C.-A. (2012). The case for single-session therapy: Does the empirical evidence support the increased prevalence of this service delivery model? *Journal of Mental Health*, Early Online, 1–12.

Kaffman, M. (1995). Brief therapy in the Israeli kibbutz. *Contemporary Family Therapy, 17*, 449–468.

Kashdan, T.B., Adams, L., Read, J., & Hawk, Jr., L. (2012). Can a one-hour session of exposure treatment modulate startle response and reduce spider fears? *Psychiatric Research, 196*, 79–82.

Kellner, R., Neidhardt, J., Krakow, B., & Pathak, D. (1992). Changes in chronic nightmares after one session of desensitization or rehearsal instruction. *American Journal of Psychiatry, 149*, 659–663.

Kirsch, I. (1990). *How expectations shape experience.* Washington, DC: APA Books.

Lambrecht, H., Laydon, C., McQuillan, C., Wisemman, S., Williams, L., Gash, A., & Reilly, J. (2007). Single-session solution-focused brief therapy and self-harm: A pilot study. *Journal of Psychiatric and Mental Health Nursing, 14*, 601–602.

Malan, D.H., Bacal, H.A., Heath, E.S., & Balfour, F.H.G. (1968). A study of psychodynamic changes in untreated neurotic patients: Improvements that are questionable on dynamic criteria. *British Journal of Psychiatry, 114*, 525–551.

Malan, D.H., Heath, E.S., Bacal, H.A., & Balfour, F.H.G. (1975). Psychodynamic changes in untreated neurotic patients. II. Apparently genuine improvements. *Archives of General Psychiatry, 32*, 110–126.

May, R. (1958). The origins and significance of the existential movement in psychology. In R. May, E. Angel, & H.F. Ellenberger (Eds.), *Existence: A new dimension in psychiatry and psychology* (pp. 3–36). New York: Basic Books.

McCambridge, J., & Strang, J. (2004). The efficacy of single-session motivational interviewing in reducing drug consumption and perceptions of drug-related risk and harm among young people: Results from a multi-site cluster randomized trial. *Addiction, 99*(1), 39–52.

McElheran, N., Stewart, J., Soenen, D., Newman, J., & Maclaurin, B. (2014). Walk-in single session therapy at the Eastside Family Centre. In M.F. Hoyt & M. Talmon (Eds.), *Capturing the moment: Single session therapy and walk-in services* (pp. 177–195). Bethel, CT: Crown House Publishing.

McLeod, S. A. (2007). Nomothetic idiographic debate. Retrieved from www.simplypsychology.org/nomothetic-idiographic.html

Meichenbaum. D. (2013). At my mother's kitchen table: Who are we, but the stories we tell? In M.F. Hoyt (Ed.), *Therapist stories of inspiration, passion, and renewal: What's love got to do with it?* (pp. 195–205). New York: Routledge.

Miller, J.K. (2008). Walk-in single-session team therapy: A study of client satisfaction. *Journal of Systemic Therapies, 27*(3), 78–94.

Miller, J.K., & Slive, A. (2004). Breaking down the barriers to clinical service delivery: Walk-in family therapy. *Journal of Marital and Family Therapy*, *30*, 95–105.

Mumford, E., Schlesinger, H.J., Glass, G., Patrick, C., & Cuerdon, T. (1984). A new look at evidence about reduced cost of medical utilization following mental-health treatment. *American Journal of Psychiatry*, *141*, 1145–1158.

Nieuwboer, C.C., Fukkink, R.G., & Hermanns, J.M.A. (2015). Single-session email consultation for parents: An evaluation of its effects on empowerment. *British Journal of Guidance & Counselling*, *43*(1), 131–143.

Nuthall, A., & Townend, M. (2007). CBT-based early intervention to prevent panic disorder: A pilot study. *Behavioral and Cognitive Psychotherapy*, *35*(1), 15–30.

O'Hanlon, W.H., & Weiner-Davis, M. (1989). *In search of solutions: A new direction in psychotherapy*. New York: Norton.

Ollendick, T.H., Oest, L.G., Reuterskiold, L., Costa, N., Cederlund, R., Sirbu, C., & Davis, T.E. (2009). One-session treatment of specific phobias in youth: A randomized clinical trial in the United States and Sweden. *Journal of Consulting and Clinical Psychology*, *77*(3), 504–516.

O'Neill, I. (2017). What's in a name? Clients' experience of single session therapy. *Journal of Family Therapy*, *39*: 63–79. doi:10.1111/1467-6427.12099.

Perkins, R. (2006). The effectiveness of one session of therapy using a single-session therapy approach for children and adolescents with mental health problems. *Psychology and Psychotherapy: Theory, Research and Practice*, *79*, 215–227.

Perkins, R., & ScArlett, G. (2008). The effectiveness of single session therapy in child and adolescent mental health: Part 2: An 18-month follow-up study. *Psychology and Psychotherapy: Theory, Research and Practice*, *81*, 143–156.

Rodda, S.N., Lubman, D.I., Cheetham, A., Dowling, N.A., & Jackson, A.C. (2015). Single session web-based counseling: A thematic analysis of content from the perspective of the client. *British Journal of Guidance & Counselling*, *43*(1), 117–130.

Rosenbaum, R. (2008). Psychotherapy is not short or long. *Monitor on Psychology*, *39*(7), 4, 8.

Rosenbaum, R., Hoyt, M.F., & Talmon, M. (1990). The challenge of single-session therapies: Creating pivotal moments. In R.A. Wells & V.J. Giannetti (Eds.), *Handbook of the brief psychotherapies* (pp. 165–189). New York: Plenum Press.

Ryan, C., & O'Connor, S. (2017). Single session psychology clinic for parents of children with autism spectrum disorder: A feasibility study. *Journal of Child and Family Studies*, *26*, 1614–1621.

Schade, N., Torres, P., & Beyerbach, M. (2011). Cost-efficiency of a brief family intervention for somatoform patients in primary care. *Families, Systems & Health*, *29*(3), 197–205.

Slive, A. & Bobele, M. (Eds.) (2011). *When one hour is all you have: Effective therapy for walk-in clients*. Phoenix, AZ: Zeig, Tucker, & Theisen.

Slive, A., Maclaurin, B., Oakander, M., & Amundson, J. (1995). Walk-in single sessions: A new paradigm in clinical service delivery. *Journal of Systemic Therapies*, *14*, 3–11.

Slive, A., McElheran, N., & Lawson, A. (2008). How brief does it get? Walk-in single session therapy. *Journal of Systemic Therapies*, *27*, 5–22.

Sommers-Flanagan, J. (2007). Single-session consultations for parents: A preliminary investigation. *The Family Journal: Counseling and Therapy for Couples and Families, 15*, 24–29.

Sproel, O.H. (1975). Single-session psychotherapy. *Diseases of the Nervous System, 36*, 283–285.

Stacey, K., Allison, S., Dadds, V., Roeger, L., Wood, A., & Martin, G. (2001). Maintaining the gains: What worked in the year after brief family therapy. *Australian and New Zealand Journal of Family Therapy, 22*(4), 181–188.

Stalker, C.A., Riemer, M., Cait, C.-A., Horton, S., Booton, J., Josling, L., Bedggood, J. & Zaczek, M. (2015). A comparison of walk-in counselling and the wait list model for delivering counselling services. *Journal of Mental Health*. Published online: 15 December 2015. DOI:10.3109/09638237.2015.1101417.

Swift, J.K., & Greenberg, R.P. (2012). Premature discontinuation in adult psychotherapy: A meta-analysis. *Journal of Consulting and Clinical Psychology, 80*(4), 547–559.

Talmon, M. (1990). *Single session therapy: Maximizing the effect of the first (and often only) therapeutic encounter*. San Francisco: Jossey-Bass.

Talmon, M. (1993). *Single session solutions: A guide to practical, effective, and affordable therapy*. Reading, MA: Addison-Wesley.

Talmon, M. & Hoyt, M.F. (2014). Moments are forever: SST and walk-in services now and in the future. In M.F. Hoyt & M. Talmon (Eds.), *Capturing the moment: Single session therapy and walk-in services* (pp. 463–486). Bethel, CT: Crown House Publishing.

Turle, G. (1992). *The art of the Maasai: 300 newly discovered objects and works of art*. New York: Knopf.

Wampold, B.E., & Imel, Z.E. (2015). *The great psychotherapy debate: The evidence for what makes psychotherapy work* (2nd ed.). New York: Routledge.

Weir, S., Wills, M., Young, J., & Perlesz, A. (2008). *The implementation of single session work in community health*. Brunswick, Victoria, Australia: The Bouverie Centre, La Trobe University.

Wells, J.E., Browne, M.O., et al. (2013). Drop out from out-patient mental healthcare in the World Health Organization's World Mental Health Survey initiative. *British Journal of Psychiatry, 202*(1), 42–49; DOI 10:1192/bjp.bp.112.113134.

Wells, R.A. & Phelps, P.A. (1990). The brief psychotherapies: A selective overview. In R.A. Wells & V.J. Giannetti (Eds.), *Handbook of the brief psychotherapies* (pp. 3–26). New York: Plenum.

Westmacott, R., & Hunsley, J. (2010). Reasons for terminating psychotherapy: A general population study. *Journal of Clinical Psychology, 66*(9), 965–977.

Young, J. & Rycroft, P. (2012). Single session therapy: What's in a name? *Australian and New Zealand Journal of Family Therapy, 33*(1), 3–5.

Young, J., Rycroft, P., & Weir, S. (2014). Implementing single session therapy: Practical wisdoms from Down Under. In M.F. Hoyt & M. Talmon (Eds.), *Capturing the moment: Single session therapy and walk-in services* (pp. 121–140). Bethel, CT: Crown House Publishing.

Section 2

Administrative

2 The Three Top Reasons Why Walk-In/Single-Sessions Make Perfect Sense

Arnold Slive and Monte Bobele

By tradition, psychotherapy services have been delivered on a by-appointment basis, whether those services take place in a private practice or in a publicly-funded mental-health agency. This is how a first session of psychotherapy is commonly arranged in a counseling agency:

(1) The client decides to talk to a mental-health professional.
(2) The client calls the agency requesting an appointment.
(3) The client gets an immediate response or leaves a message requesting a return call.
(4) The client speaks by phone to the receptionist or intake person (same day or days later).
(5) A meeting for an "intake" is arranged; this could occur shortly after the first telephone conversation or even days or weeks later.
(6) The intake process often requires the completion of intake forms and a meeting with an agency therapist or intake specialist during which the client's issues and concerns are discussed. In some settings a battery of assessment instruments may be routinely administered. That meeting may conclude with a referral elsewhere based on a decision that the client's needs are not a fit for the agency services. Or, the client may be given an appointment for a first session of psychotherapy or be placed on the agency's wait-list. This intake process may take from one to several hours.
(7) The client arrives for a first session (or perhaps not, since a significant percentage of those given a first appointment do not arrive).

By contrast, here is how the process works at an agency that offers a walk-in option:

(1) The client decides to talk to a mental-health professional.
(2) The client arrives at the walk-in service and is asked to complete a brief one-to-two page intake form;
(3) The session begins, usually less than an hour after arrival.

If you were a client, which of the above processes would you prefer? If you were an administrator of a mental-health service, would you be asking yourself about the comparative cost of these two forms of service delivery as well as the accessibility of your services and satisfaction of your clients? What if you learned that one session is the modal length of psychotherapy and that most single-session clients report high satisfaction and significant improvement? Would you then begin to consider walk-in services as one element of your agency's offerings?

Elsewhere in this volume, you will find descriptions of a variety of different implementations of walk-in services. Some operate every day and some as infrequently as one half-day per week. Some charge a fee and some do not. Walk-in services do not screen; the client decides whether or not to come. (The exception to this is that agencies do not all serve the same client populations; e.g., some focus only on children and their families.) Several psychotherapy models can be adapted to the walk-in format. Central to the walk-in concept is the therapist's firmly held belief that the walk-in session may be the only session. The focus of the session, therefore, is on what the client most wants to achieve at that particular time.

The majority of walk-in clients decide that one session is enough for the time being. It is possible that clients may return at some point in the future for a subsequent walk-in session though they may not see the same therapist. Some walk-in sessions end with a referral for on-going by-appointment counseling or other mental-health services.

Our approach aims to have a complete therapy occur in a single therapeutic encounter: no pre-session screenings or assessments, no earlier triage, and no follow-up. By *walk-in* we are referring to an experience where the client walks into the clinic without an appointment, is seen by a therapist as soon as possible, and receives a complete single-session of therapy, at that moment. We have not built in routine follow-up, whether in person or by phone, in this model. Briefly, the model that plans to have a second contact (even if it is called a follow-up) is different than our mindset that the present encounter may be the only one the therapist and client may have. Of course we follow-up in exceptional cases such as when harm to the client or others is possible.

Walking in and expecting an immediate service has become commonplace. Our clients are used to it. They walk in to hairstylists, to restaurants, to income tax services, and drive in for a coffee or banking. Twenty-five years ago in Calgary, Canada, we watched as walk-in medical services became more and more popular. If anything, mental-health professionals have been behind the times, but there are signs that we are catching up (see Figure 2.1).

We (AS and MB) have been developing and providing walk-in services at locations in Canada, the United States, and Mexico (Bobele, et al., 2008; Slive, et al., 1995; Slive & Bobele, 2012; Slive, Bobele, McElheran, Platt, & Rodriguez, 2014). Such services are developing in countries around the globe, none more so than in Canada. We strongly believe that walk-in services have found a place in the continuum of mental-health services. In this chapter, we provide food for thought for those who are in a position of wanting to advocate

"We get in, we get help, and we get out."

Figure 2.1 "We get in, we get help, and we get out" (Will McPhail The New Yorker Collection/The Cartoon Bank ©2016. Used by agreement)

for walk-in services to your constituents and funders. We will focus on three specific reasons:

(1) They seize the moment.
(2) They work.
(3) They are efficient.

But First, a Case Example

Recently, at the Community Counseling Service (CCS) operated by Our Lady of the Lake University (OLLUSA) in San Antonio, Texas, Maria, who was in her 50s walked in without an appointment with her 21-year-old daughter, Antonia. They were given a brief intake form to complete, and the session began about 20 minutes later. Maria and Antonia had heard about the walk-in service from their primary-care doctor after Maria told the doctor that she was having difficulty coping. She was sleeping more than usual, feeling sad and tearful, and regularly missing work. Antonia pointed out that she had come to the session to support her mother. Both Maria and Antonia attributed their difficulties to the fact that Victor, Maria's husband and Antonia's father, had died three months earlier after a long illness. Maria told us that she wanted to "feel well enough" to get back to work on a regular basis. Friends and family had been advising Maria that she was spending too much time dwelling on the loss of her husband, that she should forget him. However, Maria found that she was unable to stop thinking about him. She even found that in her "conversations" with Victor since his death, he had been advising her to "move on."

Following a 10-minute break in the session (some walk-in services operate with a team of therapists that are available to consult during the session) the co-therapists reflected to Maria that her well-intended attempts to forget and move on were not working. If anything, those efforts seemed to lead to more remembering. So, the therapists suggested that Maria consider "forgetting about forgetting." Surprisingly, Maria immediately agreed.

For the remainder of the session the therapists, Johanna Becho and Karla Caballero, borrowed from the work of Michael White (1988), who demonstrated that saying "hullo" can sometimes be a more effective grieving strategy than saying goodbye. The therapists encouraged Maria and Antonia to share their memories of Victor with each other. Antonia made two lists on a whiteboard in the therapy room. One list (about 15 items) described the characteristics of Victor that they most wanted to hold on to (e.g., his romantic nature). The other list (4 items) consisted of his qualities that they preferred to stay in the background (e.g., his quick temper). The therapists took photographs of each list and gave copies to them. The mother and daughter were advised to keep the list of more positive qualities with them at all times so they could refer to it whenever they needed to remember Victor. As far as the less desirable listing, they were instructed to store it somewhere in their home so that it was not always present but could be retrieved "should it be needed." At the end of the session, Maria was smiling, more energetic, and making plans with Antonia for the remainder of the week. She thanked the therapists for encouraging her to remember Victor and to not forget him too quickly. They were invited to walk-in again, if they needed. At the time of this writing they had not returned.

Now, we return to the three reasons.

They Seize the Moment

Motivated Clients

Clients who arrive at a walk-in service have not had to jump the various hurdles that are commonplace in by-appointment services. They have not been screened; the screening is done by the clients themselves. Rather than having a session at a time that is most suitable to the service provider, the clients have decided on a moment in time that best fits for them. Therefore, their motivation is usually at a high point. They are likely to be *customers* for change (de Shazer, 1988) or at the *action* stage of readiness (Norcross, Krebs, & Prochaska, 2011). The solution-focused therapists Michele Weiner-Davis and her colleagues (Weiner-Davis, de Shazer, & Gingerich, 1987) serendipitously found that clients frequently report pre-treatment change. In our own experience, we have found that asking clients, "What has gotten better since you decided to come for counseling?" identifies steps already taken to begin a resolution of the initial complaint. We are convinced that when clients walk-in for services they are at a point of maximum motivation to change. We frequently remind our student therapists that we are often seeing clients, if not on the worst day of their lives, at least during the worst week of their lives. As Duvall and his colleagues (2012, p. 17) reminded us, "When people first approach organizations for help, they are not at their best and may be at their worst." They go on to warn that this is not the optimal time to administer deficit-based assessments that may create a distorted view of the client and result in a discouraging experience for the client. Clients call for help or walk-in when they are energized and taking the first step to change. We want to keep the ball rolling at that point.

Happy Therapists

Motivated clients are rewarding to therapists. Walk-in clients tend to arrive ready to work. They have something they want to talk about and are pleased to have an interested listener. Often, they are ready to consider small steps in a new direction. Even when they are mandated to receive counseling, or when they arrive at the insistence of someone else, the therapists know that one session may be the only session. At minimum, the therapist can use that one session to give the client an opportunity to vent. The therapist can create a "less bad" experience of therapy than the client expected. We can, for example, instill hope and create a positive experience for the client by identifying, in the client's story, strengths and resources to reflect back to the client. These positive observations can be especially helpful to clients who arrive expecting to be criticized. We have adopted the *Session Rating Scale* (*SRS*) (Miller, et al., 2003) as a measure of the therapeutic alliance. Therapists get immediate feedback from clients about the quality of the therapeutic relationship, and find this information highly motivating. The *SRS* provides a way to initiate a conversation with clients about what was helpful and what the therapist might have done do to have improved the session. Clients consistently rate their walk-in experiences very highly on the *SRS*.

Happy Clients

Walk-in clients are pleased and relieved to receive a session of counseling at a moment of their choosing, without having to wait and jump through administrative hurdles. AS began providing walk-in services in 1990 at the Eastside Family Centre (EFC) in Calgary Canada (Slive, et al., 1995). He was pleasantly surprised when his very first walk-in client profusely thanked him simply for the fact that she could talk to someone about her concerns at the precise moment in time that was meaningful to her.

Positive Change Happens Early in the Therapeutic Process

Decades of research have shown that for most clients the largest gains occur in the earliest sessions of therapy (Owen, Adelson, Budge, Wampold, Kopta, Minami, & Miller, 2015). More change tends to occur in the first session than in subsequent sessions. Researchers (Harper-Jaques & Foucault, 2014) have found that 40% of clients at a walk-in service report that one session is sufficient. Furthermore, the therapist's single-session mindset can be "transferred" to the client. For example, while explaining the walk-in service at the beginning of the session, the therapist might comment that many clients find one session to be sufficient, that they leave the session with a new way of thinking and perhaps some new steps to try out in addressing their situation. With this introduction, the client and therapist might begin to share the single-session mindset.

The Walk-In Option

As mentioned earlier, "no appointment necessary" walk-in services have become a part of everyday life. People expect to be able to access services when the service is most needed or when they are most ready to change. In Calgary in 1990, when AS and others began talking about the possibility of a walk-in counseling service in, we were told that we would be overwhelmed (Slive, et al., 1995). We took that comment as a sign that we were on the right track. Now, there are over 40 walk-in clinics in the Canadian province of Ontario, alone (see Chapter 6 in this volume).

Over 20 years ago, in San Antonio, Texas, MB heard about the EFC during a visit to Calgary and brought walk-in services to OLLUSA's CCS (Bobele, et al., 2008). The CCS shares a waiting room with a family medicine practice group. Prominently displayed in the waiting room is a sign advertising our walk-in services. Many times over the years, a walk-in client has told a story that starts like this:

> Well, I was sitting out there in the waiting room and saw your sign. I knew I might have to wait a couple of hours to see the doctor, so I thought I would come over here, in the meantime, to get some help with . . .

The CCS also has a large sign outside the building on a busy neighborhood street that advertises the availability of walk-in services in English and Spanish. Other clients have told us that they had noted the sign over the years and had filed away the idea that the CCS was a place they could come to, without an appointment, whenever they needed help. In both of these examples, the idea of walking in for a service fit with the everyday lives of the CCS's clients.

They Work

Improvement in Presenting Concerns

A growing body of research indicates that many clients report an improvement in presenting concerns following a single walk-in session as well as decreased stress, increased agency, decreased problem severity and increased coping (Harper-Jaques & Foucault, 2014; Hymmen, Stalker, & Cait, 2012). As one approach to handling the demand for services and the limited therapists available, some agencies and practitioners establish a wait-list. For example, a recent study (Stalker, et al., 2015) compared outcomes of walk-in clients and wait-list clients. The researchers reported that after a four-week follow-up, walk-in clients had improved faster and were less distressed than the group of clients who were eventually served after being on a wait-list. Ten weeks later, both groups had improved and were similar. Participants receiving instrumental support such as services related to family violence, unstable housing, or financial problems prior to counseling improved more slowly. The qualitative data confirmed that participants highly valued the accessibility of the walk-in model and were frustrated by the lengthy waits associated with the traditional, by-appointment model.

High Client Satisfaction

There is ample evidence that clients are satisfied with single sessions, whether planned or unplanned (Talmon, 1990). Recent investigations of walk-in/single-sessions have consistently shown positive client satisfaction. For example, Miller (2008) surveyed 403 walk-in clients and over 80% reported they were "very satisfied" or "satisfied." Remarkably, less than 2% reported being dissatisfied. More recently, Harper-Jaques and Foucault (2014) reported that of 98 walk-in clients, 93% reported satisfaction with the service. There is little doubt that consumers of psychotherapy are happy with walk-in/single-sessions.

They Are Efficient

Reduced Wait-lists

A recent study (Malowney, Keltz, Fischer, & Boyd, 2014) conducted by researchers at Harvard found that prospective patients were stymied in their attempts to make an appointment with a psychiatrist in Boston, Chicago, or Houston. The researchers, posing as patients, called 360 psychiatrists who were listed in the Blue Cross and Blue Shield online database. The "patients" were able to make appointments with only 93 (26%) of the psychiatrists. The researchers noted that 23% of the psychiatrists' offices did not even return calls. One interpretation of this data is that in the American healthcare system, even those with excellent health insurance coverage are not able to access mental-health outpatient treatments. For the prospective patients in three large U.S. cities, even a wait-list was not an option.

Walk-in services are a useful way of obviating the cost of missed appointments. There is no reliable way of predicting which clients will not show up for their initial, scheduled appointment for therapy (Anderson, 2015) or subsequently scheduled appointments (Scamardo, Bobele, & Biever, 2004), but we know that a significant percentage of first appointments are no-shows (Barrett, et al., 2008). No-shows reduce scheduling capacity, lower the quality of care, increase staffing inefficiencies, and negatively affect the climate of care (Duvall, Young, & Kayes-Burden, 2012; Ulmer & Troxler, 2006 Robinson & Chen, 2009).

Many organizations decide to start walk-in services due to concerns that lengthy wait-lists reduce accessibility of services. In Calgary, we were increasingly worried about how much staff time and energy were expended in order to manage a wait-list. In those days, a new client first met with a staff member designated as an "intake coordinator." That staff member also had the job of "looking after" the clients on the wait-list by answering their phone calls and, sometimes, responding to mental-health crises. When an appointment finally became available, the clients sometimes declined because their need or motivation had changed. Many clients who agreed to a first appointment did not show up. When we started our service that provided all counseling through walk-in sessions (Slive, et al., 1995), we no longer needed an intake coordinator, and obviously there were no longer any declined or missed appointments.

Of course this does not mean that walk-in services are cost free. Therapists need to be available to see walk-in clients. In many agencies, those therapists are a combination of paid staff, student trainees, and mental-health professionals who volunteer. Someone also needs to be available to greet and orient clients when they walk in. This could also be a paid receptionist or a volunteer. However, like Horton, et al. (2012, discussed below), we argue the provision of walk-in services adds efficiencies and reduces costs for mental-health systems. As a result of the explosion of walk-in clinics in Ontario, for example, agencies have found that they could reduce the staff time encumbered by no-shows and cancellations, freeing up staff to handle the infrastructure demanded by walk-in services (Duvall, Young, & Kayes-Burden, 2012).

Five years ago, the Austin Child Guidance Center (ACGC) in Austin, Texas decided to start a walk-in counseling service. They, too, had a lengthy wait-list. On the day they began to provide walk-in counseling, they discontinued their wait-list. Since then, when a prospective client calls to ask for an appointment, the client is given an appointment if an ACGC therapist has an opening within two weeks. Otherwise, the client is asked to call back to check on the availability of an open appointment slot. However, they are also informed about the walk-in option. Prospective clients are told that they can walk-in, as an alternative, as often as they like, or until an appointment becomes available. In actuality, many who choose the walk-in option come just one time, are satisfied with that session, and decide not to make an appointment. Hence, ACGC now provides more efficient services with satisfied customers, serves more people, and no longer has a wait-list.

Reduced Use of Expensive Services

Pilot research (Horton, et al., 2012; also see Chapter 6 this volume) has found that introducing walk-in counseling at a Kitchener-Waterloo, Ontario, Canada counseling agency practically eliminated wait-lists and reduced costly no-shows. Horton and her colleagues found that clients' distress was decreased significantly after just one session. A large percentage of clients who attended the walk-in service were found to be "ready for change." The walk-in service diverted many clients from very expensive hospital services, connected them to community agencies, and returned them more quickly to work and social activities. The benefit of reduced hospital utilization and faster returns to work alone exceeded the cost of the walk-in services.

Reduces Overtreatment

At the beginning of a walk-in session, a therapist might say to the client that "Some people find one session is enough for now." The therapist is planting a seed that they will take full advantage of their time together and increase the chance that clients will leave with a sense that the time has been well spent and obviate the need for another visit. Perhaps there will be a new way of thinking about a problem and maybe an idea for a next step in dealing with their concerns. At minimum, we want clients to leave with increased hope and a sense that they have been heard and understood. This attitude takes advantage of the knowledge that clients enter the therapeutic process with already existing resources, extratherapeutic factors (Lambert, 2005) that can be recruited in the efforts to solve a problem. One important job of the therapist is assisting the client in discovering (or rediscovering) those resources and applying them to current life matters. This mindset assumes that the most important work rarely occurs in the therapy room alone. The important work frequently begins after the session when clients apply ideas discussed in the session. The single-session mindset encourages the client's own self-healing processes.

As noted earlier, in a walk-in service, each session is its own complete therapy. We do one session at a time and assume that each one could be the last. While some people benefit from an on-going therapeutic relationship that lasts months or even years, we do not assume that one size fits all. We believe in options and choice. Some clients who choose a walk-in option make good use of brief, perhaps single-session, therapeutic encounters. We think it is best for clients to have options for the type of service delivery that fits for them at a given point in time. These options reduce unnecessary treatment.

On Follow-Ups

Our work is based on the model of walk-in therapy developed at the Eastside Family Centre in Calgary (Slive, et al., 1995). Most of the chapters in this text that describe walk-in services have borrowed from that model. We do not make routine follow-up phone calls unless significant risk issues have been identified during the session. Nor do we routinely arrange to have sessions by appointment after a walk-in session. If the client requests another meeting, and if by-appointment services are available at the agency providing the walk-in service, we help them make an appointment. Otherwise, we invite them to walk-in again when they wish. We want our walk-in clients to know that we have confidence in their ability to carry on in their lives. The clients decide what to take from the walk-in single session. The clients decide when to seek additional mental-health services, which could be another walk-in session. Additionally, as we wrote in Slive and Bobele (2014, p. 84):

> At recent workshops that we have conducted, participants have raised some additional interesting observations about follow up contact after therapy has ended (even if it is a single session of therapy). One person noted that this could create boundary confusion since post-session contact could imply to the client that the therapist thinks therapy is continuing even when the client does not. This led to a discussion about the infrequency with which questions are raised about whether to routinely initiate follow up contact when therapy ends after 3 sessions, or 10 sessions, or six months. It is not clear why not. Does a single session of therapy somehow make follow up more necessary? Is follow up contact more the therapist's need to know or stay in contact; does it interfere with the client who endeavors to address life struggles without therapy?

There are other issues to be considered. We have limited staffing, which would make it inordinately difficult to attempt to follow-up with the high volume of cases seen. We have also found that communicating with clients by telephone is extremely difficult—they may call us for information and to schedule appointments, but calling them back to confirm appointments, to reschedule appointments, etc. is usually met with either a no-answer or a voicemail greeting; messages are rarely returned. Another factor is that a model of service delivery with a built-in follow-up, we think, could encourage therapists to conduct sessions knowing that loose ends could be resolved on follow-up; our model, instead, encourages therapists to approach each session as if it were the *last* opportunity that the therapist(s) will have to work with the client. Clinicians and researchers may be curious about what happens after clients leave a session, but we know of no research demonstrating better outcomes for clients if there is a follow-up contact. So, it is hard to justify the added cost.

Implications and Future Opportunities

We believe that the best mental-health service delivery systems are those that offer an array of service options to the community. Those options can range from the least intrusive, most accessible, briefest services all the way up to the more extensive and expensive such as inpatient and residential services. What is likely to be most helpful for a given consumer is something that the consumer believes is a good fit at that time. Walk-in/single-session counseling services are unintrusive. Walk-in services offer clients immediate access at key moments in time, are efficient, inexpensive, and encourage clients to make use of their own capabilities in the service of positive change. "By-appointment" services will and should continue to be available. Just as some people choose to walk-in for a haircut instead of making an appointment, some mental-health consumers will just walk-in rather than making an appointment. Walk-in counseling services can also link up with other mental-health services in the community. Walk-in services can help their clients to connect with other recommended services. In that sense we might consider walk-in/single-session services as one entry point into a broader range of services. In other words, often clients will leave a walk-in session with new ideas for dealing with a problem in their lives, while others may leave with a direction about where to go for additional services.

Mental-health service providers can offer walk-in counseling in unique forms that fit the local context. Some have offered walking in as the main form of service delivery on a full-time basis (Slive, et al., 1995). Others agencies and providers offer walk-in for a few hours a week. Even when it is available for limited hours, walk-in services provide a safety valve for a community. It is a place where those in need do not have to wait for an appointment, will not be screened, and to which they can return if they so choose.

We can think creatively about applications of "no appointment necessary" counseling by finding novel settings for providing the services. For example, the *Wall Street Journal* (Potkewitz, 2015) reported that the ubiquitous IKEA furniture stores are frequently the sites of couples' arguments over shopping for or assembling the iconic furniture. Although IKEA employs furniture consultants to help customers pick out furnishings, the addition of a relationship consultant on-site might be a good marketing move. In fact, the IKEA store in Calgary, Canada, in the 1990s provided just such a free service on Valentine's Day. In another iteration, free listening is offered to passersby in a number of American cities by Sidewalk Talk (www.sidewalktalksf.com). Here, "listeners" situate themselves on city streets to make themselves available for 5 to 10 minute conversations. And in Stockholm, Sweden, taxi services offer passengers free therapy with a ride-along psychologist in the back seat (Malm, 2014).

Conclusion

So, now the three top reasons why walk-in/single-sessions make sense should be obvious:

(1) Walk-in/single-session counseling reduces roadblocks and frustration, increases accessibility, and creates opportunities for meaningful therapeutic conversation at just the right moment.

(2) Walk-in/single-session counseling reduces wait-lists and other inefficiencies, produces satisfied customers, and leads to lasting change in presenting concerns. Also, consumers of services are used to the walk-in concept.
(3) Walk-in/single-session services are cost efficient, add to the range of options available to consumers, and reduce risks associated with overtreatment.

So, why not walk-in services?

References

Anderson, K.N. (2015). *Premature termination of outpatient psychotherapy: Predictors, reasons, and outcomes.* Theses, Dissertations, and Student Research: Department of Psychology. University of Nebraska—Lincoln Paper 74. http://digitalcommons.unl.edu/psychdiss/74.

Barrett, M.S., Chua, W.-J., Crits-Christoph, P., Gibbons, M.B., & Thompson, D. (2008). Early withdrawal from mental health treatment: Implications for psychotherapy practice. *Psychotherapy, 45*(2), 247–267. http://doi.org/10.1037/0033-3204.45.2.247.

Bobele, M., López, S., Scamardo, M., & Solórzano, B. (2008). Single-session/walk-in therapy with Mexican-American clients. *Journal of Systemic Therapies, 27*(4), 75–89.

de Shazer, S. (1988). *Keys to solution in brief therapy.* New York: Norton.

Duvall, J., Young, K., Kayes-Burden, A. (2012). *No more, no less: Brief mental health services for children and youth.* www.excellenceforchildandyouth.com.

Harper-Jaques, S. & Foucault, R. (2014). Walk-in single session therapy: Client satisfaction and clinical outcomes. *Journal of Systemic Therapies, 33*(3), 29–49.

Horton, S., Stalker, C.A., Cait, C., & Josling, L. (2012). Sustaining walk-in counselling services: an economic assessment from a pilot study. *Healthcare Quarterly, 16*(3) 44–49.

Hoyt, M.F. & Talmon, M. (Eds.) (2014). *Capturing the moment: Single session therapy and walk-in services.* Bethel, CT: Crown House Publishing.

Hymmen, P., Stalker, C., & Cait, C. A. (2012) The case for single-session therapy: Does the empirical evidence support the increased prevalence of this service delivery model? *Journal of Mental Health, 22*(1), 60–71.

Lambert, M.J. (2005). Early response in psychotherapy: Further evidence for the importance of common factors rather than "placebo effects." *Journal of Clinical Psychology, 61*(7), 855–869. http://doi.org/10.1002/jclp.20130.

Malm, S. (2014). The taxis in which the passengers get tips! Cab firm puts therapists in back of its cars to counsel lonely Swedes. www.dailymail.co.uk/news/article-2812359.

Malowney, M., Keltz, S., Fischer, D., & Boyd, J.W. (2014). Availability of outpatient care from psychiatrists: A simulated-patient study in three U.S. cities. *Psychiatric Services,* DOI: 10.1176/appi.ps.201400051.

Miller, J.K. (2008). Walk-in single session team therapy: A study of client satisfaction. *Journal of Systemic Therapies, 27*(3), 78–94.

Miller, S.D., Duncan, B.L., Brown, J., Sparks, J.A., & Claud, D.A. (2003). The outcome rating scale: A preliminary study of the reliability, validity, and feasibility of a brief visual analog measure. *Journal of Brief Therapy, 2*(2), 91–100.

Norcross, J.C., Krebs, P.M., & Prochaska, J.O. (2011). Stages of change. *Journal of Clinical Psychology, 67*(2), 143–154. doi: 10.1002/jclp.20758.

Owen, J., Adelson, J., Budge, S., Wampold, B., Kopta, M., Minami, T., & Miller, S. (2015). Trajectories of change in psychotherapy. *Journal of Clinical Psychology, 71*(9), 817–827. http://doi.org/10.1002/jclp.22191.

Potkewitz, H. (2015). Can your relationship handle a trip to IKEA? Retrieved from www.wsj.com/articles/can-your-relationship-handle-a-trip-to-ikea-1429724227.

Robinson, L.W. & Chen, R.R. (2009, March 17).The effects of patient no-shows on traditional and open-access appointment scheduling policies. *UC Davis Graduate School of Management Research No. 16-09; Johnson School Research Paper Series No. #43-09.* Available at SSRN: http://ssrn.com/abstract=1478736 or http://dx.doi.org/10.2139/ssrn.1478736.

Scamardo, M., Bobele, M., & Biever, J. L. (2004). A new perspective on client dropouts. *Journal of Systemic Therapies, 23*(2), 1–12.

Slive, A. & Bobele, M. (2012). Walk-in counselling services: Making the most of one hour. *Australian and New Zealand Journal of Family Therapy, 33*(1), 27–38. http://doi.org/10.1017/aft.2012.4.

Slive, A., & Bobele, M. (2014). Walk-in single-session therapy: Accessible mental health services. In M.F. Hoyt & M. Talmon (Eds.), *Capturing the moment: Single-session therapy and walk-in services* (pp. 73–94). Bethel, CT: Crown House Publishing.

Slive, A., Bobele, M., McElheran, N., Platt, J., & Rodriguez, I.J. (2014). *Walk-in services: An international perspective.* American Association of Marriage and Family Therapy Annual Meeting, Milwaukee, WI.

Slive, A., MacLaurin, B., Oakander, M., & Amundson, J. (1995). Walk-in single sessions: A new paradigm in clinical service delivery. *Journal of Systemic Therapies, 14*, 3–11.

Stalker, C.A., Riemer, M., Cait, C.-A., Horton, S., Booton, J., Josling, L., Bedggood, J., & Zaczek, M. (2015). A comparison of walk-in counselling and the wait list model for delivering counselling services. *Journal of Mental Health.* Published online: 15 December 2015. DOI:10.3109/09638237.2015.1101417. This study was funded by Canadian Institutes of Health Research (CIHR) FRN 119528.

Talmon, M. (1990). *Single session therapy: Maximizing the effect of the first (and often only) therapeutic encounter.* San Francisco: Jossey-Bass.

Ulmer, T. & Troxler, C. (2006). The economic cost of missed appointments and the open access system: Working paper. *Community Health Scholars.* Gainesville, FL: University of Florida.

Weiner-Davis, M., de Shazer, S., & Gingerich, W.J. (1987). Building on pre-treatment change to construct the therapeutic solution: An exploratory study. *Journal of Marital and Family Therapy, 13*(4), 359–363.

White, M. (1988). Saying “hullo” again: The incorporation of the lost relationship in the resolution of grief. *Dulwich Centre Newsletter*, 7–11.

3 Single-Session Therapy

The Misunderstood Gift That Keeps On Giving[1]

Jeff Young

This chapter celebrates the potential flexibility, diversity, and disruptive qualities of Single-Session Therapy (SST). Single-Session Therapy—or more accurately, a single-session attitude to service delivery—can be highly generative. Amongst a larger suite of possibilities, a SST "sensibility" can act as:

- a constructive agitator for implementing transparent client-led practices
- a convincing rationale for accessible service delivery
- a vehicle for collaborative practices across services, disciplines and therapeutic modalities, and
- in the case of the Bouverie Centre (where I serve as Director), a starting point for introducing systemic, family-based approaches into individually-focused service systems.

The above possibilities are explored through the lens of the Bouverie Centre's experience engaging with single-session ideas at both a clinical and broader service design level. I put forward the argument that a fundamental SST attitude or sensibility can generate great creative possibilities but that particular misunderstandings risk constraining the widespread potential impact of SST research and thinking. Four of the most common misunderstandings are presented prior to describing some advantages of a simple definition of SST. I then raise a vexed challenge to SST clinicians: how might SST clinical techniques be adapted to respond effectively and respectfully to clients (and others) who are suspicious of services?

The Bouverie Centre: Victoria's Family Institute

For the center I lead—an AUS$4.7 million integrated clinical, academic, research and workforce capacity builder in systemic family therapy and family-sensitive approaches—SST has been an effective and versatile service delivery model for client-led practice. It has provided a vehicle to take our work into front-line services, has helped us introduce family-based systemic approaches into over-subscribed individually-oriented services, and has helped us to work with a number of organizations, including our own, to explore ways to make services more accessible. Over the past two decades many of my Bouverie colleagues have contributed to the large body of work which forms the basis for this chapter. This work falls into five main areas of practice:

(1) Twenty-three years of clinical family therapy informed by, and delivered using, SST ideas.
(2) Training over 4,000 people from hundreds of organizations in SST via 1–2 day workshops.
(3) Implementation support to individual organizations, large and small.
(4) Large-scale, statewide implementation projects delivered in Community Health Counselling; Adult Mental Health; Alcohol and Other Drugs; and Youth Mental Health services.
(5) Implementation of SST family therapy in our own organization (twice).

Regarding Point 5, the need to repeat the implementation at our center (1994 and 2009) reflects the profound challenge SST provides to an organization's typical modes of service delivery; to clinicians' usual ways of conducting therapeutic work; and to clinicians' ideas about change and their role in the process of therapeutic change. Even where the introduction of SST has led to positive outcomes for clients and service providers, as in our service and in many others (e.g., Price, 1994; Hampson, et al., 1999), it is quite common for these services to revert to standard service delivery (assuming on-going work, especially for complex issues) over time. In our experience, if an organization does not keep SST alive with on-going activities such as evaluation, research, and/or reflective supervisory practices, and if it is not embedded in policy, core practice, and key processes, SST-inspired service delivery is lucky to survive beyond five years (Young, Weir, & Rycroft, 2012; Young, Rycroft, & Weir, 2014). This is especially likely if key supporters of the approach leave the organization.

In our clinical service, families are offered an initial session with two therapists. After the first session, one therapist drops out unless the family situation requires joint work, but remains an obvious "corridor consultant" and can return as co-therapist at a later point as a consultant or reviewer of progress. This structure has allowed our staff to enjoy co-therapy in a resource-friendly way. A pre-session questionnaire sent prior to the session helps family members prepare for key issues, indicate priorities, and begin thinking about goals for the work. As each family member may have different goals, three different options are suggested for completing the pre-session questionnaire when it is sent out: one questionnaire filled out communally (seldom happens), one questionnaire completed by the initiator of the referral (happens frequently), or separate questionnaires completed by each family member (happens most frequently). Unless risk[2] issues (e.g., suicidality, violence, neglect) are identified during the session, the decision about whether a second single session is to be organized, on-going work commenced, a referral made to another service or the work is complete is decided in discussion with key family members during a follow-up phone call, made at an agreed-upon time. The timing of the phone call is determined by the individual situation of the family. For example, if a family's teenage daughter is being bullied at school, the phone call may be scheduled once the teenager has had sufficient time back at school to notice whether or not the ideas collaboratively generated in the session successfully address the bullying. Delaying the decision about next steps to the phone call, if it is safe to do so, provides a unique opportunity for clients to take responsibility for change with the backup of professional help only a phone call away. We have an open-door policy that invites clients to ring at any time for additional help; knowing it is available, they seldom need to call.

More detailed accounts of the Bouverie Centre's SST clinical family therapy program can be found in Young and Rycroft (1997); including evaluations in Boyhan (1996), O'Neill and Rottem (2012), and client feedback in O'Neill (2017). Research, evaluation, and conceptual development help keep SST alive in our clinical program as does our training and workforce development with other organizations (see Rycroft & Young, 2014, for a description of our most effective training exercises; and Young, Weir & Rycroft, 2014, for recommendations regarding SST implementation). In addition to deciding next steps, the post-session follow-up phone calls also provide therapists with regular feedback about the impact of sessions; in effect, an on-going clinical evaluation program. Single-session follow-up phone calls have taught us that change within families is seldom predictable. A family self-referred to Bouverie in the early days of our SST development taught me that change happens both inside and outside of the therapy room; that change is unpredictable as is the number of sessions and the nature of the contact.

Case Example: Change and Contact are Seldom Predictable

Barry, a 50-year-old floor sander, his two daughters, Emily (18) and Jasmine (16), together with his second wife, Tina (52) and her son, Declan (19) attended professional therapy at Bouverie after an informal mediation attempt by Barry and Tina's next-door neighbor only exacerbated the family conflict. Arguments between Barry and Declan had escalated to the point where Declan had thrown a punch at Barry. Barry called our center, each family member completed questionnaires, and the family was scheduled to see me as therapist. The family, when they arrived for therapy, consented to a reflecting team. Although we seldom use reflecting teams in our clinical work now due to the added resource required, they were an important component of developing our early SST clinical knowledge.[3]

The session did not start well: Barry began sniping at Declan; Emily and Jasmine looked bored; Tina seemed resigned to this being a repeat of the neighbor's failed attempt at resolving Barry and Declan's dispute. The pressure of time (knowing that we might only have one encounter) combined with the fear of failing in front of my colleagues, inspired me to ask Barry directly, before I had established a strong working relationship with him, why he spoke so critically of Declan. Such directness, experienced by Barry to be in good faith and in keeping with the limited time available, ironically helped build the therapeutic relationship. Barry explained that he didn't want Declan to follow the same path that he had taken in life. Worried about Declan, Barry had given him a job in the family's small floor-sanding business and quickly promoted Declan into a management role. Unfortunately, Declan was not interested in floor sanding, which led to lackluster performance and increasing tension between him and his stepdad.

Encouraged to share the source of his protective but misplaced support of Declan, Barry revealed that his mother had taken a swipe at his head with an axe during an argument when he was 14 years old. Uninjured physically but emotionally hurt, Barry gave up on his mum at this point and left home two years later to live on the streets, ending up in prison—something he wanted to help Declan avoid. The effect on Declan of hearing the good intentions behind, and context of, his stepfather's incessant criticisms of him was palpable. He softened. Tina, usually caught in the middle of Barry and Declan's battles, appeared lighter. Emily and Jasmine looked pleased, but mainly because they weren't the focus of the session, which they had reluctantly attended.

Towards the end of the session, the reflecting team, who had been observing from behind a one-way mirror, swapped places with the family and bore witness to the power of Barry's story and how it helped them make sense of the tension between Barry and his stepson. The team acknowledged the family's struggle and their underlying concern for each other, including how Tina tried unsuccessfully to mediate between Barry and Declan, and Barry's attempted support for Declan, whilst naming the unintended consequences on their relationship. The session ended feeling productive but unfinished. I handed Barry the video recording of the session, which had been taken with the family's consent, and along with the team, bid farewell to the family.

The family was difficult to reach to complete the follow-up phone call, so after six weeks I sent them a letter asking how they had found the session and inquired whether they wanted further help. I received a letter back stating that the relationship between Barry and Tina had improved largely as a result of Barry attending AA (Alcoholics Anonymous). Tina's pre-session questionnaire had raised Barry's drinking as a secondary problem, but because of the intensity of addressing the immediate conflict in the room between Declan and Barry, I had not addressed it during the session, for which I'd felt some "professional guilt." Barry reported that the family had watched the video of the session "16 times" and during an early viewing, Declan had stood up for Barry when other family members were critical of him, which contributed to an improvement in Barry and Declan's relationship. Interestingly, in the letter the family indicated that they did not require further assistance.

However, 18 months after the session, Tina rang wanting another single session with Declan to address relationship issues he had with his friends (Declan had been asked to leave two houses by his housemates). Return visits many months or years after an initial SST encounter are not unusual in our experience (Young & Rycroft, 1997) and can be seen as a component of an efficient and accessible service—where clients feel they can respectfully decline immediate therapeutic help, but easily seek it in the future as needed. Some of our clients who return ask to speak to their therapist—even when the initial one-off session occurred years earlier.

Defining SST: Why SST is an Inaccurate Name that We Should Retain

Whilst specific definitions (see Chapter 1) have their advantages, a fundamental definition of SST is likely to make SST relevant to a greater range of services. With this in mind, a fundamental definition of Single-Session Therapy could be everything that derives attitudinally, clinically, and organizationally from accepting three findings, two backed by research and the third by our clinical experience. Finding #1: that the most common number of service contacts[4] that clients attend is one, followed by two, followed by three . . . irrespective of diagnosis, complexity, or the severity of their problem (Talmon, 1990). Finding #2: that the majority (often about 70–80%) of those people who attend only one session, across a range of therapies, report that the single session was adequate given their current circumstance (Talmon, 1990; Bloom, 2001; Campbell, 2012). Finding #3: possibly the hardest finding to accept, is that it seems impossible to accurately predict who will attend only one session and who will attend more, a proposition that has significant clinical and organizational ramifications. If it cannot be predicted who will attend only one session and who will attend more, it follows that both possibilities need to be embraced simultaneously by both the worker and by their service system. That is, the first session should logically be conducted "as if" it may also be the last. In our training programs we present these three findings and ask workshop participants the following question: "If you accept these three findings, and we are not asking you to, but if you did accept these findings, how would you conduct the first session and how would you re-design your service system?" If the responses of trainees are aggregated, a description of how Bouverie staff understand SST begins to emerge. This low-resolution map has two dimensions:

Dimension #1: A SST-informed attitude to clinical work

- Approaching the first session "as if" it could be the last; irrespective of diagnosis, complexity or severity
- Exploring what each client wants to walk away with at the end of the session at hand (rather than the usual question of what the client wants from a course of therapy)
- Prioritizing what to focus on—negotiated between client and clinician, but largely client led
- Checking in at various points throughout the session to ensure the work is on track
- Sharing directly, albeit in a tentative way, feedback, advice, strategies, commendations and information that the clinician feels is helpful, driven

by the idea "What would I want to share with this client if I never see them again?"

- Providing resources and clarifying next steps.

Dimension #2: A SST approach to service design

- Embedding SST services within the organization so that clients have follow-up support if they need and want it, whilst supporting the possibility that one session may be sufficient, irrespective of diagnosis, severity or complexity
- Creating processes that accept that clients may or may not seek further help
- Establishing a no-failure context that supports clients who choose to attend one as well as supporting those who choose to attend multiple sessions.

From the preceding, it seems clear that the term "Single-Session Therapy" is likely to be a creative and disruptive influence on clinical practice and on service design (Young, et al., 2012; Young, et al., 2014) even though the term itself is misleading. A practical example illustrates this point. Using the statistics from our service, over the years, about 50% of clients attended a single session of family therapy but the remaining 50% attended multiple sessions. We offer repeat single sessions, which are sufficient for about 25% of families (two sessions in total), leaving 25% of clients who have multiple "on-going" sessions. These figures pose two challenges; whilst the challenge for professionals new to SST is to create a context where one session may be sufficient, the challenge for SST converts is to accept that on-going work is a legitimate and a positive aspect of a single-session approach. The task for SST organizations is to create processes that reflect, promote and support this balance.

In addition to its inaccuracy, the term "SST" is a turn-off for a proportion of participants involved in our training and workforce development projects. We encourage those who feel uncomfortable with the term to generate alternative descriptions that better suit their sensitivities and service context. Examples of alternative descriptions include: "an initial family consultation" and "an opening conversation."

So, if SST as a name does not reflect the research it is based upon, leads to misunderstandings of the concept, and is potentially off-putting, why not change the name in the literature?[5] Perhaps a more accurate name would be "Therapy Reflecting How Clients Seek Help and Change" or "Therapy in Which Everybody Knows the Client Will Decide with Their Feet if They Return for More Sessions or Not." However technically apt, these alternatives fail; they do not have the in-your-face quality that "Single-Session Therapy" conveys. For better or for worse, the term "SST" has a disruptive quality which shouts out, "People can change in one session with a professional, even people with complex problems, so deal with it!" Furthermore, "If people can change in one session, therapists are not always as significant in the change process as we'd like to think, so deal with that!" And, "If a significant number of clients will not return after the first session and yet are satisfied anyway, embrace it!" In short, whilst SST is a misnomer, it is a great name for challenging the traditional thinking about the therapeutic change process and for challenging traditional ways of providing services. Notwithstanding the advantages of the term SST, the following section is an attempt to re-cast the ambit of single-session thinking.

Four Misunderstandings of SST

Four misunderstandings, reinforced by the name, risk limiting the vast potential of SST as a positive disruptive influence.

Misunderstanding #1: SST is Seen as a Specific Model of Therapy Rather than a Model of Service Delivery

SST is often described as or conflated with a particular model of therapy, such as solution-oriented therapy, narrative therapy or cognitive therapy, or as a model of therapy itself. I believe it limits the ambit of SST to think of it as a particular model of therapy. I think it is more usefully disruptive to see SST as a *service delivery model* based on the three findings described earlier in this chapter—that essentially predict how clients will respond and relate to your service, not how they will respond to your therapeutic approach *per se*. Viewed in this way, therapists can embrace SST without giving up their preferred therapeutic model; a model they have usually spent thousands of dollars and many years honing. If seen in this way, therapists from different theoretical backgrounds can work together within the one organization delivering their preferred model of therapy within a SST service delivery system, thus avoiding much of the dubious debate about which model works best (Hubble, et al., 1999). Hence, SST can be conceptualized fundamentally as an attitude or approach to practice (Campbell, 2012), informed by the three findings stipulated.

A fundamental SST attitude will influence how all therapeutic models will be delivered, but won't necessarily alter the philosophy of change particular to the therapeutic model used. The pragmatics of being aware of typical client patterns of contact, to which the SST research has drawn our attention, will invite collaborative client-led practices. As clients and therapists approach each session as if it may be the last, a natural response to the client contact data, they will work to make the most of every moment (Young & Rycroft, 1997). A SST mindset (see Chapter 1) encourages adherents of any therapeutic model to be responsive to what clients want and to be transparent about the process of therapy, including what the therapist thinks and whether further sessions are required. Essentially a SST approach to service delivery helps ensure that clients are asked about what they want and that attention is directed toward that end. This means SST is disruptive to any therapy that does not value client-led or at least client-informed practice.

Misunderstanding #2: SST is Described as Brief Therapy Rather than Responding to Clients' Natural Help-Seeking Behavior

SST ideas and client contact data can have a major influence on how services are designed, including how to best respond to resource limitations. Rather than restricting services to an arbitrary number of sessions, a SST-informed delivery system can be used to manage limited resources whilst maintaining a service responsive to clients. When we first implemented a SST-service delivery system in our organization (Boyhan, 1996), the number of clients attending only one session went from approximately 20% (pre SST implementation) to approximately 50%[6] (post SST implementation) and the overall number of sessions was reduced. The savings on our front-end allowed long-term therapy families to be seen without setting an arbitrary limit to the number of sessions. Some families required years of support, which we were able to provide. Seeing SST as an efficient therapy because it aligns with what clients want and their natural help seeking behavior rather than being a brief therapy[7] *per se* will appeal to a wider range of practitioners and will allow SST thinking to guide the provision of services to all clients; those who attend once and those who require longer-term work.

Therapist, client, and organization tend to be bonded to particular assumptions about the ideal number of sessions. For example, when the Bouverie Centre was contracted to provide SST training to Community Health Counselling Services (CHCS) across the state of Victoria, the most popular norm clinicians held was that six sessions was the ideal number of counseling sessions; a smaller subgroup believed 10 sessions was the ideal. However, contact data for CHCS statewide for the period (2002–2005) revealed that of 115,206 clients, only 6% attended exactly six sessions, (and fewer clients attended exactly 10 sessions). This contact data was for the established standard practice prior to SST training and implementation (see Figure 3.1).

The belief that SST aims to restrict services to clients, or is a brief therapy, are major reasons why some professionals remain cynical about the approach. In responding to this cynicism, we believe data is more powerful than opinion. We use data to create a clear rationale for embracing a single-session approach. For example, the client contact data presented in Figure 3.1 shows that for three consecutive years between 2002–2005, prior to SST implementation 42% of over 115,206 clients in counseling-friendly community health centers across Victoria attended only one session; 18% two sessions; and 10% three sessions and these percentages were almost identical for each of the three years. This data helped provide a rationale for our goal, which was to help clinicians respond more effectively to what they were already doing—seeing many clients in unplanned one-off sessions. And whilst SST will typically reduce the number of treatment sessions, it will never replace the need for a range of service provisions; long; short; and "intermittent therapy across the life cycle" (Cummings, 1990), as in the case of Barry's family, discussed earlier.

We have found the shape, if not the numbers, of the contact data graph in Figure 3.1 to be extremely robust across a wide range of services, including

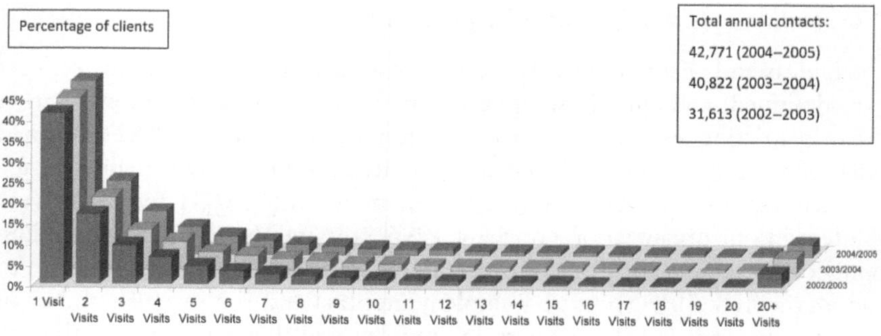

Figure 3.1 Collated statewide client visits for Victorian community health counseling services between 2002 and 2005 (used by agreement with the Bouverie Centre)

our own. For proponents of SST, it is important to remember that a significant number of service users will seek further work, and that this should not only be made available, this work should be seen as an important part of SST. Seen as a service delivery model, not a brief therapy model, SST could potentially influence provision of a range of non-therapeutic services such as physiotherapy, legal advice, financial advice, home-help, etc. In fact, any service that has similar contact data, similar satisfaction with a first meeting, and similar inability to assess who will attend one or more sessions, could be guided by SST thinking.

Misunderstanding #3: SST is Only Suitable for Clients Facing Simple Problems

Many non-SST clinicians believe the approach is not suitable for complex clients. They assume, falsely, that there is a direct relationship between complexity and the time clients remain in therapy—however, such a link does not appear to exist (Talmon 1990; Hoyt & Talmon, 2014). I recall a comment made by Moshe Talmon during his first Melbourne SST workshop in 2001 that provided a visceral example of the disjuncture between complexity and length of therapy. Talmon entreated us to compare the presenting difficulties of our friends who were in weekly psychotherapy and our clients who attended our service less frequently.

The most common question asked by participants in our training is "For whom is SST suitable and for whom is it not suitable?" We believe the best response to this question is to avoid having to answer it by embedding SST in the service system so that clients can return if they want to. Embedding SST into the service system so that all services the organization normally provides are available following an initial session, conducted as if it may be the last, allows the practitioner and the organization to avoid the "difficult if not impossible" decision of who is suitable and who is not suitable for a "one-off" session. For many therapists and some managers, the assumption that clients facing complex problems require "deep" change which can only occur in long-term work is very strong and entrenched. The SST literature continues to build data to challenge this assumption. About 15 years ago, whilst I was conducting a SST workshop, a psychoanalytically trained therapist was adamant that whilst SST may be useful for superficial change it would not be sufficient for "deep" change. During the lunch break I asked this therapist what had led to major changes in his life. Amongst other things he told me how a film he'd seen had led to a profound change in his life.

Although we, as clinicians, may think our clients need the "Rolls-Royce" treatment, often they are happy with the "Holden Ute" (an Australian icon of automotive practicability). There is no use having a great comprehensive product if the client does not want it. Many services are built on an assumption that all people with complex problems require long-term work. For example, when the Child and Adolescent Mental Health Services (CAMHS) services were established in Victoria, Australia, the first four sessions were allocated to assessment. It is an understandable approach to start work with clients facing complex difficulties by conducting a thorough assessment; however, if a significant number of clients "drop out" before the "active phase" of treatment this approach needs to be reconsidered. For example, in one Victorian CAMHS utilizing the comprehensive four-session assessment, 34% of clients didn't make it to the treatment phase (Diffey, 2007).

Focusing on what can be achieved by "making the most" of the first session, with the security of having further sessions available if needed, can help make approaching complex problems seem less overwhelming. Reportedly, when Jay Haley was asked during a workshop what suggestions he had to treat a depressed drug addict with a diagnosis of post-traumatic stress and a history of sexual abuse, he replied, "I wouldn't let that be the problem." Whilst Haley cautions us about constructing problems that can't be solved, an overly laborious focus on assessment can get in the way of responding to a client's immediate needs and wants, as defined by the client.

Misunderstanding #4: SST Means One Session

Possibly the most damaging idea to the potential expansion of SST as a responsible service delivery model is the misunderstanding that SST refers only to planned one-session treatments. Whilst in some service contexts, such as work on the streets, work in countries with limited health resources (see Chapters 8, 19, and 20), interventions may be limited to one-off sessions by necessity, considerations such as referral options, if available, are part of the broader consideration. For skeptics of SST, the idea that treatment should ideally be limited to one session, fuels cynicisms that SST is about reducing resources for therapy rather than making the most of the available health resources.[8] For adherents of SST, the idea that a good SST encounter necessarily leads to one-off sessions creates unnecessary pressure on the therapist and invalidates the significant number of people who return for further sessions. Our research (O'Neill, 2017) indicated that whilst some client families were initially concerned that the SST approach to service delivery implied limited therapeutic sessions were available, these clients were easily reassured when told further services were available and easily accessible.

Single-session services that strive to only provide "one session" options, unless the context categorically does not allow follow-up support, do not reflect the essence of SST; they simply provide a limited service. However, SST as one session is often reflected or implied in the literature; for example, "It could be argued that walk-in counseling clinics do not offer a 'pure' form of SST because clients are told that they may return to the walk-in clinic if necessary" (Hymmen, et al., 2013, p. 62). As a SST adherent, I want to provide a good service to the 42% of clients who attend community health counselors once (Figure 3.1) and an equally good service to the 58% of clients who attend multiple sessions. In fact, the skill of the SST therapist is to keep the possibilities simultaneously in mind that treatment may last one or multiple sessions, irrespective of the client's or practitioner's pre-existing perspectives on diagnosis, prognosis, severity, or complexity. Avoiding set expectations about the length of therapy has led to significant SST-inspired philosophical work by Rosenbaum (e.g., 2014), Hoyt and Talmon (2014), Slive and Bobele (2011), and others about the importance of being in the moment where therapy will take as long as it is needed and no longer.

The often-unspoken advantage of SST work delivered by either walk-in or by appointment is that clients are usually given time to see if the therapeutic session is helpful or not, before contracting for further support. The before-the-first-encounter assumption that another appointment will be automatically required is broken or obviated. This is done in our center by the decision about further sessions being made via a follow-up phone call, and in walk-in services by the person knowing they can walk in (again) at a later stage. In both cases, the client is given the responsibility for change whilst being supported in the knowledge that they can seek further help easily; a powerful context for change.

The following section looks at two different ways SST thinking has informed service delivery, each with distinctive advantages.

Different Service Delivery Models: Single-Session Therapy by Walk-In or Appointment

Although having a different historical development from that of SST by appointment services, walk-in single-session services share a radical approach to service delivery. Walk-in services have been largely designed in response to how communities want counseling services to be delivered, that is, stigma-free counseling when needed with no red tape and no exclusion criteria, available in shopping centers and other accessible community venues (Slive, et al., 2008). The same service is provided to people walking in with simple or complex problems. Whilst not offering structured follow-up phone calls or appointments, duty of care and the option of on-going work is provided by the fact that clients can just as easily return for repeat sessions. Easy access to a walk-in service, it could be argued, provides greater support and duty of care than a specific future appointment, which may or may not be kept and may not be convenient for the client. In the room, the therapeutic minutiae are determined by the therapeutic training of the therapist (and the interaction with the client), but are influenced by the same research findings underlying SST by appointment: that the client may not return. This is made overt and hence there is an incentive for the most to be made of the session by both client and therapist.

The potential power of SST by walk-in, or appointment, is that therapists trained in any therapeutic model will adapt their approach to fit the research findings of the natural client help-seeking behavior and in the case of walk-ins the feedback from the general community about the way in which people want services provided. The result, accessible and transparent services that are client-led and targeted to what clients want to achieve, consistently gains high client satisfaction rates. A meta-review of 18 refereed journals and book chapters by Hymmen, et al. (2013) found client satisfaction rates were extremely high (90–100%) for both SST by walk-in (five studies) and by appointment (13 studies). Feedback from the first 50 client families we surveyed (of which 36 were available for the study) indicated that 100% would recommend the service to others (Boyhan, 1996). We have found that once clinicians experience working within a SST program, even those who are cynical at first, find the responsiveness of SST to clients and the sense of completion at the end of each session, rewarding. Single-Session Therapy, as an efficient service delivery model, also commonly appeals to managers, making it unusual in that the approach can potentially be positive for the holy trinity of therapeutic stakeholders; clients, clinicians and managers, making implementation easier than many other models of practice.

Translating Single-Session Thinking into Practice

In the seminal systematic review on the diffusion of service innovation conducted by Trisha Greenhalgh, et al. (2004, p. 610), the authors conclude that "The evidence regarding the implementation of innovation is particularly complex and sparse" and that "the move from considering adoption to successful routinizing it is generally a nonlinear process characterized by multiple shocks, setbacks, and unanticipated events." After reviewing 235 articles on dissemination and implementation, Grimshaw and Eccles (2004) found that most implementation and dissemination strategies resulted in small to moderate improvements in care. Boren and Balas (1999) estimate that new evidence-based interventions languish for 15 to 20 years before they are incorporated (if ever) into core practice. The failure to translate the billions of dollars invested in evidence-based research into actual services on the ground is one of the great contemporary challenges of our health care system (Greenhalgh, et al., 2004).

More complex innovations are typically more difficult to implement, especially approaches that challenge workers' existing models of practice (Durlak & DuPre, 2008). Although the introduction of new ways of working is never easy, we have found that in services, especially those that embrace a social model of health, a philosophy of client-led care, and an openness to new approaches, a single-session approach to service delivery is "relatively" implementable because it does not replace workers' existing therapeutic models. For example, in Community Health Centres (CHCs), we achieved extremely high implementation success rates for individual counselors adopting elements of SST thinking (87%; 101 of 116 counselors) and for the adoption of SST as the preferred service delivery model of the CHC counseling service (55%: 55 of 101)—see Young, Weir, and Rycroft (2012) for further details. We have also gained some success in using single-session thinking as a starting point for establishing family involvement in individually focused services such as mental-health and alcohol and drug services. In the following section, several iterations of SST thinking in different work settings are described.

Putting Single-Session Thinking to Work in Diverse Settings

If SST is seen as a service delivery model based on client help-seeking behavior, the potential for one session to be helpful with options or pathways to further support, if desired by the client, the versatility of a SST approach is almost limitless. The diversity of applications of SST is clearly reflected in the chapters of this book and the edited text *Capturing the Moment: Single Session Therapy and Walk-In Services* (Hoyt & Talmon, 2014), which featured over 20 different applications ranging from equine-assisted therapy to medical family therapy to therapy for street robbery victims in Mexico City.

We find the fundamental ideas informing SST are also relevant to the work of many practitioners who do not identify or call themselves therapists—such as youth workers, support workers, and case workers. To make SST more appealing to workers who do not identify as therapists or counselors, we simply broaden the term to Single-Session Work (SSW). The fundamental single-session attitude is the same; service users may or may not return, and hence the first episode of care makes the most of the time available and completion or further assistance is considered an equally reasonable outcome if negotiated collaboratively, actively and openly with the client.

Single-Session Therapy thinking has provided a "missing link" in our efforts to introduce more systemic ways of working in strongly individually focused service systems, as outlined in the following section.

Single-Session Family Consultations (SSFC)

The Bouverie Centre has developed Single-Session Family Consultations as a key element in a comprehensive approach to engaging families in primarily individually-focused service systems, such as adult mental health services and alcohol and other drugs services. Starting with engaging the individual client about the potential benefits of involving family members in their treatment, the clinician then, with the explicit agreement of the individual client, contacts family members to determine what they would hope to achieve if such a meeting went ahead. The SSFC process has the benefits of protecting the much-prized individual client–worker relationship and creates an agreed agenda prior to the SSFC, which helps make the SSFC meeting more likely to be mutually beneficial and less conflictual. The approach combines ideas of a collaborative opportunity for families and workers to discuss how the family and service system will work together (Family Consultation; Wynne, 1994), and the SST idea of making the most of the opportunity when the family and clinician get in the room together. Single-session thinking, such as clarifying what each person in the room wants to achieve by meeting's end is relevant whether the clinician is a family therapist or a general case worker.

We have found that SSFC is an effective starting point for individually focused services to begin implementing more elaborate family-inclusive practices. Articulated in the document "From Individual to Families: A Client-Centred Framework for Involving Families" (www.bouverie.org.au), SSFC has the advantage that it can be taught relatively easily to clinicians, can build on basic family-sensitive cultural practices (Level 1), and can act as an end in itself or as a pathway to more intensive specialist family approaches (Level 3). Informed by the Family Pyramid of Care (Mottaghipour & Bickerton, 2005), the Pyramid of Family Involvement (Figure 3.2) provides guidance for professional development of the workforce that is linked to different levels of family involvement.

The framework argues that all families should receive basic family-sensitive practices (Level 1) as part of a whole-of-service family-sensitive culture, hence

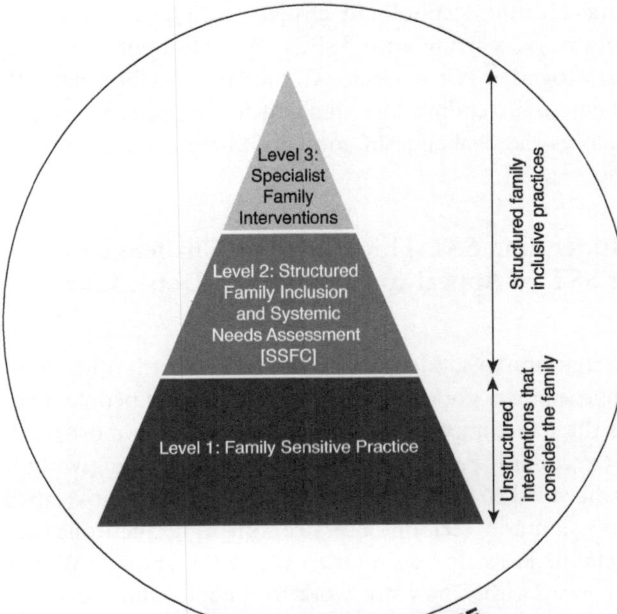

Figure 3.2 Pyramid of family involvement in "From Individual to Families: A Client-Centred Framework for Involving Families" (The Bouverie Centre, 2016. Used by agreement)

all staff are trained in this largely attitudinal and organizational cultural approach. At the second level of the framework, a significant number, but not all families, are likely to accept an invitation to participate in a structured family discussion without necessarily a long-term commitment (SSFC); hence a significant number, but not all staff, are trained in SSFC. Finally, intensive family work is required and desired by a smaller percentage of families (Level 3), so fewer staff are required to engage in extensive training required by such specialized practices.

SST: Bridging Work Across Different Settings and Modalities

It becomes clear that if SST is seen as a service delivery model, a wide range of therapeutic models and therapeutic approaches can be linked by the way these services are provided, rather than separated by the content of what they provide. Walk-in services typically allow professionals from different services to work together behind the one-way screen or as part of a team ready to be split if needed to see another client who walks in the door. SST and SSFC can fit with many different therapeutic models as mentioned earlier but can also be implemented across services, thus connecting them and leading to less siloed services—a major policy trend in Australia. Families are relevant across services (e.g., Mental Health; Alcohol and Drugs) and typically equally neglected, hence family work, starting with SSFCs, is a good entry point for helping services work together (Cross-Sector Conference, Melbourne, 2014). In line with the theme of extending SST thinking to diverse settings, the following section explores the challenge of contexts where clients are not voluntarily seeking help.

Further Extending SST Thinking: The Challenge of Adapting SST to Appeal to Clients Who Don't Like Therapy

One of the common misunderstandings of SST—that it offers less—is exactly why the approach is a good starting point to engage people who don't like therapy. As the name implies, this approach makes the most of the moment and doesn't necessarily push a long-term commitment. But, whilst SST clinical approaches have led to accessible client-directed collaborative approaches for people who voluntarily seek out a service, orienting questions such as "How can I be helpful? How do you want to spend this session? What would you like to walk away with?" may not work for people who are suspicious of us therapists and who have been mandated to seek help by the courts, their partners, or some other power.

These wonderfully facilitative questions for orienting a session with a client who wants help are likely to generate the following responses from someone who doesn't want help, if they could share their honest inner thoughts:

SST Therapist:	How would you like to work together today?
Mandated Client Thought Bubble:	I expect you'll tell me—yah %@#*!!
SST Therapist:	What would you like to get out of today?
Mandated Client Thought Bubble:	I just want to survive today!
SST Therapist:	What is the most important thing we should talk about today?
Mandated Client Thought Bubble:	How you can leave me alone and fix my wife!
SST Therapist:	What would you like to walk away with today?
Mandated Client Thought Bubble:	Just walking away would be enough.

Clinical experience has taught me that engaging clients who are extremely cynical and suspicious of therapy requires an approach almost totally contradictory to what I was taught as a clinical psychology student. Honesty (transparency) about the enterprise at hand, and a business-like directness about the situation that has brought it about (e.g., partner mandated) can do more to create trust with a person who feels forced to attend therapy than attempts at friendly collaboration. An approach that builds on the SST aspect of "cutting to the chase" (Young & Rycroft, 1997) and assuming minimal time to help, within an ethical stance of transparency and authenticity, has led to the development of an approach to engaging people who hate therapy that I have called "No Bullshit Therapy" (NBT)—see Findlay (2007). Made up of four clinical guidelines, NBT is enacted by creating a context where a therapist (and client) can be honest and direct, where the therapist can challenge from a good and caring place, can marry honesty and directness with warmth and care, and promote transparency and reduce obfuscation by avoiding jargon. NBT can be surprisingly effective, even when the person opposite you is cynical, suspicious, or not wanting to be in your presence.

Creating transparency in keeping with the philosophy of SST with mandated clients may look like stating how you prefer to work and seeking the client's response ("I like to be pretty up front and direct; how does that fit with you?"), rather making the assumption that the client wants to collaborate with you.

Creating a context where you and your client can be honest and direct can allow the sharing of tough but potentially transformative feedback. Agreeing to make the most of the initial and subsequent sessions by being honest, up front and direct can create much-needed opportunities later in the work to challenge unethical or unhelpful behavior (such as violence). Making overt that the work may only last one session can provide a boundary within which the therapist can "cut-to-the-chase" and a rationale for directness which is more likely to be experienced by reluctant customers as honorable, authentic, and respectful.

The Gift of SST

In preparing for the keynote presentation on which this chapter is based, I initially struggled to articulate why SST is such a gift. I spoke to a colleague who argued that SST promotes good basic ethical practice. Like a thoughtful gift, SST matches a therapeutic offering to what clients want. When clients get what they want, especially if they get it when they want it, they are more likely to be co-operative and eventually satisfied. If clients are driving the work, it is easier for practitioners to be transparent and authentic, which in turn allows clients to be more up front and direct about what they want and/or don't want. Matching services offered to clients' needs creates efficiencies that are good for clients, practitioners, managers and funders.

Models of clinical practice that engage practitioners, managers, funders, and clients are more easily implementable, especially if they don't replace the clinician's favored therapeutic model. A fundamental understanding of SST has the potential to influence all therapeutic models in the direction of being more transparent, authentic and client led (except in the early stages of engagement with mandated clients) whilst making services accessible and responsive to community needs. To my thinking, an implementable, efficient, accessible, client-led service delivery model that promotes transparency and authenticity across services is a considerable gift to the community.

Notes

1 My appreciation to Mark Furlong for his input regarding this chapter.
2 Risk issues are responded to in the same way risk issues are addressed in on-going work, with immediate action.
3 The reflecting team comprised Ralph Hampson, who was visiting Melbourne from the Canberra Child and Adolescent Mental Health Team, an early adopter of SST in Australia and two of the founding members of the Bouverie SST team, Colin Riess and Pam Rycroft.
4 In Chapter 11, Michael Hoyt points out that the most common number of sessions is actually zero!
5 There have been a number of attempts, without much success, to create a more accurate and attractive term for SST, for example "therapy moment by moment" (Rosenbaum, 2008), "present therapy" (Talmon, 2012), "one session at a time" (Slive and Bobele, 2011) and "making the most of every encounter" (Young and Rycroft, 2012).
6 Boyhan's (1996) research showed that 53% of client families did not require further sessions, but this was measured only after two months; over time, families would return for additional sessions, usually for another presenting problem, and the "one-session only" rate returned to about 50%.
7 When seen in this way, services are more likely to use a SST mindset to provide the most responsive service to those who decide they only need one or a few sessions but not exclude those who need and want longer treatment. In this way, SST as a service delivery model is relevant to whole-of-service provision, not just brief work; it is neither "long" nor "short" (Rosenbaum, 2008).
8 As highlighted in Chapter 1, SST is not a panacea. We strongly advocate a full range of mental-health services are needed. However, a SST service delivery approach can be a very effective starting point for many services.

References

Bloom, B.L. (2001). Focused single session psychotherapy: A review of the clinical and research literature. *Brief Treatment and Crisis Intervention, 1*(1), 75–86.

Boren, S.A. & Balas, E.A. (1999) Evidence-based quality measurement. *Journal of Ambulatory Care Management, 22*(3), 17–23.

Boyhan, P. (1996). Client's perceptions of single session consultations as an option to waiting for family therapy. *Australian and New Zealand Journal of Family Therapy, 17*(2), 85–96.

Campbell, A. (2012). Single-session approaches to therapy: Time to review. *Australian and New Zealand Journal of Family Therapy, 33*(1), 15–26.

Cross-sector Conference. (2014, August 26). *Creative cross-sector conference: Making it work for the client.* Melbourne, Australia: Organized by The Bouverie Centre, sponsored by the Victorian Responsible Gambling Foundation, supported by the Victorian Department of Health.

Cummings, N.A. (1990). Brief intermittent psychotherapy throughout the life cycle. In J.K. Zeig & S.G. Gilligan (Eds.), *Brief therapy: Myths, methods, and metaphors* (pp. 169–184). New York: Brunner/Mazel.

Diffey, C. (2007). *Incorporating single session therapy into everyday CAMHS clinical practice.* Master's thesis, La Trobe University, Melbourne, Australia.

Durlak, J.A. & DuPre, E.P. (2008). Implementation matters: A review of research on the influence of implementation on program outcomes and the factors affecting implementation. *American Journal of Community Psychology, 41*(3–4), 327–350.

Findlay, R. (2007). A mandate for honesty, Jeff Young's No Bullshit Therapy: An interview. *Australian and New Zealand Journal of Family Therapy, 28*(3), 165– 170.

Greenhalgh, T., Robert, G., Macfarlane, F., Bate, P., & Kyriakidou, O. (2004). Diffusion of innovations in service organizations: Systematic review and recommendations. *The Milbank Quarterly, 82*(4), 581–629.

Grimshaw, J.M., & Eccles, M.P. (2004, March 15). Is evidence-based implementation of evidence-based practice possible? *Medical Journal of Australia, 180*(6 Supplement), S50-1.

Hampson, R., O'Hanlon, J., Franklin, A., Pentony, M., Fridgant, L. & Heins, T. (1999). The place of single session family consultations: Five years' experience in Canberra. *Australian and New Zealand Journal of Family Therapy, 20*(4), 195–200.

Hoyt, M.F. & Talmon, M. (Eds.) (2014). *Capturing the moment: Single session therapy and walk-in services.* Bethel, CT: Crown House Publishing.

Hubble, M.A., Duncan, B.L., & Miller, S.D. (1999). *The heart and soul of change: What works in therapy.* Washington, DC: American Psychological Association.

Hymmen, P., Stalker, C.A., & Cait, C. (2013). The case for single-session therapy: Does the empirical evidence support the increased prevalence of this service delivery model and walk-in services? *Journal of Mental Health, 22*(1), 60–71.

Mottaghipour, Y. & Bickerton, A. (2005). The pyramid of family care: A framework for family involvement with adult mental health services. *Australian e-Journal for the Advancement of Mental Health, 4*(3), 210–217.

O'Neill, I. (2017). What's in a name? Clients' experience of single session therapy. *Journal of Family Therapy, 39*: 63–79. doi:10.1111/1467-6427.12099.

O'Neill, I. & Rottem, N. (2012). Reflections and learning from an agency-wide implementation of single session work in family therapy. *Australian and New Zealand Journal of Family Therapy*, *33*(1), 70–83.

Price, C. (1994). Open days making family therapy accessible in working class suburbs. *Australian and New Zealand Journal of Family Therapy*, *15*(4), 191–196.

Rosenbaum, R. (2008). Psychotherapy is not short or long. *Monitor on Psychology*, *39*(7), 4, 8.

Rosenbaum, R. (2014). The time of your life. In M.F. Hoyt & M. Talmon (Eds.), *Capturing the moment: Single session therapy and walk-in services* (pp. 41–52). Bethel, CT: Crown House Publishing.

Rycroft, P. & Young, J. (2014). SST in Australia: Learning from teaching. In M.F. Hoyt & M. Talmon (Eds.), *Capturing the Moment: Single-Session Therapy and Walk-in Services* (pp. 141–156). Bethel, CT: Crown House Publishing.

Slive, A., McElheran, N., & Lawson, A. (2008). How brief does it get? Walk-in single session therapy. *Journal of Systemic Therapies*, *27*, 5–22.

Slive, A. & Bobele, M. (Eds.) (2011). *When one hour is all you have: Effective therapy walk-in clients*. Phoenix, AZ: Zeig, Tucker, & Theisen.

Talmon, M. (1990). *Single session therapy: Maximizing the effect of the first (and often only) therapeutic encounter*. San Francisco: Jossey-Bass.

Talmon, M. (2012). When less is more: Lessons from 25 years of attempting to maximize the effect of each (and often only) therapeutic encounter. *Australian and New Zealand Journal of Family Therapy*, *33*(1), 6–14.

The Bouverie Centre (2016). *From individual to families: A client-centred framework for involving families, developed for mental health and alcohol and other drug services*. Melbourne: The Bouverie Centre: Victoria's Family Institute, La Trobe University.

Wynne, L.C. (1994). The rationale for consultation with the families of schizophrenic patients, *Acta Psychiatrica Scandinavica*, *90*(s384), 125–132.

Young, J. & Rycroft, P. (1997). Single session therapy: Capturing the moment. *Psychotherapy in Australia*, *4*(1) 18–23.

Young, J. & Rycroft, P. (2012). Single session therapy: What's in a name? *Australian and New Zealand Journal of Family Therapy*, *33*(1), 3–5.

Young, J., Weir, S., & Rycroft, P. (2012). Implementing single session therapy. *Australian and New Zealand Journal of Family Therapy*, *33*(1), 84–97.

Young, J., Rycroft, P., & Weir, S. (2014). Implementing single session therapy: Practical wisdoms from Down Under. In M.F. Hoyt & M. Talmon (Eds.), *Capturing the moment: Single session therapy and walk-in services* (pp. 121–140). Bethel, CT: Crown House Publishing.

4 Change in the Winds

The Growth of Walk-In Therapy Clinics in Ontario, Canada

Karen Young

There are at least 40 walk-in counseling clinics currently operating in Ontario, more than in any other province or likely country. In 2001, ROCK (Reach Out Centre for Kids) began operating our walk-in counseling clinic and along with two other children's mental-health centers became one of three operating clinics in Ontario that year. Since then, the number of walk-ins in Ontario is constantly growing as new clinics open their doors. In this chapter we will visit the circumstances that made this unique growth of walk-in counseling clinics possible: the backstories and history that it stands on, the inspirations and pivotal events, and the impact of brief narrative practices on the therapeutic approach at many of the clinics. We will look at the effects of walk-in therapy on service delivery for children, youth and families; the influence on and from provincial policy; and the opportunity created for developing a multi-organization evaluation project. As with any story, this is not the only story—it is a story inside of many other stories, and is influenced by the experience and context affecting the storyteller.

The development of walk-in clinics in Ontario came about as a response to challenges and dilemmas in mental-health service delivery. The problem of staggeringly long waiting lists, along with the problem of the medicalization and pathologization of people's identities at the front doors of our helping system, created an opportunity. This was an opportunity to respond in ways that were consistent with particular commitments, values, and hopes about the lives of children, youth, and families. The way to access help could shift away from the first contact with children, youth, and families being deficit-focused assessment tools and then placement on long waiting lists, to quick access to a meaningful, collaborative, and strength-oriented therapeutic encounter. Walk-in counseling clinics, many influenced by brief narrative practices, began to appear across all the regions of Ontario.

Ontario's Walk-In Clinics

The walk-in counseling clinics at ROCK, located in five different sites across the geographic region served by the organization, provide initial contact, Single-Session Therapy, and referral into further services when needed for approximately 2,000 children and their families each year. The clinics are well advertised to the community through brochures at key referral sources such as schools, child welfare, and doctors' offices, and on the agency's website. The service is described as:

> [H]elp when you need it; an opportunity to see a trained therapist in your moment of need; immediate opportunity for therapeutic conversation and problem solving; connection to other services if needed; and, for many a single session is all that's needed, but you can come more than once, you decide.
>
> (ROCK, Walk-in Counselling Clinic Brochure, 2016)

Many other walk-in counseling clinics in Ontario are described similarly; over half are operated by children's mental-health centers, with the others being operated within adult services such as Family Service agencies, Canadian Mental Health Associations and Family Health Teams, and some being collaborations between children and adult services. About 14 clinics serve adults, four clinics serve both adults and children/youth, with the remainder serving children and youth. Walk-in counseling within the adult sector has been expanding with new clinics recently started by adult health-funded organizations. Some clinics are simply named walk-in therapy or walk-in counseling clinics while others have more creative names such as Talk-in Clinic, Session at a Time Service, and the What's Up Clinic.

Backstories and Pivotal Events: Once Upon a Time . . .

Once upon a time, there was a problem called "Waiting Lists." These lists had grown ever increasingly long over the mid-1990s and early 2000s in Ontario—particularly in the area of children's mental health where, in some cases, young people had waited as long as four years to finally gain access to services (The National Infant, Child, and Youth Mental Health Consortium, 2010; Reid & Brown, 2008). The "Waiting Lists" were having devastating effects on children and families (Boyhan, 1996; Rosenbaum, Hoyt, & Talmon, 1990) as problems grew worse while people waited and then, the longer they waited, the less likely they were to eventually connect to any services (Reid & Brown, 2008; Sherman, Barnum, Buhman-Wiggs, & Nyberg, 2009). "Waiting Lists" were not only created and maintained by a lack of funding resulting in insufficient resources, but were also supported by the practices in the system that uniformly assumed the need for complex, deficit-focused assessments at the front-end of services and elaborate longer-term involvement once children and families finally entered services (Duvall, Young, & Kayes-Burden, 2012).

However, ideas that questioned these taken-for-granted assumptions and practices were circulating in the field both through publications (Harper-Jaques, McElheran, Slive, & Leahey, 2008; Slive, McElheran, & Lawson, 2008; Miller & Slive, 2004; Rosenbaum, Hoyt, & Talmon, 1990) and the emergence of radical new services such as the first walk-in counseling clinic in Canada opening in 1990 at Woods Homes in Calgary, Alberta. The "social weather" (Lynn Hoffman, as quoted in Shotter, 2015a) had been shifting in Ontario, with the introduction and enthusiastic uptake of new emerging therapies informed by postmodern (Duvall & Beres, 2011; White, 2007; Freedman & Combs, 1996) ideas and practices. Hoffman describes "social weather" as "an interwoven flow of meaning and activity . . . It fills our sails, becalms us . . . . It shapes and effects what we sense is called for in a particular context . . ." (Hoffman, 2002, p. 68). There were some very significant "weather systems" that came together in Ontario that shaped how walk-in clinics in Ontario developed.

Beginning in 1990 and going forward usually annually after that, Michael White and David Epston began teaching about narrative therapy practices in Ontario. These ideas were very resonant for many therapists, and inspired and shaped teaching and training programs in Ontario (J. Duvall, Brief Narrative Therapy with Children, Families and Adults: Year-Long Certificate Program; K. Young, The Narrative Therapy Training Certificate Program; R. Pluznick and A. Yuen, Narrative Therapy Centre of Toronto; S. Cooper, Brief Narrative Practices Project). Jim Duvall, who commenced training programs in Ontario in the late 1980s, began to organize narrative training events with Michael White, drawing larger and larger crowds of practitioners—over 800 people at a Toronto event in 1993. The richer text of a therapy philosophy articulated within narrative therapy clearly connected with a longing for more meaningful ways to work shared by so many therapists. It galvanized therapists to stand against problem-saturated pathologizing ways of working. It was like a fresh wind blowing across the province and the field.

In 2001 the new CEO of ROCK, Ron Rodgers, who arrived with a vision and commitment to implement a walk-in counseling clinic, approached me with a wonderful opportunity—the task to lead the design and implementation of the clinic at ROCK. I had already designed and implemented a brief therapy service informed by narrative practices in 1992 and had been teaching narrative therapy since 1993. This invitation was therefore in many ways the spark between narrative therapy and walk-in counseling clinics in Ontario. After this time, in many of the training programs and workshops where I was teaching, there was great interest in the use of these practices at walk-in clinics, in single sessions, and in brief therapy. Invitations to consult and train specifically in how to start up walk-in clinics and utilize brief narrative practices at walk-in clinics grew.

In 2008, ROCK invited all the organizations that were currently running walk-in clinics to a gathering to share ideas, practices, and emerging evaluation and research from the clinics. A document was posted on-line summarizing this event called "An Inventory of Walk-in Counselling Clinics in Ontario" (Bhanot-Malhotra, Livingstone, & Stalker, 2009). This created an increased circulation of knowledge and the number of walk-in clinics in the province grew more rapidly.

Policy Influence

In 2012 a policy-ready paper, "No More, No Less: Brief Mental Health Services for Children and Youth" (Duvall, Young, & Kayes-Burden) for the Ministry of Children and Youth in Ontario was sponsored by the Ontario Centre of Excellence for Child and Youth Mental Health. This paper focused on brief services implementation, purposes, philosophy, and approaches and became one of the most frequently accessed policy papers on the Centre of Excellence website. The Ministry of Children and Youth Services in Ontario then utilized this paper in its system transition process—a process implemented in Ontario starting in 2015, which includes requiring brief services such as walk-in counseling clinics to be offered by children's mental health services in every community across Ontario. A bold and inspired move by government funders! The social weather in Ontario had taken a significant turn.

Brief Narrative Practices at Walk-In Clinics

Narrative therapy was first developed by Michael White and David Epston (White & Epston, 1990; White, 2007). It is a collaborative, non-pathologizing, and competency-focused approach to therapy. It is based on the notion that stories are created to make sense of our lives, and that the stories we create then also influence our lives and relationships. Problems are viewed as separate from people's identities and part of the larger context of people's lives. People are seen as having knowledge, skills, abilities, values, and commitments that can assist them to respond to the problems that are influencing their lives. These skills and values are often hidden by the problem stories and thus require the therapy conversation to serve as an opportunity to make these visible and accessible to people. People are then in touch with an expanded or even new sense of identity that is powerfully connected to their preferences, values, and commitments.

There are many aspects of narrative practices that are a perfect fit with brief or time-sensitive services as they quickly create meaningful, useful conversations. Narrative therapy offers a clear philosophy and practice for creating an impactful, novel, and useful conversation in every session. Brief therapeutic encounters shaped by narrative therapy can shift how people view problems and themselves, expanding and changing stories, making it possible for people to see ways forward in their lives. People are invited to see themselves as knowledgeable about their own lives, and as having many skills, abilities, beliefs, values, and commitments that will assist them to reduce the influence of problems in their lives. People consistently report experiencing brief narrative practices as meaningful and useful, and often report that "aha" moments in brief narrative sessions ripple forward in their lives, creating lasting change (Young & Bhanot-Malhotra, 2014; Young & Cooper, 2008).

The influence of narrative therapy at a walk-in counseling clinic begins even before the session in that at most clinics when people arrive they are asked to complete short questionnaires. These pre-session questionnaires, influenced by narrative and solution-focused ideas, set the stage for conversations where the counselor strives to understand the problem and to find hope, new ideas, and knowledge about how to proceed. The questionnaires help people to shift into paying attention to their abilities, skills, accomplishments, and values even before the session begins. This provides important initial information for the counselor that assists in preparing for the session. The multiple focus that includes both why the client is here and what more there is to know about them is designed to reassure clients that they will be respected and seen as people who both have competencies and have a current problem or struggle that they are here to talk about (Young, Dick, Herring, & Lee, 2008). At many clinics the supervisor meets with the counselor briefly before the session to assist in preparing for the session with a competency-lens. The supervisor and/or the counselor both need to have skills to look at the questionnaire with eyes for both the problem story and the other stories that reflect the knowledge, values, skills, and preferences of the client.

Given the challenges of achieving and maintaining a competency-focus in the session, and ensuring a meaningful, impactful conversation, it is very useful to have a least two counselors. One counselor can be more in the lead of the session, while the other can focus on offering reflections that highlight knowledge, values, skills and possibilities. The pair might be a therapist or counselor paired with an intern or student. The process could follow an outsider witnessing tradition as in narrative therapy (White, 2007). The lead therapist can pause and invite the witnessing therapist to offer reflections guided by questions such the following (White, 2007; Young, 2015):

- What stood out for you that you appreciate about this person/couple/family?
- What did you hear/see that told you something about what this person/couple/family values?
- What knowledge, values, and skills did you notice so far?
- Did a picture or an image come up for you that represents something about this person/family? If so, what is it?
- What will you remember about this person/family? What have they taught you?

Narrative therapy provides an overarching "attitudinal stance" (Pare, 2013, p. 101) that assists counselors to maintain a high degree of collaboration, transparency, respect and genuine curiosity (Young, 2017). This therapeutic posture moves the counselor away from advising, problem solving and assessment, and keeps the conversation generative and energizing. The counselor's commitment to transparency and collaboration is maintained throughout the session from the beginning explanations and information about the process, to the concurrent and open in-session note-taking. Borrowing again from a narrative therapy documentation tradition, the counselor takes notes during the session in an open and transparent way onto a summary report form that is photocopied and given to the client at the end.

It is useful to create documents during every walk-in session. These notes, lists, quotes, statements, drawings, and diagrams are very engaging of people during the session, and can be sent home with them so they are available to them. This assists with "stickability" of what was talked about in the meeting (Duvall & Young, 2009).

A summary report along with any other therapeutic documents such as lists and drawings are completed within the walk-in session in a way that engages the participants in the process, is transparent, and includes their own words and understandings. Verbal summaries throughout the session serve as a way to check in about how the co-therapists' understanding of their situation, ideas, and words is going. These summaries are derived from the notes taken during the conversation and are often read back to people throughout the conversation. This holds up their words like a mirror, allowing for any corrections, and for the persons involved to reflect further on their own words and to possibly expand on them. Summarizing in this way slows the pace of the conversation and creates a place from which the next question may be asked. I have written previously (Young, 2011, 2006) about the importance of slowing down the pace in Single-Session Therapy as an important aspect of practice that contributes to effectiveness. In taking away a summary report and other documents persons are provided with a record and a reminder of their own words, knowledge, new understandings, and plans that emerged within the conversation. People often share these documents with others who are not present such as family members, friends, and schoolteachers or principals. This engages a potential support team that can assist in sustaining new ideas and plans (Duvall & Beres, 2011; White, 2007; Young & Cooper, 2008).

Narrative practice can also lend a framework for the flow and process of sessions at a walk-in clinic. The following is a guideline that I have developed and shared with many of Ontario's walk-in clinics. This guideline is meant to be used in a flexible, fluid way as the counselor responds with genuine curiosity and is artful in their practice. The guideline is informed by narrative therapy practices and is referred to as Brief Narrative Therapy (www.windzinstitute.com).

A Guideline for Walk-in Session Structure Influenced by Brief Narrative Therapy

(1) *Pre-session preparation:* This can be a brief discussion between a supervisor and the counselor, or between counselors, that looks at the client questionnaire carefully for: preferences, hopes, and values that are expressed by the client's agenda; ideas about possible externalizing language for the problem; and glimmers of stories of knowledge, values, and skills. The conversation can help to generate possible questions that could be asked.

(2) *Beginning the session:* The counselor explains the process, forms, and consents, risks and benefits to the clients. The role of everyone present is described—for example, the lead therapist and the witnessing counselor. The process of collaborative documentation is explained, including the procedure and the purposes.

(3) *Setting the agenda:* This is a time in the session when the counselor finds out more about what the client wants to focus on in this conversation today. The counselor might start with something like: "I am prepared to work hard with you for the next hour or so in relation to what it is that brought you here. What should we focus on in our conversation so that you leave feeling it was useful?" Whatever words the therapist uses to set the agenda should convey messages of collaboration, respect for what the clients want to talk about, the importance of having a focus, and especially that they can leave with something useful today.

(4) *Discover strengths:* In a brief narrative practice at a walk-in, this is a time where the counselor will seek permission from the client to pause the problem talk and explore strengths, skills, abilities, knowledge, values, commitments, and preferences. This practice comes from the belief that *the person is not the problem* (White, 2007; White & Epston, 1990). There is so much to know about the person that is different from only narrowly knowing them in relation to the problem. A narrative counselor often initiates these conversations early on in the brief therapy session through asking a question such as, "Before we talk more about 'the problem,' would it be OK with you if I ask some questions to find out about you or your child away from this problem?" In keeping with a transparent posture, they might add, "This will help us to know what you've already got with you that might be put up against this problem." Then, with the parent's go-ahead, the counselor might, for example, ask, "Of all the many stories you have about Sara [child], what is one story that you could tell so I can know what there is to really appreciate about her?" With any story or small glimmer of a story, the counselor's job is to become curious and ask questions that develop the details and create a rich story.

These conversations explore a person's qualities, skills, and ideas of how to live life, values, knowledge, know-how, and so on. This can lead to discovering what it is that the person has got to put up against the problem, which is something that the person is unlikely to be in touch with at the start of the session. This type of inquiry facilitates the development of links between stories of the person's identity and the possibilities that exist for influence over the problem and its effects. In fact, there are times when these conversations can stand on their own, in terms of being enough and sufficient for the person to find new ideas about how to respond to their concerns.

(5) *Exploring the problem:* The counselor here seeks to develop an understanding of what this problem is like for this client, and how they understand it. A narratively-informed counselor is mindful of asking questions that both seek

to understand the problem and work to create a different way of seeing and understanding the problem. It is our job to facilitate a conversation that introduces novel ways of viewing the problem. Creating novelty in therapy is an important factor in change and supported by neuroscience (Siegel & Bryson 2011; Beaudoin & Zimmerman, 2011; Young & Hibel, 2017). This is especially important in brief therapy as people come to walk-in clinics and other brief services with a problem they are struggling with and for which they want immediate assistance. Externalizing conversations, where the problem is talked about as a separate thing from the person, help to develop new, sometimes unusual, language with clients to open up new possibilities for meaning and actions. Practices such as "externalizing problems" (Combs & Freedman, 2012; White, 2007) are highly effective in brief therapies (Young & Hibel, 2017; Young, 2011; Ramey, Young, & Tarulli, 2010).

(6) *Develop details of knowledge, skills, values, and preferences:* The counselor explores the actions/initiatives/responses the clients have taken to try to reduce the problem, and their skills/strengths/abilities and values and commitments they drew upon to do this. They work hard to get the details of the client's competencies and how these can be useful in relation to the problem or concern. Opportunity is found to explore the preferences the client has for their life and relationships and why and how they want to move toward these, and any ways that they already do this.

(7) *Review and expand what was useful:* The counselor explores what stood out from the conversation and why this stood out to the client. This is generated together. The conversation is collaborative, not simply the counselor giving advice or teaching.

(8) *Co-develop next steps:* The counselor explores how any new ideas or understandings might help, and specifically how to use these new understandings or ideas. This conversation should be generative—together with the client planning for any next steps. The counselor stays away from trying to talk the client into change and instead elicits from them their reasons for change. The client and the counselor discuss how to keep the ideas/plans/next steps going and what supports are needed to do this.

(9) *Wrap up:* The counselor provides the client with a summary report and any documents developed together in the session. They may offer reflections that acknowledge the two-way phenomenon of therapeutic conversations and offer to tell the clients briefly about their effect on us, and what we will remember or have learned from them (White, 2007; Freedman & Combs, 1996). The client is offered a session evaluation to complete privately.

Evaluation

In 2014 and 2015, ROCK was the lead organization in an evaluation project of brief single-session services and walk-in clinics across Ontario. The process and outcomes of this study were published (see Young & Bhanot-Malhotra,

2014) on the website of the Ontario Centre of Excellence for Child and Youth Mental Health, which had funded the research. Working together, six partner organizations designed the very first comprehensive look at the effects of single-session and walk-in therapy for clients in Ontario. The evaluation team spanned multiple organizations, multiple ways to deliver brief single-session services, and a range of therapeutic approaches for Single-Session Therapy with an over-arching influence from brief narrative practices.

This evaluation examined outcomes from a sample of Ontario's brief single-session services: walk-in clinics at ROCK, the collaboratively run What's Up Clinic based in Toronto (East Metro, Oolagen, Yorktown, and Hincks-Dellcrest), Point in Time brief services in Haliburton, and Youth Services Bureau walk-in clinic in Ottawa. All serve children and youth 0–18, some to age 24, and their families.

The evaluation addressed the following questions:

(1) Do clients benefit from participating in a single therapy session? If so, what positive outcomes are achieved?
(2) Are the benefit(s) from a single session maintained after three months?
(3) What kinds of presenting problems are the clients experiencing who access these services?

The methodology included a pre-test immediately prior to the single session, a post-test immediately after the session, and then a three-month post-test. The surveys used included one designed by the research team, the *Brief Services Evaluation* (Young & Bhanot-Malhotra, 2014), one previously designed and published questionnaire, *The Problem Evaluation Summary* (Campbell, 1999), and one standardized measure, the *Session Rating Scale* (Miller, Duncan, Johnson, 2000) that has been widely used. All the surveys used were deliberately brief, client-centered, and competency-focused, exploring people's development of knowledge and skills to respond to problems.

Questionnaire items were designed to measure:

- the issues that brought a client to walk-in
- clients' understanding of the issue that brought them to walk-in
- clients' perceptions of their own skills, strengths, and problem-solving abilities
- clients' knowledge of their social supports and community resources
- the severity of the problem/issues, and
- clients' coping skills.

Findings

A total of 352 clients completed both pre-session and post-session measures, with 70 clients completing the three-month post-session measures.

Analysis

Overall, results suggested that clients experience a number of positive outcomes as a result of participating in brief single-session services. The following is a summary of some of these:

- The biggest areas of improvement were in clients' awareness of their own skills, ideas about how to solve the problem/issue, and awareness of community resources.
- The majority of clients (about 80%), reported having "aha moments"/ realizations from the session.
- The average three-month post-session scores were higher than the pre-session scores for every outcome that was measured.
- 86% of clients reported that they had used ideas/strategies from the session.
- Clients reported improvements in coping.
- The results of our three-month follow-up suggest that clients perceived that the problem was less severe/less frequent and that they had more control over the problem.
- The findings of our evaluation further suggest that a strong therapeutic alliance is possible during brief services. The *Session Rating Scale* (*SRS*) was used as a measure of therapeutic alliance (344 clients completed this post-session). The average *SRS* score for the sample was 35.16 (maximum possible score of 40). This suggests that there was a high level of therapeutic alliance between clients and therapists. This finding suggests that high levels of therapeutic alliance are possible during single-session and brief services. This is important because research shows (Duncan & Miller, 2000) that the most important predictor of a positive outcome from therapy is therapeutic alliance. Perhaps future research might explore any correlation between the strength of the therapeutic alliance and positive outcomes in single sessions.

Summary

Change is in the winds in Ontario. The growing number of walk-in clinics there stands for quick access to meaningful and useful help when people need it. These walk-in services depart from dominant medicalized assessment and diagnostic practices and then placement on long waiting lists. At a time in history when we all face the imposition of tick-box protocols, manualized treatments, evidence-based practices, and a host of many other diagnostic tools (Shotter, 2012), walk-in clinics are reclaiming an alternative to this. The approach has created an opportunity for client-centered competency-based evaluation from the consumers of walk-in clinics. Conversations guided by brief narrative practices at walk-in clinics are distinctly collaborative, guided by genuine curiosity and a steadfast commitment to attend to both the problem story and the other stories of people's lives that reflect knowledge, values, skills, and preferences. As John Shotter (2015b, p. 84, italics in original) writes:

> [T]herapists both speak to and listen to their clients in ways that are often *poetic*, in ways that "touch" or "move" them, in ways that stimulate clients to draw on their own resources; to develop new ways forward, fashioned in *their* terms, not in *ours*.

Both the approach to conversations with clients at walk-in counseling clinics and the very existence of these clinics as an alternative to long waits for service have moved the field forward in ways that are congruent with our values for people to have quick access to a meaningful, collaborative and strength-oriented therapeutic encounter.

References

Beaudoin, M.N. & Zimmerman, J. (2011). Narrative therapy and interpersonal neurobiology: Revisiting classic practices, developing new emphases. *Journal of Systemic Therapies*, *48*(1), 1–13.

Bhanot-Malhotra, S., Livingstone, & S., Stalker, C. (2009). An inventory of walk-in counseling clinics in Ontario. www.briefnarrative.com/field-notes/walk-in-inventory.pdf.

Boyhan, P.A. (1996). Clients' perceptions of single session consultations as an option to waiting for family therapy. *Australian and New Zealand Journal of Family Therapy, 17*, 85–96.

Campbell, A. (1999). Single session interventions: An example of clinical research in practice. *Australian and New Zealand Journal of Family Therapy*, *20*(4), 183–194.

Combs, G. & Freedman, J. (2012). Narrative, postructuralism, and social justice: Current practices in narrative therapy. *The Counseling Psychologist*, *40*(7) 1033-1060, Sage. doi: 10.1177/0011000012460662.

Duncan, B.L. & Miller, S.D. (2000). *The heroic client: Doing client-directed, outcome-informed therapy*. San Francisco: Jossey-Bass.

Duvall, J. & Beres, L. (2011). *Innovations in narrative therapy: Connecting practice, training, and research*. New York: Norton.

Duvall, J., & Young, K. (2009). Keeping faith: A conversation with Michael White. *Journal of Systemic Therapies*, *28*, 1–18.

Duvall, J., Young, K., & Kayes-Burden, A. (2012). *No more, no less: Brief mental health services for children and youth*. www.excellenceforchildandyouth.com.

Freedman, J. & Combs, G. (1996). *Narrative therapy: The social construction of preferred realities*. New York: Norton.

Harper-Jaques, S., McElheran, N., Slive, A., & Leahey, M. (2008). A comparison of two approaches to the delivery of walk-in single session mental health therapy. *Journal of Systemic Therapies, 27*(4): 40–53.

Hoffman, L. (2002). *Family therapy: An intimate history*. New York: Norton.

Miller, J.K. & Slive, A. (2004). Breaking down the barriers to clinical service delivery: walk-in therapy. *Journal of Marital and Family Therapy*, *30*(1): 95–103.

Miller, S.D., Duncan, B.L., & Johnson. L.D. (2000). *The Session Rating Scale.* Chicago, IL: International Center for Clinical Excellence.

National Infant, Child, and Youth Mental Health Consortium Advisory. The Provincial Centre of Excellence for Child and Youth Mental Health at CHEO (2010). *Access and wait times in child and youth mental health: A background paper.* Toronto: Canadian Institutes of Health Research.

Pare, D.A. (2013). *The practice of collaborative counselling and psychotherapy: Developing skills in culturally mindful helping.* Los Angeles, CA: Sage.

Ramey, H.L., Young, K., & Tarulli, D. (2010). Scaffolding and concept formation in narrative therapy: A qualitative research report. *Journal of Systemic Therapies, 29*(4), 74–91.

Reach Out Centre for Kids, ROCK. (2016). Walk-in Counselling Clinic brochure. www.rockonline.ca.

Reid, G.J. & Brown, J.B. (2008) Money, case complexity, and wait lists: Perspectives on problems and solutions at children s mental health centers in Ontario. *Journal of Behavioral and Health Services Research, 35*, 334–346.

Rosenbaum, R., Hoyt, M.F., & Talmon, M. (1990). The challenge of single session therapies: Creating pivotal moments. In R.A. Wells & V.J. Giannetti (Eds.), *Handbook of brief psychotherapies* (pp. 165–198). New York: Plenum Press.

Sherman, M.L., Barnum, D.D., Buhman-Wiggs, A., & Nyberg, E. (2009). Clinical intake of child and adolescent consumers in a rural community mental health center: Does wait-time predict attendance? *Community Mental Health Journal, 45*, 78–84.

Shotter, J. (2012). Bodily way—finding our way into the future: Finding the guidance we need for our next step within the taking of our present step. www.opendialogicalpractices.eu.

Shotter, J., (2015a). On being dialogical: An ethics of "attunement." www.developingopendialogue.com.

Shotter, J., (2015b). Tom Andersen, fleeting events, the bodily feelings they arouse in us, and the dialogical. *Australian and New Zealand Journal of Family Therapy, 36* (1), 72–87.

Siegel, D.J. & Bryson, T.P. (2011). *The whole-brain child: 12 revolutionary strategies to nurture your child's developing mind.* New York: Delacorte Press.

Slive, A., McElheran, N., & Lawson, A. (2008). How brief does it get?: Walk-in single session therapy. *Journal of Systemic Therapies, 27*(4): 5–22.

White, M. (2007). *Maps of narrative practice.* New York: Norton.

White, M. & Epston, D. (1990). *Narrative means to therapeutic ends.* New York: Norton.

Young, K. (2006). *When all the time you have is now: Narrative practice at a walk-in therapy clinic.* www.narrativeapproaches.com.

Young, K. (2011). When all the time you have is now: Re-visiting practices and narrative therapy in a walk-in Clinic. In J. Duvall & L. Beres (Eds.), *Innovations in narrative therapy: Connecting practice, training, and research.* New York: Norton.

Young, K. (2015). Guidelines for practice at ROCK's walk-in clinic. www.rockonline.ca.

Young, K. (2017). Walk-in therapy clinics: An opportunity for socially just conversations. In D.A. Pare & C. Audet (Eds.), *Social justice and counselling: Discourse in practice.* New York: Routledge (Taylor & Francis).

Young, K. & Bhanot-Malhotra, S. (2014). *Getting services right: An Ontario multi-agency evaluation study.* www.excellenceforchildandyouth.com.

Young, K. & Cooper, S. (2008). Toward co-composing an evidence base: The narrative therapy re-visiting project. *Journal of Systemic Therapies, 27*(1), 67–83.

Young, K., Dick, M., Herring, K., & Lee, J. (2008). From waiting lists to walk-in: Stories from a walk-in therapy clinic. *Journal of Systemic Therapies, 27*(4), 23–39.

Young, K., & Hibel, J. (2017). Single session therapy and neuroscience: Scaffolding and social engagement. J. Duvall & M.N. Beuadoin (Eds.), *Collaborative therapy and interpersonal neurobiology: Emerging practices* (pp. 103–115). Newcastle upon Tyne, UK: Cambridge Scholars Publishing.

5 Twenty-Five Years of Walk-In Single-Sessions at the Eastside Family Centre

Clinical and Research Dimensions

Janet Stewart, Nancy McElheran, Harry Park, Margaret Oakander, Bruce MacLaurin, Cindy Jing Fang, and Alexandra Robinson

Eastside Family Centre (EFC) of Wood's Homes has been providing immediate accessible, no-cost, self-referred, walk-in single-session therapy (SST) for 25 years. The development of the service and its clinical principles has been extensively documented in the literature (McElheran, Stewart, Soenen, Newman, & MacLaurin, 2014; Clements, McElheran, Hackney, & Park, 2011; Slive, McElheran, & Lawson, 2008), as has its effectiveness (Miller & Slive, 2004; Miller, 2008; Miller, 1996). This chapter will highlight the foundations of the EFC walk-in SST service, its years of development and evolution into the program currently offered, as well as future directions for research and training.

Service Development

The development of the walk-in SST service began in response to a dearth of community mental-health services on the eastside of Calgary, Alberta, Canada, a high-needs and low socio-economic, high-density, multi-cultural area of the city. In 1990 social service funding was drastically reduced at the same time as the population of the area in which the EFC is located was growing. In addition, Calgarians across the city were searching for accessible mental-health services as waiting lists for many counseling programs grew.

In 2015 the clients who walked into the EFC were representative of all quadrants of the city of 1.2 million residents, with 36% living in the northeast, 29% in the southeast, 19% in the northwest and 11% in the southwest. Clients, who often call the program to clarify that no appointment is needed, commonly express their relief and surprise that they are able to talk to a professional counselor in person immediately. Clients often report the immediacy of the service is one of its greatest strengths. Following each session, clients are asked where they would have gone on the day if not the EFC. Among those who respond, 30% of clients report that they had no other option, 30% report they would have attended their family doctor, and 30% report they would have attended their local hospital emergency room. Family physicians and community mental-health services remain the top referral sources as reported on the clients' information sheets. It appears that the EFC walk-in service has become an integral part of the continuum of services within the Calgary community by providing an effective, barrier-free option for mental-health assistance.

The program began as an immediately accessible, community-based mental-health service with support from local community members, physicians, schools, and the justice system (Clements, et al., 2011; Slive, MacLaurin, Oakander, & Amundson, 1995). Program developers communicated effectively with community members, promoting the benefits of the walk-in single-session approach for children and families. A community advisory committee was formed to provide ideas on program details such as the hours and days the center was open (Harper-Jaques, McElheran, Slive, & Leahey, 2008). For example, the center continues to operate on Saturdays as a result of these initial community consultations. Recently, the hours on Saturdays have expanded to two additional hours to meet the steady increase of clients requesting mental-health support on days when other services are not available.

Financial and therapeutic support for the establishment of the EFC walk-in service was initially provided by Wood's Homes, through its Board of Directors, Alberta Mental Health, through its funding to the agency and Wood's Homes clinicians. EFC is one of 35-plus services provided by Wood's Homes, a multi-service non-profit children's mental-health center based in Calgary, founded in 1914. The vision of Wood's Homes is to always be there for the well-being of children, youth, young adults, and families as reflected by its motto, "We Never Say No. We Never Give Up. We Never Turn Anyone Away." The Wood's Homes' mission is to promote and assist the development and well-being of children, youth, and families in our community. Over time other funders such as provincial and municipal human services (Alberta Health Services, Calgary and Area Children's Services, and Calgary Family and Community Support Services) have supported the center, increasing the stability of the EFC. Partner agencies have shared the center's space for the past two decades including a counseling agency (now known as Carya) offering multi-faceted services including family therapy, and the Calgary Emergency Women's Shelter Men's Counseling program. Volunteer legal services from Calgary Legal Guidance are offered to clients one day a month. Clients benefit from these on-site agencies working together as it provides continuity of care and expedited referrals.

At its inception, volunteer therapists were recruited from community mental-health professionals interested in being part of an innovative therapy approach. These professionals donated 8–10 hours per month in exchange for training in our walk-in single-session approach. Today, multi-disciplinary graduate-level students are provided with practicum placements and are supervised by full-time paid staff and therapy leaders in the agency. Wood's Homes program clinicians, community volunteer therapists, and students all work one or two four-hour shifts per month. For each period of time or shift at the EFC, a shift coordinator is identified. This clinical lead and team member has advanced experience and training in the supervision of others and experience working with multi-disciplinary teams. The shift coordinator is responsible for the quality of the service delivered, the management of risk, and also serves as a support to other therapists through session consultation and from behind a one-way mirror (McElheran, et al., 2014).

The Therapeutic Approach

Clients can walk-in to the center six days a week – Monday through Thursday, 11 a.m. to 7 p.m.; Friday, 11 a.m. to 6 p.m.; and Saturday, 11 a.m. to 4 p.m. Although clients who walk-in are self-referred, they hear about the program from their physician, community mental-health programs, family and friends, or other community resources. Over the past five years, there has been a significant increase in the number of clients who have heard about the program from social media including websites and Facebook. The volume of clients seen during a four-hour shift varies considerably, generally from three sessions to 10 sessions, and approximately 3,500 walk-in sessions are conducted per year. Typically there are two to four therapists working on each shift.

When they arrive, clients are greeted by an administrative staff member who guides them to a waiting area to complete a set of pre-session forms. The forms and questionnaires are designed to encourage clients to begin to think about their concern or problem before they meet the therapist. The forms request basic demographic information and include questions such as "Who is the most effected by the problem?" and "What have you tried to improve the situation to date?" so that the therapist and their consulting team have the opportunity to review and reflect on what the clients have thought important to write down prior to commencing the session.

Over the 25 years of operation, walk-in therapy sessions at the EFC have followed a five-part sequential organization consistent with the Milan model for conducting a session (Boscolo, Cecchin, Hoffman, & Penn, 1987), as described in McElheran et al. (2014):

(1) pre-session, where the forms the client has completed are reviewed by the team, hypotheses are generated as to the possible nature of the issues presented, and a plan of action for the session is formed;
(2) the session with the client, wherein the therapist and client collaborate on addressing the presenting issue;
(3) an intersession consultation, where the therapy team reviews the problem construction that has been co-created with the client and therapist and an intervention is formed;
(4) delivery of the intervention by the therapist on behalf of the whole team;
(5) a post-session debriefing, in the absence of the client, that focuses on whether, from the team's perspective, the session met the client's needs and suggestions made as to future directions, should the client return.

The hoped-for outcome of the walk-in SST at the EFC is for individuals, couples, and families to leave the session with a sense of emotional relief and some sort of positive outcome. Slive and Bobele (2012) remind us that positive outcomes differ from client to client or family to family. For one client, it may be as simple as having someone hear his or her story. For a family it could be a new way of thinking about their concerns for a family member. Another family may leave the session with a specific task designed to address their main concerns.

The clinical principles underlying the walk-in approach have been well-articulated by Slive and Bobele (2011) and Slive, et al. (2008). These principles include the following:

- Viewing a walk-in single-session of therapy as a whole therapy in one hour is key to the approach. Building a therapeutic alliance quickly is essential. Alliance is promoted by attending to the common factors articulated by Duncan, Miller, and Sparks (2004), including exploring a client's readiness for change and their personal motivations as well as addressing a client's expectations for the session.
- The therapist guides the conversation to the present and assists the client to address his/her immediate concerns by narrowing the database and keeping a focus on the current problem or most pressing issue. The therapist can refer to the client's forms or ask questions such as "How can we be the most helpful today?" and "If we were to focus on what brought you in today, what would that be?"
- Determining what is the best fit for the client rather than rigidly adhering to one model of therapy; this assists with effectively moving a session forward. Although each session at the EFC is organized in the Milan style, no one model of therapy is considered more effective than another. Therapeutic influences are tempered with pragmatism, which supports the therapist being aware of and using what will work for each client in the moment (Amundson, 1996).
- The therapist and the client are engaged in a collaborative process. Therefore, the session is seen as a consultation. The therapist offers ideas but creates a context that encourages clients to decide if they will accept, reject, or think about these ideas or find new ones as an outcome of the conversation.
- The therapist is creating a context for the client to discover his/her own resources and solutions.

Training and Supervision

From its inception, the EFC has actively developed a culture of teaching and learning among the therapists providing walk-in mental-health services and has extended this culture to members of the therapeutic community and to graduate-level students. The approach to training and supervision provided at the EFC, as described in this section, helps therapists to develop the skills necessary to provide effective walk-in SST.

Practicums are available to approved educational institutions for mental-health and medical disciplines including master's and doctoral students from applied psychology, clinical social work, nursing, counseling, marriage and family therapy, as well as medical family practice, psychiatric, and genetics residents. The multi-disciplinary students who are chosen for a practicum at the EFC have generally had career or volunteer experiences working with children and families within community, medical or educational crisis and counseling settings prior to starting their practicums. A practicum at the EFC meets these students' goals of learning therapy skills, participating in multi-disciplinary teams, and receiving effective supervision.

The training and supervision offered at the EFC are inclusive of supervisory practices specific to social work and marriage and family therapy, and also draw from counseling psychology and medicine. Students are assigned a supervisor from their respective discipline while community volunteer therapists are guided and/or supervised by the EFC staff therapists. A guided training process is provided to each student and volunteer therapist. This process starts with students and volunteers observing sessions with clients presenting a variety of concerns across a range of severity, acuity and risk factors. The supervisor or staff therapist can be active throughout the observation by pointing out aspects of the session to which the student should attend. They are encouraged to listen and then participate in the multi-disciplinary team during each part of the session organization including the pre-session, intersession, and debrief.

Live supervision is a cornerstone of the teaching and training at the EFC. Live supervision has become an integral and highly-valued form of supervision in therapist training in the 40 years since its origins in marriage and family therapy settings (Mauzey & Erdman, 1997). Since its inception, the center has installed and consistently used two observation rooms equipped with one-way mirrors and a call-in system. This infrastructure has supported staff therapists and supervisors at the EFC to consistently observe the progress of graduate students or community volunteer walk-in therapists who are new to the walk-in SST service. Graduate students and volunteer therapists in the walk-in SST service have the opportunity to receive specific and immediate feedback following each walk-in single session by the consulting team and the shift coordinator. All sessions are monitored for quality and risk by the shift coordinator.

Student supervisors and staff therapists offer suggestions to help guide the novice walk-in therapist by using the telephone system during a session or intervening by entering the session room. At the EFC, a combination of live observation of sessions from behind a one-way mirror with telephone input as well as co-therapy with supervisory-level staff are most consistently used to supervise students and new community volunteer therapists.

When clients complete their pre-session information forms, they are offered a choice of a session in a room with a one-way mirror and a team observing their session, or a room without a mirror. Although not used as often as telephone or call-in supervision, co-therapy is used to support a student when clients request a non-mirror room.

During a co-therapy session, a supervisor or an experienced therapist is present in the room with a student, observing the session and asking questions of the client when appropriate (in place of calling in questions on the telephone from behind the one-way mirror). This form of supervision has been found to alleviate anxiety and to build confidence for novice therapists (McGee & Burton, 1998).

A recently-developed tool called the *Supervisor Evaluation Form* (Matheson & McElheran, 2013) identifies 16 items related to the skills and processes necessary for an effective walk-in therapy session at the EFC. It is suggested that students and supervisors use this form as a learning tool as it outlines the skills supervisors and staff therapists will use to guide each new therapist to develop. The following items are assessed as "not at all," "minimally," "somewhat," "mostly," and "completely" present in the session with space available for supervisors to write specific comments to the student.

- Demonstrates ability to engage the client system.
- Is able to clarify all and the most pressing issues for the client.
- Able to determine *with the client* his/her needs in the first 15–20 minutes of the session.
- Is able to build upon and add depth to the issues noted.
- Demonstrates empathy.
- Demonstrates ability to ask good questions and reach the heart of the matter.
- Demonstrates ability to conceptualize the issues into a hypothesis.
- Demonstrates ability to understand and act upon non-verbal or hinted messages.
- Demonstrates an understanding of and pays attention to the therapeutic process and flow (the beginning, middle and end of a session).
- Shows interest and engagement while encouraging and listening to the client's story.
- Is able to draw out the strengths and resources (past and present) of the client system.
- Is able to assess risk effectively, quickly determine any intent and plan, assess resiliency and protective factors.
- Offers creative tasks or develops interventions that engage the client system.
- Is able to end the session smoothly, positively, and with hope for the future.
- Uses time wisely and ends the session in a timely fashion.
- Demonstrates an ability to succinctly and credibly document the activities and results of the session.

During initial observation of sessions, a student of the EFC walk-in SST service is encouraged to make note of how therapists execute the 16 skill-related items listed above. The supervisor also encourages the supervisee to attend to general counseling skills being used by the therapist (e.g., use of verbal and non-verbal skills, common factors in developing the relationship). The number of sessions a student or new community volunteer therapist observes prior to conducting their first session depends on the individual experience of each supervisee in consultation with their identified supervisor or the team of staff therapists.

When a student or a therapist new to the EFC walk-in SST service is chosen for a client, the needs of the client are always prioritized. The supervisor or shift coordinator assesses the competency of the therapist in relation to the presenting concerns identified on a client's pre-session form. For example, a novice walk-in therapist would not be allocated to a client who has identified suicidal ideation as their primary reason for coming to EFC. A student's supervisor or the shift coordinator works with students to develop the skills to explore fully with their client any concerns related to risk including: suicide, self-harm, domestic violence, homicide, and child protection concerns. Typically, it may take up to several months before a supervisee is considered ready to conduct a walk-in session without live supervision. This is one way that both the quality of the service delivered is ensured across the 3,500 sessions conducted at the EFC each year as well as the quality of the therapists' developing skills.

Individual in-office supervision is used in conjunction with live, behind-the-mirror supervision. Individual supervision is often required by a student's educational institution and is an integral part of the culture within Wood's Homes. The supervisee comes to the meeting with a list of concerns to discuss in supervision focusing on three areas: administration, support, and education (which would include working on clinical skill development). Students may wish to discuss topics such as therapeutic strategies used in session, personal reactions to client's presenting concerns, effective clinical writing skills, or other professional development.

Team consultation during pre-session, at the mid-session, and after the session at the EFC allows for a student or new community therapist to draw from multiple perspectives in a multi-disciplinary context. In addition, supervisees gain invaluable skills in learning to maximize inter-professional collaborations, which is an important but often neglected skill in mental-health delivery systems (Arthur & Russell-Mayhew, 2010; Ruddy, Borresen, & Gunn, 2008). A multi-disciplinary team can be directive in case conceptualization and planning with students or therapist new to the SST service. As therapists becomes increasingly skilled at walk-in SST, risk assessment, and case conceptualization, the team typically becomes less specific in its direction. The team increasingly encourages novice therapists to present their own case conceptualization during intersession, thus supporting students in their on-going development.

The Case Consultation Model

An essential part of the walk-in single-session approach practiced at the EFC is the intersession break, which is an opportunity for the team and therapist to have a consultation about the case. This is where the multi-disciplinary aspect of the team really comes to light, as clinicians from a variety of backgrounds come together to discuss the client's situation and develop an intervention that suits the individual client or family's needs. The EFC multi-disciplinary team has always included social workers, psychologists, family therapists, nurses and psychiatrists.

The number of psychiatrists on the EFC team has varied throughout the years. At this time, EFC offers 5 days per week of psychiatric consultation during the intersession, provided by 3 community psychiatrists. A psychiatric consultation may be important to the development of effective interventions for clients who are concerned about their mental-health, those who share questions about their current diagnosis in the session, which was given by another service, and/or their current treatment, including medications, prescribed by a community physician. With a psychiatric consultation, general suggestions to clients with specific medication and treatment concerns can focus on returning to their prescribing physicians or treatment provider with clearer questions. Psychiatric consultation can also be utilized when there is a concern regarding risk or safety of any client who has walked in, to discuss clients who return for more sessions, and who may have complicated mental-health backgrounds. About 40% of clients return for additional sessions, either years after their initial walk-in SST session or several times during a situational crisis. Several clients return periodically during the year, using the EFC as part of their mental-health support system.

The clinical break during a therapy intersession can serve many purposes. Its primary use is to allow time for therapist–team discussion in order to develop an intervention that will be useful for the client. Other uses of the clinical break may include making a transition in the session (e.g., from discussing problems to discussing possible solutions) or as a time for training and teaching. A novice walk-in therapist may benefit from hearing about effective anxiety-reducing strategies during the consultation or hearing suggestions as to how to share an intervention such as a "thinking" or "doing" task with a client.

As stated earlier, the practice of an intersession break is not new as many family therapy models (Hoyt, 2015) were using the method in the early 1980s and the current approach to the walk-in single-session approach was based on the Milan family therapy five-part team model (Boscolo, Cecchin, Hoffman, & Penn, 1987). At the beginning of the session, the therapist informs the client that at 35–40 minutes into the session, the therapist will take a break to consult with the team. The client is invited to remain in the session room where they have privacy, return to the waiting room, have a complimentary beverage, go to the bathroom and then return to the room—whatever suits their needs.

At the EFC, the consultation break has become a standard practice since the center began conducting a walk-in sessions. Every therapist is expected to consult about their case with at least the shift coordinator and most often with the team of therapists who are assigned to the shift. At any one time, the consultation team may comprise a shift coordinator, a psychiatrist, one or two permanent staff members, and one to three postgraduate students, one to three medical residents, and one to three community volunteer therapists. On average, there are between three and nine team members offering intervention suggestions and thinking about the clients' situation during the consultation break.

The intersession break creates a transition point to move from information to suggestions and is intended to take about 10 to 15 minutes. When the therapist meets his or her team, the therapist provides a quick synopsis of the session. A therapist's consulting team during the intersession may include therapists who were not present during the pre-session or they may have not been watching from behind the mirror. They may have been leading their own session at the time or were supporting another team member behind another one-way mirror. When clients decline to have their session conducted with a mirror, a synopsis and discussion of the content of the session is necessary for the team. The synopsis brings everyone on the team up to a common point of conversation in readiness to fashion an intervention. This consultative process supports the therapist to review their interactions and experience with the client.

At the EFC, each team member brings with them their own varied professional background and perspective. Therefore, each intervention is unique to the therapist–client and also unique to the team that was involved in its creation. Interventions are based upon client type and readiness for change and style of change (Prochaska & DiClemente, 1982). The consultation can strengthen the quality of the intervention as multiple therapists hear the client's story. Risk issues and legal requirements in areas related to custody and access of children and child protection concerns are addressed as needed. The clinical consultation can be a rich resource for therapists and clients.

A common challenge for a shift coordinator is to ensure that each team member has the opportunity to express his or her perspective, while a client's stated goals for the session are prioritized, not the team's perception of the client's goals. The shift coordinator's role is to oversee this process and may prompt the therapist and the team with a question such as, "What did the client say they wanted from today's session?" after the synopsis of the session is provided.

The team encourages the therapist to be reasonably succinct with the delivery of the intervention. An intervention with numerous ideas can be overwhelming to some clients, so care must be taken to tailor the content of the intervention so it can be clearly understood and meets the specific goals of the client. Given many ideas are typically raised during a team discussion, the therapist usually finds it useful to write down the ideas generated by the team. This can help link concepts together and to craft the delivery to the client. Working within a team and absorbing multiple perspectives during the intersession consultation can be overwhelming to a novice therapist. It is the shift coordinator's role to manage the contributions of each team member to ensure that the student or new volunteer therapist can benefit from the multi-disciplinary collaboration. A shift coordinator may review the ideas presented by the team for the therapist at the end of the intersession.

The efficacy of using a consultation break has been researched by Knott and Espie (1997, p. 437) who reported that of the 43 families surveyed "over 80% either thought the discussion break was useful or did not mind it." Validation for this statement is seen at the EFC as many clients give specific feedback on the usefulness of the team and actually give a "thank you" to the team at the end of the session either in person or on the feedback form. Consistent with Knott and Espie's research, 82% of the EFC clients report satisfaction with the team approach.

The following case examples highlight the experience of a student therapist, the processes of supervision and training, as well as the case consultation model used at the EFC.

Three Case Examples

Case #1: One Time Visit and All is Well—for Now

Cynthia came to the Eastside Family Centre to talk about her concerns for her husband, Jeff. Jeff had been laid off from his job with an oil and gas company. The team noticed that Cynthia was not overly distressed (about 5 on a scale of 1–10) but that she was experiencing a range of symptoms such as problems with sleeping, eating, and feeling as if she had let her family down and described the symptoms as quite intense. Cynthia was focused on getting support for Jeff while he was experiencing joblessness and hoped a session with us would be a good place to start. Some questions raised by a relatively small team of a shift coordinator and a social worker included:

- "How long have you been experiencing the symptoms you described on the information sheets?"
- "What do you think about your overall level of distress compared to the symptoms you described?"

Dean was Cynthia's therapist. Cynthia and he began by sharing the story of how she and Jeff met, all of his qualities, and what made him a good oil and gas engineer. Dean asked questions about Cynthia's symptoms and how the situation was impacting her life. She responded by describing her sleeping problems and how she was overeating; however, she quickly turned the conversation back to how Jeff was handling the situation.

The shift coordinator, Greg, who was watching behind the one-way mirror, called in a question to Dean. He wondered if Cynthia had experienced a job loss herself or if a family member had experienced a job loss in the past. Cynthia began to cry as Dean asked about her experiences with job loss. She shared that her father had lost his job when she was a teenager and described how the family supported him. Her mom and siblings had rallied around him and made sure he was feeling happy and strong so he could continue to look for a job. Cynthia was not sure, but now that the question was asked, she thought she was doing the same thing for Jeff. She identified that she was not really talking about her own worries but keeping them to herself in support of Jeff. She wondered if she was experiencing most of her symptoms because she was trying to keep a "stiff upper lip."

Prior to the intersession, Dean asked Cynthia what she was hoping for from today's session. Cynthia stated that her thoughts had changed. Before the session, she wanted to know about supports for Jeff and now she thought they both needed some help. Cynthia shared that her thoughts were racing all day long and "worst possible scenario" thoughts were interfering with her sleep. She was hoping that the team could provide her with some ideas to calm her mind.

At the beginning of the team consultation, Dean provided a short synopsis as context for other team members who did not view the session. During the intersession, the team members commended Cynthia on her quick insight and that she connected some of her life experiences that seemed to be helpful to her. They also recognized the challenges of supporting a partner as he or she goes through a potentially life- and family-changing transition. One team member was particularly impressed with Cynthia's openness to new ideas which could serve her and Jeff well during this time in their lives.

Dean shared this intervention with Cynthia as well as some specific strategies. The team suggested that Cynthia practice blocking her worries—giving herself time in the morning, afternoon or early evening to worry about their situation but also giving herself time off from worrying every day. The team suggested she could also write out her worries before bed so that they were out of her head. If she thought it might be helpful, she and Jeff also were invited to return to talk about how they would work together. Cynthia expressed her satisfaction with the session, saying that talking was so helpful to clear her mind. She was not sure if she and Jeff needed another session as she would pass on the information shared with her today to Jeff. Jeff and Cynthia did not return to the Eastside Family Centre for a session; however, Cynthia did return six months later to discuss a situation of bullying in her workplace that was causing her significant distress. Cynthia shared that the Centre had supported her when she was worried about her husband's situation so she was certain the walk-in single session therapy could help this time as well.

Case #2: Intermittent Visits as Needed

Sarah and John returned to the EFC to continue talking about how to improve their relationship. As in their previous visit, they shared on their information sheets that they were both committed to remaining together as a couple given they were parents to two young children. Sarah and John reported on their information sheets that communication was their most pressing concern. The team of a psychiatrist, a social worker, a psychologist, and a student met for the pre-session. The session note written following the couple's first session at the center was available to the team. It was discovered that John had told Sarah that he had shared some texts with a woman from work. The texting did not lead to a physical affair as John ended the texting but for a few weeks the relationship was more than a friendship and they continue to see each other at work. Given the student had not yet developed the skills to engage in a couple therapy session at the walk-in SST service, Barbara, the psychologist, saw the couple. Questions developed during the pre-session were:

- "What has happened since the last time you were at the EFC?"
- "Was there something the team said that was helpful last time?"

Barbara acknowledged the couple's return visit to the EFC and wondered what had happened between the first session and today. Sarah shared that she agreed with the suggestions of the team at their first session—that she and her husband were not communicating effectively as there were new holes and gaps in how much she trusted her husband with other women. John stated that he understood he had broken Sarah's trust and he was willing to build that back up again. He also agreed with the team's assessment from the previous session. However, both shared that their distress levels returned to very high levels as they were raising their voices at each other, and this had never happened in their relationship before. They both stated that they were feeling unprepared and unable to cope with these kinds of interactions. It was especially distressing to them that they are doing this in front of their children.

The team called in from behind the one-way mirror asking Barbara to check if their discomfort with each other extended to any worries about safety. The couple both denied any physical safety concerns. John shared that he did not feel it was safe to share his emotions, thoughts, and feelings about how to improve their relationship with Sarah considering the hurt he has caused her. He reported that when he begins to share these ideas the arguing starts.

Barbara continued to explore Sarah and John's values and beliefs about how to build a relationship after one partner's trust has been eroded and how a loss of trust impacts all areas of a relationship—including communication. Prior to the intersession, Sarah and John were asked what they wanted to hear from the team today. They both said that they had returned as they appreciated the team's point of view but would like some specific strategies today to use when they argue and raise their voices.

During the intersession, the team commended the couple for their commitment to their relationship as well as to do something specific to address what is causing most of their distress. Each team member validated the hurt Sarah must feel given John's choices and John's trepidation to discuss their relationship as he recognizes the impact of those choices. They also suggested that it must be difficult to know how to have a productive argument when you have never before had one with your partner.

During the intervention, Barbara shared the team's point of view with the couple. She also provided them with several ideas of how couples can argue without further damaging feelings of trust or, to put it another way, how to "fight fair." Specific suggestions of setting aside time to talk after the kids are in bed, using "I" statements, no name calling, and taking time outs when overwhelmed were shared. It was also suggested that the couple could find other times to begin to listen to each other. They were told of an exercise during which one partner shares their thoughts for a few minutes then the other partner repeats what was heard and then they reverse. It was believed this exercise could allow each partner to be validated for their thoughts and feelings away from arguments and raised voices.

Both Sarah and John were excited to try these specific strategies and stated that they planned to return the next week to report on their progress. Two weeks later, Sarah and John returned to the EFC to report that the strategies they were using were working very well. Both expressed delight in catching each other using "I" statements, with John laughing the loudest when Sarah noticed him using the strategy. They wanted to return to the Centre to tell the therapist "Thank You" and to hear about any other strategies that they could use to solidify the improvements in their relationship.

Case #3: Significant Risk and the Role of the Supervisor

Tran (not his real name), a Chinese man in his early 50s, came to the EFC upon referral from his doctor. The team reviewed the pre-session forms in which he identified his presenting concern as having difficulty with his supervisor. He indicated that he was in extreme distress (he rated his distress as a "10" on a scale of 1–10). Jenny, a social work student, saw the client as she was becoming skilled at assessing risk. Tran had indicated on his information forms that he felt extreme distress regarding his job environment but it was not clear if risk was a presenting concern. A large consulting team was available including a psychiatrist, a supervisor, a social worker, two psychologists, and two students. The team assessed risk based on his level of distress and brainstormed important questions to ask during the session such as:

- "How long have you been experiencing extreme distress?"
- "How worried are you for your well-being and for the well-being of others around you?"
- "Why did you come today?"
- "How can we be most helpful?"

English was not Tran's first language, making it a challenge to understand him. However, early in the session, it became clear that he was in extreme distress over how he was being treated at work. He explained to Jenny that he felt like an abused animal backed into a corner. Tran began to cry and explained that he could not get thoughts of murdering his supervisor out of his head. He said that he thought he would get a gun or make a bomb, or get some acid to throw on the supervisor's face. Worryingly, Tran reported that he had thoughts of going after the supervisor's whole family and had followed his supervisor from work to figure out where he lived and where he goes. He explained that on the day prior to attending the walk-in session he had gone to his foreman and manager to tell them that he was so upset at how he was being treated that he had thoughts of killing his supervisor if he was provoked again. He begged his manager and foreman to lay him off so that he would not have to work with the supervisor anymore. They responded by offering for him to take a day off. Knowing that a day off was not all he needed, Tran used the day to go to see his doctor who sent him directly to the EFC.

Jenny listened carefully to Tran, hearing his level of distress and encouraged him to tell his story, asking him several times, and in several different ways, if he had a plan to kill his supervisor next time he encountered him; each time the therapist asked, Tran explained that he was bound to. He repeatedly asked the therapist to help him. The psychiatrist who was listening to the session from behind the mirror immediately notified the shift coordinator. The team called in and requested that the therapist ask several different questions to try to assess how imminent the risk was.

Tran reported that he has had thoughts about killing his supervisor for the past year. For the past several days, it was all he had been able to think about. It was difficult for the therapist to ascertain if Tran was "hearing voices" or if Tran was clear that these were his own thoughts. Perhaps the most convincing statement Tran made to attest to his resolve to harm his supervisor was when he said that even if he spends the next half of his life in jail, he would be smiling because that horrible man would be gone. He also reported having a terrible headache that would not go away, even with a well-known over-the-counter pain-relief medication.

Despite these alarming statements, throughout the session Tran presented as a kind and gentle man. In the session he indicated that he had dedicated his life to raising his children after arriving in Canada. He made sure that his children had a good education and his son had become a pediatrician, his eldest daughter an engineer, and his youngest daughter a chartered accountant. He explained that he had never gambled, drank, or smoked since arriving in Canada so that he could have a good life there with his family. The therapist thought it may have been that Tran's perception of the years of discrimination and abuse at work had simply become too much for him to tolerate and were overwhelming at this point in time.

During the intersession, the entire team was present for the discussion. The team, led by the shift coordinator, talked about their interpretation of the level of risk and the possibility of speaking to the police given the duty for professionals to warn of potential harm. The decision to call the police was made collectively by the team. As a result, the shift coordinator and therapist sat together to make this call. The police supported the therapist and shift coordinator's decision to have Tran assessed at one of the local hospitals and stood by.

The shift coordinator accompanied the therapist after the intersession. The therapist explained to Tran that the team could see how difficult his situation was and that we believed him when he told us that he was afraid he could act on his thinking. The therapist then explained that we were committed to keeping everyone safe, and that we would get Tran the help he was asking for. The therapist told Tran that the hospital would be able to help him. At this point, Tran began to cry and thanked us. Tran was then told that the police would be escorting him to the hospital and assured him that he was not in any trouble. When the police came into the room, he bowed to them. As the police escorted him out, he began to cry again and repeatedly thanked the police officers, shift coordinator, and therapist. Tran did not return to the Eastside Family Centre after this session.

Quantitative Evidence from EFC Supporting Walk-In Single-Session Therapy

The EFC has supported a number of independent research initiatives over the past 25 years. While these initiatives contributed greatly to the evidence supporting walk-in SST, there was emerging demand for an on-going and systematic approach for data collection. During 2012, a study team was established to develop an on-going outcome framework using primarily data that was currently being collected.

For data collection, the EFC has historically used a range of forms including the *Client Demographic Form*, the *Client Confidential Questionnaire*, and a *Distress Scale* based on the *Session Rating Scale* (Duncan, et al., 2004). These forms and questionnaires have been used for decades as part of the pre-session team consultation as well as for data collection. In 2012, two additional scales were added to assist in understanding risk and acuity: *Patient Health Questionnaire* (*PHQ-9*) and *Generalized Anxiety Disorder* (*GAD-7*). Data were also collected as clients completed a feedback form with a post-measure of distress as well as feedback reflecting their engagement with the session and therapist. The lead therapist also contributed to the data at the EFC by providing information on acuity of risk, severity of concerns, client resources, form of intervention, and use of psychiatric consultation (McElheran, et al., 2014).

Data were then imported into SPSS, a statistical software program commonly used for analyses. Since 2012, we have data on more than 3500 sessions for over 2600 unique clients. Following minor revisions, data collection continues.

Between 2012 and 2015, approximately 60% of primary adult clients were female. Adults reflected all age groups, most notably ages 25–39 (41.7%) or 40–59 (35.6%). About two-thirds of the clients resided in the northeast or southeast quadrants of Calgary. Primary presenting concerns identified mental-health, couple/relationship, family relationship, and parent/child relationship issues. Mental-health issues included clients wondering if they were experiencing symptoms of depression and clients requesting support to manage symptoms of an anxiety disorder. Family relationship issues revolved around adult family members while parent/child relationship issues focused on parents and children under the age of 18.

Clients came to the EFC as individuals (71.6%), families (17.9%), and couples (10.5%). Fifty-seven percent of clients visited the EFC for the first time; however, many EFC clients noted previous (70.4%) or current (16.8%) involvement in counseling. Therapists used this information to explore clients' motivation and expectations for the walk-in session based on past experiences in counseling, both positive and negative.

On the *Client Confidential Questionnaire*, clients reported their level of distress by crossing a 10 cm line ranging from 0 (no distress) to 10 (extreme distress). Following the session, clients were asked again to rate their level of distress to determine if there is change in distress. Since 2012, among all the clients participating in the research study, 86.7% noted a decrease in distress after the intervention. The mean distress scores for all clients were 7.0 out of a possible 10.0 at pre-test, and 4.1 out of a possible 10.0 at post-test. Using an independent samples T-test[1] a significant difference ($p<.001$) was noted between the mean distress change for males and females, with males showing a 2.72 point change in distress compared to a 2.97 point change for females. Along with a difference in distress changes between male and females, it was also noted that 40% of the clients who walked into the center were male. Typically one-third of clients who sought support through counseling were male (Cox, 2014). Further investigation into differences of men and women walking into the EFC SST service may enhance the services provided to all.

Client-reported satisfaction with services using a rating scale ranged from 0 (Strongly Disagree) to 10 (Strongly Agree). Clients reported they felt heard, understood, and respected (8.98), the therapists worked on and talked about what they wanted (8.90), the therapist's approach fit well (8.84), and they overall were satisfied with the session (8.54). A client's overall satisfaction with the session was also associated with a number of related factors. Some of these variables included: the client's pre- and post-session level of distress ($p<.001$) and distress improvement ($p<.001$). Clients who were the most distressed before their session and who had a greater reduction in distress appeared to be most satisfied with their experience with the walk-in SST service of the EFC.

The *Patient Health Questionnaire* (*PHQ-9*) is used as a screening and diagnostic tool for mental-health disorders specific to depression. *General Anxiety Disorder* (*GAD-7*) is a standardized rating scale designed to measure severity of various symptoms of generalized anxiety disorder. Both the *PHQ-9* and the *GAD-7* were filled in by clients prior to their session only and have been helpful in highlighting the acuity of the clients using the walk-in SST at the EFC. Over half of the clients reported moderate or severe severity on the *PHQ*. Significant differences were noted for *PHQ* severity for males compared to females using T-test ($p<.05$), with females reporting more symptoms of depression. Findings indicated that nearly half of the clients reported severe scores for the *GAD*. Significant differences were noted for *GAD* severity for males compared to females using T-test ($p<.01$).

Preliminary findings identified a range of factors associated with a change in level of distress as measured by chi-square.[2] Statistically significant variables related to more change include: if the client noted someone who was most emotionally affected by the presenting concern ($p<.001$); if the client had previously tried things to address the presenting concerns ($p<.001$); if the client identified prior to the session the specific things that would tell them the session helped them head in the right direction ($p<.001$). Overall, it seemed that a client had a more significant reduction in distress when they were able to express details about their most pressing concern on the information sheet and was consistent in filling in this information from the top to the bottom of the page.

The EFC plays an important role in serving an acute population with relatively high severity in anxiety and depression. Preliminary findings indicated that clients had a significant decrease in their level of distress following the completion of their session and were highly satisfied with services of the EFC. Further studies will inform our understanding of which factors are most predictive of positive outcomes.

Documenting positive change over the course of a walk-in single session is a critical step in intervention research. Equally important, however, is understanding the impact of the sessions on clients over extended time periods. The study team met during 2015 to develop and implement a follow-up study of clients accessing the EFC. Specifically, this work will include a randomly-selected sample of clients who agreed to be contacted one month post-session for a telephone interview related to longer-term outcomes of walk-in SST. These findings will further inform best practices and contribute to the development of walk-in single-session services.

Summary

Over the course of 25 years the Eastside Family Centre has developed a walk-in single-session mental-health services delivery approach. Clients and their concerns are placed at the center of this approach by offering barrier-free, immediate access to professional therapists and a multi-disciplinary consultation team. This notion of consultation is not limited to the team aspect of the session. It is one of the principles of the session itself – therapists offer themselves as consultants to the clients and their concerns. Clients continue to report high satisfaction with the overall service as well as the use of consultations with a team of professional mental-health providers. Family physicians and community mental-health agencies remain satisfied with the service as well as they continue to recommend the EFC to their clients and patients. Psychiatrists continue to provide consultation to clients as part of the consultation team and community volunteer therapists continue to value the team consultation experience and training. Graduate students and medical residents continue to seek out the EFC as an internship.

Given this data, it appears that the EFC provides a service that has become part of the continuum of mental-health services in the Calgary community. Since 2012, the EFC has also committed to collecting data on an on-going basis rather than periodically. Exploring connections between client differences and the clinical dimensions of walk-in SST can enrich our understanding of the impact of this approach as more than 3500 therapy sessions are conducted each year at the EFC. The more we understand from clients what it is about a walk-in single session of therapy that works in the moment, the more we can do what works in the moment of a single session of therapy.

Notes

1 T-test is a measurement designed to assess the statistical significance of the difference between two sample means. Probabilities less than .05 ($p < .05$) suggest that the differences did not occur by chance.
2 Chi-square is used to examine the differences with a number of categorical variables, and it indicates how well an observed breakdown of people over the various categories fits the breakdown that was expected.

References

Amundson, J. (1996). Why pragmatics is probably enough for now. *Family Process, 35*, 473–486.

Arthur, N. & Russell-Mayhew, S. (2010). Preparing counselors for interprofessional collaboration through supervision and lateral mentoring. *Canadian Journal of Counselling, 44*, 258–271. Retrieved from http://cjc-rcc.ucalgary.ca/cjc/index.php/rcc/article/view/937.

Boscolo, L., Cecchin, G., Hoffman, L., & Penn, P. (1987). *Milan systemic family therapy: Conversations in theory and practice.* New York: Basic Books.

Clements, R., McElheran, N., Hackney, L., & Park, H. (2011). The Eastside Family Centre: 20 years of single-session walk-in therapy. In A. Slive & M. Bobele (Eds.), *When one hour is all you have: Effective therapy for walk-in clients* (pp. 109–127). Phoenix, AZ: Zeig, Tucker, & Theisen.

Cox, D. W. (2014). Gender differences in professional consultation for a mental health concern: A Canadian population study. *Canadian Psychology, 55*(2), 68–74. Retrieved from http://ezproxy.lib.ucalgary.ca/login?url=http://search.proquest.com/docview/1548766962?accountid=9838.

Duncan, B.L., Miller, S.D., & Sparks, J.A. (2004). *The heroic client: A revolutionary way to improve effectiveness through client-directed, outcome informed therapy.* San Francisco: Jossey-Bass.

Harper-Jaques, S., McElheran, N., Slive, A., & Leahey, M. (2008). A comparison of two approaches to the delivery of walk-in single session mental health therapy. *Journal of Systemic Therapies, 27*, 40–53.

Hoyt, M.F (2015). Solution-focused couple therapy. In A.S. Gurman, J.L. Lebow, & D.K. Snyder (Eds.), *Clinical handbook of couple therapy* (5th ed., pp. 300–332). New York: Guilford Press.

Knott, F. & Espie, C. (1997). Families' perception of the one-way screen in the first meeting. *Journal of Family Therapy, 19*, 431–439.

Matheson, J. & McElheran, N. (2013). *Supervisor Evaluation Form.* Calgary, Alberta, Canada: Wood's Homes.

Mauzey, M.A. & Erdman, P. (1997). Trainee perceptions of live supervision phone-ins. *The Clinical Supervisor, 15*, 115–128. Doi:10.1300/ J001v15n02_09.

McElheran, N., Stewart, J., Soenen, D., Newman, J., & MacLaurin B. (2014). Walk-in single session therapy at the Eastside Family Centre. In M.F. Hoyt &

M. Talmon (Eds.), *Capturing the moment: Single session therapy and walk-in services* (pp. 177–194). Bethel, CT: Crown House Publishing.

McGee, M. & Burton, R. (1998). The use of co-therapy with a reflecting mirror as a supervisory tool. *Journal of Family Psychotherapy, 9*, 45–60.

Miller, J.K. (1996). Walk-in single session therapy: A study of client satisfaction. *Dissertations Abstracts International, 58*, 421.

Miller, J.K. (2008). Walk-in single session team therapy: A study of client satisfaction. *Journal of Systemic Therapies, 27*, 78–94.

Miller, J.K. & Slive, A. (2004). Breaking down the barriers to clinical service delivery: Walk-in family therapy. *Journal of Marital and Family Therapy, 30*, 95–105.

Prochaska, J.O. & DiClemente, C.C. (1982). Transtheroretical therapy: Toward a more integrative model of change. *Psychotherapy: Theory, Research and Practice, 19*(3), 276–227.

Ruddy, N., Borresen, D., & Gunn, W. (2008). *The collaborative psychotherapist: Creating reciprocal relationships with medical professionals.* Washington, DC: APA Books.

Slive, A. & Bobele, M. (2011). Making a difference in fifty minutes: A framework for walk-in counseling. In A. Slive & M. Bobele (Eds.), *When one hour is all you have: Effective therapy for walk-in clients* (pp. 167–183). Phoenix, AZ: Zeig, Tucker, & Theisen.

Slive, A., & Bobele, M. (2012). Walk-in counseling services: Making the most of one hour. *The Australian and New Zealand Journal of Family Therapy, 33*(1), 27–38.

Slive, A., MacLaurin, B., Oakander, M., & Amundson, J. (1995). Walk-in single sessions: A new paradigm in clinical service delivery. *Journal of Systemic Therapies, 27*, 5–22.

Slive, A., McElheran, N., & Lawson, A. (2008). How brief does it get? Walk-in single session therapy. *Journal of Systemic Therapies, 27*, 5–22.

Talmon, M. (1990). *Single session therapy: Maximizing the effect of the first (and often only) therapeutic encounter*. San Francisco: Jossey-Bass.

6 The Walk-In Counseling Model

Research and Advocacy

Leslie Josling and Cheryl-Anne Cait

> Some of the greatest discoveries . . . consist mainly in the clearing away of psychological road blocks which obstruct the approach to reality; which is why post factum, they appear so obvious . . . This operation of removing a problem from its traditional context and placing it into a new one, looking at it through glasses of a different color as it were, has always seemed to me of the very essence of the creative process. It leads not only to a revaluation of the problem itself but often to a synthesis of much wider consequences, brought about by a fusion of the two previously unrelated frames of reference.
>
> (Arthur Koestler, *The Sleepwalkers*, 1959, p. 207)

Matters of the Heart

In 1949, two doctors, William Sewell and William Glenn, built the first prototype of the modern artificial heart at the Yale School of Medicine. They built this prototype using bits and pieces from the five- and ten-cent store and what is now known as the popular toy Meccano (Lavietes, 2003). A dog lived on this heart for more than an hour (ConnecticutHistory.org, 2017). In the past 65 years there have been numerous iterations of the artificial heart, possible only with extensive and costly research and design. Yet it has limited use with approximately 1500 transplantation patients benefiting from this to date (SynCardia, 2014).

Research and design and the iterative process are generally recognized as the cost of advancement. Yet, this level of design has rarely been supported in the counseling field (Canada, Parliament, The Standing Senate Committee on Social Affairs, Science and Technology, 2006, p. 252), where "matters of the heart" such as emotions, mental health, relationships, family functioning and parenting affect millions of people.

The fact that research has been woefully inadequate in the mental-health sector is borne out in our years of experience in this industry where attention to design has typically been overshadowed by the need to simply keep our programs afloat. After all, it is difficult to entertain research and advancement while struggling to keep programs open. It is easy to become discouraged with the perpetual cycle of promising service development that only ends in premature decline due to lack of funding.

This chapter is about university community collaboration between KW Counselling Services, researchers from Wilfrid Laurier University, the University of Waterloo in Ontario, and the opportunities for advocacy that may support the expansion of emergent walk-in counseling globally.

Background

KW Counselling Services is a not-for-profit agency located in Kitchener-Waterloo, an urban community of approximately half a million residents in southern Ontario, Canada. The agency was founded in 1950 and has a long history of offering individual, couple and family counseling. In 2006 KW Counselling Services, like many other counseling agencies, had developed an extremely long wait for service with close to 1,000 people on the list. The wait had become an immense barrier to timely access and a tremendous burden to the organization that felt helpless to address the needs of its community.

When our Walk-In Counselling Clinic (WICC) was launched in 2007, it was one of the first of its kind in Ontario. The WICC model was developed with consideration of human needs and wants and with a refreshing view to the client's experience. Born out of fiscal restraint and with a desire to make our services more useful and accessible, clients at the WICC are seen immediately, which we speculated would speak to our current culture of the drive-thru and 24/7 services. By seeing people in their moment of need we also hoped to capitalize on "Readiness to Change," a clinical measure of the Transtheoretical Model of Change (TTM; Prochaska and DiClemente, 1982) that is a predictor of improved clinical outcomes. The WICC also eliminates costly "no shows" which account for far too much of therapists' time and our agency's resources (see Slive, et al., 2008, p. 6). In developing the WICC we moved outside of traditional contexts for counseling, envisioning possibilities. In retrospect, the capacity and capability for accessible counseling existed within our system; we simply needed to recombine our resources in a new way.

The Model

The WICC operates every Thursday from noon to 8 p.m. with the last client arriving by 6 p.m. The average wait for service is 15 minutes. Clients are seen first by an Intake Resource Consultant for 10–20 minutes. This consultant conducts a screening interview and determines either a funding subsidy or a fee based on income. Screening is conducted for harm to self or others, intimate partner violence, and addictions. A director assigns the client to a therapist. Assignment is based on presenting issue and risk, client preference, and therapist skill and availability. Service is available to all families, couples, and individuals.

The sessions are typically scheduled for 1.5 hours. Interventions used include a diverse range of counseling approaches (narrative, cognitive-behavioral, solution-focused, etc.) building on client strength and capacity. The client walks away with a concrete, written, co-created plan, which includes referrals to other resources. The client is encouraged to implement the plan after the session. If they feel that more support is needed, they are welcome to either return to the WICC or call for on-going therapy. Should the therapist and client deem that risk is high at the close of the session there is the option of immediately assigning the client to on-going therapy. Very rarely, if risk is imminent, involvement of emergency services (i.e. ambulance, police, shelter) may be warranted.

Funding

The existing single day of WICC each week at KW Counselling Services is made possible with existing provincial and municipal funding as well as grants, donations, and clients' employee benefits (employee assistance programs and employee insurance benefits) which allow us to offer full to partial subsidy to most clients on a sliding scale. The agency commits to never turn anyone away based on means to pay.

The ongoing challenge is to strike a delicate balance between ensuring adequate staffing (reception, intake, and therapists) to meet the ebb and flow of visitors over the course of the day, while not overstaffing which results in a loss of revenue. In the early WICC days this was not always well calculated and waiting times resulted. With years of experience there is seldom a mismatch of staff to clients. The challenge is never fully put to rest given the startling growth in the service. The agency would have long ago failed to keep step if it had not been for the introduction of interns, externs, and volunteer-psychotherapists seeing a large volume of our clients every week.

The Growing Need

The WICC has grown in popularity over the course of the past nine years with the number of visitors steadily climbing from an average of 30 visitors per day in 2007 to as many as 96 clients per day in 2016. To the best of our knowledge there is no other WICC globally that serves more clients in a single day. The agency is currently looking for funding to expand the WICC to a second day. Research has been a valuable tool in advocating for this support.

Two Generations of Research

Research conducted at KW Counselling Services includes both an initial pilot study and a second study using mixed methods (which involved a qualitative case study and a comparison group). Objectives of the pilot study were: to learn more about the clinical effectiveness of single-session therapy (SST) as delivered in a WICC; to identify if the WICC model was cost-effective; and to better understand how the quality of research on this model of service delivery could be improved. We measured psychological distress through a

12-item version of the *General Health Questionnaire* (*GHQ-12*) (Goldberg, 1972); stage of change as posited by the Transtheoretical Model of Change (TTM) and measured by an 18-item *Stages of Change Questionnaire* (*SOCQ*) (Bellis, 1994); recent use of health and social services; and recent ability to work and undertake normal activities in a sample of clients attending the KW Counselling Services WICC. In this unfunded pilot study, the sample size was small, efforts to collect data from a comparison group were not successful, and it should be noted that some of the measures did not attain 5% significance level. What we were able to ascertain was that clients presented at the walk-in service with significant psychological distress and that those who returned the questionnaire indicated that they were significantly less distressed one month later and four months later (Horton, Stalker, Cait, & Josling, 2012; Stalker, Horton, & Cait, 2012).

In terms of cost-effectiveness, other differences were observed (KW Counselling Services, 2011):

- 33% of the 225 clients reported that the issue that brought them to the WICC prevented them from working. Lost days of work declined by 79% after four months representing (of 24 clients) a cost savings to society of CAN$70.00 per client attending the WICC (assuming minimum wage).
- 53% of clients reported that they were unable to participate in their usual family and community activities when they first visited the WICC. Close to 80% of 24 clients had resumed their usual activities at four-month follow-up.
- 19% of the base-line sample (225) reported that they would have visited the Emergency Room if the WICC had not been available. Eight percent said they would have visited their family doctor. The cost savings by averting these emergency and doctors appointments was calculated as saving the healthcare system CAN$90.00 per WICC client when compared to the costs of the WICC session. A visit to the local Emergency Department was calculated to be three times as costly as a visit to the WICC. One-third of clients visiting Emergency with mental-health issues are admitted as in-patients. Averting just one in-patient stay saves CAN$8,000.
- WICC clients used more community services following their visit than they did prior to their visit (Stalker, Horton, & Cait, 2012). The WICC is acting to aid clients in referral and system's navigation.

The Second Study

The purpose of our second study was to compare outcomes for clients of KW Counselling Services with those of another counseling service, both agencies serving similar client populations in two separate cities using two different models of service delivery. The models were: (1) the WICC service delivery model, described above; and (2) a traditional service delivery model, wherein clients telephone to request service, and after talking with an intake worker, are usually placed on a wait list (Stalker, Riemer, Cait, Horton, Booton, Josling, Bedggood, & Zaczek, 2016). The second study included an additional question about which clients benefit most from the WICC model (Riemer, Stalker, Dittmer, Cait, Horton, Booton, & Kermani, 2015). As in the pilot, this study also measured cost-effectiveness. Our research team integrated a qualitative case study component into the study to provide a more comprehensive account of both models of service delivery. The qualitative component sought to understand past counseling experiences of participants, the nature of their personal difficulties and the significance of these for current service use, and their assessment of the model of service used.

Equipped with our initial learning from the pilot study and new funding, the follow-up questionnaires and interviews were done by phone, greatly increasing the rate of response by participants. In the second study 359 WICC clients completed the baseline questionnaire; of these, 221 (72% of those consenting to follow-up) completed data collection at the four-week follow-up, and 229 (75%) completed the data collection at the 10-week follow-up. At the comparison agency, 151 individuals (28%) completed the baseline data collection. At four weeks follow-up, 146 of the 151 (97%) completed the data collection, and at 10 weeks, 142 (94%) completed the data collection (Stalker, et al., 2016).

From the initial quantitative findings, we created three different categories, based on *GHQ-12* scores, for qualitative interviews: (1) participants who improved; (2) participants who did not change; and (3) participants who deteriorated. Some prior studies of single-session counseling excluded clients presenting with more severe mental-health issues, including issues around trauma, because it was believed this approach might not be helpful for this group (Cameron, 2007). We knew that people dealing with trauma did utilize WIC (walk-in counseling) and from the initial quantitative analysis we did see improvement with this group based on their *GHQ-12* scores. Because previous research had not included this group we were particularly interested in understanding why these participants found WIC helpful and took this into consideration in selecting cases for the qualitative study. We conducted 48 telephone audio-recorded (with client consent) interviews (Cait, et. al., 2016).

Both agencies involved in the study have made efforts to reduce barriers to access for new Canadians. The study sample was comprised of 26.8% of people utilizing the WICC and 22.7% at the comparison agency identifying being born outside of Canada, figures similar to the general immigrant populations where the study agencies were located. Thus the samples from both agencies are reasonably representative of the local communities in terms of cultural diversity. The participants attending the WICC were more likely to be male (40.5% vs. 26.1%) and slightly younger than the comparison group. Among participants attending the WICC, the proportion of the immigrant group who were male (35.1%) was not significantly different from the proportion born in Canada (41.3%). The mean age of immigrant males was also similar to non-immigrant male participants. Similar proportions at both sites were employed full-time (23%) or unemployed (17.3% at WICC and 15.2 at wait-list model) but those attending the WICC were more likely to report attending school and less likely to report being on either social assistance or the provincial disability support program. More than half of the people in the sample, 59.1% from the WICC and 64.9% from the comparison agency, had a household income of CAN$19,999 or less. From this we concluded the people in this study did not have the financial resources to obtain mental-health services privately, thus limiting their options for counseling (Stalker, et al., 2016).

Quantitative findings of the second study using multi-level modeling established that clients of the walk-in model improved more rapidly and were significantly less distressed as assessed by the *General Health Questionnaire-12* (*GHQ-12*) at the four-week follow-up compared to clients of the traditional service delivery model. At the 10-week follow-up, both groups were less troubled compared to baseline, and mean *GHQ-12* scores for the two groups were similar (Stalker, et al., 2016).

Findings from the qualitative case study using a thematic analysis revealed that the effectiveness of walk-in counseling is strikingly influenced by accessibility; we would miss the nuance and complexity of participants' experiences, however, if we were to suggest WICC was only helpful because it was accessible (Cait, et al., 2016). One participant attending the WICC explained looking for some help around his relationship with a former girlfriend:

> I was just looking at options for what we could do to kind of help the situation and get an outside opinion . . . It was nice when you have these things on your mind, you kind of want to get if off right away . . . So it was nice to have somebody there that day to, you know, vent a little bit . . . Uh just to I guess talk and, you know, see if I can get some answers out of myself almost just from kind of saying everything out loud instead of in my head . . .

This participant was able to "vent" about his experience, and through articulating his thoughts aloud he came to his own answers. The timeliness of the service and this participant's ability to take advantage of the nature of the service was helpful. Feeling a strong connection with the counselor was also significant. He said she was

> very comforting in the way that she would ask questions and it didn't come across as invasive or uncomfortable like. Yeah, like almost like I'd known her for a long time. Or she knew my history or something like that.

Another participant reported having used the WICC service previously for "anything and everything really. Anything that was troubling me that I didn't feel I had the coping skills or know-how to push through an issue." For her the process of getting into the WICC was "easy-breezy" and "really reasonable." When she had called for counseling at other agencies, and even including KW

Counselling Services, she was told there was a two- to three-month waiting list. She further clarifies why accessibility is so important:

> It's optimal because I would say that if I couldn't have gotten in when I needed help I would have been overwhelmed and probably been at the point of self-harm. Pretty much any time that I've ever gone and I've gone in because I just don't have the coping skills to get through a situation.

We also asked and learned how she had found the session helpful:

> I definitely need empathy. I just need someone to give me real good direction so that I can get the skills to be able to cope without returning over and over again . . . I come out feeling, um, so relieved and that I truly have enough skill to, um, be able to cope with the situation and if it was to arise again the know-how of what to do and basically to get validation that you don't just feel like, um, you are alone with this situation . . . I'm quite visual, so, um, it was helpful to draw some things out on paper. Writing them down to give me a set of know-hows and to-dos, to kind of go home and work on and she [the counselor] recommended a couple of books, too, which I got and read . . . You don't just walk away, you do have a game plan.

This participant speaks to the critical nature of timely and accessible service when she said that she would have been at the point of self-harm if she were not able to speak to someone. She was able to regain a sense of control over her life after having a directive session focused on skills acquisition and a written plan with which to move forward. Also important for this participant is not having to return "over and over again" (Cait, et al., 2016).

Our second objective for this study was to better understand who benefits from walk-in counseling. A moderator analysis suggests that, on average, clients with mood issues (i.e., anxiety and depression) benefit more from the walk-in model compared to those with other issues, at least during the weeks immediately following the single session. Challenging our assumptions, clients presenting with issues we termed "complex needs" (participants who at baseline reported they were coping with abuse, or indicated they had a child welfare issue, trauma/PTSD, serious mental illness or harm to self) who received service from the WIC model also improved more quickly than clients presenting with complex needs at the agency employing the wait-list model. The difference between the clients of the two delivery models in the rate of change over time for those without complex needs was less pronounced (Riemer, et al., 2016).

Two examples, discussed in the text that follows, from the qualitative research both allude to increased hope that the participants felt through their walk-in counseling experience, which can influence the decrease in indicators of distress (Cait, et al., 2016). One participant from the WICC voiced that after five years of being sober, she had started to drink again and this was increasing along with her depression. Her boyfriend had just gone to jail and she was having difficulty leaving her apartment. She explained that her "depression and anxiety and PTSD has always been there." This participant spoke about not really wanting help but still accessing WICC: "Like I just hated the world and I just really didn't want help, I just wanted to sit in my own self-pity." In spite of this participant's lack of interest in services, she attended the WICC based on encouragement from a friend and the ease of accessing the counseling and found it helpful:

> Just talking to somebody for even that little bit of time . . . having her [the counselor] write down things and tell me things. She was very positive with me and that I know a lot, because I do know a lot.

The walk-in counseling session for this woman who said she really didn't want help seems to have been both motivational and hopeful because of both the direction and the affirmation it provided for the participant. This woman identified her need for service and then followed through without unnecessary rules or agency policies impairing her readiness.

Another participant described going to WICC because she was suffering from depression and anxiety for over two years. She was a university student but decided to attend WICC instead of the university counseling center. She voiced feeling somewhat embarrassed because she had not told anyone she was coming to the WICC and also felt nervous, not knowing what to expect. Discussing her feelings after the session this participant explained:

> I guess that like there was help for me and . . . um, that was the first time I've ever like really talked to anyone about anything. And I guess I just felt like, um, it was a step in the right direction. And I just felt really comfortable with the counselor.

When asked what made her feel comfortable she said:

> She was just, um, really compassionate . . . She, she told me about stories of like other people that have been through it and like that: "You can do it!" and she was, um, as I was telling her the story, you could tell that she was getting, she felt for me and like that was really nice of her.

The client was given sheets to work on, numbers to call, and tips to think about when she was feeling down. She explained, having never been to counseling before to deal with her depression and anxiety, that it was difficult to integrate all the feedback:

> Well, it was my first time going and I only, I was experiencing it for like almost over a year so it was very hard to incorporate it like right away

> . . . it just sort of gave me a little bit of hope but I didn't really practice anything that she gave me.

While this participant was not able to completely use all the resources made available, it did give her hope that there were things she could do. Throughout the follow-up interview we learned that this woman decided to withdraw from university temporarily, to relocate closer to home and begin to work. She also told her family about her anxiety and depression two weeks after she had been to the WICC. After re-locating she re-entered counseling, feeling that her positive experience at the WICC made going to counseling much easier. She reported that she later re-enrolled in another university.

An important part of walk-in counseling is the *creation of hope* in the single session (Harper-Jaques & Foucault, 2014; Slive, et al., 2008; Young, Dick, Herring, & Lee, 2008), which can be what makes the service significant for some.

Snyder, Michael, and Cheavens (1999) delineate two components of hope: "pathways thinking" and "agency thinking." The first component involves believing that ways to attain one's goals and objectives exist. In this situation, a person does not have to have established the pathways to experience hope. The perception that these paths are available is what is important. For the first participant described earlier, delineating a plan with clear directions was helpful; for the second participant, the session gave the young woman a bit of hope even though she had not actually used any of the papers provided by the counselor. It was enough to know that, not only were there other people who had dealt with similar situations, but also there were a variety of routes to address the problem. The second component of hope, "agency thinking," involves people thinking they will be able to follow through with particular roadmaps to help them obtain their goals. It is the combination of these two that Snyder (1994) has theorized leads people to meet their goals (Cait, et al., 2016).

The second research study (Stalker, et al., 2016) has provided evidence that participants in the WICC group improved faster than participants in the comparison group at the four-week follow-up point. The findings of this study also confirm previous claims that walk-in SST may be a good fit for ethnically diverse communities (Slive, McElheran, & Lawson, 2008). For example, a female client from a minority cultural community in 2013 wrote the following on a *Session Feedback Form*, the data collection tool used at WICC as part of ongoing program evaluation:

> I feel that my counselor possesses a remarkable understanding of my culture and religion and is always prepared to learn more about the various dimensions and intricacies of my cultural and religious identity.

The proportion of males in the immigrant group attending walk-in counseling is also higher than usually seen in psychotherapy research, suggesting the attractiveness of walk-in for men may be a cross-cultural difference.

Qualitative findings help corroborate the importance of many concepts woven into the design of the walk-in counseling model. In particular, we note the timely provision of service, the walk-in session as a therapeutic consultation, emotional release, the infusion of hope, the importance of feeling heard, and the need to have confirmation of one's own resources and strengths (Slive & Bobele, 2012). The narratives told by participants elucidate that many people can benefit from a pragmatic consultation session (Slive & Bobele, 2012; Winnicott, 1971) with suggestions and feedback from the counselor. The service user then works collaboratively with the counselor to identify which option might be best. This type of session is akin to what is discussed in the literature as a "consultation process" (Slive, et al., 2008, p. 11). The value of a walk-in single session also lies in its philosophy of a whole therapy in a single session. For some individuals who are not interested in returning to counseling on an ongoing basis, having a whole therapy in one session is meaningful and beneficial. Extracts from the interview data also demonstrate the importance of accessibility. Fewer barriers to receiving services at the WICC made the experience for many clients much more satisfactory. Readily accessible single-session walk-in counseling is of benefit to people when in need and is also beneficial to the system as a whole by alleviating the pressure of waiting lists. The walk-in model can also serve to mitigate the crises and more complex consultations that ensue when difficulties fester.

Advocacy Efforts Utilizing the Research Studies

Many emergent WICC programs struggling with sustaining a new and unrecognized service, as KW Counselling Services is, may find that these two generations of research strengthen advocacy efforts. The following findings may be useful in articulating the value of WICC to a variety of funders:

- WICC is clearly perceived as accessible by clients in both studies. Accessible services are often valued by funders who recognize the barriers clients face in getting their needs met in a world of lengthy waiting lists and difficult to navigate service systems.
- WICC is accessed more by men than are traditional services. It is recognized that men seek help and use health services less frequently than women do (Smith, Braunack-Mayer, & Wittert, 2006, p. 81). This is known to negatively impact their well-being. The development of responsive and effective interventions for men has great potential for improving both men's lives and reducing health costs (Galdas, Cheater, & Marshall, 2005, p. 616). The WICC represents such an opportunity.
- Healthcare funders are often interested in diversion from costly medical services such as emergency departments and doctors. The first study, although small, offered some counterfactual evidence that a WICC may divert from emergency rooms and doctor's office. Further research is

required as cost effectiveness was not clearly evident in the second round of research.

- The research demonstrated that those with "complex needs," which included those with histories of abuse, did better clinically at the WICC than in traditional services. Although not captured in the research, internal agency program evaluation has highlighted that approximately 20% of our WICC visitors are women who present with a history of or current intimate partner violence (Walk-In Counselling for Violence against Women Proposal 2014). The WICC may offer a new and clinically potent service alternative to these women.
- WICC clients presenting with depression and anxiety fared somewhat better than those in traditional settings. Funders of mental-health services may find this to be of interest.

Future Research Directions

Our university-community collaboration has sought to conduct research that furthers both our understanding of WICC, as well as advocacy efforts, to provide a service that evidence clearly suggests is both effective and accessible. Future research is needed. Questions that we are eager to explore include:

- What are men's experiences of walk-in counseling? It appears that proportionately more men may come to the WICC compared to an agency requiring an appointment. What can these men tell us? What are the implications for men's health?
- We are also curious about the experience of women attending walk-in counseling who are living with intimate partner violence. How effective is walk-in counseling in supporting these women? What is the role of the WICC in the spectrum of services?
- What role does walk-in counseling have on return to work for clients living with disability and in receipt of social assistance? Does walk-in counseling result in faster return to work or poverty reduction for these populations?
- Are there better ways to track costs and benefits of walk-in counseling than those used to date?
- What are the experiences of newcomers using the service? Is this a useful model of service?

Conclusion

Walk-in counseling represents a paradigm shift and challenges long-held assumptions about how best to provide effective counseling services. In spite of research suggesting that across modes of service provision a majority of service users attend counseling for one or two sessions (O'Neill & Rottem, 2012; Perkins & Scarlett, 2008; Slive & Bobele, 2011; Talmon, 1990; see Hoyt & Talmon, 2014), it is difficult to transform long-held beliefs about service delivery. Our research (see Riemer, Stalker, Dittmer, Cait, Horton, Booton, & Kermani, 2016) provides encouraging evidence in terms of the effectiveness of walk-in counseling. Those at KW Counselling Services have a deeply held belief that the agency is doing something that is right and valuable as is evident not just in our formal research but in the many visitors who attend the service one day a week. If we hope to see this new model benefit those struggling with "matters of the heart" it is necessary for our global pioneers in WIC to continue to pursue further research and advocacy.

References

Bellis, J.M. (1994). The transtheoretical model of change applied to psychotherapy: A psychometric assessment of related instruments. Doctoral dissertation, University of Rhode Island, 1994. *Dissertation Abstracts International, 54*, 3845B.

Cait C.-A., Skop, M., Booton, J.A., Stalker, C.A., Horton, S., & Riemer, M. (2016). Practice-based Qualitative research: Participant experiences of walk-in counselling and traditional counselling. *Qualitative Social Work*. DOI: 10.1177/1473325016637910.

Cameron, C.L. (2007). Single session and walk-in psychotherapy: A descriptive account of the literature. *Counselling and Psychotherapy Research, 7*(4), 245–249.

Canada, Parliament, The Standing Senate Committee on Social Affairs, Science and Technology (2006). *Out of the shadows at last: Transforming mental health, mental illness and addiction services in Canada*. May.

ConnecticutHistory.org (2017). Heart pump out of an Erector Set—who knew? http://connecticuthistory.org/heart-pump-out-of-an-erector-set-who-knew/. Retrieved December 25, 2017.

Galdas, P.M., Cheater, F., & Marshall P. (2005). Men and health help-seeking behavior: Literature review. *Journal of Advanced Nursing, 49*(6), 616–623.

Goldberg, D.P. (1972). *The detection of psychiatric illness by questionnaire*. London: Oxford University Press.

Harper-Jaques, S. & Foucault, D. (2014). Walk-in single-session therapy: Client satisfaction and clinical outcomes. *Journal of Systemic Therapies, 33*(3), 29–49.

Horton, S., Stalker, C., Cait, C., & Josling, L. (2012). Sustaining walk-in counseling services. *Healthcare Quarterly, 15*(3), 44–49.

Hoyt, M.F. & Talmon, M. (2014). What the literature says: An annotated bibliography. In M.F. Hoyt & M. Talmon (Eds.) (2014). *Capturing the moment: Single session therapy and walk-in services* (pp. 487–516). Bethel, CT: Crown House Publishing.

Koestler, A. (1959). *The sleepwalkers: A history of man's changing vision of the universe*. New York: Macmillan.

KW Counselling Services (2011). Annual report 2010: Celebrating 60 years of making better lives possible. Kitchener-Waterloo, Ontario, Canada.

KW Counselling Services (2014). *Walk-in counselling for violence against women proposal*. Submitted to the Ministry of Community and Social Services.

Lavietes, S. (2003). William Glenn, 88, surgeon who invented heart procedure. *New York Times*, March 17.

O'Neill, I. & Rottem, N. (2012). Reflections and learning from an agency-wide implementation of single session work in family therapy. *The Australian and New Zealand Journal Family Therapy, 33*(1), 70–83.

Perkins, R. & Scarlett, G. (2008). The effectiveness of single session therapy in child and adolescent mental health. Part 2: An 18-month follow-up study. *Psychology and Psychotherapy: Theory, Research and Practice, 81*(2), 143–156.

Prochaska, J.O. & DiClemente, C.C. (1982). Transtheoretical therapy: Toward a more integrative model of change. *Psychotherapy, Theory, Research, and Practice, 19*, 276–288.

Riemer, M., Stalker, C.A., Dittmer, L., Cait, C., Horton, S., Booton, J., & Kermani, N. (submitted). Single-session walk-in counseling: Who benefits the most? Submitted for publication.

Slive, A. & Bobele, M. (Eds.) (2011). *When one hour is all you have: Effective therapy for walk-in clients.* Phoenix, AZ: Zeig, Tucker, & Theisen.

Slive, A. & Bobele, M. (2012). Walk-in counseling services: Making the most of one hour. *Australian and New Zealand Journal of Family Therapy, 33*(1), 27–38.

Slive A., McElheran, N., & Lawson A. (2008). How brief does it get? Walk-in single session therapy. *Journal of Systemic Therapies, 27*(4), 5–22.

Smith, J.A., Braunack-Mayer, A., & Wittert, G. (2006) What do we know about men's help-seeking and health service use? *Medical Journal of Australia, 184*(2): 81–83.

Snyder, C.R. (1994). *The psychology of hope.* New York: Free Press.

Snyder, C.R., Michael, S.T., & Cheavens, J.S. (1999). Hope as a psychotherapeutic foundation of nonspecific factors, placebos, and expectancies. In M.A. Hubble, B. Duncan, & S. Miller (Eds.), *The heart and soul of change: What works in therapy* (pp. 205–230). Washington, DC: American Psychological Association.

Stalker, C.A., Riemer, M., Cait, C. A., Horton, S., Booton, J., Josling, L., Bedggood, J., & Zaczek, M. (2016). A comparison of walk-in counselling and the wait list model for delivering counselling services. *Journal of Mental Health, 25*(5), 403-409.

Stalker, C.A., Horton, S., & Cait, C. (2012). Single-session therapy in walk-in counseling clinics: A pilot study of who attends and how they fare afterwards. *Journal of Systemic Therapies, 31*(1), 38–52.

SynCardia (2014). www.syncardia.com/2014-multimedia-releases/7-things-about-artificial-hearts-that-you-should-know/itemid-1715.html.

Talmon, M. (1990). *Single session therapy: Maximizing the effect of the first (and often only) therapeutic encounter.* San Francisco: Jossey-Bass.

Winnicott, D.W. (1971). *Therapeutic consultations in child psychiatry.* New York: Basic Books.

Young, K., Dick, M., Herring, K., & Lee, J. (2008). From waiting lists to walk-in: Stories from a walk-in therapy clinic. *Journal of Systemic Therapies, 27*(4), 23–39.

7 Development of a Single-Session Family Program at Child and Youth Mental-Health Services, Southern Melbourne

Rachel Barbara-May, Paul Denborough, and Tess McGrane

Single-session consultation with young people and their families has been practiced in Australia for over 20 years in a variety of settings. In this chapter, we describe how a single-session model has been implemented in a Child and Youth Mental Health Service (Alfred CYMHS), a tertiary child and youth mental-health service, and in a federally-funded youth mental-health service (Headspace).

Alfred CYMHS is one of five state-funded services in metropolitan Melbourne covering a catchment area of around 600,000 people. Our mandate is to see the most severe and complex young people and their families and those requiring a multi-disciplinary team. We see between 1–2% of the child and youth population and also support other services that help another 10–12% who have mental-health difficulties.

Alfred Health also runs a local Headspace center which provides early intervention for 12–25-year–olds. These Headspace centers were initiated by the Australian government in 2006 and there are now about 100 centers across the country in regional towns and larger metropolitan cities. The model usually includes a lead agency (such as Alfred Health) and a local partnership of not-for-profit organizations. The centers cover four core areas: mental health, physical health, work and study support, and alcohol and other drugs services. These centers are designed to be "youth friendly" and easily accessed in order to minimize the stigma associated with mental-health services. Headspace has an inclusive "no wrong door" approach for young people and their families. Families who have mild or moderate problems are ideally linked early into Headspace and families facing more severe and complex problems are linked into the state-funded CYMHS system.

Single-Session Work at Alfred CYMHS

We initially tried to set up single-session practice at Alfred CYMHS in 2004 but this did not work. Intake clinicians were not involved in the family sessions but rather just asked to identify suitable cases. As they weren't part of the actual sessions they found it difficult to speak confidently to families about the rationale behind the approach or how the process might unfold. We also did not have a regular group of clinicians who set aside time each week to meet and therefore appointments were made on an *ad hoc* basis.

At that time, there were longstanding practices with underlying philosophies and beliefs which impacted on the success of this initial attempt of implementation. Such beliefs about what constitutes effective therapy and therapeutic change included "more is better," "real changes happen slowly and gradually," and "effective therapeutic relationships take time to develop." (These impediments and others—such as the overvaluation of "deep insight" and the confusion of clients' and therapists' interests—have been catalogued by Hoyt, 2009, pp. 6–7.) Working in a single-session framework requires a willingness to work with partial knowledge and relinquishment of the expert position about what change is required to alter the problems families present with and what needs to happen in order for "real change" to occur.

Two years later (2006), in a second attempt to implement a SST framework we involved our intake clinicians plus a couple of other clinicians and set aside a regular two-hour weekly time slot. There was still a great deal of skepticism from staff and referrers about how we could possibly help families with such complex presentations within one session. Having the intake clinicians involved in a dedicated single-session team allowed new clinical processes to develop. The intake clinicians were well positioned to carry a thread of information about the family and their concerns from the first point of contact, through to the session and follow-up. From the first phone call, the intake clinicians were able to begin preparing the family's readiness for the session, thereby helping the family to make the most of the time spent in the session. Part of the flaws of the earlier attempt at implementation was the absence of this preparatory work undertaken with the family by the intake clinicians.

The decision to embark on a SST approach to treatment when a young person and family first seek help is made collaboratively with families. The decision is made in an informed way, with various options presented to the family. Families are reassured about the availability of alternate pathways for treatment in the service, should the goals of the single-session intervention not be achieved or if the family feels that further assistance is required at follow-up. Families being able to *choose* this approach places them in a position of authority about their own needs and what might work best for them. Families actively choosing a SST approach also possibly reduces the risk of them experiencing the offer of the single-session consultation as a diminishing of the seriousness of their problems. Some other factors that are appealing to families choosing the single-session consultation are "getting started quickly" and "focusing on solutions rather than problems."

The single-session program at Alfred CYMHS focuses on a meeting with the entire family unit, including parental and sibling systems. We encourage all to attend even in the case of divorced, separated, or blended families. Getting everyone together to help the young person is a powerful intervention in itself.

Sometimes this has meant the getting together of family members who have, up until the session, struggled to come together in any other way. The intake clinician, who is dealing with the initial contact with the family and responsible for the setting up of the family session, works hard with the family to determine who is in the family and who might be an important participant in the family session. Sometimes there may be some reluctance from different members of a family to come together for the session, particularly when there has been separation or divorce and when those members of the family remain estranged from each other. The intake clinician will discuss the possible benefits of everyone coming together for a one-off session. We have found that estranged family members are often prepared to come together for a one-off session in the interests of the troubled young person. The intake clinician will collaborate with each family member about how to manage the coming together in the interest of the young person. Although this can be a lengthy process, the investment that the intake clinician makes in helping this be possible for estranged families assists the young person to experience a significant coming together of those that care about them most. On those occasions where this is unsuccessful or not possible, the family session will proceed with those family members willing or able to participate. An extended family session provides young people with an opportunity to experience a strong support network of family members and professionals who are willing to do what they can to help them overcome the difficulties they are facing. It creates an opportunity for change that may be otherwise difficult to achieve.

We use a "one-way screen" (mirror) with a reflecting team (see Anderson, 1991, 1992; Friedman, 1995; Jenkins, 1996) in which, with the clients' permission, a group of observers watches the session and then shares their observations with the clients. Two therapists work together with the family for an extended period of time, usually about 1 hour and 20 minutes, before they switch places with the team of usually about four observers. Families can then listen in as the team discusses their observations. The reflecting team speaks for about 5–10 minutes before swapping back over with the family. The therapists then invite the family to respond to what they have heard from the team. The idea of "many heads working on the problem" increases the capacity to make the most of the consultation session. It elicits multiple viewpoints and perspectives. The reflecting team is able to provide reflections back to the family about what they have noticed the family members doing well, what they have already been doing to fight the problem, and also to reinforce the views about change and solutions that the family and therapist have identified throughout the process. While observing the session, one of the reflecting team members will be preparing a summary of the session that aims to capture the main themes discussed throughout the session, capturing the family's ideas and the team's reflections. The family is provided with a copy of this summary to take away at the end of the session.

Our program has now expanded to three teams, each with six or seven members. The reflecting team is such a rich training ground for clinicians who are new to this way of working. Much of the work in our mental-health service is carried out by clinicians working on their own with families, and this approach allows staff to work directly with their colleagues. It is an excellent way to provide in-house family therapy training and experience for new staff and trainees, who have reported satisfaction from the multidisciplinary teamwork and the on-going learning this provides. Three families per week are seen through the single-session program, with each of the teams working with one family per week for an extended time, with the entire process taking just over two hours per session. During busy periods the sessions can be booked up a few weeks in advance, but most families can be seen quickly, usually within one to two weeks of the initial contact. All the families seen through the single-session program have either self referred or have been referred to our service by the community. Being the only public mental-health service for children, youth and families in the region, the service is well known in the community and has a central role in the system of care in this area. All three single-session teams have a set time and day that they meet each week and the intake clinicians book families into the next available slot. All team members are scheduled recurrently for the session time each week and participation in the program is accounted for in the overall workload management system and time allocations.

Each of the three separate teams will schedule a team review session every six to eight weeks, so that they can discuss their work together. These meetings help the team stay on track with following up families that they have seen previously and for the team to hear about the progress of the families since their session. During these meetings, the team will consider together how to support those families who require more intervention at follow-up and make plans for this as appropriate. These meetings are quite important to check in on the team's processes and for the team to pay attention to the co-therapy relationships and practices. All three teams come together once a month for a two-hour peer supervision meeting with an external facilitator, with one of the teams presenting a case for discussion with the rest of the group. These processes are important in the continued development of the teams, clinicians, and the program overall.

We have collected outcome data, not just because this is useful clinically to learn what is effective, but also because we needed to prove the worth of the program to our funding agencies. Evaluation of the single-session program is conducted via the Miller and Duncan (2002) *Outcome Rating Scale* (*ORS*) and *Session Rating Scale* (*SRS*). These are routinely completed at the beginning and end of the session and also at follow-up.

Arrangements for the follow-up after the single-session are made with the family at the end of the session. Families decide with the team the timing of the follow-up, with consideration given to the outcomes of the session and presenting concerns. Usually the follow-up will occur between two and four weeks after the session.

Now nearly 25% of all new referrals start with a family single-session and reflecting team. Influenced by our single-session practice, the first contact with families—often a phone call—is welcoming and encouraging with strength-based and solution-focused leanings rather than a clinician running through a problem-saturated checklist trying to determine whether the family meets some rather arbitrary eligibility criteria. We have found that implementing single-sessions has been a practical way to ensure that recovery-orientated practice happens "on the ground."

Case Example: The Jones Family

Jake, a 16-year-old boy, was referred to Alfred CYMHS by his stepmother, Nicole. Jake presented with increasing behaviors of concern, including angry outbursts, disengagement, having trouble following rules, poor attendance at school, and getting into a bit of trouble with teachers. Nicole described feeling worried that Jake was isolated in the family, wasn't really getting along well with others, and that he seemed very unhappy. Jake lived with his father, Mike, younger sister, Karen (who had Down's syndrome), and stepmother, Nicole. Jake and Karen's mother had died approximately two years ago from cancer. Prior to her death, Mike and Jake's mother were described as being happily married. Mike and Nicole had married a few months prior to the session. All four members of the family attended the two-hour single-session family consultation involving the reflecting team.

Initially, Jake was difficult to engage in the session because despite Mike and Nicole's expressed concern for him and for the breakdown in his relationships in the family, he was concerned that the session was going to target him and his bad behavior. He agreed that things had changed for him and that he was often "wagging" school [Aussie slang for "truancy"], getting angry, and feeling angry a lot of the time. Jake was struggling to be able to understand or explain why this had been happening. He seemed saddened by the loss of his relationship with his dad and was struggling to accept Nicole and her place in the family.

Mike and Nicole approached the session with care and concern. Mike described a sense of loss of Jake, really missing his relationship with him. He told us how Jake used to be fun and caring, that he would make a lot of effort to look after his little sister, and how he and Jake would enjoy many activities together. Mike also noticed that Jake, who once "got along with everyone" seemed to be having a bit more trouble getting along with others and that he was angry a lot of the time. Mike and Nicole told us how they had tried a few different things to help work this out with Jake but nothing seemed to be working. They had tried giving him more space but this only seemed to isolate him more from them. They had also focused a bit more on limit setting and consequences, feeling as though they needed to be tougher on Jake but this also seemed to only cause more conflict in their relationship with him. Karen talked about feeling quite sad and confused about what was happening with Jake and also talked about missing having fun times with him.

We heard from Mike and Nicole how Jake and Karen had been through a difficult few years, with their mother's illness and then death. Nicole talked about feeling worried that Jake thought she was trying to replace his mother and how much she cared for Jake and Karen. Jake started to talk about feeling angry at his dad, because he thought his dad had "forgotten" his mum and that he no longer missed her or felt sad about her death. Jake said his dad no longer visited his mum's grave and that they hardly ever talked about her anymore. Mike listened to Jake and was very surprised to hear that Jake was feeling this way. They spent a great deal of time talking about Jake and Karen's mother, the kinds of things that they miss about her, what she was like and the kind of mother she wanted to be to Jake and Karen. Mike talked to Jake about how he still misses her and thinks about her every day. Nicole did a great job at helping Mike share his grief and sadness with Jake and Karen.

Jake started to express his sadness to his dad and how he had been feeling angry at Mike and Nicole. The family talked about grief and sadness and the different ways that they manage it. Mike suggested to Jake that they make a plan to visit his mother's grave together. Jake thought that this would be a good idea and asked his dad if they could start doing something together again regularly.

When the team followed up with Mike and Nicole a few weeks after the session they reported great progress. Mike felt that Jake and he were getting back on track in their relationship and that they were communicating more and spending time together. Mike was making a lot of effort to talk about their mother with Jake and Karen and they had visited her grave together and planned on doing so again sometime in the future. Jake had been opening up to Nicole and they were making steps towards a respectful and warm relationship. Jake was getting on better at school and his behaviors had settled. Jake was more connected in the family and was cooperative and pleasant to be around. The family felt that they had gotten what they needed from the session. No further contact was planned and the family were encouraged to contact the service should they want any further assistance in the future.

Single-Session Work at Headspace

Traditionally, clinical practice at Headspace has been more about individual counseling with young people rather than involving the whole family. The way the Headspace model is funded through Medicare tends to encourage more individual practice and mental-health care plans tend to be written with individual counseling in mind rather than family therapy. Most clinicians operate on a time-limited, fee-for-service model which makes seeing individuals more appealing for clinicians.

Recent Australia-wide Headspace data indicated that about 50% of clients attended for one to two sessions only (Rickwood, Telford, Mazzer, Parker,

Tanti, & McGorry, 2015). This is consistent with other local and international data which have consistently showed that a significant proportion of clients attend for one session only (Diffey, 2007; Hoyt, Rosenbaum, & Talmon, 1992; Hoyt & Talmon, 2014; Perkins, 2006; Slive & Bobele, 2011).

We wanted to set up family single-session work at our Headspace Southern Melbourne service for several reasons, not just because of the clinical effectiveness of the approach. Other reasons included these:

- Families were telling us that a large gap in the system was that they were not being supported if the young person refused to attend (i.e., under the existing system, the young person needed to be present for the clinician to be reimbursed by Medicare).
- It was clear to the Headspace intake workers and many of the counseling clinicians that many of the young persons' issues and difficulties were relational in nature and all family members were affected.

In 2013 we had a chance, with some one-off funding (from a budget surplus due to salary underspend) to employ two senior family therapists to help set up single-session practice within Headspace, Southern Melbourne. They were salaried rather than fee-for-service so had some time to set up the program supported by the appropriate processes. The initial program quickly expanded to include the salaried senior intake clinicians along with the original two family therapists (who were able to stay long term) and now we regularly have six single-sessions per week, in a co-therapy or reflecting team format. The clients are young people (ages 12–25), parents only, or families, either at the first point of contact with Headspace or referred by the clinician who provided individual treatment to the young person. Significantly, the program is able to support parents and families where the young person may decline or refuse to attend. The program has been very positively received by the community, and now serves as a stand-alone treatment, an adjunct to existing individual counseling, or as a "soft entry" to individual support for the young person.

At the point of intake, Headspace staff email information about the session and also the pre-session questionnaire which aims to seed a solution-focused approach. We generally allow two hours for the sessions. If we are working as co-therapists without the extended team, we generally take a short break before offering a reflection to the family. We try to make the reflection strengths-based and comment positively on the resources within the family. Because of the way we work in taking a "non-expert" approach and in seeking to empower parents, we generally try to address any risk issues or concerns within the session, and a safety plan, if needed, is talked about with the young person and parents.

A summary of the session is written in real time by a member of the reflecting team and either emailed or given to the family at the end of the session.

This summary serves as the clinical documentation for the client file. We have a follow-up phone call after a few weeks and talk then about what else, if anything, is needed or wanted by the family. Sometimes the family will contact us sooner to talk about options, which may include having another family session, individual counseling for the young person, or very occasionally, referral to CYMHS.

Data for the first 18 months indicated that of the total 174 sessions conducted the large majority included either the young person and family (55%) or the parents only (41%). Furthermore, 70% attended once only, 20% attended for two sessions, and the remaining 10% had three or more sessions. Most referrals came directly from families contacting Intake (75%) rather than from other Headspace clinicians (25%) and slightly more males (57%) than females (43%) were the identified client. All ages up to 21 years old were well represented, with the largest cohort being the 15–16-year-old age group.

As with the CYMHS service, evaluation of the single-session program is conducted via the Miller and Duncan (2004) *Outcome Rating Scale* (*ORS*) and *Session Rating Scale* (*SRS*). The *SRS* is a measure of client satisfaction and is routinely completed at the end of each session. As shown in Figure 7.1, the SST sessions during the first 18-month period were consistently rated highly by the participants. The *ORS* is routinely completed at the beginning of the session and also at follow-up (typically two to four weeks after the session). As shown in Figure 7.2, follow-up *ORS* data indicated a statistically significant improvement in the young person's functioning. (For full discussion of data analyses in Figures 7.1 and 7.2, see Hopkins, Lee, McGrane, & Barbara-May, 2017.)

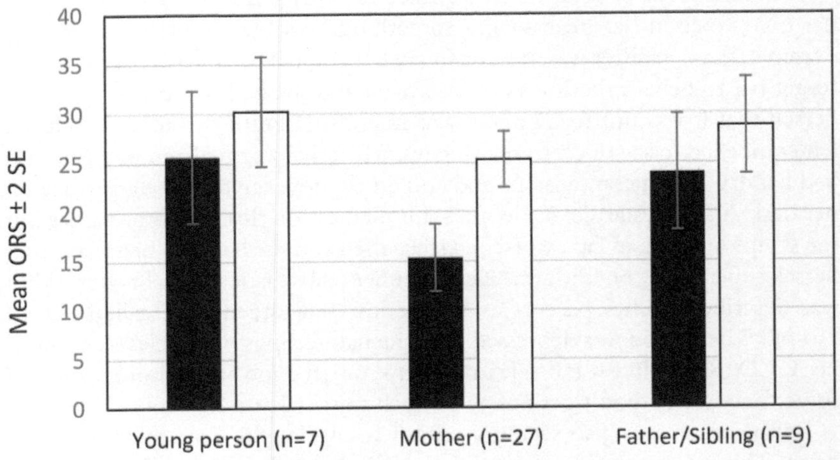

Figure 7.1 Mean *Session Rating Scale* scores for the young person, parent and sibling/other (Hopkins, et al., 2016)

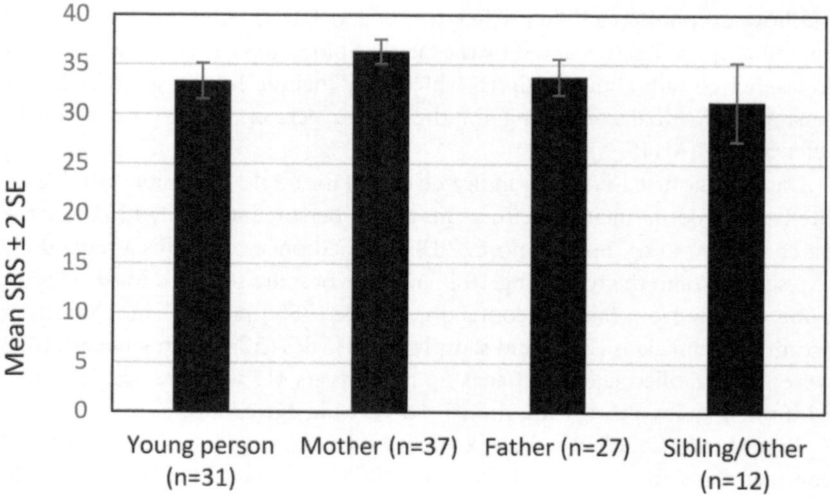

Figure 7.2 Mean *Outcome Rating Scale* scores for the young person rated by the young person, mother, or father/sibling pre-SST (black) and at follow-up (white) (Hopkins, et al., 2016)

Case Example: The Reed family

Edith, a 17-year-old girl, had been seeing a private psychologist for several months for individual treatment of her obsessive-compulsive symptoms. She lived with her parents, Tanya and Arthur, her 20-year-old brother, James, and her 15-year-old sister, Sarah.

The OCD involved what Edith described as "mental rituals." She experienced her own voice in her head saying something horrible about someone—for example, that her sister was ugly, or to kill her sister. The voice apparently tried to get her to believe the things it was saying and she had to work to convince herself that it was not true or to make amends. If Edith passed a church she felt compelled to say or do something immediately in a ritualized way. She also had hand-washing compulsions and could not move anything out of place on her desk. She had started anti-depressant medication three months earlier but the symptoms had, in fact, worsened since then and she had also begun cutting herself superficially on one arm. Picking at her scabs made her feel better. Edith was described by her parents as having low self-esteem; she called herself "stupid," her mood was depressed, and she had feelings of hopelessness about her OCD. She didn't want to learn to drive or get a job and although she had some friends, she didn't get out very much to socialize with them.

Edith's sister was also seeing a school counselor for depression and self-harm. The sisters were close but did not talk about their "mental issues" with each other and did not discuss them with their brother.

Edith's private psychologist initially referred Edith to Headspace because she had run out of "funded sessions" and the family could not afford to continue the therapy. Both parents and Emily attended a single-session soon after with two co-therapists (Rachel and Tess) in the room and one reflecting clinician (Campbell) behind the one-way screen. After about an hour the three clinicians had an in-room reflection with each other in the presence of the family and a letter was sent to the family the following week.

During the single-session, the co-therapists talked at some length about how the family expressed little conflict. The family emphasis on niceness and politeness became clear and was explicitly commented upon by the therapists. During the reflection, the clinicians wondered how the family could have some playfulness with anger and "bad" thoughts. Thus, we were drawing on a number of therapeutic ideas, including the narrative externalizing of the OCD, and exposure with a paradoxical approach. We explained the ideas to the family in the letter below sent to the family after the session. The widespread use of therapeutic letters was introduced by narrative therapists David Epston and Michael White (Epston, 1994; White & Epston, 1990). Their informal research showed that a single letter was worth approximately three to five face-to-face counseling sessions. More recent formal research has found that therapeutic letters make a substantial contribution to positive outcomes and have significant value for clients (Moules, 2009).

> Dear Edith, Tanya, and Arthur,
>
> Thank you for coming along and meeting with us a few days ago. You came to see us because you wanted to find a way to help Edith fight her OCD. You told us about all the things you and she have done to fight against the OCD, and some of the successes you have had along the way.
>
> Arthur, you described yourself as trying to pull Edith up from above and that Tanya is often beneath her trying to stop her from falling; you think that with time Edith will overcome the OCD, as she moves through life and progresses through school. Tanya, you said you are probably the family member most aware of how the OCD impacts on Edith as you are with her when it is at its strongest. You worry that it is getting worse for Edith and that she needs more help to fight against it. Edith, you said that the OCD makes it really hard for you to "be a normal person" and that it really gets in the way of your life and makes you not like yourself. You seemed hopeful that the OCD would one day get out of the way and let you get on with your life. Edith, you told us about your "ritualizing" and that you often have "bad thoughts" that trigger it.
>
> Often the thoughts are nasty things about other people. The OCD makes you think you need to ritualize in order to prevent something bad from happening or to counteract the nasty thought. We wondered if it might help you, Edith, to start telling your parents what kind of bad thoughts you have and what you think might happen if you don't ritualize. We worried that having to keep it a secret made the OCD more powerful.
>
> Tanya and Arthur, you told us how you helped Edith overcome her fear of churches through exposure. Exposure to thoughts isn't so straightforward, so we wondered about some of these ideas:

- The more unwanted and unacceptable thoughts are, then the more dangerous and powerful they feel; how can you as parents help Edith to accept her "bad thoughts" and know that everyone has them. Perhaps other family members can share with Edith some of the "bad thoughts" they have from time to time.
- Play with your thoughts. For example, the family could play thought charades, practice saying them in funny voices, draw a thought cartoon, and write them down in colorful fonts.
- It seemed to us that the OCD might be "attacking your niceness"; it sees that you care what people think, that you don't want to be angry or unkind to people and it uses that against you. We thought it might help to build resilience against this by practicing expressing angry or not nice things. This way you might be able to experience this as quite normal and harmless.

We look forward to hearing how things have progressed in your fight against OCD when we talk to you in a couple of weeks.

Regards
Rachel, Tess and Campbell

During the session, we had arranged to call Tanya on the phone after a couple of weeks. The family had agreed that this was a suitable time interval for them to start to practice some of the ideas that we had talked about in the session. At the follow-up call, we heard from Tanya that Edith was "starting to get her head around her OCD" and was saying things like "thoughts are just thoughts, everyone has them." She was more involved with activities and going out socially and generally seemed more happy and relaxed. In a phone call with Edith, she confirmed her parent's observations, and said that she was less distressed by her "bad thoughts" and was practicing playing around with thoughts and noticing that they seemed less powerful.

It was agreed that no further session was needed at that point. The clinician expressed optimism about the family's ability to continue to tackle and tame the OCD, and also encouraged the parents to make contact again at any time in the future if another session could be helpful. The clinician also advised the parents to make contact with the prescribing doctor to review and discuss Edith's medication.

Conclusions

The single-session programs at Alfred CYMHS and Headspace continue to grow and improve. Each week we see approximately three single-sessions at Alfred CYMHS and six single-sessions at Headspace, Southern Melbourne. We are now much more respectful of clients' assessment of their own needs and work with a greater degree of openness and transparency. We now provide a written summary of each session, reflecting the family's and team's thoughts and focusing more on strengths, as well as providing recommendations. We measure our outcomes using the *SRS* and *ORS* (Miller & Duncan, 2004) and report these back to our staff group.

SST has been an excellent way to improve collaboration and move away from the so-called "expert" position which unintentionally often left clients disempowered and feeling blamed. The majority of our clinicians are now involved in single-session work and over time we have come to see the values and attitudes of SST as being part of everyday practice.

References

Andersen, T. (Ed.). (1991). *The reflecting team: Dialogues and dialogues about the dialogues.* New York: Norton.

Andersen, T. (1992). Reflections on reflecting with families. In S. McNamee & K.J. Gergen (Eds.), *Therapy as social construction* (pp. 54–68), Newbury Park, CA: Sage.

Diffey, C. (2007). *Incorporating single session therapy into everyday CAMHS clinical practice.* Master's thesis, La Trobe University, Melbourne, Australia.

Epston, D. (1994). Extending the conversation. *Family Therapy Networker, 18*, 30–37.

Friedman, S. (Ed.) (1995). *The reflecting team in action: Collaborative practice in family therapy.* New York: Guilford Press.

Hopkins, L., Lee, S., McGrane, T., & Barbara-May, R. (2017). Single session family therapy in youth mental health: Can it help? *Australasian Psychiatry, 25*(2), 108–111.

Hoyt, M.F. (2009). *Brief psychotherapies: Principles and practices.* Phoenix, AZ: Zeig, Tucker, & Theisen.

Hoyt, M.F., Rosenbaum, R., & Talmon, M. (1992). Planned single-session psychotherapy. In S.H. Budman, M.F. Hoyt, & S. Friedman (Eds.), *The first session in brief therapy* (pp. 59–86). New York: Guilford Press.

Hoyt, M.F. & Talmon, M. (2014). What the research literature says. In M.F. Hoyt & M. Talmon (Eds.), *Capturing the moment: Single-session therapy and walk-in services* (pp. 487–516). Bethel, CT: Crown House Publishing.

Jenkins, D. (1996). A reflecting team approach to family therapy: A Delphi study. *Journal of Marital and Family Therapy, 22*(2), 219–238.

Miller, S.D. & Duncan, B.L. (2004). *The Outcome and Session Rating Scales: Administration and scoring manual.* Chicago, IL: Institute for the Study of Therapeutic Change.

Moules, N.J. (2009). The past and future of therapeutic letters: Family suffering and healing words. *Journal of Family Nursing, 15*(1), 102–111.

Perkins, R. (2006). The effectiveness of one session of therapy using a single-session approach for children and adolescents with mental health problems. *Psychology and Psychotherapy: Theory, Research, and Practice, 79*, 215–227.

Rickwood, D., Telford, R., Mazzer, K., Parker, A., Tanti, C., & McGorry, P. (2015). The services provided to young people by Headspace centres in Australia. *Medical Journal of Australia, 202*(10), 533–537.

Slive, A. & Bobele, M. (Eds.) (2011). *When one hour is all you have: Effective therapy for walk-in clients.* Phoenix, AZ: Zeig, Tucker, & Theisen.

White, M., & Epston, D. (1990). *Narrative means to therapeutic ends.* New York: Norton.

8 Single-Session Therapy in the Majority World

Addressing the Challenge of Service Delivery in Cambodia and the Implications for Other Global Contexts

John K. Miller, Jason J. Platt, and Kevin M. Conroy

Each year for the past decade, we have been leading student educational exchange and human services trips to Cambodia at the invitation of the psychology department at the Royal University of Phnom Penh (RUPP) and non-governmental organizations (NGOs) in the country. During these exchanges, we endeavor to take Western graduate therapy, social work, and counseling students to Cambodia to conduct service-learning projects. One of our aims is to promote meaningful educational, cultural, and therapeutic experiences in collaboration with graduate students and faculty at RUPP. The students we bring to Cambodia are predominantly from North America, although we have taken students from all over the world. This chapter examines our efforts to engage with the Khmer (Cambodian) people during these exchanges to address needs without over-imposing our national values (sometimes referred to as "colonialism"). We also work to understand and promote the natural healing methods and rituals of the Khmer people. Many of our activities in Cambodia involve single-session therapeutic encounters. We have employed single-session therapy methods in other international contexts such as Mexico and China (see Miller, 2014; Platt & Mondellini, 2014) as well as other unique situations such as post-disaster settings (Miller, 2011). In this chapter, we will present several different types of single-session therapy (SST) modalities we have discovered or modified in collaboration with our Khmer colleagues over the past 10 years working in Cambodia. None of our SST methods occur in traditional Western-style office settings, as this would be inconsistent with current cultural norms or be simply impractical given the available economic resources. Instead, we adapted our SST methods to fit the surroundings and the cultural mores.

While two of us grew up and were trained as therapists in the U.S., we have traveled and worked extensively outside the U.S., including Latin America (Platt) and Asia and Canada (Miller). One of the challenges of our work has been making use of the methods and theories from our Western training in non-Western contexts. While the Western world dominates the field of therapy, it ironically is designed to fit for only a minority of the world's population. The Western world from which most models of psychotherapy emanate represents only about 5% of the global population (Arnett, 2008). It has been our experience that while there are many fundamental therapy constructs that transfer meaningfully between cultures, others do not or are completely inappropriate. For example, the importance of the free and well "differentiated" individual is a cornerstone of Western therapy, but will often seem inappropriate or even bizarre in most collectivistic cultures where family and community interconnectedness are of priority importance and individualism is a shrinking consideration. Additionally, the Western single vision of therapy as a service delivered from well-appointed professional offices on an appointment-only, fee-for-service basis is impossible to appreciate for the majority of the world's population. A recent report from the World Health Organization (WHO) predicts that within the next few decades depression and other untreated mental-health issues will be the predominant contributor to the total burden of disability globally. One of the main reasons for this dilemma will be inadequate clinical service delivery systems in non-Western (majority world) contexts. In our view, SST methods of clinical service delivery may represent one type of innovative strategy to overcome these barriers in parts of the world where the concept of therapy as a treatment for mental issues is still developing. The SST modalities we describe in this chapter represent our humble insights regarding our best efforts to apply SST as it might be conducted for some of these "majority" world settings. We reflect on some of these ideas specifically with regard to our decade-plus experience in Cambodia.

Cambodia in Context

The Kingdom of Cambodia is a Southeast Asian country roughly the size of the state of Missouri, with a population of nearly 14 million people. About 10% of the population live in Phnom Penh, the capital, with 80% of Cambodians living in rural communities as farmers and manual laborers. The recent history of the country is one of war and genocide[1] as a result of the infamous Khmer Rouge (KR) regime from 1975–1979. The rise of the KR had its roots in the Vietnam War.

In 1965 the U.S. Johnson administration was engaged in the Vietnam War that strove to limit the spread of communism in the region. In an effort to combat the Viet Cong Army (VC) and the North Vietnamese Army (NVA) the U.S. began a bombing campaign in Cambodia in 1965 that escalated under the Nixon administration in 1969 with carpet bombing deep into Cambodia (Brinkley, 2011). The United States ultimately dropped more explosives on Cambodia than all those dropped during the entirety of World War II (Owen & Kiernan, 2006). Conservative estimates list civilian casualties between

50,000 and 150,000 as a result of the bombings. The bombings traumatized the civilian Cambodian population, driving them into the arms of the KR who seized upon the bombings as anti-American propaganda. One-third of Cambodia's population (about 5 million) are survivors of the 1975–1979 reign of the Khmer Rouge, under which an estimated 25% of the Cambodian population died from starvation, overwork, disease, and execution. During the four years that the Khmer Rouge leader Pol Pot was in power, the country suffered massive brutality and complete restructuring of its society where formal education was closed down, religion and class distinctions were abolished, and lawyers, doctors, teachers, engineers, scientists and professional people in any field were systematically murdered, together with their extended families (Hinton, 1998; Miles & Thomas, 2007; Um, 2008). It has been documented that much of the torture and executions were carried out by children and young people, many of whom are now parents (Miles & Thomas, 2007). The Khmer Rouge were overthrown by the Vietnamese army in 1979, but the civil war between the Khmer Rouge and the government of Cambodia continued from 1979 to 1996 and resulted in more traumatizing experiences (Bureau of East Asian and Pacific Affairs, 2011; Hsu, Davies, & Hansen, 2004).

The Psychological Scars of Genocide in Cambodia

Cambodia's lasting legacy of genocide, prolonged armed conflict, and enduring poverty has left many suffering from post-traumatic stress disorders and other psychosocial problems (Hinton, 1998; Palmieri, Marshall, & Schell, 2007; Um, 2008; Zimmer, Knodel, Kim, & Puch, 2006). A number of studies have described mental-health problems and the psychological scars left by the genocide. Survivors of the Khmer Rouge regime were found to have experienced 12–16 major trauma experiences, including torture, long periods of malnutrition, slave labor, imprisonment, and witnessing atrocities (Kinzie, Fredrickson, & Ben, 1984; Mollica, Wyshak, & Lavelle, 1987; Realmuto, Hubbard, Grotelchen, & Chhun, 1992). A 12-year follow-up study of Khmer youth by Sack, Him, and Dickason (1999) showed that when the children of the Khmer Rouge era of genocide grew up, the symptoms of post-traumatic stress disorder (PTSD) and depression were still very high, 50% and 47% respectively, at the first interview in 1983–1984 (four years after the end of the regime). Sack and colleagues (1999) also found that 12 years after the Pol Pot and Khmer Rouge regime, the percentages of the same individuals affected by PTSD and depression were still very high, at 35% and 34% respectively. A study conducted in 2008 by Pham and colleagues (2009) found 35% of Cambodians suffer from some kind of severe psychiatric problem (e.g., schizophrenia, epilepsy, severe depression, and psychosis) and 45% suffer from psychosocial problems (e.g., anxiety, grief, and stunted emotional development). There is little question that the genocide of Cambodia still haunts Cambodian people today (Hinton, 1998; Miles & Thomas, 2007).

The Need for Sufficient Training and a Skilled Workforce in Mental Health

Despite the grave need in the country for mental-health care, Cambodia lacks sufficient information and resources to provide facilities or treatment for its population (van de Put & van der Veer, 2005). The basic psychiatric services and facilities that had been established in Cambodia prior to 1975 were entirely destroyed by the Khmer Rouge regime. It was not until 1993 when the Cambodian government, with the help of the United Nations, established its first National Health Plan as an effort to address the high prevalence of mental disorders among Cambodians (Somasundarm, van de Put, Eisenbruch, & de Jong, 1999; Stockwell, Whiteford, Townsend, & Stewart, 2005). The dominant method of handling mental-health issues in Cambodia is heavily influenced by the medical model, largely originated in the West (Stevens & Wedding, 2004; Stockwell, et al., 2005). As such, the selection of these models is not always designed to address the needs of the communities facing poverty. Further, the very constrained public mental-health services that currently exist are hampered by a shortage of a skilled workforce, insufficient training programs, and no professional regulation for professionals that provide counseling and therapy. Mental-health professionals are especially needed in Cambodia, a country that is recovering from the trauma of war and genocide, and experiencing high rates of associated mental-health issues.

Historically there has been no concept of "psychotherapy" in the Cambodian language of Khmer, and no equivalent Khmer term for "therapist." In 2007, the faculty in the Psychology Department of the RUPP began inviting Western experts in family therapy and psychology to help develop their psychology curriculum, in collaboration with RUPP faculty and administrators. Courses and trainings were offered by the authors, a collection of Western experts, and advanced graduate students brought to RUPP to cover topics such as trauma, brief therapy, child–parent relationships, systemic therapy, play therapy, domestic violence intervention, intergenerational therapy, cognitive behavioral therapy, substance abuse treatment, experiential therapy, structural family therapy, solution-focused therapy, couple therapy, and crisis intervention.

While it is sometimes attractive for the newcomer to Cambodia to concentrate on the recent history of trauma, the story of Cambodia begins long before the Khmer Rouge. Cambodia's story is also one that must include the fact that it was once a powerful Buddhist and Hindu empire that ruled most of the Indochinese Peninsula between the 11th and 14th centuries and represented a rich culture with tremendous natural beauty and societal harmony that continues to this day. Before the Vietnam War, it was a thriving modern country with a progressive and peaceful society, often referred to by Westerners as the "smiling nation" due to the peaceful and welcoming demeanor of the people. As it is often true in therapy, we believe it is important to remember the multitude of stories and qualities of those we work with, instead of only seeing the single story of the trauma or problem.[2] We have found that it is essential to maintain some balance of viewpoint that recognizes the multiverse of realities including the problems that often draw our attention, as well as the beauty and resources that often existed long before and are often the most powerful and impressive resources to overcome challenges.

The following section outlines several single-session (or single-encounter) strategies that we have piloted, developed, adapted, and explored in the Cambodian context. We hope that our experiences may benefit others who endeavor to engage with various "majority world" contexts where about 85% of the people on the planet reside. We believe the efforts to adapt, modify, or sometimes reject, Western modes of intervention will be an important step in the next stages of development of mental-health intervention in the global context.

Mobile Mental Health Unit

Several years ago the graduates of the RUPP psychology program started a Mobile Mental Health Unit (MMHU) to journey into the countryside to meet with families who have a member who is mentally ill. The unit is essentially a van that carries several mental-health staff members into the countryside to meet with families in need of help. While a portion of the population of Cambodia lives in the capital city of Phnom Penh, the majority of people with mental-health issues live in the countryside where there are almost no services. The mobile unit was created to address this need, and travels to these areas on a frequent basis (often monthly) visiting with families and offering assistance where possible. The road conditions are rough by Western standards, and the trip to the countryside often takes all day, or several days. These meetings with individuals and families often involve a single-session with a family. The team works in coordination with the local doctors, officials and resources in Phnom Penh, Siem Reap, and other big cities in Cambodia. Beginning in 2006, we began lecturing at RUPP about our work with Single-Session Therapy (SST) in other contexts (China, Mexico, U.S., Canada, and post-disaster settings) and our Khmer hosts were very interested in the strategies we had employed given the need for access to services in the country. Yet, we must hasten to add that their methods with the MMHU were of their own creation, and we found that we learned more from them (the Khmer graduates and staff) than we believe they learned from us. Over the past several years, we have accompanied the staff members of the MMHU during their trips into the countryside and herein offer a few abbreviated and amalgamated examples to illustrate what we learned. We have changed many of the details and collapsed some of the examples to clarify essential concepts and conceal the identities of those involved.

Example #1: The Family and Son in Chains

During one trip into the countryside with the MMHU, the team had been alerted that there was a family in need of help. Often those in need of help are aware of the unit and ask for help directly, or others in the village are aware of a need and inform someone on the team that a family may need help. In these rural villages, there is often a collective informal network of communication that, while rarely formalized, works efficiently to communicate what is happening in the community. Small villages in the countryside of Cambodia are often comprised of a handful of families that struggle to survive through subsistence farming. Their family dwellings are typically made of grass huts that are built on posts about 6 feet off the ground to keep them dry during the floods of the rainy season. Many of these homes are clumped together around the main road. As a rule, the entire family works together, and in collaboration with the other families in the village. In this situation, the MMHU was summoned by a middle-aged couple who asked for help for their 18-year-old son. The son had become increasingly delusional and prone to wandering off into the road or the countryside. The parents were desperate since they were unable to constantly watch their son (both worked in the fields). Out of this desperation, the parents had chained their son to his bed to prevent him from hurting himself. While this is shocking to see and, we imagine, to read about here, it is often the only recourse for families with a severely mentally-ill member. In the Western world, this may seem abusive. Yet, in Cambodia this drastic action may be the family's only way of caring and providing safety for the family member. We have observed this type of family intervention happen many times throughout these "majority world" contexts given the limited alternatives for the families involved. The team met with both the parents first to get an idea of what had happened to lead to the current situation and find out what might help. While the desperation of the situation for this family was easy to appreciate, the team worked to help the family prioritize their list of concerns and possible ideas about what was needed. The family members were eager to talk with the team and seemed calmer as they shared some of their concerns about their son and their situation in general. The team discussed things that had helped in the past, and what was needed for the future. There were several moments in the interaction between the family and the team that seemed helpful. The parents were very worried for their son and did not understand what was happening for him. The team helped by providing basic mental-health information about what could be happening with his mental-health condition and encouraged the parents to take him to a hospital. The team listed the resources they could provide, including transportation, a referral for help, and possible medication. One of the Khmer team members was also willing to go with the family and help explain things to both the doctors and the family. The family agreed to accept the help and arrangements were made to take him to the hospital. The team also examined what the family could do in the meantime to help manage the son until they could get further help. The family members were greatly calmed to have this chance to talk with someone and to make a plan for the future.

While the single-session encounter with this family would not solve all the dilemmas this family was facing, the team was able to provide a valuable connection to hospital resources that were previously unattainable or unknown to the family. The utility of the single-session for these types of situations has been highlighted in the past in other settings, such as post-disaster (Miller, 2011).

The WHO and the U.S. Surgeon General have commented on the three main barriers to service globally: stigma, cost, and limited access. In this situation the cost and access were predominant obstacles to getting help. The resources often exist for these families in Cambodia through the important work of NGOs and the church who do the majority share of social services work in the country, yet connecting the resources to the people who most need it is problematic. Also, the family seemed to be helped by the simple act of witnessing their problem, reviewing their situation with an objective and caring professional who assisted them in organizing their thoughts and making plans. The panic this family was experiencing was palpable, and the connection with the staff of the mobile mental-health team and the information about mental-health treatment calmed them greatly. This utility of single-session therapy has been documented in the West since the 1970s with the work of Spoerl (1975) who studied the health records of hundreds of clients to find that many were assisted by reviewing their life situation, education about the therapy process, and allaying irrational fears so as to make it easier for them in future treatment. We believe we saw these factors at work with this family. We followed up with the family a year later and were happy to learn that the son was no longer chained to the bed, had been taking medication for his delusions, and that the family had continued to meet periodically with the MMHU staff on subsequent trips to their village.

Example #2: Family Imprisoned and Ostracized by Mental Illness

As in Example #1, the MMHU was summoned to a village in the countryside by a mother and father to help with their 24-year-old son. During the daytime the parents had been keeping their son locked in the space under their home, roughly 10 square feet in size. This family had walled-in this area and had been locking their son under the home each day for the past six months during the times that the father was away from the home working in the fields. The team met with the parents and the son to help understand what had led up the current situation. The son sat quietly with the family and team during the meeting. The family explained that over a year ago the son had become delusional and while the father was working the field he was left alone in the home with his mother. The son had become increasingly aggressive and sometimes violent with his mother in his delusional state, so the father had taken to locking the son under the home every time the father went away to work in the fields. Compounding the problem, the family had become ostracized by the other villagers as a result of the son's bizarre behavior. Understanding of mental-health issues among the village population is sparse, and many families still hold stigmatizing, prejudicial, and superstitious views of mental-health problems.

The father wept as he told the team about this situation because of his worry for both his son and his wife. Yet, he also explained that the problem of the son's delusional behavior had been helped in the preceding months since he had begun taking anti-psychotic medication that another NGO had helped arrange. He felt that it was likely that the son was no longer dangerous to his wife or the villagers, but that he could not be sure nor would the villagers accept him even if he was better. So, the father continued to lock his son up when he was away. The meeting with the team took place in front of the home in view of several other village families' homes. Several of the other village families came out to see what was happening, as it is a fairly rare occurrence for a car with strangers to stop in the village. During the meeting the Khmer MMHU workers talked with the son directly, which seemed a surprise to him as most people had stopped talking to him. He welcomed the chance to talk and became more comfortable talking as the conversation proceeded. The team asked him directly about his delusions and whether he felt he was a danger to others. He expressed that he knew that he had concerned people in the past but that he felt he was better now with the medications he had been taking. He expressed that, like his father, his main concern now was that the other villagers did not seem to accept that he had changed and continued to ostracize the whole family. In the village being ostracized is a threat to their fundamental survival as a family, as the only way to survive in the village is through collective sharing of resources and collaboration with other families. The team asked if the problem of violence were to return for the son, how did they imagine that it might happen. The family all agreed that it would only happen again if the son stopped taking his medication. As the team talked with the family they asked if it was OK to go and sit next to the son while they talked. Later in the conversation the team member asked if it was OK to take the son's hand as they talked. The son welcomed this. In Khmer culture it is more common than in the West for friends to hold hands when talking together. Later one of the team members explained that they did this to show the other villagers that it was OK to sit next to the son without fear of being hurt by him and to try to normalize talking with him. The team continued to talk with the family about ways to connect with the other villagers again and a plan to make sure that the son would continue to take his medication. They all made an agreement together that they would ensure he continued to take his medication. The team discussed with the family the concepts of "habits" and that changing habits often takes time. They offered possible plans for letting the son out during the times when the father was away and how they might know if this plan was working. The meeting concluded with the family agreeing to slowly let the son out more frequently to give him a chance to show that he was safe. They discussed things that he and others might notice if he was leading up to being unsafe and an agreement was made that they would all work together to look for these signs that he might become violent again.

This case demonstrates some of the ways single-session therapy can be helpful. This family seemed to us to be stuck in a situation where the original problem (the son's delusions and aggressive behavior) had created a secondary problem of discrimination and being ostracized by others in the village. This secondary problem threatened the very existence of the family. Even if it was certain that the son's delusions and violent behavior were under control, the family still had the problem of assuring the rest of the people in the village that the change had occurred and that it was OK to be with the family and the son again. The Khmer team member's sensitive realization of this problem and his effort to normalize the son by sitting next to him and taking his hand seemed to us to be a powerful intervention to help lead the family out of the prison they had all found themselves in. It has been our experience that in some single-session encounters such as this, the simple introduction of a "source of the new" (to paraphrase Gregory Bateson) can help create new possibilities for families (and villages) that have become stuck in an undesirable situation. Normalization, safety planning, making agreements, and providing information all seemed to be meaningful interventions we witnessed. We followed up with this family a year later and found that they were no longer locking the son up each day and that he had continued to respond well to his medication. The family had begun to engage more with the other villagers and felt they were on their way to becoming more accepted in the community.

Example #3: Mother with Newborn All Alone in the Jungle

The MMHU was summoned to an extremely rural village in a remote jungle location. While most villages have limited plumbing and electricity, this village seemed especially rustic. There were no visible running water, electricity, or sewer facilities. The team was summoned to a hut comprising a single 10 foot × 10 foot grass and bamboo room on stilts about 4 feet off the ground. The team met with the residents of the hut—a young mother, and her infant son to whom she had recently given birth. The team was joined by a female neighbor who knew the mother and offered her support. The team talked with the mother who seemed mildly psychotic, occasionally answering to voices that only she could hear. Yet she was able to communicate effectively with the team who learned that the baby was her first child and had some medical issues that had not yet been treated. The neighbor who joined the meeting said that she was very worried for this young mother and the baby as she felt that the mother was alone and vulnerable. The neighbor had noticed that the mother would become especially delusional in the dark hours of the night and would wander off into the jungle. There was no father or other family members to support her. The neighbor had tried to do what she could to help the young mother, but was unsure if she could be available every time the mother had a need. The team reviewed the mother's concern about the baby's medical issue and asked if they could help arrange for a medical evaluation and treatment for the child. In the remote villages like this one, there is often a village elder who must be consulted before such an action can be taken. While part of the team went to meet with the village elders to get permission to take the mother and child to the hospital the rest of the team met with the mother and a gathering group of women who lived in the other huts in the area. The neighboring women (all of them were themselves older mothers) shared their concern for the young mother and their observation that she would sometimes wander off leaving the baby alone. The team collected these women together and asked for their help with the mother, knowing that it would take several days to arrange to take the mother and child to a hospital facility. The team made a plan with the women that they would take turns being with the mother and the baby, and a schedule was established for the following week. The women seemed eager to help, and welcomed the organization that the team members offered through setting up a schedule so that the closest neighbor was not always the one on watch. The team discussed with the collection of neighbors that they had an important role here and that the mother and baby were in danger. The team complimented them on what they had done so far and agreed that the team would do what they could to get the mother help but that it would take time. In the meantime, these neighboring mothers' help would be essential. All agreed and plans were made for eventual transport to the hospital.

This case highlights several elements of what others have documented regarding the utility of single-session meetings in Western-world contexts. First, the single-session meeting often serves as a "safety net" for the community, helping draw resources to critical situations that might otherwise go unnoticed (Miller & Slive, 2004). This situation posed a severe risk to the mother and especially the infant, who was often left alone in the jungle with unknown and untreated medical issues. Secondly, the single-session intervention served to capitalize on existing but underutilized resources. In this situation, the neighboring women who offered help were the most important resource for the survival of this mother and child. The team was not legally able to remove the child and/or mother without the consent of the village elders, which often takes some time to secure. A short-term safety strategy was required, and the neighboring women were important existing resources that simply needed some organization to be most effective. Another existing resource was medical intervention for the infant and psychological support for the mother. The team was able to provide this; yet as in the previous examples this would not have been possible without the single-session consultations provided by the MMHU. The authors have followed up on this case over several years and found that the team was able to get the mother and child to a hospital for treatment. The team connected the mother to other resources that allowed her to move to a larger city and into an apartment with modern conveniences such as running water, electricity, and a bathroom. The team had found a way for the child to spend each day in a daycare facility, and arranged for the mother to get a job in the facility so that she could be with her son. The mother had been prescribed medication that was effective in dealing with her psychotic symptoms, which had completely passed.

Example # 4: Single-Session Consultations for Victims of Acid Burn

Over the past decade we have helped organize and participated in several other single-session consultation meetings that have their foundations in our previous single-session work in other contexts. One example includes a single-session consultation day we organized in collaboration with an NGO created to help with the victims of acid burn, a tragic form of domestic violence. In Cambodia industrial strength acid is available with little regulation. The acid is sometimes used as a weapon by splashing it on others, often when they are asleep. The effects of these attacks are ghastly, as the acid will eat away any skin and flesh it makes contact with. The tragedy of acid-burn victims continues after the original assault, as many victims are subsequently ostracized from their families and communities because of their appearance. The Acid Burn Charity is a special NGO that works to help these victims. One activity they organize includes yearly week-long meetings with victims to get together for a jamboree-type event where they can share some time together doing fun activities like singing songs, playing games, and engaging in group activities. This may sound mundane to some, but we witnessed that this was a very special time for many of these people as in their own community back home their injuries are so distracting to others that they rarely feel normal and they end up hiding inside most of the time. At the jamboree, they could be out in the open and be free to focus on things other than their injuries. We worked with the Acid Burn Charity NGO and the Khmer graduates from RUPP to offer a free single-session consultation day for these acid-burn victims at the invitation of the NGO. To our surprise most of the participants welcomed the chance to talk with us. During our time we conducted about a dozen interviews working in therapy teams including one Western therapist paired with one Khmer RUPP graduate. Interviews were conducted in Khmer and translated by the graduate student. Many of the people asked to simply tell the story of how they had been burned and what their life was like before the attack, the attack itself, and what had happened afterwards with their family and relationships. For most people, the relationships with family and community were of most importance. They talked about how their appearance (often very severe scarring) had changed their relationships and that this was the thing that was most hurtful. They also felt that they were no longer able to participate in the community and missed talking and connecting with others. Several carried pictures of themselves that were taken before the acid attacks that they would hold to their chest as they talked as if to say "This is who I am, the one in the picture; not what you see me as now." Several others cried when they talked with us, taking our hands (which is common in Cambodia when talking with friends) and thanking us for the chance to tell their stories.

Finally, we believe it is important to make sure we try our best to take care of our Western participants/students during the exchange experience. Given the sometimes stressful nature of the work, we believe "self-care" issues and "caring for the caregiver" are important considerations. Part of this process, for us, is organizing a debriefing meeting at the end of every day to discuss our Western participants' reactions and reflections to what we experience each day. A few days before the meetings with the acid burn survivors we also met with the Western students to discuss what would likely happen during our visit in an effort to help them mentally prepare. We talked about the phenomenon of vicarious traumatization and secondary traumatic stress, how to recognize it in yourself, and how to minimize its negative effects.[3] Finally, we gave our Western participants the choice to opt out of conducting the interviews and arranged for other activities that day if they wished.

These single-session meetings with the acid-burn victims were very powerful for us and the Khmer staff we worked with. We believe that the single-sessions were important for these people in that it simply gave them a chance for catharsis, or the purging of emotions, feelings, and tensions through speaking them out (or other forms of expression like art or mime). Fortunately, in the years following our single-session consultations, the incidence of acid-burn attacks has dramatically declined in Cambodia partly due to increased regulations restricting the availability of industrial strength acid and increased punishments for those who commit such attacks. We believe that these changes were due in part to the efforts of important NGOs such as the Acid Burn Charity.

Example #5: Other Single-Session Interventions: The Theater of the Oppressed

Humility and trusting in the local experts is the best foundation for presenting single-session interventions. They know the context, cultural values, and how difficulties are conceptualized in Cambodia better than any visiting scholars could possibly know. Those preparing Cambodian students for clinical practice must be mindful that many educational and psychological approaches were developed in and for wealthy communities. In order to be relevant and effective, both mental-health education and clinical practices need to be adapted for the economic reality of Cambodia and more approaches need to be developed within and drawn from communities living in poverty. Salvadorian psychologist Martín-Baró (1994, p. 23), a major voice for the need to reconsider the assumptions of mainstream mental health, challenged the field of psychology stating that:

> What is needed is for our most basic assumptions in psychological thought to be revised from the bottom up. But this revision cannot be made from our offices; it has to come from a praxis that is committed to the people.

Not only do we need to do this type of revision with mental-health interventions, but also how we go about teaching them.

A pedagogical method we have found useful for avoiding educational colonialism is "Theater of the Oppressed," a Brazilian-originating approach to creating social change developed by Augusto Boal (1974) that can also be effective as an educational tool. Theater can facilitate a reconsideration of Western conceptualizations of mental health and open dialogues about Cambodian views of problem conceptualization, healing, and change. This process is important because clinical practices primarily reflect only the known world of the wealthy, whereas theater as an educational and clinical approach is helpful in exploring conceptualizations and interventions to problems that may not yet exist in the professional literature (Boal, 1974).

One way we have employed the Theater of the Oppressed began by dialoguing with the Cambodian students about the social problems they have seen within their local community. Once they had identified the ones they found most relevant, we asked them to create human sculptures with members of the class that illustrated those issues. This created a space for brainstorming and experimenting regarding what approaches might work best for addressing different problems faced by Cambodian individuals and families.

"What educators need to understand is that it is not about the performance at the end, but the process of using drama, the techniques and exercises, that can open up a world of possibilities in the classroom" (Schaedler, 2010, p. 142). In our experience, theater can help tap into the creativity and resourcefulness of Cambodian students, which is obviously invaluable in moving toward the goal of developing mental-health conceptualization and practices relevant for their context.

Theater of the Oppressed is not only a powerful educational tool within classrooms, but has been used in more than seventy countries as a way of directly engaging in dialogues with the community. This is often done through the use of varying forms of street theater. Similar to how it is used in classrooms, these public performances can be a powerful tool for assisting members of communities to identify and brainstorm ways for addressing issues impeding their full expression of basic humanity and the resulting mental-health implications (e.g., domestic violence, human trafficking, homelessness, poverty, etc.). Given the heaviness of the topics that Theater of the Oppressed can often touch on, single-session therapy may complement and provide additional resources to community members desiring additional support (Platt & Bobele, 2017, unpublished manuscript). We have found that creating three teams of mental-health workers with three distinct roles has been helpful. One group is engaged as actors who create a performance based on common presenting problems. For example, this first group may create a sculpture depicting a scene related to domestic violence. The second group acts as facilitators of street dialogues and engages with community members that begin observing the scene. This second group may offer community members who express interest or appear in distress the option of talking one-on-one with a member of the third group, therapists guided by the concepts of a single-session approach. We have found it useful to either set up a small, perhaps more private, space off to the side of where performances are taking place, or to have the street performances occur near existing traditional mental-health clinics.

Second-Order Intervention in a Majority World Context

While we, as Western outsiders, have tried to introduce something useful during our work in Cambodia, we have also benefitted greatly from the indigenous Khmer ways of healing and the creative work of other NGOs we have observed over the years. We have witnessed many efforts by NGOs to intervene in Cambodia, many with regrettably limited or what would seem to be only "first-order" solutions. First-order strategies are often those that offer content help (such as giving someone a meal) but are not sustainable in the long run (like teaching someone to fish and therefore feeding themselves). We have observed that outsiders often resort to first-order solutions but struggle, as we have at times, to find "second-order" sustainable interventions. This, we believe, is often the dilemma of the single-session therapist, so we will share some our reflections on this issue here.

One interesting "second-order" effort we have observed includes the work of *Friends*, a local organization working with Cambodian street children, their families, and the community to develop creative projects that effectively support the children to become independent and productive members of the community. The pathway that leads many children to become trafficked in Cambodia (and around the world) is that they have no other way to make a living. While giving them money in the short term may help a little, helping them find healthy ways to make a living on their own is much more effective. There are dozens of activities that *Friends* engages in to help these families, but one of the most effective activities we have observed is that they teach young people to earn a living on their own by training them to be restaurant workers. To the outsider it may seem unremarkable, but in our view it is very remarkable. *Friends* accomplishes this by running one of the best restaurants in Phnom Penh, staffed by formerly homeless children that they have taken in and trained to run the restaurant. Meanwhile, they also provide other important educational and support services for their families that lead to healthy self-support. During each visit to Phnom Penh we have taken our U.S. students to the *Friends* restaurants, met with their staff to learn about their methods, and enjoyed some of the finest meals we have had during our visits to Cambodia.

We believe that another way to create second-order solutions is through education. Over our decade of work in Cambodia we have endeavored to provide important educational experiences for the Khmer students at RUPP, that in some instances we believe capture some of the elements of single-session therapy. SST has its roots in attempting to provide a meaningful and lasting impact through a time-limited therapeutic experience. This is the spirit of our educational exchange experiences at the RUPP. During our lectures at the university we are always mindful to ask, "What is needed and wanted?" instead of what we want to talk about. We defer predominantly to what our Khmer hosts want versus what we want to do, unless we believe what is asked for might be harmful. We were once asked by a Khmer hospital to give them the machinery to conduct electro-convulsive therapy (electroshock therapy).

While one of our team members actually had the resources to make this happen we declined, because we could not clearly see how it would helpful, and could see many ways it might be harmful. This has also been our orientation in our single-session therapy: find out what the client wants and, when possible, give it to them unless we believe it might be harmful.

Another second-order type activity we have engaged in is teaching by taking U.S. students and training them how to become teachers and interventionists themselves. During our first delegations to Cambodia we took professors. Yet it seemed to us that what was needed was student-to-student cultural and academic experiences, which led us to limiting our Western delegations to students or recent graduates only. We thought the Khmer students would be helped more by exposure to their peers from other cultures (other students learning to become therapists) instead of exposure to Western professors telling them what to do. In this way, there is an efficiency to the experience and we avoid the "banking" experience of education that often occurs when there is a larger hierarchical difference between the "teacher" and the "student." In our exchange experiences we are all "students" and "teachers" and strive to create true two-way sharing of information and expertise. Occasionally our Western participants return to Cambodia to continue working with the Khmer students or Cambodian NGOs, eventually developing a career as international therapists. Sometimes, the students we bring decide to simply stay in Cambodia for a term to volunteer with an NGO or work at RUPP. Sometimes the Khmer students we meet with make important connections during the trip that allow them to come to the U.S. to continue their education and one day return to Cambodia and become the first generation of U.S.-trained professors to teach in the country post-Khmer Rouge. Like in single-session therapy, we are always looking for efficiencies in the way we work so as to capitalize on the therapeutic potential of the moment we have together, realizing that this moment will lead hopefully into some brighter future.

Closing Thoughts About *Minority World* Therapists Working in the *Majority World*

Our work in Cambodia has been some of the most powerful and impactful work of our careers. Yet, at times it has been some of the most discouraging and heart-wrenching work. When encountering the severe and seemingly hopeless situations we have seen in these majority-world contexts it can be easy to become overwhelmed and be tempted to give up. The Western students we bring to Cambodia are often overwhelmed at first and sometimes deal with their anxiety about what is happening by simply giving up, or pronouncing overarching judgments. Yet, we know it is not helpful to let these feelings win out, as it only leads to other similar feelings and little action in the direction of growth and change. Instead we advise others entering this work to *maintain a sense of optimism* about the work. Get involved, and believe that your efforts can and will make a difference. Avoid sitting back and criticizing what is happening because we have found doing so is often linked to the overwhelming sense of helplessness and need to gain control over the situation. While it may offer some comfort to do so, it will not help.

Likewise, we advise that therapists ***avoid providing more help than is being asked for***. We have found that, as in single-session therapy, more is not better, *better is better* (Miller & Slive, 2004). Sometimes when becoming overwhelmed by the desperate situations that people encounter in the majority world it can be tempting to try to run in and provide more help than is requested, or even healthy for the situation. For instance, we have found that simply giving money in poverty situations is not always helpful, and many times is even harmful. Sometimes the child who is begging for money on the street is trapped in a situation where he or she is kept as a beggar by an older handler who profits from the child's efforts. Simply giving the child money in this situation might help in the moment, but almost certainly will not help that child to escape an overall situation. Likewise giving money to NGOs that are simply fronts to collect money and do little to address problems only perpetuate the problems.

Seek sustainable solutions over short-term fixes. As Thoreau (1854) admonished, "It is not enough to be busy, we must be busy doing the right things." Simply intervening without respecting the system as it is, can create worse situations. For example, condemning the mother that sells her child into slavery is easy for a Western outsider. However, often mothers in this situation are trying to feed the remaining children they have at home. Sustainable solutions are harder to come by, but essential for meaningful change.

Our work in the majority world has also taught us the importance of maintaining a position of ***humility and curiosity*** about what is happening. Often things that initially seem strange or unexplainable to us will make sense once we know the entire context that led up to the current situation. As privileged Westerners, it is common for those we work with in the majority world to imbue us with more power, intelligence, and ability than we deserve. It can be tempting for the Western therapist to accept this invitation to power, but our advice is to reject it and instead maintain a position of humility and "not knowing" curiosity as is common among some the best single-session therapists.

We encourage therapists engaging in this work to recognize the healing power of simply creating a place or space for people to *tell their stories* and appreciate their sorrows and accomplishments. Some situations that therapists will encounter in the majority world become overwhelming, or fill the Western therapist with the desire to fix the situation. Many times there is no easy "fix" to the situation. Yet it is very helpful to provide a chance to witness the story and provide the ability for people to tell it out.

In closing, we agree with Ignacio Martín-Baró (1994) when he insisted that psychology should be developed in relation to the social and historical conditions and aspirations of the people it is meant to assist. Martín-Baró insisted that psychology should be developed in relation to the social and historical conditions and aspirations of the people it is meant to assist. He believed that students of psychology should learn to analyze human behavior in the particular contexts where it happens. In his writings and lectures he rejected the comfortable yet false idea of an impartial psychology of the minority world in favor of what we have come to think of as a "majority world" practice. Single-session therapy seems one ideal strategy for better meeting the needs of those living in majority world contexts.

Notes

1 French author, Jean Lacouture coined the term *autogenocide* to refer to the extermination of a group's members by its own people or government (Chandler, 1999). The term was coined to describe killings by the Khmer Rouge to denote that they were carried out by Cambodians, on Cambodians across all society. This is opposed to other descriptions of extermination carried out on a targeted group by "other" groups.

2 Adichie, C. (2009). The danger of a single story. TED Talks. See www.ted.com/talks/chimamanda_adichie_the_danger_of_a_single_story.html

3 See Miller's (2011) description of self-care strategies for SST therapists in the wake of Hurricane Katrina.

References

Adichie, C. (2009). The danger of a single story. TED Talks. See www.ted.com/talks/chimamanda_adichie_the_danger_of_a_single_story.html

Arnett, J.J. (2008). The neglected 95%: Why American psychology needs to become less American. *American Psychologist*, *63*, 602–614.

Berryman, P. (1987). *Liberation theology: The essential facts about the revolutionary movement in Latin America and beyond*. New York: Pantheon.

Boal, A. (2008). *Theater of the oppressed*. London: Pluto Press (originally published 1974 in Spanish as *Teatro del oprimido*).

Brinkley, J. (2011). *Cambodian curse: Modern history of a troubled land*. New York: Perse Books.

Bureau of East Asian and Pacific Affairs (January 28, 2011). *Background note: Cambodia*. Retrieved February 19, 2011, from www.state.gov/r/pa/ei/bgn/2732.htm.

Chandler, D. (1999). *Brother number one: A political biography of Pol Pot*. Thailand: Westview Press.

de Jong, J.T. , Komproe, I.H., Van Ommeren, M., El Masir, M., Araya, M., Khaled, N., van de Put, W. & Somasundaram, D. (2001). Lifetime events and posttraumatic stress disorder in 4 postconflict settings. *Journal of the American Medical Association*, *286*(5), 555–562.

Freire, P. (2007). *Pedagogy of the oppressed*. New York: Continuum.

Hinton, A.L. (1998). A head for an eye: Revenge in the Cambodian genocide. *American Ethnologist: Journal of the American Ethnology Society*, *25*(3), 352–377.

Hsu, E., Davies, C., & Hansen, D. (2004). Understanding mental health needs of Southeast Asian refugees: Historical, cultural, and contextual challenges. *Clinical Psychology Review*, *24*, 193–213.

Kinzie, D., Fredrickson, R., & Ben, R. (1984). Post-traumatic stress disorder among survivors of Cambodian concentration camps. *American Journal of Psychiatry*, *141*, 645–650.

Mair, M. (1988). Psychology as storytelling. *International Journal of Personal Construct Psychology, 1*, 125–138.

Martín-Baró, I. (1994). *Writings for a liberation psychology.* Cambridge, MA: Harvard University Press.

Miles, G. & Thomas, N. (2007). "Don't grind an egg against a stone": Children's rights and violence in Cambodian history and culture. *Child Abuse Review, 16*, 383–400.

Miller, J.K. (2008). Walk-in single-session team therapy: A study of client satisfaction. *Journal of Systemic Therapies, 27*(3), 78–94.

Miller, J.K. (2011). Single-session intervention in the wake of Hurricane Katrina: Strategies for disaster mental health counseling. In A. Slive & M. Bobele (Eds.), *When one hour is all you have: Effective therapy for walk-in clients* (pp. 185–202). Phoenix, AZ: Zeig, Tucker, & Theisen.

Miller, J.K. (2014). Single session therapy in China. In M.F. Hoyt & M. Talmon (Eds.), *Capturing the moment: Single session therapy and walk-in services* (pp. 195–214). Bethel, CT: Crown Hoe Publishing.

Miller, J.K. & Slive, A. (2004). Breaking down the barriers to clinical service delivery: Walk-in family therapy. *Journal of Marital and Family Therapy, 30*(1), 95–103.

Mollica, R., Wyshak, D., & Lavelle, J. (1987). The psychosocial impact of war, trauma and torture on Southeast Asian refugees. *American Journal of Psychiatry, 144*, 1567–1572.

Owen, T. & Kiernan, B. (2006, October). Bombs over Cambodia. *The Walrus Magazine*, 62–69.

Palmieri, P., Marshall, G., & Schell, T. (2007). Confirmatory factor analysis of posttraumatic stress symptoms in Cambodia refugees. *Journal of Traumatic Stress, 20*(2), 207–216.

Pham, P., Vinck, P., Hean, S., & Stover, E. (2009). So we will never forget: A population-based survey on attitudes about social reconstruction and the extraordinary chambers in the courts of Cambodia. Human Rights Center of California Berkeley. Retrieved on February 20, 2011, from http://escholarship.org/uc/item/74x685xm#page-1.

Platt, J.J. (2012b). A Mexico City-based immersion education program: Training mental health workers for practice with Latino communities. *Journal of Marital and Family Therapy, 38*, 352-364. doi: 10.1111/j.1752-0606.2010.00208.

Platt, J.J. (2013). Stepping over a baby's head: Thoughts on privilege, humanity and liberation. In M. E. Gallardo (Ed.), *Developing cultural humility: Embracing race, privilege and power* (pp. 199–221). Thousand Oaks, CA: Sage.

Platt, J.J., & Bobele, M. (2017). Therapeutic spaces in public places: *Pláticas en la plaza.* Unpublished manuscript.

Platt, J.J. & Laszloffy, T.A. (2012) Critical patriotism: Incorporating nationality into MFT education and training. *Journal of Marital and Family Therapy*, 1–16, Retrieved from doi: 10.1111/j.1752-0606.2012.00325.x

Platt, J.J. & Mondellini, D. (2014). Single-session walk-in therapy for street robbery victims in Mexico City. In M.F. Hoyt & M. Talmon (Eds.), *Capturing the moment: Single session therapy and walk-in services* (pp. 215–231). Bethel, CT: Crown House Publishing.

Realmuto, G., Ann, C., Hubbard, J., Grotelchen, A., & Chhun, B. (1992). Adolescent survivors of massive childhood trauma in Cambodia: Life events and current systems. *Journal of Traumatic Stress, 5*(4), 589–599.

Sack, W.H., Him, C., & Dickason, D. (1999). Twelve-year follow-up study of Khmer youths who suffered massive war trauma as children. *Journal of the American Academy of Child and Adolescent Psychiatry, 38*(9), 1173–1179.

Schaedler, M.T. (2010). Boal's theater of the oppressed and how to derail real-life tragedies with imagination. *New Directions for Youth Development, 125*, 141–151.

Spoerl, O.H. (1975). Single-session psychotherapy. *Diseases of the Nervous System, 36*, 283–285.

Stevens, M.J. & Wedding, D. (Eds.) (2004). *Handbook of international psychology.* New York: Brunner-Routledge.

Stockwell, A., Whiteford, H., Townsend, C., & Stewart, D. (2005). Mental health policy development: Case study of Cambodia. *Australasian Psychiatry, 13*(2), 190–194.

Thoreau, H.D. (1854). *Walden.* Chicago, IL: University of Illinois.

Somasundaram, D., van de Put, W., Eisenbruch, M., & de Jong, J. (1999). Starting mental health services in Cambodia. *Social Science & Medicine, 48*, 1029–1046.

Um, K. (2008). Cambodia: A decade after coup. *Southeast Asia Affairs, 2008*(0), 107–120.

Van Maaren, P. (2012). Mental health a tough challenge for Cambodia. *Phnom Penh Post.*

van de Put, W. & van der Veer, G. (2005). Counselling in Cambodia: Cultural competence and contextual costs. *Intervention, 3*(2), 87–96.

Zimmer, Z., Knodel, J., Kim, K., & Puch, S. (2006). The impact of past conflicts and social disruption on the elderly in Cambodia. *Population and Development Review, 32*(2), 333–360.

9 Walk-In Counseling Center of Minneapolis/St. Paul

The Magic of Our Model for Clients and Volunteers

Mary Weeks and Lori Zook-Stanley

Walk-In Counseling Center, in Minneapolis/St. Paul, Minnesota, has offered free, anonymous, walk-in counseling since 1969—one of the first walk-in counseling centers in the world! All of the people who deliver our counseling services volunteer their time, and team consultation is a primary way these volunteers support each other and provide quality services to clients. This chapter explores the model, values, and unique elements that, on many days, seem synergistic and magical.

Situating Ourselves: Our History

In the middle of the United States in Minneapolis, Minnesota, sits a house: home to Walk-In Counseling Center. Walk-In (WI) first opened its doors in 1969. As reported in Schoener (2011), one evening in 1969 a young psychologist stood up at a meeting of the Minnesota Chapter of Psychologists for Social Action and offered a radical invitation: "Anyone who wants to open a free walk-in counseling clinic, meet me in the corner" and Walk-In Counseling Center was born.

Since its inception and continuing today, Walk-In Counseling Center's mission and service delivery have rested on three foundational structures:

- we offer free, anonymous, no-appointment-needed, mental-health counseling
- all of our service providers—counselors, team consultants, receptionists—are volunteers or advanced (clinical) graduate students, and
- these volunteers are organized onto regularly scheduled teams for each walk-in clinic shift, making team consultation and team work a central method for support and accountability.

The early work with clients at Walk-In Counseling Center revealed the issue of sexual abuse of client by therapist (Schoener, Milgrom, Gonsiorek, Luepker, & Conroe, 1989). A strong consultation and training focus was formalized—later named as Walk-In's Consultation and Training Institute—to prevent, intervene, and resolve professional boundary and ethical violations. This work continues today. In addition, Walk-In Counseling Center has played a critical role in identifying and shaping early public discourse, policy, and service development around topics such as rape and sexual assault, domestic violence, and LGBTQ issues.

Our Model: All the Elements That Make Us Who We Are

Just Walk-In—No Appointment Needed

It's simple: if you come during a walk-in clinic, you will see a counselor. There is no need for intake interviews or appointments or paperwork. (However, because of limited staffing, if a client needs counseling in Spanish, an appointment can be made for this purpose.) There are walk-in clinics in Minneapolis and St. Paul; depending on location, clinics are open weekday afternoons and evenings. This is particularly important for people who experience situational crises and need to see someone quickly but for whom a hospital emergency visit is inappropriate. Now, even with insurance, wait times for an appointment with a traditional provider can be weeks. Walk-In Counseling Center offers a more immediate alternative or support while clients are waiting for a traditional appointment time.

Free

One of the concepts many people—especially clients—struggle to understand is that our services are free to everyone. No income requirement, no sliding fee, no insurance necessary. Even if a client has insurance and is willing to use it, we have no mechanism to accept it. If a person wishes to make a donation—maybe the amount of a co-payment—it is gratefully accepted. If a client doesn't or can't make a donation, no one ever knows, and service is never affected.

Anonymous

The keystone of Walk-In's approach, and the feature that sets us apart from many other providers, is the guarantee of anonymity. Unlike traditional clinics, we don't ask for identifying information. Instead, we ask: "Have you been here before? Can I get you some coffee or tea? What brings you in today?" Even if a client provides a name or contact information, we never ask for proof of identity. In a client survey, 68% of respondents indicated they value the option of anonymity. "Anonymous" or a first name only is typical in our database.

Of course, anonymity may pose a challenge for legally mandated reporters, which the Walk-In Counseling Center is. Meeting with an anonymous person who poses imminent risk of harm to self or others requires sophisticated therapeutic skills of engagement, calm, and alliance. The type and level of risk evolves out of the assessment of reported experience or intent. Although situations are different and may require differing responses, these may include: encouraging the client to provide contact information, with an explanation of why this is important; the client and therapist calling Child Protection together; the police being called to come to Walk-In with or without the client's knowledge; and a call to police (if a client has left the premises) to inform them of the lethality of a threat and provide any descriptive information we might have.

Volunteers Carry Us

Volunteers deliver all of the counseling services at the WICC The counselors and team consultants are licensed professionals in the counseling/mental-health fields (psychology, social work, or marriage and family therapy), or are advanced clinical graduate students. Volunteer receptionists often have experience in a human service field or are considering an advanced degree. Volunteers are organized into teams that staff each walk-in clinic. This important element of our model will be discussed in more detail in the next section.

Who We Serve

Each year approximately 2,000 clients are served in some 6,000 of walk-in and brief counseling sessions. Clients are equally men and women, and one-third are people of color. More than half have household incomes of less than U.S.$30,000/year and half are multi-person households, so many of our clients/families survive on very low incomes. To support them, each year 180 volunteers contribute some 18,000 hours, equivalent to over one million U.S. dollars' worth of counseling services (based on 2015 statistics).

Our Sites

Walk-In Counseling Center operates in four sites—the main house in Minneapolis and three other partnership satellite locations in St. Paul, Minnesota. Over these four locations there are a total of 22 walk-in clinic times during weekday afternoons and evenings.

Single Session/Brief Treatment

We deliver our counseling services in single sessions, sequential single sessions, or on-going brief counseling by appointment. Approximately half of the WICC's clients choose to schedule an appointment after the initial walk-in session and may be seen up to 10 times, or as needed. Many clients who choose a single session return at a later date for additional sessions. Depending on the person's situation and/or desires, referrals to ancillary or more appropriate services are made.

Team Consultation: Central to the Model and the Magic

Team Composition and Structure

All volunteers are assigned to one or more of our 22 walk-in clinic teams for a four-month trimester period. Each team is composed of:

- a receptionist, who welcomes clients and manages the flow of the clinic
- two to five counselors, depending on the site, who provide counseling services, and
- a team consultant who offers guidance, perspective, and facilitates the collaboration of the team to achieve high levels of professional care.

Most volunteers continue at the WICC for a number of years, and some teams have remained very stable with the same people over many years. When composing team assignments, goodness of fit is as important as volunteer availability. Our Volunteer Coordinator strives to balance team composition with counseling experience and approach, education, gender, race, and personality style.

Almost all clinic teams meet every other week. The clinic shift begins with a two-hour period during which anyone who walks in sees a counselor. Following the walk-in clinic session, the team re-convenes to consult about the cases of the day. Although clients have no paperwork to complete, counselors document demographic and assessment information, and write progress notes and therapeutic goals. A team meeting, described a little later, concludes the end of each walk-in shift.

Collective Wisdom

Counselors are encouraged to use the collective wisdom of the team or team consultant even as they meet with clients. This practice is not routinized or required but is encouraged and modeled; e.g., a counselor might excuse him/herself to confer with the team about additional ideas or for emotional support. The conversation a therapist may have with a client might sound something like this:

> We work on a team model here at Walk-In. I would like to take a bit of a break and talk with my team members to see if they have other ideas that we are not thinking of. There might be other ways to address the problem or other referral ideas. I want you to be able to leave with the best ideas all of my team can come up with. Can I get you some coffee or tea while you are waiting? You may also want to think about whether this conversation is going in the way you were hoping, or whether there are other things you want to make sure we talk about.

Sometimes, following this mid-session break, the team consultant, at the request of the counselor or at the consultant's own initiation (and with the client's consent), may join the client session either as an observer or as a co-facilitator.

Team Meeting

The team consultant facilitates the team meeting at the end of the shift, with the expectation and value that everyone has an active voice at the table. For example, the receptionist—whose contact is limited to the waiting room and the welcome and farewell to each client—often has rich observations regarding encounters with clients. In addition, team members strive for collaborative language and representation of clients, bearing witness to their lives, hopes, and struggles. Some teams attend to this respectful consideration by imagining clients are actually present and listening to the consultation and the ways they are represented.

All clients who walk-in are reviewed during the team meeting at the end of each shift. Moreover, counselors are encouraged to discuss the status of their work with on-going clients at least every five sessions (on-going clients are seen an average of five times). Team consultation offers feedback, support, and new ideas. At critical times, team members provide back-up for counselors who are working with a client in crisis—assisting with calls to a hospital or to summon ambulance transportation, as well as debriefing afterwards. The team approach helps minimize counselor errors such as not adequately assessing and addressing risk factors for harm. Counselors feel supported by the team debriefing, errors are seen as a learning opportunity for everyone involved, and when we have client contact information, we initiate further assessment, intervention if appropriate, and referrals.

The team is a powerful presence even at a broader level. For example, a counselor who saw a client who had intent and ability to "go out and kill someone" found great support from the team's input. The client gave convincing detail about the gun and the ammunition he intended to use. Although the client's admission did not require a duty-to-warn since there was no identified victim, it was clear to the counselor ***and the team*** that the intent and means were in place for imminent harm. The team decided to alert police to the potential danger and gave as much detail and description as they could. It was fortunate. The police found the person, armed and ready to randomly shoot to kill. Someone's life was saved that day.

Benefits of the Team Model

The team model leads to a range of benefits for clients, volunteers, and the organization, including:

- diverse ideas, perspectives, and referrals regarding services and resources for the client

- immediate support for the counselor, typically one of the primary points of volunteer satisfaction
- on-going skill development for all volunteers, even those with experience
- assurance of ethical and high standards of care and
- support of volunteers (which helps volunteer recruiting).

The team model fosters quality of services and offers a direct channel to communicate and monitor agency policy and protocol. In an agency with 180 volunteers and 2,000-plus clients in a given year, teams are the primary vehicle to acculturate and strengthen the values and practices that we call "The Walk-In Way."

But, because we have 180 volunteers in a given year, ranging from advanced clinical graduate students to senior practitioners, all with varying education, training, and experience, it is also impossible to standardize our counseling practices. We do not prescribe any one model or philosophy, but ask each volunteer counselor to use the approach she or he believes will work best for the client at that unique moment. While respecting individual professional differences, we also clarify and train our volunteers in the values and practices of "The Walk-In Way." These values and practices are highly resonant with single-session and solution-oriented work being done around the globe, including:

- staying in the present: "What brings you in today?"
- staying with the client's goals and not the therapist's assumptions: "What are your hopes for today? How can I help?"
- accessing the client's hopes and ideas: "What have you tried so far? Do you think these changes are possible?"
- engaging support people and agencies: "Who or what supports do you have in your life?"
- traveling with, not leading, the client on the journey
- seeing the client as the expert; honoring the client's choices
- focusing on client strengths
- not focusing on previous history if/when it is not relevant to today's events
- describing, not diagnosing, and
- recognizing that every interaction is a multicultural interaction.

Diagnoses

Our counselors do not conduct diagnostic assessments. Diagnoses are not required of us since we do not take insurance, and many clients do not need, or want, a diagnosis. In addition, a diagnosis may not be helpful. For example, a recent client introduced himself in this way: "Hi. I'm Brian and I'm (diagnosis)." Brian was over 30 years old and had received a diagnosis, as a young teenager, that became his identity for half his life. From the perspective of the counselor, the diagnosis didn't even seem appropriate. Our thought at the time: perhaps the Walk-In Counseling Center should *un-diagnose* clients!

But we also do not discount diagnoses entirely. Clients may describe a diagnosis that they have received previously that can inform the therapeutic work. However, we pay closer attention to how problems manifest in daily life. For students in particular, this can provide a challenge and an opportunity for learning: honoring the client's story and descriptions over someone else's diagnosis.

Culture

"Every interaction is a multicultural interaction." This phrase is part of the Walk-In Way. To see and understand multiculturalism can be a formidable task. Culture's impact on how we see ourselves and see others is often invisible and taken for granted. This is true whether it spans identities or differences in race, sexuality, income, gender, religion, etc. When we add to this the power differential of client and therapist, the possibility for misunderstanding and lack of connection becomes greater. At the WICC, we try to see every interaction as a multicultural interaction, and we strive to keep the conversation about a multicultural lens going, primarily through team consultations and agency-wide trainings. Like most of our U.S. society, we certainly have a long way to travel—but at the Walk-In Counseling Center, we are at least on the road.

Examples of "The Walk-In Way"

It's difficult to express the magic that happens at the Walk-In Counseling Center. The diversity of clients and problems is exceptional, so several stories of our work with clients may help.

Case Example #1

Five siblings—two young adults, plus a 13- and 15-year old, plus an even younger sister—came out of concern for the sadness and potential for suicide (based on Facebook postings) of the youngest sister. Though there was no imminent risk, this single session allowed the two younger siblings to express to their older siblings how difficult their home life was (dysfunctional family dynamics, loss of housing, etc.), and for the older sibs to offer support to the younger ones. There was extensive support and "loving language" during the session, and the youngest sister's affect was "positive and bright" when her sisters expressed their love and support. The younger brother said it "felt good to talk" and was encouraged to reach out to them. There was significant renewed bonding among the five, and commitment of one older sib to be the "go-to" person for the youngest sister. The counselor followed up with referrals for additional services more appropriate for their Asian culture, for child/adolescent crisis intervention, and for medical insurance for the family.

Case Example #2

A single woman presented with extremely high anxiety. She had tried medication and other talk-therapy with little result. One of our clinical graduate students worked with her over several sessions to provide support and teach her mindfulness and anxiety reduction techniques. Her beginning baseline on the *Beck Anxiety Inventory* (Beck, et al., 1968) was almost off the charts, but when she re-took the test after the fifth session, her anxiety score was significantly lower—a visual record of her progress and her success in using the skills she learned during just a few sessions by appointment.

Case Example #3

A single, family session was initiated by a teenage son who was furious with and refused to speak to his father after his father's affair was revealed. The mother/wife felt helpless to get the two to talk, and was, of course, angry, so she asked the father to leave the home. The father was very regretful, and feared the son might not be willing to re-connect. They generally enjoyed doing things together as a family, so the father and son agreed to try seeing each other only one day a week. At the conclusion of the session the father and mother decided to pursue marital counseling to determine next steps of the separation. As they had insurance, they felt confident in pursuing other resources after the initial crisis session, knowing they could come back if they need to.

Case Example #4

An undocumented Hispanic man was injured at work and received disrespectful and unscrupulous treatment by his employer. He was forced to quit, and when the family (mother and several children and adolescents) brought him to the Walk-In Counseling Center, they were very worried about his level of depression and despair. He was working with an attorney to make a claim for unemployment, which his employer was fighting. He could not work and support his family, and he felt hopeless about the future. Our counselor was an English-speaker, so we engaged one of our Spanish interpreters. As noted earlier, WICC clients may be seen for a single session, sequential single sessions, or on-going brief therapy by appointment as needed. After about 10 sessions a bilingual counselor became available and the client was offered this as an option. He declined. He reported that he greatly appreciated his counselor and interpreter, and had no need to change counselors. We saw him for 18 sessions, and ultimately he was successful in winning his unemployment case. The depression subsided, and the family came with him to his last session at WICC to celebrate.

Case Example #5

A woman walked in during an afternoon when there was no formal clinic. She had just been terminated from or left (questionable circumstances) an inpatient chemical abuse treatment program and had all her possessions with her in a suitcase. The only counselor who was here had an appointment, but the appointment client did not show, so the counselor offered to see the woman. Although there was not an immediate mental-health issue the therapist could help with, this woman needed a supportive ear and kindness, which she received in abundance from her counselor. When she left, despite the fact she had virtually nothing, she put a $1 bill in our donation box, and commented that she wished it was more. She promised to come back again if she needed to.

Case Example #6

A young adult woman in her late teens/early 20s came at the encouragement of her mother. The girl lived at home, was unemployed, depressed, and anorexic. Her story was confusing and at first made little sense, but over several sessions she felt more trust and confidence. Ultimately, with much gentle urging and support from the counselor, the truth about her experience of being sexually victimized as a young girl by her stepfather came out. And the stepfather was still in the home. The woman's symptoms began to make more sense. Soon after she disclosed the abuse to both her sister and her boyfriend, she moved out of the family home. A referral for more intensive therapy regarding the abuse was made immediately. Her intent was to reveal the abuse to her mother as well, but at this time we are not sure if she did so. A dilemma of short-term therapy is that, sometimes, we do not know the end of the story. Will she reveal to her mother? What will be the mother's response to her daughter? To her husband—her daughter's abuser? We may never know these outcomes! But through her work here, this young woman has begun her journey and faced some huge personal/interpersonal challenges. She has new resources to pursue. She is on the road to healing. And she can always come back.

Case Example #7

A young adult male came to Walk-In during a time of major life adjustment. He was slowly losing his eyesight. And though he was doing well in his work with services for the visually impaired, his difficult experiences as a child exacerbated his current situation. He was a foreign-born adoptee, and his adoptive father had murdered his two siblings. Now, in his 20s and going blind, he was struggling with trust issues: trust of others and trust in himself, survivor's guilt, pain, self-confidence, etc. Over 15 sessions by appointment with a very mature therapist, the young man moved through adjustments to his new reality, developed increased understanding of social clues, higher confidence in his capabilities, began to understand emotions and the possibility of an intimate relationship, and developed significant hopefulness about his future. The counselor expressed what a great honor it was to work with this young man. This is one of the unique ways Walk-In clients give back . . . they succeed!

And Not So Much "The Walk-In Way"

As is true in any organization, things aren't always perfect, and with 180 volunteers, it's difficult to ensure that the Walk-In Counseling Center's philosophy and protocol are interpreted and/or implemented consistently. We see clients referred by probation officers (POs). Though we avoid court-ordered referrals (to reduce the chance that our volunteer counselors would have to appear in court), it's often unclear if the referral is a suggestion by the PO or a true order by the judge. To complicate matters, some probationers referred by their PO come with no intent to work, but just to fulfill the expectation and document their "___ # of sessions." When this is the case, little progress happens. It's frustrating for our counselors and a poor use of our time when we could be seeing other clients who are eager to do the work. And despite the fact that some probationers don't want to work, there are others who take full advantage of this opportunity to deal with their problems and avoid the criminal justice system in the future. Unfortunately, on occasion everyone on probation may get painted with a broad brush.

Case Example #8

A legitimate complaint was made by a client who came not as a requirement of the PO, but out of the PO's sincere concern for his emotional health in a difficult situation. He came about once a month for recurring walk-in sessions as he was able, saw several different counselors, and he reported benefitting greatly. However, on his seventh visit he was confronted by a member of the clinic team and told that he must see only one counselor and that we needed a release of information so we could to talk with his PO.

Although it's true that it is helpful to know what a PO might have in mind when she or he refers to the Walk-In Counseling Center, and it's usually more beneficial for a person to see the same counselor over time, neither are requirements, and we do not demand that clients follow these protocols, especially if they are sincere about their willingness to work. The client described his last experience as an "interrogation," and does not intend to come back. We regret that we can't make it right with him, but it is a reminder that occasionally, we misstep on fulfilling our own "Walk-In Way" model. Our hope is that this client will understand that there are nearly 100 other counselors who might see and treat him very differently, as did the counselors he saw previously.

The Bigger Picture: The Community

At the Walk-In Counseling Center the "team" concept goes beyond that of the client, counselor, and clinic team. A number of formal and many informal relationships enhance the mental-health continuum of care in the Twin Cities, of which the WICC is an integral part.

Students and Their Educational Institutions

Each year the WICC hosts 15–20 students in their advanced (master or doctoral) clinical graduate programs. Formal agreements with between four and seven educational institutions ensure that students have ample opportunity to see diverse clients, experience inter-disciplinary teams, and receive excellent supervision.

Relationships with Community Agencies and Professionals

The WICC is well-known in the Twin Cities because of its longevity, history, and availability to serve all clients on a walk-in basis and without cost. Because of this, we are an important safety-net service for the clients of many community agencies and private practitioners who refer clients and/or who call us to consult. Likewise, Walk-In relies on other providers as we seek to provide comprehensive and/or crisis services for each person who walks in, many of whom are marginalized socially and economically. We are thrilled when these systems work together.

Case Example #9

A couple came during the beginning of a walk-in shift. The woman was a Spanish-speaker with no English; the man spoke little English. It was clear through their behavior that she was experiencing an emotional crisis, but we had no Spanish-speaking staff available at the time. One of our graduate students volunteered to try to work with them. It became clear the woman needed further assessment for suicide/self-harm. Consultation resulted in a call to a local, county-operated outreach crisis program. We identified ourselves as the Walk-In Counseling Center and asked if they had a Spanish-speaker available. In minutes, we were connected with a bilingual staff person who talked with the client and counselor by phone. He determined that he had actually seen her the week before, assessed her level of risk and arranged for an outreach visit to her home the following day. During the team consultation, the team decided the most important outcome and learning from that event was to "Never Say No." At the WICC, we believe there is always a way we can try to help and people we can engage, even if it's outside our immediate skill base. Over many years, that's become our reputation. It is, in part, why clients come. We help.

The Magic of The Model

The WICC's work spans nearly 50 years. While we conduct annual client and volunteer satisfaction surveys, in such a small organization (3.7 FTE paid administrative staff), we can't do the research that "proves" that what we do works. We believe it does. And, thankfully, others are doing this research about single session and other forms of brief therapy.

However, we can point to an interesting study that did happen here. A doctoral student who had done a clinical practicum at WICC came back to do his dissertation research (Marsh, 2014). Although there were significant challenges in his pre/post-test study (due to our very transient client population), his outcomes surprised both him and us! His overall findings were that: *regardless of* the (a) number of times a client came, (b) similarity of client/counselor socioeconomic status, or (c) affinity between client and counselor, *clients who came to the Walk-In Counseling Center for counseling got better!* And not just a little better: "moderately to substantially better" and "the short-term therapy focus of Walk-In does provide real, tangible changes to clients who seek out services" (correspondence between M.A. Marsh and Walk-In Counseling Center, 2014).

We believe a combination of factors contribute to making our Walk-In Counseling Center effective: free, anonymous, easily accessible mental-health counseling; team wisdom, camaraderie, and support; and, last but certainly not least, a strong volunteer ethic. Walk-In counselors are volunteers—here for and with each client purely because they want to be. Surely there is magic in that!

References

Beck, A.T., Epstein, N., Brown, G., Steer, R. A. (1988). An inventory for measuring clinical anxiety: Psychometric properties. *Journal of Consulting and Clinical Psychology, 56*, 893–897.

Marsh, M.A. (2014). *The relationship between the therapeutic alliance and outcome in short term therapy* (Unpublished doctoral dissertation). Eagan, MN: Argosy University.

Schoener, G.R. (2011). Walk-In Counseling Center: Minneapolis, Minnesota. In A. Slive & M. Bobele (Eds.), (2011). *When one hour is all you have: Effective therapy for walk-in clients* (pp. 95–108). Phoenix, AZ: Zeig, Tucker, & Theisen.

Schoener, G.R., Milgrom, J.H., Gonsiorek, J.C., Luepker, E.T., & Conroe, R.M. (1989). *Psychotherapists' sexual involvement with clients: Intervention and prevention.* Minneapolis, MN: Walk-In Counseling Center.

Section 3
Clinical

10 The Eternal Now

On Becoming and Being a Single-Session Therapist

Moshe Talmon

This year I will conclude 42 years of practicing psychotherapy. I have been privileged to attend to the lives of thousands of individuals, couples, and families. In a few cases, I have had the opportunity to work over the course of many years with three generations of families that were created, grew-up, and aged with me. In many instances, I met my patients intermittently throughout their lifecycle. Thus, I believe I can qualify to be a long-term therapist. I even dare to say that I am among the longest-term therapists. I followed closely the lives of many of my clients much longer than the most renowned long-term therapists, simply because I was fortunate to have had a long career in one small, troubled, closely interconnected, highly conflictual state (Israel). I'm proud to state: Sigmund Freud was a much briefer therapist than me! I have had the luck to be still alive and active even in post-retirement age and still carry a deep sense of presence, engagement, and purpose with every new patient.

On the other hand, my colleagues and I have published a few books (Talmon, 1990, 1993; Hoyt & Talmon, 2014), chapters, and articles on Single-Session Therapy (SST), so I am better known as an advocate of the briefest form of psychotherapy. For the past 32 years (since 1986) I have seen about one-half of my patients in a "one-at-a-time," SST manner, while the other half I have seen for on-going therapy, ranging from a few weeks to a few years at a time.

For now, I consider this as my final chapter on the subject of SST. In all the previous ones, I made sure to present all the research and clinical data on the subject. This one is limited to my very subjective personal notes, based on my perspective on the experience of becoming and being a single-session therapist.

On the Essence of Psychotherapy

The essence of any psychotherapy is the same as that of SST. It is based on the abilities of a therapist and patient to create a therapeutic alliance in the here-and-now of each therapeutic encounter. The magic of the moment is based on the fact that when two (or more) people meet for the first time anything can happen.

The therapist may contribute to the therapeutic alliance by utilizing three main roles:

- The first is the "privileged listener"—to be attentive, caring, warm and non-judgmental while encouraging the patient to open up as the therapist expresses her/his understanding of the patient's deepest concerns/feelings or inner or external conflicts.
- The second is the therapist as a "facilitator" of the patient's inner strengths, abilities, adjustments and resilience both within themselves as well as with any social or familial support system. In doing so, the therapist is not only uncovering a patient's authentic strengths, but also often serves as a reliable optimist and positive "cheerleader."
- The third role of the therapist is the role of the constructivist, where the therapist together with the client re-constructs, re-labels and re-authors the patient's original "transcript." Persuasion, suggestion, interpretation, and joint "brain-storming" are often used under this role.

On Teaching SST

In the two books I wrote, plus the several articles and chapters my dear and longstanding partners Michael Hoyt and Robert Rosenbaum wrote with me, we presented all the scientific and clinical data. Those findings have been replicated over and over again (see Chapter 1 this volume), all indicating the following:

(1) When planned ahead at least half of psychotherapy users are likely to elect only one session at a time while up to 80% are likely to select one session when using "no appointment necessary" walk-in clinics. A large part of the rest of the patients are likely to use only two or three sessions even when more sessions are offered. When SST services are not available, a single session is still the most common length of therapy, ranging from 20% to 33% of all other lengths of therapy.
(2) About 90% of patients, using planned and mutually agreed-upon SST, will benefit from such lengths of therapy and will be highly satisfied with the session as well having short- and long-term positive outcomes.
(3) By far, the first session is the most cost-effective relative to all the sessions that follow. Although the "law of diminishing returns" is often found in psychotherapy outcome measures, most therapists continue to expect therapy to last much longer than it does in reality.

During the many years of teaching SST (all over the world) I realized again and again how organizations, clinics, and universities greatly developed and improved our work (e.g., see other chapters in this book). A one-at-a-time (OAAT) approach is embraced successfully where the need is much larger than the supply and where the therapists are working as a team with training and research being an active part of the process, and where the therapist's income is not based on a fee-for-time nor based on the assumption that more is always better. The most intriguing lesson I learned from teaching SST is that those services are greatly needed with the most challenging cases: homeless youngsters living on the streets, sexually abused women, hard-core addicts, unemployed poor single mothers as well as hospitalized cancer patients in stage four of the illness. Initially I insisted that I have no experience using SST with such difficult and complex cases. The heads of those services provided me with statistics of only-one-session frequency in their services indicating that SST is often of a higher frequency than found in my private practice with relatively high-functioning and well-to-do patients. I learned that very often people in great need (who clearly can and should be helped for the longest possible periods) are often best treated in an OAAT manner. Using a OAAT approach, the services could both reduce their waiting lists while, at the same time, reducing the percentage of "drop-outs" from their services. OAAT patients get more accessible, readily available services in a timely manner and nobody is ever considered as a "drop out." In medicine, every medical student first learns primary and internal medicine and knows early on how critical and common are the first hours of care—often called the "golden hour" or "golden day," particularly in the emergency rooms.

On the Concept of "Cure"

When someone chooses to become a clinical and medical psychologist, as I elected in my 20th year, one soon realizes that life is a painful, difficult, and complex journey. One learns to be a privileged and empathic listener and witness to human suffering and pain, and soon begins to comprehend the deep meaning of our being here temporarily. As a young therapist, I had a great need to rescue my patients and cure them. Later on I realized that very few patients are ever "cured" by therapy.

The more I got devoted and committed to seeking *psychohealth* instead of psychopathology, resources over deficiencies, strengths and abilities over disabilities and disorders, the less convinced I got about the concept of "cure" as a goal in psychotherapy. Most people (including myself) continue to be challenged by difficult and at times traumatic life events. In some cases, my own clients met life challenges by themselves and at other times returned for one or a few sessions as necessary. After four decades of practicing psychotherapy I need to acknowledge that the notion of "cure" is often a myth and the hope that psychotherapy process will have a natural ending with a measurable and sustainable outcome rarely "holds water." The pathogenic-medical model that therapy should start when a patient is properly diagnosed as being ill or having a mental disorder and should end when that patient is cured is, at best, misleading both for therapists and patients.

A great force in me to become a therapist stemmed from my need to rescue and cure others. Today I know that whenever a healer plays a guru or a surgeon plays God we miss a critical part of our role. The struggle against death and dying is not one that human beings can win. Gracefully accepting death and, on the way, many goodbyes, breakups, and necessary and unnecessary losses are all a meaningful *part* of our lives both as therapists and as patients. This is, at times, the hardest but yet a very significant role in our work. Not every illness can be defeated and not every problem can be resolved.

On "Time is Money"

One does not need to learn accounting in order to know how many single-session patients you need in order to match the fees you collected from one patient committed to intensive long-term therapy. From 1992 on, half of my solo private practice has been on a OAAT basis.

Here are a few alternative options I have used in my private practice in order to challenge the problematic concept of "fee-for-your-time" in psychotherapy:

(1) "You will pay me a retainer for keeping you healthy and I will work for free for as long as you are sick."
(2) "You will pay me at the end of therapy only for the results of therapy and not for the time of therapy."
(3) "I am committed to creating a change in the direction you have chosen. Since much of the therapeutic progress is a result of what happens after the session and between sessions you will be asked to carry out certain agreed-upon tasks and goals. In case progress is made and tasks are completed, we will stay with a basic low fee, but each time you don't work between sessions or simply stay stuck or regress the fee goes higher by 20% until progress is returned."
(4) With people who graduated many kinds of therapies prior to the first session with me: "What was the total cost of your last therapy? I will see you on a one-at-the-time basis and will charge you for only one-half of what you paid for your last treatment and will be available whenever a session is needed."
(5) Last but not least: I don't have a fixed fee and try to find the right "therapeutic fee" for each client. I always keep 10% reserved in my practice for no-fee patients. At times I may feel that no-fee or a nominal, symbolic amount is much more therapeutic, in some cases, than my "market value" fee. Furthermore, volunteering one's time is extremely rewarding for the giver. In order to afford it I did set a high base fee for my services so I can gladly be using a flexible and sliding scale when appropriate or even feel rewarded when I volunteer my time for free. In summary, I found that despite my creative efforts no fee structure fits all patients. In doing so, I know that I often take "the road less travelled" and yet prefer my concern for my clients' well-being over my own financial benefit.

On Being a Competent Expert

When I was a psychotherapy trainee, I believed that first I needed to learn all the scientific data and the relevant theories. Second, I had to train myself how to conduct the relevant skills and therapeutic procedures (joining, intake, dream interpretations, expressing empathy, hypnotic suggestions, enactment, utilizing eye-movement or other non-verbal cues, giving directives, etc.). Recently the tendency has been to believe that if you publish a detailed evidence-based protocol for a specific disorder, you will improve the expertise and cost-effectiveness of the therapist. While having great respect for the long training I (and many other able therapists) got in a variety of therapy methods, I eventually learned that more often than not such protocols, guidelines, and textbooks distance the therapist from the here and now of each client and each therapeutic moment. Furthermore, you miss the fact that the real expert and the real hero of every amazing therapy is more likely to be the person who sits in front of you: your patient.

On Creativity

I am much more natural in my role as an open-ended therapist than as a time-limited therapist—although, as every existentialist can teach us, we all live on a very time-limited basis, and we rarely know, in advance, how limited is our time on this earth. In this way, treating each session as the *first* session (for the rest of therapy), while knowing it could be also the *last* one (accepting that one day it will be also true), has been the most creative force in my work as a therapist. Holding these two poles (beginnings and endings) together and working with both at once—a fresh beginning and possible ending—has proved for me to be very critical for the creative force clients and therapists bring into each therapeutic session. I have found that OAAT therapy is the best force for my creativity in psychotherapy. Such creativity often takes place when I walk in curious and open-minded and allow patients to surprise me and teach me something new in each session.

As I grew to appreciate the significant role of creativity in effective psychotherapy, I could better work with the dynamic poles in the therapist's job. I could write a whole new book on the creative art of the here and now in psychotherapy. For the purposes of this chapter, let me present here a few of those opposite poles. On one pole to validate a patient's story via empathic listening and on the other pole to challenge the problematic elements in the same storyline. On one pole to increase a sense of hope or a realistic sense of optimism, and on the other pole helping him/her to accept certain parts of the harsh reality. There is an essential balance between offering neutral (and at times passive, silent) listening in one part of a session, and in another part, presenting active, focused questions. Similarly, between being non-directive at one point of the session, while at other times giving prescriptive-like directions.

The creative element here is the ability to work with both poles, or as creative psychotherapists like Milton Erickson or Salvador Minuchin might have suggested: lead the session by following your patient's language, culture, personality, and preferences. This way you are not only engaging in both/and options (over either/or therapeutic styles), you also allow each session to develop and evolve in unique, surprising, and flexible ways.

Conclusion

Psychotherapy is a creative art you never cease to learn. Any knowledge you acquire and any skill you may learn via on-going training and practice is going to be challenged and tested in your next session or when meeting your next patient.

Once you take a humble stand, realizing that you may cure nobody, that you are no great master and you appreciate how much you don't know, then you can better relax and open up to the ever-learning process each new patient and each new session offers you. Life and therapy are an eternal now. Although more often than not, therapy is a very brief process, it should not be viewed as either short or long. As my partner and friend Bob Rosenbaum (in Hoyt, Rosenbaum, & Talmon, 1992, p. 80) noted: "My desire is not to see everyone for one session; my desire is to see everyone for one full moment, as long as that takes."

When therapy is good, every session is a "golden hour" to be cherished, used, and remembered for a long time; and when it is bad, it may not worth a penny and years of therapy may make no difference. When you look at your patients as your main partners, you may find them to be your best-ever teachers and supervisors; you may not only respect and love them more, but it also allows yourself to enjoy your work and love what you do for a living and find it (as I do) as the most enriching job you will ever have. My main hope is that the "one-at-a-time'" approach advocated in this volume will further help in developing new directions and service-delivery systems, which leads to a more individually-tailored treatment for each patient's needs and choices and soon his/her unique being will be replacing many of the evidence-based and statistically-based therapeutic procedures.

References

Hoyt, M.F., Rosenbaum, R., & Talmon, M. (1992). Planned single-session psychotherapy. In S.H. Budman, M.F. Hoyt, & S. Friedman (Ed.), *The first session in brief therapy* (pp. 59–86). New York: Guilford Press.

Hoyt, M.F. & Talmon M. (Eds.) (2014). *Capturing the moment: Single session therapy and walk-in services.* Bethel, CT: Crown House Publishing.

Talmon, M. (1990). *Single-session therapy: Maximizing the effect of the first and often only) therapeutic encounter.* San Francisco: Jossey-Bass.

Talmon, M. (1993). *Single session solutions: A guide to practical, effective, and affordable therapy.* Reading, MA: Addison-Wesley.

11 Single-Session Therapy

Stories, Structures, Themes, Cautions, and Prospects

Michael F. Hoyt

Being a single-session therapist and having read Monte and Arnie's chapter on "One Session at a Time" in *Capturing the Moment* (Bobele & Slive, 2014; also see Slive & Bobele, 2011), I should say, "We have a WHOLE 30 minutes!" As we all know, lots can get done in one session, so I'd like to address a few issues.

The most common length of therapy is zero sessions—most people think about seeing a therapist, but never do. Among those who actually do seek counseling, ONE is the most common length of treatment. Consequently, we ought to figure out how to make the most of that—how to "capture the moment," so to speak.

Dr. Sigmund Freud, the father of psychoanalysis, can rightly be said also to have been the first modern single-session therapist: he met one time with an emotionally upset young woman named Katharina while Freud and his family were on vacation in the Alps (the innkeepers were Katharina's parents); and in another instance, he met one time with the great music composer Gustav Mahler, who had sexual and marital problems that seemed related to issues Mahler had with his mother. We don't know exactly what Katharina and Freud, and Mahler and Freud, talked about, but we do know that they knew they would only have the one meeting and we know, from reports (Breuer & Freud, 1893–1895/1953; Kuehn, 1965) that the single sessions were helpful.

Many of Dr. Milton Erickson's cases were also one session long. In fact, while all of his single-session cases did not produce good results (see Hoyt, 2000a, pp. 189–194), the great majority did and one session is actually the most common length of treatment in all of Erickson's known cases.

My own involvement with planned or hoped-for Single-Session Therapy began with the study at Kaiser Permanente Health Plan, a large health-care organization based in Northern California, when Moshe Talmon, along with Bob Rosenbaum, invited me to be part of the SST research project we did in the late 1980s. Here, by the miracles of video, is the first minute of what may have been my first, or certainly one of my first, SST sessions. It's from 1988.

Hoyt: Well, as I said outside, I'm Dr. Michael Hoyt. The purpose of our meeting today is what in our department we call an intake or screening interview. It's to find out briefly what problems you are having, what brings you here, and then to figure out what services we have that would be helpful.

Client: Yeah, that's what I need.

Hoyt: Okay. Sometimes we can get everything solved in one visit. If you are really motivated and want to get right down to figuring out what to do, we may be able to get everything dealt with today. If we are not able to, then we will figure out what the next steps are.

Client: Okay.

Hoyt: So, fill me in. I know we spoke briefly on the phone the other day—but what brings you here, what's cooking?

As can be seen, I "seeded" the idea of one session possibly being enough, but did not assert that we would necessarily have only one meeting. There are some things I see that I wish I had done differently—like not implying that if we didn't finish in one session it was because she wasn't trying hard enough; and not beginning with a vague, problem-inviting "What's cooking?"—but, there you have it. I'll have more to say about it later. (A report of the case appears in Talmon, 1990, pp. 78–96, with some elaboration in Hoyt, 2000a, pp. 169–188.)

SST Concepts: Definitions, Theories, and Models

In the book *Capturing the Moment* (Hoyt & Talmon, 2014), there are various definitions of Single-Session Therapy. Some prefer to restrict the term "SST"

Figure 11.1 The first minute of my first SST session in the Kaiser research project, circa 1988 (screen shot from video)

to those cases that, from the get-go, are clearly only going to be one session long—which is usually the case when folks come to a walk-in clinic. Jeff Young and Pam Rycroft (2012) estimate, however, perhaps 50% of SST clients will eventually return for another session or sessions—Rubin Battino (2014, p. 405) has thus contributed the useful term "SSST", Sequential Single-Session Therapy. Others have aggregated data showing that some percentage of all general clinic cases finish after one visit. They are one-session therapies, but did not start out—at least in the clinician's mind—with the understanding that they would be only single meeting "one-offs." In our study at Kaiser, we implied and invited—"Maybe in one visit; are you interested in that?"—but did not insist on a one-session format. Insistence produces resistance, imposition produces opposition, push produces pushback—so I think it is important to offer and invite, but not demand, one visit. In our studies of SST, we have been careful to refer to the "POSSIBILITY of one session being enough" and to say "When the first session MAY be the last." When therapy takes more than one session it is NOT an SST failure—it just means it took more than one session.

I'm a big fan of *competency-emphasizing* therapy—be it called solution-focused, narrative, strength-oriented, resource-based, positive psychology, or whatever.[1] In a discussion (Hoyt, 1994/2001a, p. 11) I had with Steve de Shazer (co-originator of solution-focused therapy) and John Weakland (co-originator of the Mental Research Institute approach), they agreed that we should endeavor to function as mental-health, not mental-illness, professionals. For me, this is also the basis of Milton Erickson's therapeutic approach: the respectful and creative *utilization* of whatever the client brings to help the client achieve what the client wants to achieve. At the first SST international symposium in Melbourne, I said, "Our primary therapeutic effort and expertise should be directed toward encouraging, eliciting, evoking, exploring, and elaborating whatever the client brings that can be helpful to get them to where they want to go" (Hoyt, 2014, p. 69).

We humans create our sense of reality (our "story" or "narrative") through language and imagination, and constructive therapists are largely in the business of helping clients to rewrite their stories by highlighting the clients' preferences and competencies. Alterations in the "language-scape" help to open space for new perceptions and new behaviors (the "viewing and doing," as O'Hanlon and Wilk, 1987, put it); "change" occurs when the client begins to live these different understandings.

Twenty years ago, while teaching in Japan, a small earthquake awakened me in Kyoto one night. Shaken and stirred, at 4 a.m. I wrote (Hoyt, 2000b, p. 167; Hoyt, 2009, p. 197) the following haiku:

> Focusing language
> On solutions, not problems
> Miracles happen.

Solution focus
Find exception and increase
Otherwise stay same.

More of same, no change
More of difference, not same
When will you notice?

I know it's strange, but that's what I did. Legend has it that three Japanese lords of old revealed their very different characters when asked what they would do with a nightingale bird that did not sing. With this in mind, I also wrote:

Single session now
Kill it, make it sing, or wait
The cage is open.

In other words: *Invitation, not imposition.*

As Moshe (Talmon, 2014, p. 34) has succinctly said, *one size does not fit all.* General principles are good, but what may be perfect for one person may not be good for another. Ultimately, I think each therapy is BESPOKE—that is, custom-made, uniquely tailored to the individual, using whatever skills and resources the client and clinician can bring to bear. Much of what we call *resistance*, I think, is what Steve de Shazer (in Hoyt, 1996/2001b, p. 162) called "therapist error"—the therapist wasn't listening carefully, and so told the client to do something the client didn't want to do. Among other issues, there are strong implications here for the significance of cultural competence, not suggesting something that goes against the grain of the person's values and beliefs.

Invitation, not insistence, is key. If one approach doesn't work, don't blame the client—try something else. In *Capturing the Moment*, there are examples of solution-focused and narrative therapies, of course, but there are also worthy examples of helpful psychodynamic, cognitive-behavioral, family systems, NLP, EFT, MRI, Haley's problem-solving, and Ericksonian hypnotherapeutic one-session approaches. There are also SST reports for Gestalt therapy, motivational interviewing, logotherapy, ACT, REBT, EMDR, and Redecision Therapy, among others. How and where you look influences what you see, and what you see influences what you do (Hoyt, 2000a, 2009)—multiple theoretical perspectives allow for multiple intervention strategies. One size doesn't fit all.

When you watch a lot of effective therapy sessions, whether they're SSTs or otherwise, you do begin to notice certain patterns. I would like to suggest some general guidelines. Many groups (e.g., Slive & Bobele, 2011; Boscolo, et al., 1987; de Shazer, 1988; McElheren, et al., 2014; Talmon, 1990) describe a sequential organization that moves from a pre-session review of client forms to beginning the session to an intersession consultation with the team to the delivery of an intervention by the therapist and then a post-session debriefing. Hillary and Brad Keeney (2014) see each session as a whole therapy and conceptualize a three-act dramatic structure for deconstructing therapy (for therapeutic purposes): Act One identifies the problems and crisis as the client presents them; Act Two bridges to more choices of understanding and action which, in turn, enables further movement toward an Act Three that is more resource-focused. For Bob Goulding, the co-developer of Redecision Therapy (see Hoyt, 1995/2001c; Goulding & Goulding, 1979), the usual successful trajectory went from *Contact* to *Contract* to *Change* to *Encore*. In several of my books (Hoyt, 1995a, 2000, 2009) I describe a schema for organizing the temporal structure of brief therapy, and note a parallel between the structure of each therapy session and the overall structure of a therapy. All this comes together, of course, when one session comprises the entire therapy, and in *Capturing the Moment* (Hoyt & Talmon, 2014, pp. 517–522), we adapted the scheme for organizing the temporal structure of Single-Session Therapy, in which we describe five phases or stages: pretreatment, early, middle, late, and follow-through (see Figure 11.2).

They tend to be pyramidal or epigenetic—that is, they tend to occur in sequence and each flows from the preceding so that successful work in one preconditions the next. The client elects therapy before forming an alliance; the therapeutic alliance establishes the ground for defining goals; goal setting leads to focusing on specific change strategies; goal attainment leads to discussion about homework, relapse prevention (which I prefer to call "relapse management"), and leave-taking; and points toward continued growth and possible return to treatment.

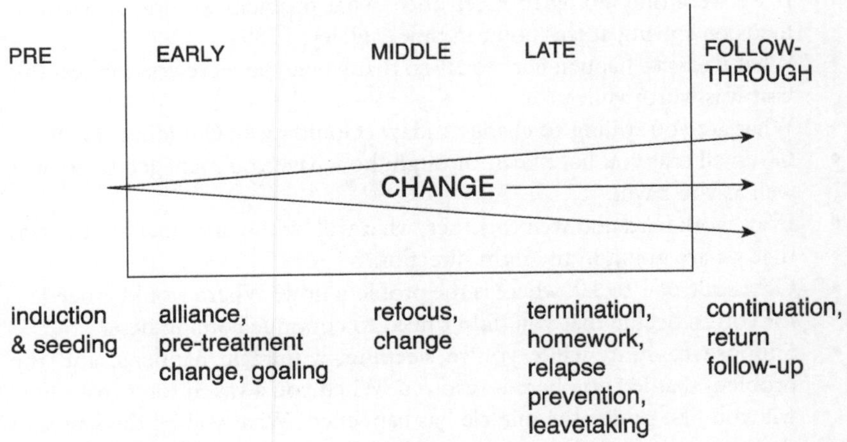

Figure 11.2 The temporal structure of SST (adapted from Hoyt, 2000, p. 218. ©2000 Taylor & Francis. Used by agreement)

There are many useful questions to ask for each phase. For example, thinking of my first SST client shown in the video, we might, in a pre-treatment contact on the telephone, be asking questions such as these:

- What's the problem—why now have you called (rather than earlier or later)?
- How do you see or understand the situation?
- What do you think will help?
- How have you tried to solve the problem so far—how did that work?
- When the problem isn't present (or isn't so bad), what is going on differently?
- Please notice between now and when we meet, so that you can describe it to me, when the problem isn't so bad, what are you doing differently then? (Weiner-Davis, de Shazer, & Gingerich, 1987)

And then, recognizing that first meetings allow new beginnings, a definitional opportunity to focus on solutions and the future more than on problems and the past, when she was in the office, guideline questions such as these might be helpful early in the session:

- Since we last spoke, what have you noticed that may be a bit better or different? How did that happen? What did you do?
- When is the problem not a problem?
- What do you call the problem? What name do you have for it?
- When (and how) does the problem influence you; and when (and how) do you influence it? (White, 1989)
- What's your idea or theory about what will bring about change? How would your life be better with these changes?
- If we were only going to meet once, what problem would you want to focus on solving at this point in time? (Haley, 1989)
- What needs to happen here today so that when you leave you can feel this visit was worthwhile?
- What are you willing to change today? (Goulding & Goulding, 1979)
- Given all that you have been through, how have you managed to cope as well as you have?
- If we work hard and well together, what will be the first small indications that we are going in the right direction?
- On a scale of 1 to 10, where is the problem now? Where would it need be for you to decide that you didn't need to continue coming here?
- Suppose tonight, while you're sleeping, a miracle happens, and the problem that led you here is resolved. When you awaken tomorrow, how will you first notice the miracle has happened? What will be the first sign that things are better? And the next? And the next? (de Shazer, 1988).
- What are your best hopes for today's meeting? (Iveson, George, & Ratner, 2014).

The questions we ask, starting with the first, do much to structure and guide the therapeutic conversation—toward problem or solution; toward past or future; toward dysfunction or health. We should pursue "solution talk," not "problem talk" (Furman & Ahola, 1992). There is a myriad of questions that could be keyed to each phase—pre-treatment, early in the session, in the middle of the session, late in the session. Finishing well is important, and when ending a session, it is usually helpful to get a sense of closure, to ascertain the client's satisfaction, to emphasize their capacities, and to discuss what may be the next steps the client plans to take—while leaving the door open for possible return. If the client feels that the one session has been sufficient, no need to gild the lily; as Shakespeare said (*King Lear*, Act I, Scene 4), "Striving to better, oft we mar what's well."[2] Again, there are lots of questions to help structure these discussions—see Hoyt, 2000c; see also Chapter 21 this volume.

When attempting to help clients via brief intervention, it is particularly important to appreciate and help them utilize their own strengths. Effective SST helps people to organize and catalyze, integrate and motivate, so that they can better access their own resources. Guidelines are OK, but the moment can't be scripted. We have to pay attention and be creative and flexible. This is the art and craft of therapy. SST is precise "good practice" (Rycroft & Young, 2014, p. 156) in a form akin to a one-act play.

To my mind, there is a "Context of Competence" that we co-create with clients, in which effective therapy—in one session, or more—takes place (see Figure 11.3).

In this Venn diagram, there are three overlapping circles, labeled ALLIANCE/GOALS/RESOURCES. Therapy takes place where the three intersect. If you have GOALS and an ALLIANCE but don't access RESOURCES, nothing happens. If you have RESOURCES and an ALLIANCE but don't have GOALS,

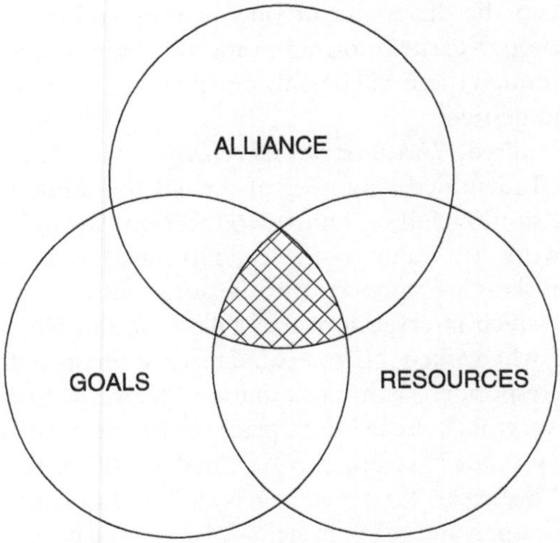

Figure 11.3 Context of Competence (from Hoyt, 2014, p. 67. ©2014 M.F. Hoyt. Used by agreement)

there's nothing to do, no purpose. If clients could match up their GOALS and RESOURCES on their own, they wouldn't need you. Hence, all three are needed. The *Context of Competence* is where GOALS and RESOURCES come together through the ALLIANCE. The work is collaborative. Effective therapy, one session or otherwise, involves all three.

Three Interrelated Themes

SST, provided in a walk-in clinic, or by appointment, or in some other situation (such as a clinical demonstration, a "second opinion" interview, or an emergency room or hospital consultation), has been helpful with a wide variety of problems—including anxiety, medical problems, depression, eating disorders, and substance abuse, as well as various relationship issues. There is a robust research literature (see Slive & Bobele, 2011; Hoyt & Talmon, 2014) supporting the effective use of SST with a wide range of diagnoses and problems.

There are three common themes that cut across and underlie different effective SSTs (Talmon & Hoyt, 2014, pp. 468–472)—mindset, time, and client empowerment—each covered in more detail below.

Mindset

This has to do with hope and expectation, the belief that one session can be sufficient, that the client has the capacity (and the opportunity) to make a significant change *in the moment*. As Battino (2006, 2014) has written, expectation is the essence of brief therapy. Bobele and Slive (2014, p. 98,) have explained, "We do not conduct any session as if there will be another session. In other words, we do *one session at a time*." SST, by appointment or walk-in, is *planned* (Bloom, 1992) or *by design* (Budman & Gurman, 1988): the client expects the therapy to be one meeting and the suggestion of one session being enough excites motivation and concentrates the mind—although we operate as though there will be only one meeting, more sessions can be had if necessary and desired.

In a book I edited, *Therapist Stories of Inspiration, Passion, and Renewal* (Hoyt, 2013), I identified a number of themes that underlie and renew our therapeutic passion, including human connection, strong feelings, curiosity, humor, hard work, the value of service, and most important, the power of love. Technical skills are important, to be sure, but a deep abiding caring is the ground in which interventions may take root and blossom. I agree with Jay Haley who, when asked, "If you could teach students only one thing, what would it be?" responded without hesitation: "Love. I'd teach them to love their clients. Everything else falls into place once a therapist loves their clients" (quoted by Davis, 2011, p. 26; also see Snyder, 2000). Shakespeare said, in *Hamlet* (Act V, Scene 2), "The readiness is all." And so I ask: Is your heart and soul (and mind) open and ready to help the client today? Do you truly expect that something good will result from the one-session meeting? Do you really affirm and "believe in" your clients?

Time

"Parkinson's Law in Psychotherapy" notes that clinical work often expands or contracts to fit the time allotted (Appelbaum, 1975). Shakespeare also said in *Hamlet* (Act II, Scene 2), "Brevity is the soul of wit." Yogi Berra, when asked what time is it, said "Do you mean NOW?" and Dr. Martin Luther King spoke of "the fierce urgency of now." Karen Young (2011), a keynote speaker (see Chapter 4) at the Banff conference, has written a lovely chapter called "When All the Time You Have is NOW: Re-visiting Practices and Narrative Therapy in a Walk-In Clinic." Bob Rosenbaum wrote: "My desire is not to see everyone for one session; my desire is to see everyone for one full moment, as long as that takes" (in Hoyt, et al., 1992, p. 81). And, he went on to remind us (Rosenbaum, 2014) in *Capturing the Moment*, that this is "the time of your life." In Single-Session Therapy, we're "on time" (Hoyt, 1990/2017; also see Ritterman, 2014). Clients walk in when they're "ready" and we should "capture the moment" and "strike while the iron is hot."

Client Empowerment

This entails having a truly respectful attitude and an awareness, to use one of my golf metaphors (Hoyt, 2000d), that we are the caddie and not the player—our primary job is to hand the client one of their clubs and maybe proffer some advice and encouragement.

Empowerment involves the co-creation of achievable therapeutic goals. What are the clients' preferences? Their intentions? (Another golf metaphor: *It's a long day on the course if you don't know where the hole is!* Have specific goals for the session.) What would tell them that the work is done—and done well? Whose therapy is it, anyway? Negotiating achievable goals is empowering: it actively involves the client from the beginning. It excites expectations and motivation, highlights their personal autonomy, calls upon the client's skills, and sets a template for our continuing client–therapist alliance.

When therapists emphasize the client's skills, resources, and strengths (rather than the client's weaknesses and problems) they are enhancing the often self-fulfilling belief, "Yes, I can." Thus, as Dan Short, et al. (2005, p. 16) report, Milton Erickson advised "Let patients know that they *are* going to be cured and that it will take place *within* them." Short, et al. pp. 16–17 (emphases in original) go on to amplify: "*Healing is the activation of inner resources during the process of recovery* . . . A great deal of healing comes from emphasizing positive attributes located in the individual and then building on it incrementally." This is the fundamental attitude shown in Figure 1.1 (see Chapter 1, page 14) where the doctor says to the patient: "Basically, there is nothing wrong with you that what's right with you can't cure."

Hope is the energizing idea that "things can get better." Recognizing one's powers helps to restore morale and builds hope and the motivation to change (Frank, 1968; Duncan, et al., 2010; Snyder, 2002; Tschudy, 2010). People sometimes face big challenges—bad relationships and jobs, serious medical illnesses, difficult situations. In therapy—one session, or more—we don't really change clients; we create therapeutic conversations in which, with our facilitation, they can change themselves. This is what we mean when we say "the power is in the patient" (Goulding & Goulding, 1978) and "your clients hold the keys" (Goldfield, 1998, p. 245). Without ignoring the reality of the situation, we endeavor to awaken the person inside. Does your client come away from the session feeling larger or smaller, more capable or less?

Did you notice the epigraph that opens this book? It quotes Lao Tzu from the 6th century BCE: "A journey of a thousand miles begins with a single step." Most of the time, in one session of therapy we clinicians endeavor to get people "unstuck"—we help them to take a new direction, or make a shift or a change. It doesn't mean everything will be solved.

Cautions

Single-Session Therapy is just right for many clients—it's what they want and it helps. There are some potential SST pitfalls, however, of which to be aware. A well-known cartoon (reproduced in Hoyt, 2017, p. 303) with the caption "Single Session Therapy" shows a therapist smacking a client across the face with the command "Snap Out of It!" Comedian Bob Newhart also produced a funny skit (available on YouTube) that spoofs one-session therapy as the therapist threatens a client with her worst fears if she doesn't just "Stop It!" Donald and Wampold (1986) tongue-in-cheek suggested "thanatotherapy" (Thanatos was the Greek god of death) as a one-session approach to brief therapy.

In addition to forcing, instead of inviting, SST, I see several other possible problems. One, already mentioned, is insisting on your theoretical model. What's the *client's* model? We therapists also often have a "need to be needed" and it may be hard for us to accept that a client can get "unstuck" and may not need us to "be there" throughout their journey (Hoyt, 1985/1995). Another potential problem, however, is insisting on everything being single-session, including rigidly using a single-session approach to avoid patients who may truly require more meetings. It is important that SST not be *imposed* when more sessions are needed. Insurance companies could unethically seize upon the evidence that SST is often helpful as a way of denying appropriate care when additional sessions are truly required, including care needed by usually undertreated or disenfranchised populations. Thus, Nick Cummings (2000, p. 77) rightly advised: "Indeed, sometimes there are single-session treatments that can be the right thing for some patients, but this should not be interpreted too broadly. It is for those who choose a single session that the benefits can be significant."

Many clients, when the choice is available, do choose to have a single meeting.[3] While psychotherapy clients (and therapists) may generally assume that therapy will be longer, clients usually come to walk-in and by-appointment

Single-Session Therapy clinics already with the expectation that there will just be the one meeting. Still, at the end of the session, there is usually some option for the client to return (for another single-session or for more). Hence, there are essentially three ways to have it be a Single-Session Therapy: (1) unilateral termination on the side of the client—that is, when the client stops and we think they should continue (although our initial chart review research at Kaiser [Talmon, 1990, pp. 8–11] found that a lot of cases we thought were "premature termination" actually were cases where the clients had achieved what they sought and were satisfied); (2) unilateral termination on the side of the therapist—that is, when the client wants to continue and the therapist won't let them (which occurs only rarely, we hope, and probably when the client can't afford to pay or even if they can pay, the therapist doesn't want to see them because they are too strange or difficult); and (3) when client and clinician mutually agree that the one session has been sufficient—at least for now. Obviously, we prefer the third. The choice of a single-session (or more, or less) should, whenever possible, be left to the client. We like to meet people in their frame of understanding and let them choose the length of therapy they prefer. "Crisis intervention is often ultra-brief, but SST is not necessarily aimed to be a crisis intervention unless this is what the client needs at the moment" (Hoyt & Talmon, 2014, p. 13). Risk factors (e.g., suicide, abuse) are treated just as they would be in any therapy (Bobele & Slive, 2015).[4] SST is a form of brief therapy (Budman, 1981; Hoyt, 2009), and can get more complicated if third-party payment requires "*DSMing*" (Battino, 2014, p. 395) the client and we are working in a manner that eschews pathologizing descriptions.

Prospects: Where Are We Heading?

I think it was Mark Twain who said that he didn't like to make predictions, especially about the future, but I'm sure there are going to be more SSTs. In *Capturing the Moment* (2014) Moshe and I documented extensively (pp. 487–516) studies that demonstrate the effectiveness and efficiency of SSTs. I'm looking forward to more research that helps us both to understand what works and what to do differently, particularly in one session, for folks who do not register high satisfaction from SST interventions.

Walk-in, no-appointment-needed clinics are burgeoning (see Bloom & Tam, 2015), and we can expect more symposia, workshops, and publications. Walk-in SSTs fit so well, especially nowadays in our speeded-up world of microwaves, instant messages, and nanosecond metrics. It seems that computers and related technology are here to stay, so get ready for more "click-ins" as well as "call-ins" and "walk-ins." An article in the *International Review of Sport and Exercise Psychology* (Pitt, et al., 2015; also see Giges & Petitpas, 2000) highlights many links between SST and the brief interventions used by sports psychologists. Used appropriately, walk-in SSTs will allow many folks, including traditionally undertreated populations, to receive mental-health services. When they see the clear cost-effectiveness evidence for return on investment—both the quantitative data and the many human stories—policymakers and politicians who care about both costs and their constituents should embrace services that offer Single-Session Therapy.

The belief that therapy should be a long, drawn-out, and expensive proposition is largely a middle- and upper-class expectation. Different cultural and social groups may be more comfortable with in-and-out, self-contained, one visit, pragmatic approaches, and we can expect to see the practice of walk-in and by-appointment SSTs expand both here in North America and around the world.

Two SST Stories with Lessons

Please allow me to briefly recount two Single-Session Therapy incidents during which I realized valuable lessons. In one, during our original Kaiser SST study, Bob Rosenbaum and I were watching Moshe and a client through a one-way mirror and were consulting by phone. Moshe and the client were doing fine, but we were calling in overly clever, overly complicated, intrusive suggestions. What I discovered was that it was often more helpful if we aligned ourselves with the therapist's intention—making suggestions to help the therapist to do what they were trying to do—rather than reframing and redirecting the whole enterprise into our pet theories and techniques and making suggestions that jerked the process around to where we wanted to go. I thought about it some, then realized that there was a parallel process going on: the therapist did better with the patient, just as we did better with the therapist, when we supported the other person's intention and worldview (see Hoyt, 2011).[5] This has many implications, especially for supervision and consultation.

In the other incident, I was the therapist and got stuck (not untypical), and I rushed out into the hallway and asked Bob: "What the hell should I do?" He calmed me down, then said: "Well, Michael, isn't this case kind of like the one last week you told me about? That was a man and this is a woman . . . but what did you do then?" He provided some support, reminded me of some past success and skills that could be useful, and gently redirected me back into the room. If we do this with other colleagues, we call it "hallway consultation" or "a little help from our friends"; if we do it with clients, we call it "Single-Session Therapy"!

So, Where is the Magic?

In a joint paper (Rosenbaum, Hoyt & Talmon, 1990) we wrote long ago, Bob quoted Herman Hesse (1943/1969, *The Glass Bead Game*):

> He felt a faint shiver, a matutinal coolness and sobriety which told him that the hour had come, that from now on there could be no more hesitating or lingering. This peculiar feeling, which he was wont to call "awakening," was familiar to him from other decisive moments of his life. It was both vitalizing and painful, mingling a sense of farewell and of setting out on

new adventures, shaking him deep down in his unconscious mind like a spring storm . . . A line of verse suddenly sprang into his mind:

In all beginnings dwells a magic force
For guarding us and helping us to live.

Others have said similar things:
Carl Jung (1949/1977, p. xxix) wrote: "There is only one first time."[6]
Cat Stevens (1967) sang: "The First Cut is the Deepest."
Nikos Kazantzakis (1965, p. 478, *Report to Greco*) penned:

> This was another divinely beautiful day. Each morning the world rediscovers its virginity: it seems to have issued fresh from God's hands. At that very instant it neither recalls what it did the day before nor frets about what it will do the day after. It experiences the present moment as an eternity. No other moment exists: before and behind this moment is Nothing.

Maya Angelou (1993), in her beautiful poem "On the Pulse of Morning" also said:

Each new hour holds new chances
For a new beginning.
[. . .]
The horizon leans forward,
Offering you space
To place new steps of change.[7]

SST involves both "capturing the moment" and "creating the moment." It's really about imagination, creativity, freedom. We are more gardeners than mechanics. We are not in the business of fixing people, as though they were cars broken and needing to be restored to their one mechanical function. Instead, they have possibilities and creative potentials to be nurtured and brought forward (Ratner & Yusuf, 2015). To paraphrase the Greek philosopher Plutarch (50–120 CE; the quotation is often mistakenly[8] attributed to William Butler Yeats): "Students [and clients] are lamps to be lit, not cups to be filled."

Awaiting skillful facilitation—in one session or more—THE MAGIC IS WITHIN, BETWEEN, AND AROUND. This single-session walk-in therapy stuff really works, and we're going to help many, many more people. As the last sentence of the editors' conclusion (p. 482) in *Capturing the Moment* (2014) says: "As many clients and therapists have discovered, SST can be as up-to-date as tomorrow's sunrise."

And that is why, on the cover of *Capturing the Moment* (see Figure 11.4), the sun is rising.

Figure 11.4 New day, new hour, new chances (©2014 M.F. Hoyt and M. Talmon. Used by agreement with Crown House Publishing and Fotolia.com)

Note: A version of this chapter first appeared in M.F. Hoyt (2017), *Brief Therapy and Beyond: Stories, Language, Love, Hope, and Time.* It has been adapted and reprinted here by agreement with Routledge (Taylor and Francis).

Notes

1 In recognition of their positive, creative, and constructivist bases, such approaches are sometimes called *constructive therapies* (see Hoyt, 1994, 1996, 1998). I like the way Insoo Berg and Yvonne Dolan (2001, p. 1) described solution-focused brief therapy: "If we had to define the SFBT approach in one sentence without talking about philosophy or techniques, we would describe it as 'the pragmatics of hope and respect.' Rather than focusing on deficits, SFBT therapists view clients as competent and in possession of resources. SFBT therapists do not attempt to educate or 'enlighten' clients; instead, they prefer to view clients as having positive rather than negative intentions. Completely accepting of the client's view, the SFBT therapist uses the client's perceptions as valuable resources to help create the change the client desires." Berg and Michael White (Duvall & Beier, 1995; also see White & de Shazer, 1996), respective co-originators of solution-focused and narrative therapy approaches, also made it clear that there are multiple ways to support clients' voices and choices.

2 Thanks to Bob Rosenbaum for calling this quotation to my attention.

3 In Talmon and Hoyt (2014, p. 481) we wrote: "In single session and walk-in services, clients come when they want, most report that they got what they came for, and they know that they can return when they want to. We hope that readers will be attracted to the elegance of doing more with less. In 1656 the French philosopher Blaise Pascal (quoted in Benham, 1914, p. 718) finished a letter to a friend by writing: 'I have only made this letter rather long because I have not had the time to make it shorter.' ('*Je n'ai fait celle-ci plus longue que parceque ju n'ai pas eu le loisir de la faire plus corte.*') Indeed, it takes time and skill both to write concisely and to practice therapy concisely, especially in a single session!"

4 Whether one proceeds in a conventional, straightforward manner or with a more idiosyncratic or unusual approach, keen clinical judgment is required; as Jay Haley (quoted in Crenshaw, 2004, p. 46) said when asked how he knew to use a certain intervention with a certain client, "Well, you wouldn't use it on someone it wasn't going to work on!" I recall long ago watching Carl Whitaker interview a teenage girl in the E.R. who had taken a little overdose to spite the boyfriend who had just dumped her. Carl asked a series of questions, like if she were dead who would get her favorite hairbrush, who would get her clothes, how long did she think it would take before the ex-boyfriend was dating someone else, etc. She got self-righteously incensed and declared, "My sister's not going to get my favorite brush, and I'm not gonna let that #%&^#%$ have the satisfaction of seeing me dead!" A few more minutes and we discharged her from the E.R. as "no longer a threat to self." Milton Erickson (see Haley, 1973, pp. 270–273) and Frank Farrelly and Jeff Brandsma (1974) also reported successful SSTs using provocative, seemingly paradoxical methods. For some other examples of SST interventions in potentially risky circumstances, along with discussions of appropriate cautions, see Bobele (1987, 1988), Weakland (1988) and Hoyt and Bobele (in preparation).

5 I subsequently read Brett Steenbarger (2012, p. 123, emphasis in original) saying something similar: "My goal . . . is not to enable you to conduct brief therapy in the manner of recognized practitioners. I also do not intend to encourage you to do therapy my way. Instead, I wish you to *consider becoming*

more of the effective helper that you already are when you are at your best. Identify what you are already doing when you are an efficient, effective facilitator of change, and then do those things more consistently and intentionally." For an exercise to help identify what we do that works, see Hoyt and Nylund (1997/2000).

6 Actually: "A repetition of the experiment is impossible, for the simple reason that the original situation cannot be reconstructed. Therefore, in each instance there is only a first and single answer."

7 "On the Pulse of Morning" from *On the Pulse of Morning* by Maya Angelou, copyright ©1993. Used by permission of Random House, an imprint and division of Penguin Random House LLC. All rights reserved.

8 Including by me (Hoyt, 2009, p. 292)!

References

Angelou, M. (1993). *On the pulse of morning.* New York: Random House.

Appelbaum, S.A. (1975). Parkinson's Law in psychotherapy. *International Journal* of Psychoanalytic Psychotherapy, 4, 426–436.

Battino, R. (2006). *Expectation: The very brief therapy book.* Bethel, CT: Crown House Publishing.

Battino, R. (2014). Expectation: The essence of very brief therapy. In M.F. Hoyt & M. Talmon (Eds.), *Capturing the moment: Single session therapy and walk-in services* (pp. 393–406). Bethel, CT: Crown House Publishing.

Benham, W.G. (1914). *Cassel's book of quotations* (rev. ed.). London: Cassell & Company.

Berg, I.K. & Dolan, Y.D. (2001). *Tales of solution: A collection of hope-inspiring stories.* New York: Norton.

Bloom, B. (1992). Bloom's focused single-session therapy. In *Planned short-term psychotherapy: A clinical handbook* (2nd ed., pp. 97–121). Boston: Allyn & Bacon.

Bloom, K. & Tam, J.A. (2015). Walk-in services for child and family mental health. *Journal of Systemic Therapies, 34*(1), 61–77.

Bobele, M. (1987). Therapeutic interventions in life-threatening situations. *Journal of Marital and Family Therapy, 13,* 225–239.

Bobele, M. (1988). Reply to "Public policy in life-threatening situations." *Journal of Marital and Family Therapy, 14,* 139–141.

Bobele, M. & Slive, A. (2014). One session at a time: When you have a whole hour. In M.F. Hoyt & M. Talmon (Eds.), *Capturing the moment: Single session therapy and walk-in services* (pp. 95–119). Bethel, CT: Crown House Publishing.

Bobele, M. & Slive, M. (2015). Walk-in psychotherapy: A new paradigm. *The Milton H. Erickson Foundation Newsletter, 35*(2), 9.

Boscolo, L., Cecchin, G., Hoffman, L., & Penn, P. (1987). *Milan systemic family therapy: Conversations in theory and practice.* New York: Basic Books.

Breuer, J. & Freud, S. (1953). Studies on hysteria. *Standard Edition of the Complete Psychological Works of Sigmund Freud* (Vol. 2). London: Hogarth Press (work originally published 1893–1895).

Budman, S.H. (Ed.) (1981). *Forms of brief therapy.* New York: Guilford Press.

Budman, S.H. & Gurman, A.S. (1988). *Theory and practice of brief therapy.* New York: Guilford Press.

Crenshaw, W. (2004). *Treating families and children in the child protective system.* New York: Brunner-Routledge.

Cummings, N.A. (2000). The single session misunderstanding. In *The collected papers of Nicholas A. Cummings. Vol. 1: The value of psychological treatment* (p. 77). Phoenix, AZ: Zeig, Tucker, & Theisen.

Davis, S. (2011, November/December). Models or therapists? Power from a common factors perspective. *Family Therapy Magazine, 10*(6), 26–28.

de Shazer, S. (1988). *Clues: Investigating solutions in brief therapy.* New York: Norton.

Donald, K.M. & Wampold, B.E. (1986). Thanatotherapy: A one-session approach to brief psychotherapy. *Journal of Polymorphous Perversity, 3*(2), 3–6.

Duncan, B.L., Miller, S.D., Wampold, B.E., & Hubble, M.A. (Eds.) (2010). *The heart and soul of change: Delivering what works in therapy* (2nd ed.). Washington, DC: APA Books.

Duvall, J.D. & Beier, J.M. (1995). Passion, commitment, and common sense: A unique discussion with Insoo Kim Berg and Michael White. *Journal of Systemic Therapies, 14*(3), 57–80.

Farrelly, F. & Brandsma, J. (1974). *Provocative therapy.* Cupertino, CA: Meta-Publications.

Frank, J.D. (1968). The role of hope in psychotherapy. *International Journal of Psychiatry, 6*, 383–395.

Furman, B. & Ahola, T. (1992). *Solution talk: Hosting therapeutic conversations.* New York: Norton.

Giges, B. & Petitpas, A. (2000). Brief contact interventions in sport psychology. *The Sport Psychologist, 14*, 176–187.

Goldfield, J. (1998). The master of faster. In M.F. Hoyt (Ed.), *The handbook of constructive therapies* (pp. 243–245). San Francisco: Jossey-Bass.

Goulding, M.M. & Goulding, R.L. (1979). *Changing lives through redecision therapy.* New York: Grove Press.

Goulding, R.L. & Goulding, M.M. (1978). *The power is in the patient.* San Francisco, CA: TA Press.

Haley, J. (1973). *Uncommon therapy: The psychiatric techniques of Milton H. Erickson, M.D.* New York: Norton.

Haley, J. (1989). *The first therapy session: How to interview clients and identify problems successfully* [audiotape]. San Francisco: Jossey-Bass.

Hesse, H. (1969). *The glass bead game.* (R. Winston & C. Winston, Trans.) Troy, Mo: Holt, Rinehart & Winston (work originally published 1943).

Hoyt, M.F. (Ed.) (1994). *Constructive therapies.* New York: Guilford Publications.

Hoyt, M.F. (1995a). On time in brief therapy. In *Brief therapy and managed care: Readings for contemporary practice* (pp. 69–104). San Francisco: Jossey-Bass. Reprinted in M.F. Hoyt, *Brief therapy and beyond: Stories, language, love, hope, and time* (pp. 6–32). New York: Routledge, 2017.

Hoyt, M.F. (1995b). Therapist resistances to short-term dynamic psychotherapy. In *Brief therapy and managed care: Readings for contemporary practice* (pp. 219–236). San Francisco: Jossey-Bass (work originally published 1985).

Hoyt, M.F. (Ed.) (1996). *Constructive therapies, Vol. 2.* New York: Guilford Publications.

Hoyt, M.F. (Ed.) (1998). *The handbook of constructive therapies.* San Francisco: Jossey-Bass.

Hoyt, M.F. (2000a). *Some stories are better than others: Doing what works in brief therapy and managed care.* Philadelphia, PA: Brunner/Mazel.

Hoyt, M.F. (2000b). Solution-ku. In *Some stories are better than others* (p. 167). Philadelphia, PA: Brunner/Mazel.

Hoyt, M.F. (2000c). The last session in brief therapy: How and why to say "when." In *Some stories are better than others* (pp. 237–261). Philadelphia, PA: Brunner/Mazel, 2000. Reprinted in M.F. Hoyt, *Brief therapy and beyond: Stories, language, love, hope, and time* (pp. 153–176). New York: Routledge, 2017.

Hoyt, M.F. (2000d). A golfer's guide to brief therapy (with footnotes for baseball fans). In *Some stories are better than others* (pp. 5–15). Philadelphia, PA: Brunner/Mazel. Reprinted in M.F. Hoyt, *Brief therapy and beyond: Stories, language, love, hope, and time* (pp. 33–43). New York: Routledge, 2017.

Hoyt, M.F. (2001a). On the importance of keeping it simple and taking the patient seriously: A conversation with Steve de Shazer and John Weakland. In *Interviews with brief therapy experts* (pp. 1–33). New York: Brunner-Routledge (work originally published 1994).

Hoyt, M.F. (2001b). Solution building and language games: A conversation with Steve de Shazer (and some after words with Insoo Kim Berg). In *Interviews with brief therapy experts* (pp. 158–183). New York: Routledge (work originally published 1996).

Hoyt, M.F. (2001c). Contact, contract, change, encore: A conversation about redecision therapy with Bob Goulding. In M.F. Hoyt, *Interviews with brief therapy experts* (pp. 121–143). New York: Routledge (work originally published 1995).

Hoyt, M.F. (2009). *Brief psychotherapies: Principles and practices.* Phoenix, AZ: Zeig, Tucker, & Theisen.

Hoyt, M.F. (2011). Foreword. In A. Slive & M. Bobele (Eds.), *When one hour is all you have: Effective therapy for walk-in clients,* (pp. xix–xv). Phoenix, AZ: Zeig, Tucker, & Theisen.

Hoyt, M.F. (2014). Psychology and my gallbladder: An insider's account of a single session therapy. In M.F. Hoyt & M. Talmon (Eds.), *Capturing the moment: Single session therapy and walk-in services* (pp. 53–72). Bethel, CT: Crown House Publishing. Reprinted in M.F. Hoyt, *Brief therapy and beyond: Stories, language, love, hope, and time* (pp. 272–286). New York: Routledge, 2017.

Hoyt, M.F., & Bobele, M. (Eds.) (in preparation). *Creative therapy in challenging situations: You said WHAT?* New York: Routledge.

Hoyt, M.F. & Nylund, D. (1997). The joy of narrative: An exercise for learning from our internalized clients. *Journal of Systemic Therapies, 16*(4), 361–366. Reprinted in M.F. Hoyt, *Some stories are better than others* (pp. 201–206). Philadelphia, PA: Brunner/Mazel, 2000.

Hoyt, M.F., Rosenbaum, R., & Talmon, M. (1992). Planned single-session psychotherapy. In S.H. Budman, M.F. Hoyt, & S. Friedman (Eds.), *The first session in brief therapy* (pp. 59–86). New York: Guilford Press.

Hoyt, M.F. & Talmon, M. (Ed.) (2014). *Capturing the moment: Single session therapy and walk-in services.* Bethel, CT: Crown House Publishing.

Iveson, C., George, E., & Ratner, H. (2014). Love is all around: A single session solution-focused therapy. In M.F. Hoyt & M. Talmon (Eds.), *Capturing the moment: Singe session therapy and walk-in services* (pp. 325–348). Bethel, CT: Crown House Publishing.

Jung, C.G. (1977). Foreword. In R. Wilhelm (Trans.), *The I Ching, or book of changes* (pp. xxi–xxxix). Princeton, NJ: Bollingen/Princeton University Press (work originally published 1949).

Kazantzakis, K. (1965). *Report to Greco.* New York: Simon & Schuster (work originally published 1957 in Greek).

Keeney, H. & Keeney, B. (2014). Deconstructing therapy: A case study of a single session crisis intervention. In M.F. Hoyt & M. Talmon (Eds.), *Capturing the moment: Single session therapy and walk-in services* (pp. 441–461). Bethel, CT: Crown House Publishing.

Kuehn, J.L. (1965). Encounter at Leyden: Gustav Mahler consults Sigmund Freud. *Psychoanalytic Review, 52*, 345–364.

McElheran, N., Stewart, J., Soenen, D., Newman, J., & Maclaurin, B. (2014). Walk-in single session therapy at the Eastside Family Centre. In M.F. Hoyt & M. Talmon (Eds.), *Capturing the moment: Single session therapy and walk-in services* (pp. 177–194). Bethel, CT: Crown House Publishing.

O'Hanlon, W.H. & Wilk, J. (1987). *Shifting contexts: The generation of effective psychotherapy.* New York: Guilford Press.

Pitt, T., Thomas, O., Lindsay, P., Hanton, S., & Bawden, M. (2015). Doing sport psychology briefly? A critical review of single session therapeutic approaches and their relevance to sport psychology. *International Review of Sport and Exercise Psychology*, DOI: 10.1080/1750984X.2015.1027719.

Ratner, H. & Yusuf, D. (2015). *Brief coaching with children and young people: A solution-focused approach.* New York: Routledge.

Ritterman, M. (2014). One-session therapy: Fast new stance using the slo-mo three-minute trance. In M.F. Hoyt & M. Talmon (Eds.), *Capturing the moment: Single session therapy and walk-in services* (pp. 373–392). Bethel, CT: Crown House Publishing.

Rosenbaum, R. (2014). The time of your life. In M.F. Hoyt & M. Talmon (Eds.), *Capturing the moment: Single session therapy and walk-in services* (pp. 41–52). Bethel, CT: Crown House Publishing.

Rosenbaum, R., Hoyt, M.F., & Talmon, M. (1990). The challenge of single-session therapies: Creating pivotal moments. In R.A. Wells & V.J. Giannetti (Eds.), *Handbook of the brief psychotherapies* (pp. 165–189). New York: Plenum Press.

Rycroft, P. & Young, J. (2014). Single session therapy in Australia: Learning from teaching. In M.F. Hoyt & M. Talmon (Eds.), *Capturing the moment: Single session therapy and walk-in services* (pp. 141–156). Bethel, CT: Crown House Publishing.

Short, D., Erickson, B.A., & Klein, R. E. (2005). *Hope and resiliency: Understanding the psychotherapeutic strategies of Milton H. Erickson, M.D.* Norwalk, CT: Crown House Publishing.

Slive, A. & Bobele, M. (Eds.) (2011). *When one hour is all you have: Effective therapy for walk-in clients.* Phoenix, AZ: Zeig, Tucker, & Theisen.

Snyder, C.R. (2002). Hope theory: Rainbows of the mind. *Psychological Inquiry, 13*, 249–275.

Snyder, M. (2000). Mutual love in therapeutic process. *Journal of Systemic Therapies, 19*(4), 4–19.

Steenbarger, B.N. (2012). Solution-focused brief therapy: Doing what works. In M.J. Dewan, B.N. Steenbarger, & R.P. Greenberg (Eds.), *The art and science of brief psychotherapies: An illustrated guide* (2nd ed.; pp. 121–155). Arlington, VA: American Psychiatric Publishing.

Stevens, C. (1967). "The first cut is the deepest." Song on *New masters* record album. London, England: Decca Records.

Talmon, M. (1990). *Single session therapy: Maximizing the effect of the first (and often only) therapeutic encounter.* San Francisco: Jossey-Bass.

Talmon, M. (1993). *Single session solutions: A guide to practical, effective, and affordable therapy.* Reading, MA: Addison-Wesley.

Talmon, M. & Hoyt, M.F. (2014). Moments are forever: SST and walk-in services now and in the future. In M.F. Hoyt & M. Talmon (Eds.), *Capturing the moment: Single session therapy and walk-in services* (pp. 463–485). Bethel, CT: Crown House Publishing.

Tschudy, J.D. (2010). Finding, nurturing and instilling hope in family therapy. Logan, UT: Utah State University. *All Graduate Theses and Dissertations* (p. 558).

Weakland, J.H. (1988). Letter to the editor: Weakland on the Woodys-Bobele exchange. *Journal of Marital and Family Therapy, 14,* 205.

Weiner-Davis, M., de Shazer, S., & Gingerich, W.J. (1987). Using pre-treatment change to construct the therapeutic solution: An exploratory study. *Journal of marital and Family Therapy, 13,* 359–363.

White, M. (1989). The externalizing of the problem and the re-authoring of lives and relationships. In *Selected papers* (pp. 5–28). Adelaide, Australia: Dulwich Centre Publications.

White, M. & de Shazer, S. (1996, October 10-11). *Narrative solutions/ Solution narratives.* Conference sponsored by Brief Family Therapy Center, Milwaukee, WI.

Young, J. & Rycroft, P. (2012). Single session therapy: What's in a name? *Australian and New Zealand Journal of Family Therapy, 33*(1), 3–5.

Young, K. (2011). When all the time you have is NOW: Re-visiting practices and narrative therapy in a walk-in clinic. In J. Duvall & L. Beres (Eds.), *Innovations in narrative therapy: Connecting practice, training, and research* (pp. 147–166). New York: Norton.

12 One . . . Two . . . Three Ways to Help You Today

Therapeutic Models in a Single-Session Therapy Program

Monica Barnes, Patricia Carruthers, and Maja Gigovic

South Calgary Health Centre (SCHC) is a community-based health clinic located in Calgary, Alberta. Calgary is the largest city in this western Canadian province, with a population of approximately 1.23 million people. Housed within South Calgary Health Centre are multiple services, including several mental-health services. These include an addictions therapist, Child and Adolescent Addictions and Mental Health Program, Geriatric Mental Health, Adult Mental Health, and Single-Session Walk-In (SSWI). Mental-health clinicians are also present in the Urgent Care Department.

Adult Mental Health is a brief therapy program, staffed by six full-time and four part-time therapists, all of whom are prepared at a master's or doctoral level as clinical nurse specialists, psychologists, and social workers. These therapists, along with therapists from the Child and Adolescent Addictions and Mental Health Program, staff the SSWI Program, which runs Mondays through Thursdays 4:00 p.m. to 7:00 p.m., and Fridays 10:00 a.m. to 1:00 p.m. Each SSWI shift is staffed by two therapists and one shift coordinator. The shift coordinator supports the other therapists and oversees the flow of clinical activity. Calgary is served by a centralized mental-health information and options call-center called Access Mental Health. Callers are assisted by clinicians in navigating mental-health services. The clinicians are well-versed in services that fall both under and outside of the umbrella of provincial healthcare. Access Mental Health is the point of entry to many of the city's mental-health services, including our SSWI program. Clients may also hear about SSWI from their family doctors, schools, community advertising, other mental-health programs in the community, or online. Access Mental Health and community mental-health programs often advise clients of SSWI as a resource while they are awaiting services or between appointments with other services.

Clients are deemed suitable for the SSWI service by virtue of their presence; there is no age limit or geographical catchment area. We are open to seeing clients individually, as couples, families, and/or their chosen small groups. Clients from every quadrant of the city, as well as the surrounding rural areas, utilize the service. Since the inception of the program in 2004, there has been a steady increase in the number of clients seen annually. In 2014–2015, nearly 900 sessions were conducted Many clients attend more than once, knowing that they will likely not see the same therapist. When clients arrive and request the SSWI service, they are asked to complete two short forms which gather demographic information, invite the client to provide a focus for the session, and provide a quick view of present functioning using a 5-point rating scale. These ratings give clues to possible risk, including suicidal or homicidal ideation, domestic violence, and substance abuse. Should these risks be evident, further exploration is pursued by the therapist and the team during the session. Like any other mental-health service, safety plans are developed in collaboration with the client and family. If the therapist and team feel doubtful about the client's capacity to maintain safety, other services are consulted and the client may be escorted to the Urgent Care department at our site where a physician is available should involuntary certification and transport to hospital be necessary. In very rare circumstances, city police are summoned if a client presents a danger to him/herself and refuses further care.

The forms also contain information about the service, most notably that the therapists function as a team with at least one member observing the session in whole or in part. Clients are advised that there is no physician associated with our clinic and we do not have the capacity to order, review, or recommend medication.

Two or three therapists are available during each SSWI shift. Typically, the match-up of therapist to client is random. At times, we do have the luxury of matching clients who present with problems for which a therapist may have particular education or experience. For example, a youth may be seen by a therapist who also works in the Child and Adolescent Program.

At the start of the session, the therapists review limits to confidentiality, explain the team approach and the structure of the session. Therapists work to establish an agenda for the session, based upon what the client desires. Each session involves a pre-session, an intersession break, and time permitting, a post-session discussion. Often, the post-session discussion happens informally. Sessions are typically 50–60 minutes in length. In addition to differing professional disciplines, therapists practice from diverse therapy frameworks, including narrative, solution-focused, emotion-focused, and cognitive behavioral. We are often asked how we reconcile our varying therapy worldviews in order to deliver comprehensive service. Given that 35% of clients who attended SSWI in 2014–2015 indicated previous attendance at a walk-in service, they undoubtedly encountered different clinicians and theoretical frameworks of therapy (Walk In Annual Report, 2015). Despite varying theoretical frameworks, clinicians at SSWI are consistent in a strength-based stance.

Case Illustration: Using Three Models in Three Single-Sessions

The following discussion will demonstrate the use of differing therapeutic models in single-session therapy with our client, Ivana. She was a 39-year-old married mother of one son who worked full time as a therapist in our Adult Mental Health and SSWI program. She gave her informed consent both to participate as a client and to have the following personal information made public. Ivana had been diagnosed with open-angle glaucoma of her right eye, a progressive condition that causes increased eye pressure and subsequent optic nerve damage, potentially leading to blindness. Ivana required multiple ophthalmic interventions, most recently the insertion of a small pump to move fluid out of her eye and prevent pressure from building. Ivana experienced considerable anxiety regarding her eye condition.

Ivana agreed to be interviewed by three therapists in a single-session format for three separate 60-minute sessions. As we developed this chapter, our goal was to demonstrate the ease with which varying theoretical perspectives could be utilized in a single-session format. Alberta Health Service's policies regarding video and audio recording of clients involved in Mental Health and Addiction services are very prohibitive. We would not have been able to feature an actual SSWI client. Rather than create a role-play scenario, which we felt would be inauthentic, we elected to interview Ivana about a real problem she was experiencing. Ivana participated in therapeutic conversations with three therapists for three separate sessions. The approaches utilized were: (1) cognitive behavioral therapy; (2) solution-focused brief therapy; and (3) narrative therapy.

Ivana's situation was one of a wide range of problems that bring clients to SSWI. As previously mentioned, many of the clients who seek SSWI services attend more than once, seeing a different therapist and experiencing a different therapy approach. Therapists may refer to content of previous SSWI sessions and may build on recommendations and suggestions offered in previous sessions, but function from their own therapeutic stances. Therapists may "borrow" strategies from other schools of therapy. They may build on interventions suggested in previous sessions, or they may approach the session as purely stand-alone, depending on the clients' needs.

Cognitive-Behavioral Therapy (CBT)

Cognitive-Behavioral Therapy (CBT) has not been typically associated with the single-session walk-in approach (although there have been reports of one session of CBT being helpful; see Dryden, 2016; Ellis & Joffe, 2002; and Hoyt & Talmon, 2014). However, CBT has managed to find an important role within the SSWI program at South Calgary Health Centre. The fundamental propositions of CBT suggest that: (1) cognitive activity affects behavior; (2) cognitive activity may be monitored and altered; and (3) desired behavior change may be affected through cognitive change (Dobson, 2001).

These propositions lend themselves to specific, targeted, and evidence-based interventions which can easily be incorporated within the single-session model (Bond and Dryden, 2002). When working from a single-session framework, what underlies all theoretical approaches are a set of common questions and ideas that provide structure to the session (Slive & Bobele, 2011):

- What does the client want from the session?
- How will the client know that the session has been helpful?
- Why is the client presenting today, as opposed to the previous day, month or year?
- What could make the smallest difference?
- What is the client's motivation for change?
- What are the client's strengths and resources?
- What solutions has the client attempted already?

To decide if a cognitive behavioral intervention might be a good fit, it is important to listen for the following:

- Is the client using specific cognitive language to describe his/her problem? (e.g., "My thinking is very negative.")
- Does the client conceptualize his/her problem in cognitive-behavioral terms? (e.g., "I know my anxiety is caused by irrational fears, but I don't know how to fight it.")
- How much education does the client have about his/her issue?
- Could this client's goal for the session be addressed through a cognitive-behavioral intervention? (e.g., Is the client looking to improve his/her mood, think more positively, solve a problem, learn strategies to manage anxiety?)

Along with these questions, a therapist would also be listening for the client's distorted cognitions, maladaptive beliefs, behavioral patterns, and even dysfunctional schemas that might be underpinning the individual's presenting concern. The most challenging aspect of the session involves finding the right fit between the interventions, the client's goal, and his/her readiness to engage in the suggested intervention. For example, a client may present with concerns regarding depression without having awareness of the triggers or factors contributing to his/her symptoms. This person might benefit from hearing a therapist describe the basic cognitive model which hypothesizes that people's perception of situations or events influences their emotions and behavior (Beck, 1964; Ellis, 1962). Exploring the influence of thoughts on emotions, identifying automatic thoughts contributing to low or anxious mood, and introducing the idea of cognitive distortions might be an effective intervention (Beck, 1995). Similarly, a client who presents with increased awareness of his/her cognitions may wish to focus on learning how to complete a simple thought record, analyse and challenge cognitive distortions, and evaluate alternative perspectives.

Ivana and CBT

Ivana, the previously mentioned client, described a struggle with a medical condition over which she does not have much control. As the CBT session progressed, it became clear that she was engaging in cognitive distortions, exaggerating potential negative outcomes, engaging in black-or-white thinking, fortune-telling, and emotional reasoning. The client was introduced to the CBT model that was illustrated on a whiteboard, highlighting the connection between thoughts, feelings, behaviors, and physical sensations. Cognitive distortions were identified and their connection between low mood and high anxiety was explored. Ivana and the therapist focused on generating evidence for Ivana's thoughts and she was taught how to challenge and/or question her distorted cognitions. An alternative cycle, focusing on more realistic and factual thoughts, was identified. Ivana was instructed to engage in this intervention on bad days when she notices that her mood is more irritable and/or anxious. The following is a brief excerpt from the cognitive-behavioral therapist's conversation with Ivana:

CB Therapist: To summarize, on a bad day there are more physical symptoms with your eye, there are more negative thoughts and more uncomfortable feelings to deal with. On a good day there are less physical symptoms and your thoughts tend to be more positive. When you have a bad day and you want to turn it into a better day, do you think that consciously focusing on some of these realistic thoughts—things that you can still do, thoughts that are supported by facts, taking a different perspective, taking care of yourself, taking care of your eye, taking something for the pain, doing something pleasurable, being aware of thoughts that lead to more withdrawal, do you think a bad day could turn into a better day?

Ivana: Yeah, I mean on a bad day I won't be very social because people get on my nerves when I am not feeling good, but I tend to talk to people more, respond and I read which seems counterintuitive (*laughs*), when your eye is hurting . . . but it makes me feel like I am doing something that I like to do so those days are not too bad.

CB Therapist: Good.

Ivana: If I am able and my eye is not hurting too much.

CB Therapist: OK, like you said with the physical symptoms, "there are things that I can't change," right? But there are some things you can change in how you react to the physical symptoms and a lot of days you have the skills and you know what to do. Some days it will take a little more effort and we identified and drew on the board what that might look like.

Other cognitive-behavioral interventions that can be easily altered to fit the single-session format include: completing a simple thought record; making a behavioral activation plan; challenging cognitive distortions; writing down coping statements/thoughts; perspective taking; practicing a breathing, grounding, or relaxation exercise in the session; challenging intermediate or core beliefs; generating a phobic hierarchy along with set exposure schedule; and assertiveness training.

Solution-Focused Brief Therapy (SFBT)

Solution-focused brief therapy (SFBT) lends itself quite naturally to the single-session format in that it focuses on the present and future, targeting the desired outcome of therapy, a future in which the problem is absent or less influential. The SFBT approach begins with a well-developed and personalized version of what the client's life would be like without the problem. Once the preferred future is elucidated, one can plan the smallest practical steps that can be taken immediately towards desired change.

The therapist's role is to inquire about the solution. This can be approached in many ways. The Miracle Question, developed by de Shazer (1988, p. 5; see De Jong and Berg, 1998) can be very useful in helping the client create a vision of his or her preferred future. Conceivably, an entire session might evolve around the miracle question. In hearing the client's idea of what life would be like without the problem, it is possible to also elicit the steps to getting there.

A solution-focused single-session involves careful listening and asking questions to elicit exceptions—times when the problem is absent or less influential. "Exceptions are scattered throughout the client conversation and it takes a well-trained ear to recognize and appreciate the opportunities they offer" (Pichot & Dolan, 2003, p. 17). When exceptions can be distinguished and explored, the client can deliberately plan to create the circumstances or engage in the behaviors that are already working.

Although not exclusive to SFBT, scaling questions are often used to invite the client to assign a value in order to conceptualize where she sees herself in relation to her *miracle* or preferred future. Consistent with SFBT's focus on desired outcome, rather than the problem, the highest point of the scale is always anchored to the solution or preferred future (Bertolino & O'Hanlon, 2002).

Ivana and SFBT

The following is a brief excerpt from the solution-focused brief therapist's conversation with Ivana:

SFB Therapist: If you could leave with one thing today that would tell you that coming was a good use of your time, what would that one thing be?

Ivana: I'm thinking it would be good to leave with . . . an idea, maybe, of how to . . . I guess . . . ride through [the anxiety] when it hits. Not so much get rid of it, because I've noticed that if I try to get rid of it, it becomes bigger. If I could do that . . . because it feels like I can't ride through it on a bad day.

SFB Therapist: Okay. So, some days aren't as bad?

Ivana: Definitely. There are some days I can handle this.

SFB Therapist: If you were to imagine a scale of "riding through it". . . 10 would be totally successfully riding through it, exactly the way you want to be doing it, and 1 would be not riding through it at all, where would you say you are at right now?

Ivana: I would say I'm about a 4.

SFB Therapist: On that "riding through it" scale how do you manage to be at a 4 and not a 3 or 2? Or even a 1? (*pause*)

Ivana: Well . . . I think that 1 (*laughing*) would be losing it completely going totally berserk and part of it is saying, "You couldn't do your work if that happens."

SFB Therapist: And when you get yourself to a 4.5 or 5, what will you be doing differently?

Ivana: At a 4.5? I probably wouldn't be . . . being hard on myself for having a bad day. And at 5 I think I would be able to do more things that are regular, daily tasks . . . like cook a meal for my family instead of picking up something already prepared. On a bad day, I do more things to check out . . . .instead of being present. At a 5 I'd be more present.

SFB Therapist: What good comes of being more present?

Ivana: When I'm more present, I'm able to recognize that . . . I'm doing well. I'm doing what other people do, and sometimes more, with one eye and with discomfort.

SFB Therapist: When you're able to have that recognition . . . what good comes of that?

Ivana: The times that I do more and feel more normal, I don't negotiate with myself so much. I do things instead of thinking about them.

Relationship questions play a significant role in SFBT. "Solution-focused therapy is a systemic approach rooted in the belief that a small change by one person will result in changes throughout the system" (Pichot & Dolan, 2003, p. 33). In asking Ivana about the impact of the small changes towards her preferred future, she noted that when she is more present, her son is more easy-going.

Without extensive exploration of the problem or its history in the single-session, Ivana's resources, competencies and preferred way of being are highlighted. In one session, steps to solutions are developed.

A Narrative Approach

Narrative therapy seeks to help people identify their values and skills and to create knowledge to emphasize value-based living (White & Epston, 1990; Freedman & Combs, 1996). When people are able to effectively confront problems, they can move away from the problem-saturated story and adopt more preferred ways of being. There is an assumption that narratives shape a person's identity and become the dominant story. The therapist helps the person to co-author a new narrative by investigating the history of these qualities. Narrative therapy promotes a social-justice approach to therapy, challenging dominant discourses that shape people's lives in destructive ways. Other common elements in narrative therapy are:

- An externalizing emphasis, naming a problem so people can assess its effects, come to know how it operates in their lives, relate the history of the problem, evaluate it to take a definite position on its presence, and choose their relationship with it. Externalizing the problem is a primary tenet of narrative therapy.
- A focus on unique outcomes, times when the problem would not be predicted by the problem's story itself.
- An awareness of the impact of power relations in therapeutic conversations with a commitment to checking back with people, seeking to mitigate the effects of assumptions or beliefs of the therapist.
- An appreciation of the creation and use of documents, as when people and therapists at the Bouverie Centre in Melbourne, Australia, create "Take Aways" which are similar to physicians' duplicate prescription pads. These documents summarize the main points of the session, homework and next steps, and self-care ideas.

Ivana and a Narrative Approach

The following is a brief excerpt of a narrative therapy conversation. The therapist began with externalizing the problem. Through the lens of a narrative therapist, the person is not the problem; the problem is the problem. A person's relationship with the problem is the matter of interest. Externalization, in a narrative therapeutic sense, refers to the distancing position taken in relation to the problem (White, 1989). As the session evolved Ivana was invited, via relative influence questioning, to help separate her life and relationships from the presenting problem.

Narrative Therapist: Hello, Ivana. How might I help you today?

Ivana: My anxiety is out of control. I have to get a grip.

Narrative Therapist: Are *you* saying anxiety has wrestled away your grip; does anxiety not have the grip?

Ivana: Yes, it's a bad day. I have pain in my eye, a wicked headache. I can't self-soothe. I need help to ride it through today.

Narrative Therapist: You have been able to self-soothe and ride through it before but today anxiety has taken charge; do I have this right?

Ivana: Anxiety is totally in charge today.

Narrative Therapist: And when anxiety is totally in charge, are there differences in your life?

Ivana: Yes, I'm not able to do the things I want to do.

Narrative Therapist: Are you saying that anxiety steals your pleasure? Would that be a fitting statement or is it too broad?

Ivana: It is not too broad. I can't ride my motorcycle when anxiety is in charge; I can't focus on my reading or writing. I'm irritable, cranky, you know?

Narrative Therapist: It sounds as though anxiety might portray you as a different person than you see yourself being.

Ivana: Yes. Anxiety portrays me as jumpy, not confident, maybe even lazy. That's not me.

Narrative Therapist: Has there been a time when you have refused to allow anxiety to portray you in this way? Have you ever refused to listen to anxiety and just gone for a motorcycle ride or read a book or written your thesis?

Ivana: Maybe once or twice. I'm not sure.

Narrative Therapist: Really! Are you able to think back and tell me more about a time? What did you do? How did you do what you did?

Ivana went on to explain how she gathered every bit of personal agency she could, refused to accept anxiety's invitation to make way for fretting, hopped on her motorcycle and headed for the mountains. She was able to appreciate this unique outcome and thought she might be able to recreate the outcome again. At the end of the session the therapist offered to read Ivana a healing story entitled "The Seedling" from a book by Lee Wallas (1985).

The story reflected the resilience of a tiny, neglected plant that matured into a healthy, flowering beauty because of its strong root system. Ivana expressed appreciation for the metaphorical relevance to her situation.

Conclusion

> All therapists operate according to certain beliefs or assumptions about what facilitates positive outcomes.
>
> (Ogles, Anderson, & Lunnen, 1999, p. 202)

Our worldviews draw us to particular therapeutic models. While we gravitate towards therapeutic approaches that make the most sense to each of us, we are unified by important overarching beliefs. We believe that change can be facilitated in one session. We believe that a client's engagement with the therapeutic service matters more than a specific model of therapy. "Effective therapy provides a safe setting, information and skills and an extended 'workspace' for thinking through problems and experimenting with potential solutions" (Hubble, Duncan & Miller, 1999, p. 14). This is the case, regardless of the therapeutic model. A wise colleague once said about single-session therapy: "Find out what they want, give them what they want, and give them more of what they want" (Maureen Osis, 2006, personal communication). We may look through different therapy lenses but our aim is to engage well with the people who consult us in SSWI, and hearing their wishes is the center of our practice.

References

Beck, A.T. (1964). Thinking and depression: II. Theory and therapy. *Archives of General Psychiatry, 10*, 561–571.

Beck, J.S. (1995). *Cognitive therapy: Basics and beyond.* New York: Guilford Press.

Bertolino, B. & O'Hanlon, B. (2002). *Collaborative, competency-based counseling and therapy.* Needham Heights, MA: Allyn & Bacon.

Bond F.W. & Dryden W. (2002). *Handbook of brief cognitive behavior therapy.* Chichester, West Sussex, England: Wiley.

De Jong, P. & Berg, I.K. (1998). *Interviewing for solutions.* Pacific Grove, CA: Brooks/Cole.

de Shazer, S. (1988). *Clues: Investigating solutions in brief therapy.* New York: Norton.

Dobson, K.S. (2001). *Handbook of cognitive-behavioral therapies* (2nd ed.). New York: Guilford Press.

Dryden, W. (2016). *Single session integrated cognitive behaviour therapy (SSI-CBT): Distinctive features.* New York: Routledge.

Ellis, A. (1962). *Reason and emotion in psychotherapy.* New York: Lyle Stuart.

Ellis, A. & Joffe, D. (2002). A study of volunteer clients who experience live sessions of rational emotive behavior therapy in front of a public audience. *Journal of Rational-Emotive and Cognitive-Behavior Therapy, 20*, 151–158.

Freedman, J. & Combs, G. (1996). *Narrative therapy: The social construction of preferred realities.* New York: Norton.

Hoyt, M.F. & Talmon, M. (Eds.) (2014). *Capturing the moment: Single session therapy and walk-in services.* Bethel, CT: Crown House Publishing.

Hubble, M., Duncan, B., & Miller, S. (Eds.) (1999). *The heart and soul of change: What works in therapy.* Washington, DC: APA Books.

Ogles, B.M., Anderson, T., & Lunnen, K.M. (1999). The contribution of models and techniques to therapeutic efficacy: Contradictions between professional trends and clinical research. In M. Hubble, B. Duncan, & S. Miller (Eds.), *The heart and soul of change: What works in therapy* (pp. 201–225). Washington, DC: APA Books.

Pichot, T. & Dolan, Y. (2003). *Solution-focused brief therapy: Its effective use in agency settings.* New York: Haworth Press.

Slive, A. & Bobele M. (Eds.) (2011). *When one hour is all you have: Effective therapy for walk-in clients.* Phoenix, AZ: Zeig, Tucker, & Theisen.

Wallas, L. (1985). *Stories for the third ear: Using hypnotic fables in psychotherapy.* New York: Norton.

White, M. (1989). The externalizing of the problem and the re-authoring of lives and relationships. In *Selected papers* (pp. 5–28). Adelaide, Australia: Dulwich Centre Publications.

White, M. & Epston, D. (1990). *Narrative means to therapeutic ends.* New York: Norton.

13 Working Within the Client's Cultural Context in Single-Session Therapy

Terry Soo-Hoo

Currently in the field of psychotherapy there is much interest in the idea of Single-Session Therapy (Talmon, 1990; Hoyt & Talmon, 2014). During times of economic distress many individuals and families see psychotherapy as low priority, both due to financial issues as well as time constraints. Consequently, when the need for therapy arises it is likely many people will prefer a very cost- and time-efficient approach. Even without managed-care medical systems adding pressure by continuing to restrict the types of psychological services reimbursed as well as the number of sessions deemed reimbursable, some clients simply prefer to be seen for a single visit. Furthermore, many cultural groups view Western psychotherapy (particularly long-term psychotherapy) as something alien to their views of mental-health and illness (Atkinson, et al., 1978; Sue & Sue, 2013). Oftentimes people from these cultures enter therapy reluctantly. Even if they come to therapy for help there is the expectation that treatment will be done quickly, perhaps in one session. Their message is, "Give me something practical that will solve my problems, then I can go back to work." There are also clients that request medication to cure their psychological problems. While medications to treat psychological problems such as depression have made some progress, there are many problems that medications just cannot treat. Subsequently, these clients are surprised to hear that to solve their problems they have to come to therapy for many sessions, perhaps for many months. These are just some of the instances where a Single-Session Therapy (SST) approach might be quite useful. However, as is true with psychotherapy as a whole, the therapist working within a SST model also must work within the client's cultural context or framework. This is especially true due to the time constraints of the model. There really is very little time to cultivate a therapeutic alliance with the client. The therapist must very quickly assess what are the important cultural factors to consider in helping clients find solutions to their presenting problems. This chapter will discuss how working within the client's cultural context is critical in conducting SST. It will focus specifically on working with Asian-American clients—although the general principle of attending to cultural context is applicable across various groups. The example presented demonstrates the importance of understanding a client's view of the family and her role in the family.

Collectivist Cultural View

In the minds of many modern Americans there is an assumption that when a person reaches adulthood he/she moves out of the parent's home. However, with the changing economic difficulties in the past two decades there have been reports of more adults returning home to live with their parents. Unfortunately, both parents and adult children have viewed this as odd and even embarrassing—as if once someone leaves home they should not ever come back? Perhaps it is this notion that guides many psychotherapists to counsel young adult clients struggling with conflicts with their parents to separate from their parents and leave home. It appears that this is a common phenomenon. However, many clients have reported that this guiding towards separation from one's parents creates even greater distress and conflict. In fact, many clients, particularly Asian-Americans, have ended therapy prematurely. The reason for this is that many Asian cultures have a different view of connection versus separation from one's family. In fact, many people who come from a collectivist culture are much more likely to value *interdependence* as opposed to *independence.* Thus, it is often not helpful to counsel Asian and Asian-American clients towards individuation and separation from one's family.

An effective therapeutic approach must be able to consider the client's cultural context (Soo-Hoo, 1999). For instance, many Asian cultures have no expectation that the adult child leaves the family. In fact, in traditional Asian cultures such as Chinese, Japanese, Korean, and Vietnamese cultures, the expectation is that the adult son is supposed to stay at home to take care of the rest of the family. Particularly as the parents age, the first-born son is to care for the aging parents. The daughters are to stay home until married. Then, upon marrying, they are to become part of the new groom's family and take care of the "in-laws." Compared to typical European-American cultures, there is less of a notion of becoming a separate person living an independent life away from the family. While it is true that the first-born has more responsibility, it is also true that every member of the family is responsible for every other member. There is a strong sense of interdependence. Even if someone does live separately away from the family there is not that feeling of separateness. One is always a part of the family, regardless of the living arrangements and where that person resides.

Furthermore, even when Asian-American clients become more acculturated to certain aspects of American culture they often continue to believe in the traditional values of diligence, harmony, taking responsibility, respect for authority, emphasis on education, respect for elders, family loyalty, self-discipline, and self-reflection (Lee, 1995). In Western cultures, there is often more of an emphasis on "individual goals" in life. Each adult should have their own goals and this should be separate from family goals. However, it should also be acknowledged that there is great diversity and range of values and behaviors within any particular culture. On the one extreme, there are those who assume that the family should have limited influence on the future life of the adult children; on the other extreme, there are those who believe that the family should dictate how an adult child should live his/her life. There are also those who believe that there should be collaboration, a joint venture. Parents support their children to succeed with emotional and financial support. The level of collaboration is a continuum that varies from family to family. Problems might arise if parents take a totalitarian position and the adult child has no say in how his/her life will be structured and what goals he/she is allowed to pursue. Bowen (1978) would call this *fusion*, and Minuchin (1974) called it *enmeshment*.

The definition of *family enmeshment* was the blurring of boundaries between different family members so that members are over-involved with each other to the detriment of each member and to the family as a whole. However, in the last 30 years it has become increasingly clear that the term *enmeshment* must be understood within a cultural context. Boyd-Franklin (2003) points out that in African-American families the grandmother often plays a huge role, often taking on great burdens and assuming great responsibility and power. She questioned Minuchin's early position that it was important to "get grandmother to step aside." In fact, with feedback from Boyd-Franklin and others, Minuchin modified his position and stated that it was important to "help grandmother to renegotiate her role in the family." This was particularly true when the grandmother needed to allow the young mother in the family to take on more responsibility for raising her children. The point was not to push the grandmother aside so that she had no role to play in the family, but to change the roles that each person played in ways that allowed them to participate in the family more effectively.

If the notion of boundaries and enmeshment is a continuum, then the point that defines where healthy, or workable, family connectedness drifts into unhealthy or problematic enmeshment varies between cultures. Thus, any assessment of this type of family dynamic or process must be conducted within a cultural context.

An Intergenerational Problem

Many young Asian-American clients who live at home often complain that they feel over-controlled by their parents or families. They have difficulty negotiating and resolving differences. This is particularly true when adult children are more acculturated to American culture and parents are more traditional and faithful to the culture of their homeland. They often report to the therapist that they feel controlled, dominated, and stifled without a sense of freedom to make their own decisions and choices. Parents do not allow them to pursue their own career interests. Social activities such as going out with friends and staying out late generate a great deal of conflict. Dating can be a volatile issue between many young Asian-American adults and their parents. Asian parents want to have some control over the dating process to the chagrin of the young Asian-Americans. This is particularly true for Asian-American women. Asian-American women face difficult challenges in the U.S. They have the role of caretakers in the family, so they take on much responsibility; yet, they have lower status then their male counterparts. The first-born daughter has tremendous pressure as mother's assistant and is responsible to take care of the family, especially the younger siblings. This is particularly true when mother is not available (which can be quite often if mother is working long hours and not home). There is usually more concern for the welfare of Asian-American women in the family (particularly concerns about dangers that lurk outside the family) as well as more restrictions (Baruth & Manning, 1999). Furthermore, if the family still needs the first-born daughter's assistance at home, a crisis can develop when the daughter begins to "date" and get serious about a romantic relationship. This can threaten the stability of the family as each family member experiences the possibility of losing the family "caretaker." Conflict can intensify as the daughter struggles with balancing her own individual needs and personal goals with that of her family's needs and goals. In addition, the Asian-American young woman is faced with conflicting cultural values as she is pressured by mainstream American society to become more assertive and to strike out on her own, to become more "independent." Furthermore, racism and prejudice against ethnic minority groups and specifically against Asians in this country further harms the young women's self-image and her struggles to achieve positive self-identity (Fernando, 1984; Kitano and Maki, 1996). Many therapists interpret these complaints as the young Asian-American clients struggling with "individuation and separation" from their families. These clients are seen as having very poor boundaries and being overly enmeshed with their parents and nuclear family. Thus, the therapist typically counsels the Asian-American clients to separate from their parents. The daughters need to develop their own interests and ideas, "to pursue your own dreams." They are often told, "You need to stop worrying about your parents. You should think of yourself."

It is important for a therapist to appreciate the cultural and social-political-economic context in which these issues occur. In fact, Asian-American clients view culturally sensitive counselors as being more credible and culturally competent than less sensitive counselors (Gim, Atkinson, & Kim, 1991; Zhang & Dixon, 2001). This is especially true in a brief therapy setting and even more critical when the therapist has only a single session to find ways to assist these clients.

Theoretical Framework

There has yet to be a unifying theory that defines the field of SST (Hoyt & Talmon, 2014). Therefore, a therapist can best approach SST by having a clear set of concepts about what leads to successful therapy in general. Once the therapist has this set of ideas, then it is possible to apply these principles to working with clients as efficiently as possible with the intention of tailoring the therapy to fit the time frame available. If the client enters therapy with notions that there is limited time (for whatever reason), then the therapist can apply these therapeutic principles to fit these time constraints. The following is a model of therapy, which I call *Strength-Based Multicultural Integrative Therapy*, that can easily be adapted to working within a SST framework (Soo-Hoo, 1999, 2005a, 2005b, 2013). While many of the concepts are drawn from the Mental Research Institute (MRI) model of therapy, this approach also incorporates concepts from other models as well.

(1) Develop a working alliance and working contract

As in most models of therapy, the first step is the development of a working alliance with the client. All the principles of good therapy apply here, such as empathy, positive regard, respect, and so on. This also involves engaging the client to allow the therapist to enter his/her world, particularly aspects of that world that are related to the presenting problem. Duncan, Miller, Wampold, and Hubble (2009) found that as much as 30% of the variance in successful treatment outcomes in therapy can be attributed to the positive therapeutic relationship between therapist and client.

(2) Identify the problem

Engage the clients to tell their stories that are related to the presenting problem. The task here is to identify and define a problem the client can agree to work on and try to resolve. The problem needs to be highly focused and specific. Vague, unfocused problems are extremely difficult to solve. It should also be defined in a here-and-now context with the expectation that the outcome or resolution of the problem can be clearly observed or measured.

(3) Identify the client's perception of the problem

It is important to understand how the client views the problem. This involves understanding aspects of the client's cultural background, belief system, value system, language, and other factors that influence how the client views the problem. This is also called the client's *frame of reference* (Soo-Hoo, 1999). It is important to *acknowledge* and *validate* that the client's story is *heard* and *understood*. The therapist listens to what has special meaning. Milton Erickson (Rossi & Ryan, 1985) proposed that the therapist focus on what the client presents rather than defining the problem from the therapist's perspective. This is particularly important since it is the client's perceptions of the problem situation that determines how he/she will behave toward the problems. The therapist *enters the client's world* by understanding these perceptions and what they mean. It is important to assess which *client* perceptions block effective solutions to the problem.

(4) Identify what solutions have been attempted

This step focuses on what the clients have tried in their attempts to solve the problem. There is an exploration of what has "worked" to some degree and what has definitely "not worked." A basic tenet of the MRI interactional-strategic approach (Watzlawick, et al., 1974; Fisch, et al., 1982; Fisch & Schlanger, 1999) is that *continued application of attempted solutions that are ineffective often compounds the problem and thwarts new, more effective solutions.* It is important to *encourage* the continuation of behaviors or solutions that have worked and *discourage* behaviors or solutions that do not work. This is referred to as "breaking the problem cycle" or "interactional cycle" that perpetuates the problem. Problems do not occur inside just one person. They occur because of the way key people view these problems then interact with other key people around these problems.

(5) Activate the client's strengths

It is very common for a client to enter therapy with feelings of being overwhelmed, exhausted, powerless, helpless, hopeless, and a sense of incompetence partly due to the inability to solve the presenting problem. Before the client is ready to take on new ideas about new ways to approach the problem, the therapist needs to help her get in touch with her strengths and resources. While Duncan, Miller, Wampold, and Hubble (2009) found that 30% of the variance on treatment outcome can be attributed to the "positive relationship" between client and therapist, they also found that 40% was related to "client factors." These client factors consist of the client's *strengths and resources* that are brought to therapy along with the client's *motivation*. When the therapist is able to assist the clients to bring out her *strengths and resources* and *motivations*, mastery over the presenting problem is also activated and enhanced. The goal is to help the client feel, "I know I am a *good* and *strong* person and with the right kind of help, I know I have the ability to solve this problem!"

(6) Shifting client's perception of the problem

Once the therapist understands the client's *frame of reference* or the meaning she is attributing to the problem situation, the therapist also needs to determine which elements of this frame of reference are rigidly held and unshakable and which elements might be open to possible shifting in perception. The presenting problem is embedded in the ways the client perceives the problem situation and subsequently interacts with others in the situation. This ineffective interactional pattern keeps the problem from being resolved (Fisch, et al., 1982). Thus, the goal is to assist the client to adopt new ways to view herself and the problem situation. This new *framing* (or *reframing*) of the problem must both fit the client's culture, belief system, and value system *and* provide a cognitive shift in her perceptions of the problem. These shifts are designed to allow the client to view the problems in new and more productive ways, subsequently allowing for more effective solutions (Soo-Hoo, 1999, 2005a, 2005b). In this step, a client's strengths and weaknesses are also assessed with the intention of drawing on the strengths to overcome the weaknesses.

(7) Generate new solutions to the problem

Having entered the client's world in previous steps, the therapist subsequently works within that world to explore new solutions. Building on the shift in perception, the therapist collaborates with the client to generate new behaviors or approaches to the problem that will represent a significant change in direction from the ineffective solutions that have been tried before. The goal is not simply to stop those solutions that are not working, but to generate new solutions that are in a different direction or category. This is often referred to as the "180 degree" turn or *second-order change*, which will free the client from the *problem cycle* (Watzlawick, et al., 1974). The focus is on small steps, which will build to larger steps. Once again, any new solution must fit within the client's cultural context (Soo-Hoo, 1999, 2005a, 2005b).

The following case example provides a detailed description of how to apply this model in a SST format by working effectively within a client's cultural context.

Case Example: The Young Caretaker

Mai was a 26-year-old woman who was born in Vietnam of Vietnamese parents. She was 5 years old when the family immigrated to the United States. She came to therapy stating that she had rather negative ideas about therapy. Her first experience with a therapist three months earlier was not helpful and left her feeling more distressed. She did not return to that therapist for a second session. Mai explained that the therapist did not understand her culture and made suggestions that "really turned me off!" So, she wanted to try an Asian-American therapist, hoping for better results, and she sought an appointment with me. She was referred to me by a Chinese-American social worker who had worked with Mai's father. The social worker explained to Mai that she might benefit from working with a Chinese-American psychologist who had a lot of experience with many different Asian-American clients.

As I have written elsewhere (Soo-Hoo, 2013), I was born in Hong Kong and moved to the U.S. when I was age 6; after working in direct clinical services for many years I am now a psychology professor at a university in Northern California. One might wonder if there is a specific advantage for a Chinese-American therapist in working with a Vietnamese-American client? While there are differences in terms of language, culture and history in the United States, etc. both Chinese and Vietnamese culture share similar patterns (Sue & Sue, 2013; Lee, 1997). The greatest commonality is that both cultures are very collectivistic. In addition, both Vietnamese and Chinese cultures follow family patterns and values that can be closely tied to traditional Confucian values. These cultural similarities allow a Chinese-American therapist to demonstrate multicultural competence by addressing the cultural beliefs of Vietnamese clients. Wang and Kim (2010) found that this ability was viewed by clients as a therapist being more competent. Asian-American therapists (Chinese-American, Japanese-American, Korean-American, Vietnamese-American) were also found to be effective in helping Asian-American clients develop culturally appropriate strategies to cope with their problems (Sue, 1981).

Mai was in crisis and wanted something concrete to do to solve her problem as soon as possible. She felt she could not continue the way things had been going. She also stated that she had very little time and it was very difficult even to come to the first appointment. It was clear she was receptive to some immediate assistance and did not know if there would be future sessions. I expressed to her that in many instances there is much that can be accomplished in one meeting and that we could explore her situation and see what we could come up with to help her.

Her main complaint was her feelings of being overwhelmed at home. She was responsible for taking care of her 60-year-old father. She described her father as having "post traumatic stress" from many hardships and crisis situations he endured during the Vietnam War. He was a wealthy businessman in Vietnam, but he had lost everything to the communists and was imprisoned for a short period. His spirit was broken—the father would say, "I left everything in Vietnam and there is nothing for me anymore." As a result, her father was clinically depressed and refused to take his antidepressant medication or to get further treatment. He had high blood pressure but refused to take his high blood pressure medication or to eat a healthy diet. He was quite isolated and stayed at home with very little social contact. Mai reported she *needed to* take care of all his needs and also to keep him company. He was refusing to even come downstairs to socialize with anyone. This isolation furthered his depression. Mai had to take his meals to his room upstairs. She worried that he would waste away soon unless she did something to bring him out of his depression. However, nothing she did worked. Furthermore, despite his depression he was still very controlling of her life. Even though she tried to be a good obedient Vietnamese daughter, he still criticized much of what she did. She had just developed a relationship with a "boyfriend" and the father had escalated his criticism and hostility towards her because of that. He was totally against this boyfriend even though, according to Mai, "the boyfriend is a very nice guy." Mai suspected the father was threatened by the prospect that this boyfriend would take her away from him and her family. Mai's mother was also against the boyfriend. Mai felt extremely responsible in the role of caretaker for her family, which was made more intense because her mother and the three other younger siblings had given up on the father. The eldest son was married and had a 2-year-old daughter and was living in his own home. Two younger sons lived at home and attended a local community college. Mother was working long hours and had limited emotional energy to devote to caring for her husband. The rest of the family basically ignored her father and expected Mai to take care of him. He vented his frustrations and anger on his family but on her particularly because she tried to help him and so spent a lot more time with him, trying to nurse her father back to health by taking care of his every need. All the pressure and distress were taking a heavy toll on her. Mai was attending graduate school at the local university, but she was having trouble focusing and concentrating at school and was having difficulty sleeping at night. She felt powerless and helpless; no matter what she did, nothing seemed to work.

The previous therapist had told her that she was over-involved with her family. He advised her that she needed to individuate and separate from her family, particularly her father. He said she could not take care of her father for the rest of his life that she had to think of her own life! She told the therapist she did not want to abandon her father or her family. She explained that her father would die if she was not there to take care of him. In fact, her entire family, mother and siblings, would not survive if she only thought of herself. Since she was the eldest daughter it was her responsibility to take care of the family, particularly since mother was too overwhelmed with work.

The following sections describes how the model of therapy outlined earlier could, with cultural awareness, be applied effectively in this situation.

Problem Cycle

The *problem cycle* or *interactional cycle* revolved around Mai's attempts to rescue her father from his depression. These "*attempted solutions* that do not work," as the MRI approach would call them, stemmed from her sense of her role in the family as the family caretaker. The problem was that the more she tried to rescue him by doing things for him the more incompetent and dependent he became. For instance, by taking meals to his room he got the message that he did not have to do anything for himself, not even come downstairs to eat in the dining room; the daughter will take care of his every need. Yet the previous therapist's suggestion that she separate from him and think of her own needs, perhaps even leaving home, was seen by Mai as abandoning her father and condemning him to a slow, agonizing death.

Develop the Therapeutic Alliance by Entering the Client's World

The first task was to engage Mai to tell her story about what it had been like to be so responsible for her family. The therapist acknowledged and validated how overwhelmed she felt. It must have been very frustrating to work so hard to take care of everyone in the family! But no one seemed to appreciate her efforts! She became very emotional and stated that part of her wanted to just leave, but she knew she would never be able to live with herself if something bad happened after she left. I entered her cultural world by acknowledging how she was very faithful to her cultural values. I reflected that she was a very dutiful daughter and she must have really loved her father. She was very devoted to helping him. In many ways she had sacrificed so much of her own life to take care of him. She replied that no one knew how much she cared and how much she had done to try to help him—but she was exhausted and overwhelmed. She felt trapped with no way out.

Activate Strengths

I focused on how Mai had been so strong and resilient and managed to hold the family together through many crisis situations. How had she managed to "keep herself together" during all these difficult times? It was amazing how much she did for everyone in the family! Despite all this she had managed to go to graduate school! Where did she get her inner strength? She replied that her loving and caring for her family kept her going. She had always been a strong and resilient person. I also asked about how she managed to get into graduate school despite all the pressure and distress. And how did she manage to find a great boyfriend who was very supportive of her? She stated that she wished she could spend more time with him. Also, she exercised at the gym, which helped a lot. She began to appear more focused and calmer as the conversation continued about her strengths and all that she had achieved over the years.

Changing Perceptions

Mai's *frame of reference* or perception of the problem situation was "My father needs me to take care of him" and "He will die if I do not do that!" This was a strongly held frame, and the previous therapist was unsuccessful in prying her away from this belief. This frame was deeply rooted in her culture, as well as in her family experience. So my task was not to pry her away from this belief by telling her she needed to take care of herself and leave her father. For her to be open to a different approach to this problem it was important for me to help her to develop a new view of her role. But this new view must have fit within her cultural context.

Changing View of Her Role

Since Mai was not going to give up her role as caretaker, it was more helpful to ask her, "How can you be *more effective in caring for your father*?" Her efforts to help him thus far had been unsuccessful and only seemed to make things worse. The more she took care of him, such taking meals to his room, the more he became helpless and dependent.

Changing View of Her Father

I explored with the client how her father was suffering from "trauma." Trauma is an injury to the mind, body, and spirit. Western psychological approaches only treat the mind, and it had not been very effective with her father. What I suggested was for Mai to help her father rebuild and strengthen his mind, body, and spirit. She readily agreed with this. When she did things for him that he could do for himself she reinforced the idea that he was too weak to do even the smallest things. His mind, body, and spirit were further weakened. Therefore, what father needed most was for her to help him become stronger and take more care of himself. But this needed to happen in very small steps.

Strengthening the Body

Since the daughter was very involved in "physical fitness" (exercise and light weightlifting), I asked if she had heard the term *muscle atrophy*. "Muscles deteriorate over time without exercise." If her father did not even come downstairs for meals his leg muscles would wither and die. "When you lift weights have you ever thought of asking someone to come over to lift your weights for you?" She laughed and said that would be silly! I agreed: "So your father needs to rebuild and strengthen his muscles by lifting his own weights!"

Strengthening the Mind

Traumatized people are stuck in a cycle of negativity. They are constantly saying negative message about themselves such as "I cannot do anything!", "I am helpless and hopeless!", "I am useless!", "No one cares about me!" etc. The key to helping her father strengthen his mind, I explained, was to counter these messages. I asked Mai to think about, "How can you send messages to him about how he is a good person, strong, and competent? People care about him and love him." I clarified, "However, these messages need to be not only through words but also through behavior and actions. What behaviors can you engage in to communicate these messages to him?" I also cautioned: "When he is ready he can talk about his successful business. However, he may not be ready initially."

Strengthen the Spirit

Pressuring her father to take care of himself would not work, I explained to Mai. "His traumatized spirit is still afraid and does not believe in himself. That part of him will put pressure on you to keep taking over for him and treat him like a child. You need to be strong for him. You need to resist this pressure to take over for him and to 'baby' him! Think of ways to activate his spirit by appealing to his love and caring for his family. His family needs him!"

The "180 Degree Turn" in Solutions

One way Mai could activate her father's strength was by becoming less available, but not in a rejecting, harsh, or hostile way, but in a caring way. The first step would be to help him come out of his room more often, to reduce his isolation. Since lecturing him, verbally criticizing, and chastising him for not coming down stairs to eat did not work, it was best to take a very different approach. "The very first step would be to cook each meal with very strong fragrances. Then open all the doors to his room so that the fragrances and wonderful smells of the food will be sure to arrive in his room. Then the family is to wait in the downstairs dinner table. It might take time but eventually he will have difficulty resisting the smells and his hunger will take over. When he finally comes downstairs to eat his meal everyone is to not be surprised but go about their business as if his presence was perfectly normal and expected."

Another key was to change his role, to appeal to the strong father inside of him. "Can you convey to your father that you are not as strong as the family thinks? In fact, you need his help much more then he realizes. Convey to him that he can take care of himself and others more not by using words but by behavior. You are only now realizing that you need a father's guidance and reassurance."

Changing the Interactional Cycle

To help interrupt the cycle I elaborated, "However, he might continue to send controlling messages to you. He might say you never listen to what he says. 'I told you that it was a bad idea to get involved with that boyfriend.' His trauma is affecting his judgment. Furthermore, he is entitled to his more traditional beliefs. It is important to develop your own judgment. Is your relationship with this boyfriend good for you and in the long run will that be good for the family? It is important *not* to try to defend yourself and argue with your father at this point. Communicate to your father, 'I respect you and appreciate you and know that you care about me. I am still working on finding myself, struggling to find the right path.'" I encouraged Mai to engage her father to share his experiences in Vietnam so they could feel closer. When the time was right, she could say to her father, "I know your life has been filled with tragedy, hardship, and disappointment. I want to learn from your life and draw strength from your experiences. As your daughter, I want to draw on your strength." I explained, "Your father might initially resist talking about his past experiences in Vietnam. However, you can encourage him by expressing your interest in learning more about your family since you were very young and did not know what was happening at the time." Mai actually expressed interest in writing a paper for one of her classes describing her family's journey.

Further Change in Role

Mai was also to encourage her father to spend more time with the eldest son's 2-year-old daughter. The family had previously felt that the father was not to be trusted, and they worried he was not a good influence on the 2-year-old. With some safeguards implemented, Mai was able to work out ways for her father to spend more time with his granddaughter. This would further change his role from "useless withdrawn hermit" who had nothing to offer, to a "loving grandfather" who could provide positive nurturance to his granddaughter.

Case Example Outcome

We met this one time. Mai said that it was "helpful" and did not schedule another appointment. However, she did take notes and wrote down some important ideas to remember them when she went home. One month later, Mai called. She reported a remarkable transformation. She had entered therapy feeling overwhelmed, oppressed, helpless, depressed, and anxious. Over the telephone she sounded significantly more confident and self-assured and much more energetic and happy. There was clarity in her thinking and judgment. She reported that her father had significantly improved. He was much more self-sufficient. In fact, he was less isolative and going out to visit friends at least two times a week. I supported her efforts and guided her to follow-up with the next steps that were discussed in the therapy session.

Three months later, she called again to report further progress with her father and their relationship. In fact, he was driving his automobile again and drove one hour to visit a friend. He was also spending much more time babysitting his 2-year-old granddaughter. He really seemed to enjoy this. Her relationship with her father was much more enjoyable and less conflicted. He still tried to exert his fatherly opinions onto her, by telling her what to do. However, she was much better in handling these fatherly assertions. She reported that her friends and family were saying she seemed to be much more outgoing and socially much more pleasant to be with. On the telephone, I continued to support her progress and further assisted her to plan out the next steps to improve her family situation.

At six months post-session, she called for the last time and reported her father's health was also improving and he was taking better care of himself. She was able to talk to her father more and engaged him to talk about his experiences in Vietnam. He had spoken of his imprisonment which, even though it was for just a few days, was quite traumatic. He was terribly mistreated physically and psychologically. He also told stories of his many hardships and disappointments, about how he lost the family business, and how devastating that was for him. He felt like a failure and now he had nothing left. Mai also asked about his successes as well. How did he manage to get his entire family out of Vietnam and to America? What was he proud of? He told her of the good times and how he was really good at his business. What did he want for his children? Did he want his children to grow up like him? Her father cried in telling some of the more poignant stories. These storytelling times became (for both Mai and her father) wonderfully "healing journeys." Her father had started to work part-time helping out his friend who had an import/export business. As her father became more energetic and was bringing home money, her mother was able reduce her work hours. This reduced pressure allowed her to be less stressed and less resentful and therefore more pleasant and positive towards her husband. As a result, the relationship between her mother and her father significantly improved. Mai began to spend more time with her boyfriend and less time at home. She also reported doing much better in her graduate program at the local university.

Summary

The case example in this chapter demonstrates how meeting with a client for a *single-session* can produce very successful results. This therapy lasted two hours, however, rather than the more typical one-hour session. There are situations when a client presents in a particular way that suggests she is ready for serious work on solving a particular problem. These are times when it is important, as Hoyt and Talmon (2014) have put it, to "capture the moment"—in other words, for the therapist to make use of the opportunity to be helpful to someone who is seriously seeking help. Positive changes were set into motion that produced other positive changes.

The case report also describes how to adopt a clinical approach that avoids the pitfalls of guiding young Asian-American clients towards individuation and separation from their parents. Instead the approach assists the young Asian-American client to stay engaged with her parents, but in a more effective manner. In the case presented here, everyone in the family realigned their roles and their boundaries and, as a result, these relationships became more satisfying. This certainly was more compatible with the client's "cultural context." Ultimately, clinical interventions will work only when clients accept them as consistent with their cultural frameworks. There may be situations in which counseling a daughter to leave home actually might be the best strategy. However, in such cases there should be collaboration between the therapist and client to determine what solutions will work within the client's cultural context rather than based upon the therapist's cultural bias.

This example involved an Asian-American therapist working with an Asian-American client. One might raise the question, what if the therapist was of a significantly different cultural background to the client? The key to successful therapy is the ability of the therapist to enter the client's world and be able to work within that unique world as opposed to forcing the client to work within the therapist's world. This means that the therapist sees the world the way the client sees it, particularly related to the presenting problem. This also means to understand that world to a certain degree, especially what has special meaning in that world. In this case, there were a number of key cultural concepts that the therapist needed to consider. One was the understanding that the client viewed family involvements and relationships through the lens of a collectivist culture. The second important point was to listen to the client about what she wanted. On the one hand, she wanted to help her father as a dutiful daughter. On the other hand, she also wanted more independence and freedom to live her own life. It was tempting for me to encourage her to act on one desired goal versus the other without fully understanding the nature of her conflict. Finally, it is important for therapists to pay careful attention to how clients react to therapeutic interventions. The previous therapist had suggested that she was over-involved with her father and needed to individuate so she could focus more on her own life. Although he was well-intentioned, he ignored the cultural nuances of the situation. However, the challenge for therapists is to be able to gauge the client's reactions to such interventions. This first therapist could have recognized that the intervention was not being received in a positive way and could have reassessed his clinical approach. A culturally competent therapist is able to be flexible and adaptable in finding ways to assist clients that are consistent within their cultural context.

References

Atkinson, D.R., Maruyama, M., & Matsui, S. (1978). The effects of counselor race and counseling approach on Asian Americans' perceptions of counselor credibility and utility. *Journal of Counseling Psychology, 25*, 76–83.

Baruth, L.G. & Mannings, M.L. (1999). *Multicultural counseling and psychotherapy: A lifespan perspective* (2nd ed.). Upper Saddle River, NJ: Prentice-Hall.

Bowen, M. (1978). *Family therapy in clinical practice.* New York: Jason Aronson.

Boyd-Franklin, N. (2003). *Black families in therapy: A multisystems approach* (2nd ed.). New York: Guilford Press.

Duncan, B.L., Miller, S.D., Wampold, B., & Hubble, M. (2009). *The heart and soul of change: Delivering what works in therapy* (2nd ed.). Washington, DC: American Psychological Association.

Fernando, S. (1984). Racism as a cause of depression. *International Journal of Social Psychiatry, 30*(1–2), 41–49.

Fisch, R. & Schlanger, K. (1999). *Brief therapy with intimidating cases: Changing the unchangeable.* New York: Wiley.

Fisch, R., Weakland, J.H., & Segal, L. (1982). *The tactics of change: Doing therapy briefly.* San Francisco: Jossey-Bass.

Gim, R.H., Atkinson, D.R., & Kim, S.J. (1991). Asian-American acculturation, counselor ethnicity and cultural sensitivity, and ratings of counselors. *Journal of Counseling Psychology, 38*, 57–62.

Hoyt, M.F. & Talmon, M. (Eds.) (2014). *Capturing the moment: Single session therapy and walk-in services.* Bethel, CT: Crown House Publishing.

Hsu, F.L.K. (1970). *American and Chinese.* Garden City, NY: Doubleday.

Kitano, H.L. (1985). *Race relations.* Englewood Cliffs, NJ: Prentice-Hall.

Kitano, H.L. & Maki, M.T. (1996). Continuity, change and diversity: Counseling Asian Americans. In P.B. Pedersen, J.G. Draguns, W.J. Loner, & J.E. Trimble (Eds.), *Counseling across cultures* (pp. 124–146). London: Sage.

Lee, E. (Ed.) (1997). *Working with Asian Americans: A guide for clinicians.* New York: Guilford Press.

Lee, F.Y. (1995). Asian parents as partners. *Young Children, 50*(3), 4–8.

McGoldrick, M., Preto, N. G., & Carter, B. (2016). *The expanding family life cycle: Individual, family, and social perspectives* (5th ed.). Boston: Pearson.

Minuchin, S. (1974). *Families and family therapy.* Cambridge, MA: Harvard University Press.

Rossi, E.L. & Ryan, M. O. (1985). *Life reframing in hypnosis: The seminars, workshops, and lectures of Milton H. Erickson.* New York: Irvington.

Soo-Hoo, T. (1998). Applying frame of reference and reframing techniques to improve school consultation in multicultural settings. *Journal of Educational and Psychological Consultation, 9*(4), 325–345.

Soo-Hoo, T. (1999). Brief strategic family therapy with Chinese Americans. *American Journal of Family Therapy, 27*, 163–179.

Soo-Hoo, T. (2005a). Transforming power struggles through shifts in perception in marital therapy. *Journal of Family Psychotherapy, 16*(3), 19–38.

Soo-Hoo, T. (2005b). Working within the cultural context of Chinese American families. *Journal of Family Psychotherapy, 16*(4), 45–63.

Soo-Hoo, T. (2013). In search of the spirit: A therapist's journey. In M.F. Hoyt (Ed.), *Therapist stories of inspiration, passion, and renewal: What's love got to do with it?* (pp. 263–276). New York: Routledge.

Sue, D.W. (1981). Evaluating process variables in cross-cultural counseling and psychotherapy. In A.J. Marsell & P.B. Pedersen (Eds.), *Cross-cultural counseling and psychotherapy*. New York: Pergamon.

Sue, D.W. & Sue, D. (2013). *Counseling the culturally diverse: Theory and practice* (6th ed.). Hoboken, NJ: Wiley.

Sue, S., McKinney, H., Allen, D., & Hall, J. (1974). Delivery of community health services to Black and White Clients. *Journal of Counseling Psychology, 42*, 794–801.

Talmon, M. (1990). *Single session therapy: Maximizing the effects of the first (and often only) therapeutic encounter*. San Francisco: Jossey-Bass.

Wang, S. & Kim, B.S.K. (2010). Therapist multicultural competence, Asian American participants' cultural values, and counseling process. *Journal of Counseling Psychology, 57*, 394–401.

Watzlawick, P., Beavin, J.H., & Jackson, D.D. (1967). *Pragmatics of human communication: A study of interactional patterns, pathologies, and paradoxes.* New York: Norton.

Watzlawick, P., Weakland, J., & Fisch, R. (1974). *Change: Principles of problem formation and problem resolution*. New York: Norton.

Weakland, J.H., Fisch, R., & Bodin, A.M. (1971). Brief therapy: Focused problem resolution. *Family Process, 13*, 141–168.

Zhang, N. & Dixon, D.N. (2001). Multiculturally responsive counseling: Effects on Asian students' ratings of counsellors. *Journal of Multicultural Counseling and Development, 29*, 253–262.

14 "Coming In for Tune-Ups"

A Family's Experience of Episodic Long-Term Single-Session Therapy at the Bouverie Centre, Melbourne[1]

Karen Story

> My desire is not to see everyone for one session; my desire is to see everyone for one full moment, as long as that takes.
>
> (Robert Rosenbaum, *The First Session in Brief Therapy*, in Hoyt, et al., 1992, p. 80)

> Psychotherapy is not long or short; to view it this way sets up a false dichotomy. Psychotherapy depends instead on "good moments" where something profound shifts for a client. All the rest is preparation and consolidation . . . Because we feel psychotherapy needs to focus more on these critical incidents of change, we no longer talk of "single-session therapy" but prefer, instead, to examine "therapy moment by moment."
>
> (Robert Rosenbaum, "Psychotherapy is Not Short or Long," in *Monitor on Psychology*, 2008, p. 8)

This chapter examines one family's experience of Single-Session Therapy (SST) in a context where participants were being challenged by complex and multiple needs (Keene, 2001). The use of a single-session approach encouraged resilience and adaptation—qualities that were essential if this family was to manage the difficulties which arose as a result of the brain damage suffered by one of the parents. A form of single-session contact, one that was tailored to meet client needs as they evolved over several years, was recommended to the family, presented later in the chapter, and normalized in the following way: "It makes sense, and it really is OK, for some, or all of you, to drop in for occasional 'tune-ups.'"

Providing irregular, family-initiated contact makes sense: such a pattern of service provision is designed to be sensitive to the evolving nature of a family's developmental demands and responsive to personal and family crises. The focus of this chapter examines whether e*pisodic, long-term Single-Session Therapy* can be useful for a diverse range of long-term complex "conditions" including Acquired Brain Injury (ABI).

The family who is at the center of the current case discussion—the Anderson family—reported that *they believed* the long-term single-session approach was one that addressed emerging difficulties in a timely manner and in a way which prevented more serious problems from developing. The Andersons' discussion of the impact of intermittent therapy on their confidence and sense of capability was recorded, and parts of the transcript from the DVD material are included in what follows. In building upon key texts that privilege the consumer's perspective (Mayer & Timms, 1969 Maluccio, 1979), we dedicate this case study to honoring the experience of the family who participated in the therapy process.

The case study focuses on three key questions:

- Do persistent problems necessarily require long-term (continuous) therapeutic interventions?
- Do families who have such difficulties actually need or want long-term (continuous) therapy?
- Can moment-by-moment therapy, with each session discrete and complete in itself, be meaningful and useful for families and individuals with apparently intractable conditions such as ABI?

The Context of Practice

The ABI team was established in 1983. Funded (since 2000) by Victoria's Department of Human Services: Disability Services to provide a specialized family therapy service for families where a member has sustained an ABI, the team is located within a state-based unit—The Bouverie Centre, a public provider of family therapy, academic training, and short-course professional development. Over its 33-year history, despite the team's changing personnel, the ABI team has maintained a leading role in theorizing, researching, and providing services (Furlong, et al., 1991; Perlesz, et al., 1992; Charles, et al., 2007; Charles & Butera-Prinzi, 2008; Butera-Prinzi, et al., 2010 Butera-Prinzi, et al., 2014).

SST, introduced to the Bouverie Centre in 1994 and implemented by the ABI team in 2005, has become a routine part of families' engagement with the ABI service. SST also informs the team's approach to longer-term work that is undertaken with some families. That is, for some families, one session is enough; for other families, attendance is long-term, but episodic, at times over many years. This latter practice may involve focused work that was identified in the initial session, or it may address unidentified issues that emerge over time or as the family passes through various developmental stages.

Initially, all families are seen for a consultation of 1.5 to 2 hours. This consultation is structured to follow an established SST intake procedure (Young & Rycroft, 1997). The initial session uses a team approach, often utilizing a one-way screen. Pre-session questionnaires are sent out prior to an initial intake meeting. This material is designed to (1) engage each family member, and (2) to define what the family wishes to ultimately achieve in the session if it is to be successful in reaching its goals. Consistent with SST practice, the sessions were organized around these questions:

- What is the main issue to address today?
- What is the second biggest issue?
- The context question: Are there other difficulties you are coping with now?
- A version of the "magic wand" question: If therapy was successful, what would you and your family be doing differently?

At the end of sessions, individuals and families are always asked: "What is one thing/the main thing you will take away from today's session?" This may be something the therapist or one of the family members has said or a personal revelation.

These questions are either explicitly asked of the family or may structure the therapist's thinking and questioning at the start of, during, and at the end of the session. Therapeutic input will be determined by the answer to this question. Depending on the family's response, "one-off" input has been offered such as has been described in a previous paper (Butera-Prinzi, et al., 2014) detailing how the team has integrated family therapy and group work (F2f link-up program), using the *Tree of Life* (Ncube, 2006; Denborough, 2008)—a half-day, multi-family experience.

Families can directly self-refer to the team, or are referred by outside professionals including rehabilitation staff, counselors, neuropsychologists, social workers, case managers, or general medical practitioners (GPs). As well as family therapy, the team provides consultation and training to professionals in the acute, rehabilitation, and community sectors in the ABI field. With practice-based research, the team has consulted broadly, published their work, and has continually reviewed and re-modeled its approach to practice. The team currently consists of myself, Franca Butera-Prinzi (team manager), and Nella Charles, who have both been part of the team for over 15 years.

Although the Bouverie Centre introduced SST in 1994, it was not implemented by the ABI team until 2005. Perhaps there was the "view that serious difficulties always require ongoing work" (Young & Rycroft, 1997, p. 20). Assumptions regarding the intensity, complexity and persistence of issues related to ABI, given it is a life-long challenge for the person with ABI and the family, may also have been behind this decision.

Acquired Brain Injury and SST

An ABI is a catastrophic event that changes lives forever, both for the person with the injury and their family members. Changes in cognitive (memory, concentration, planning, organizational skills), physical, emotional, and/or independent functioning profoundly challenge the identity of the affected person and puts extraordinary stress on family relationships. Sequelae of these changes generally persist over the lifespan and families, children, and adolescents with brain-injured parents have significantly more emotional and behavioral problems than the general population (Smiton, 2005). This profile does not immediately seem to fit with the idea of SST.

In our work with a significant number of families we observed that the SST framework appeared to provide flexible, timely, focused, and non-pathologizing points of entry which, in turn, created a climate of safety enabling families to "drop in" on an infrequent basis according to need or when they needed help in navigating key developmental stages or transitions. While long-term therapy had been thought to be the treatment of choice for more serious conditions such as ABI, our observations were that short-term therapies including SST can very useful, especially in addressing emerging difficulties. There is some support for this view in the research literature (Fisher, 1980, p. 389; Perkins, 2006, p. 225). We also observed that the timeliness, flexibility and responsiveness of SST were helpful in preventing the development of the more serious conditions common in vulnerable families with a parental ABI—conditions such as depression, suicidality, anxiety, peer relationship difficulties, school and academic difficulties (including school dropout), feeling different, social isolation, and feeling silenced by the lack of understanding and stigma.

The team found that SST provided a structure within which the various frameworks used by the team could be incorporated, such as the Family Tasks Model (Perlesz, et al., 1992; Charles & Butera-Prinzi, 2008), narrative therapy, solution-focused work, EMDR (Eye Movement Desensitization and Reprocessing), emotion coaching, sibling and family therapy, and group work including Family-to-Family (f2f) link-ups (Butera-Prinzi, et al., 2010). Therapists were able to remain focused on the presenting agenda without becoming problem saturated, while using these other frameworks. This approach maximized the use of families' own resources and promoted resilience. Because the SST approach had been seen as successful by the team, I decided to interview the Anderson family to determine what elements of their experience might benefit other families.

The Anderson Family

The Anderson family attended sessions with the ABI team at the Bouverie Centre over a five-year period at an average of 6.5 times a year in various presenting combinations. Whilst the 32 sessions might be considered long-term therapy, the focus of each session was determined by the client family, and was considered as a stand-alone session by the therapist. Each session addressed different things as determined by individual and family needs. Consistent with SST practice, the sessions were organized around the four main questions shown earlier in this chapter.

When the team first met the Anderson family—John (40), his wife Sue (40), Patrick (14), Abbey (12), and Rosie (9)—we were struck by John's t-shirt, which he had had made, that clearly and accurately stated "Insufficient

Memory." This public flag was a dramatic declaration that signaled John's everyday experience as a result of sustaining a brain injury two years earlier at the age of 38. Whenever John was asked a question about the future or the past, he would simply point to his t-shirt.

John had contracted a flesh-eating bacteria from pathogens entering an uncovered wound in his arm that had attacked his arm and many of his internal organs, leaving permanent damage and a foreshortened life expectancy. The acute onset of his illness was extremely traumatic for the family as well as the horror of witnessing the exposed bone and flesh of the arm and the risk of amputation. The bacterial infection was difficult to contain and was potentially life threatening. He was placed on life support and, unbeknownst to staff, suffered hypoxia and developed an ABI. Sent home alive, but with a permanent physical disability and a misdiagnosis of PTSD, John's ABI was not diagnosed until two years later. John was a "tall, strong-looking man, articulate and good-humored. His profound difficulties were not evident on first appearances, but were profoundly impacting on his life and his family" (Butera-Prinzi, Charles, & Story, 2014, p. 52).

John's experience was as follows:

> Two or three times a day I have the experience of waking up (after walking around the house in a daze) and wondering how did I get here, what am I doing here—on a bad day this can happen up to 7 or 8 times or wondering what I should be doing . . . I get upset and angry but then I remember why. I have a weekly and daily running sheet and phone reminders ... I have a note on the fridge to remind me what year it is. I remember the kids more from 4 years ago.

An exploratory study by O'Neill (2017) noted that: "(i) most clients found SST had been helpful and responsive to their needs and (ii) most respondents did not report being discomforted or discouraged at the prospect that their contact with the service might involve one or two contacts." Consistent with this finding, when John was interviewed about the SST process he reported:

> Because they [the children and Sue] can come [on an as-needed basis] . . . they can vent I suppose (*laughs*), they can find out that there's nothing wrong with how they feel . . . they've got a place where they can . . . remember that it's not normal, and they're not going to feel normal all the time (and that) . . . you sort of forget how to look after yourself. I just don't know really how to look after myself (*laughs*). It helps me to understand the value in what I do . . . Unfair to the kids in particular that they have to support their dad, but I'm still their dad and so I'm still trying to support them as much as I can, but I can't do it, I just can't. It's not that I'm not trying, its insufficient memory, I just can't do it . . . and that's where coming here, the sessions for them become that missing support.

> . . . I have one gammy arm so I'm holding them up with one hand and Bouverie's holding them up with the other.

John's comments indicated that SST being offered on an "as-needs," intermittent basis relieved him of an area of responsibility (for his children's mental health, past memories, and future plans) that he was no longer able to perform. He also valued it as a normalizing experience for him and his family. This, in turn, reduced his anxiety and agitation, resulting in less conflict and tension at home. At the same time, this also allowed him to be the best father he could be under his changed circumstances. This was confirmed by 16-year-old Patrick:

Karen: (therapist/author)	And what about your Dad, have you noticed anything different as a result of you guys coming (to Bouverie)?
Patrick:	He does seem to function better when we're all functioning well, and having no real problems going on for us, he then works better.

Do Long-Term Problems Require Long-Term Intensive Interventions?

Although the Bouverie Centre had been trialing, adopting, and evaluating SST (Young & Rycroft, 1997) since 1994, in the 1980s and 1990s postmodern thinking was challenging traditional therapeutic practices and assumptions (Luepnitz, 1988; Amundson, 1996; Bubenzer, et al., 1994; Sanders, 1998). Local pressures around funding and scarce resources raised managerial concerns about which therapies could maximize efficiency and efficacy. At that time, SST was being experimented with internationally, as were other brief and time-limited psychotherapeutic options (e.g., Fisher, 1980). Objections to SST (and brief therapies more generally) included the possibility that hard-won knowledge, expertise, and therapies might have to be given up by their practitioners. Additionally, some thought that "brief therapy . . . is a second-rate treatment, to be offered only when long-term therapy is not available" (Wolberg, 1965; quoted in Fisher, 1980, p. 377; also see Hoyt, 1985).

Since SST's introduction, Bouverie's staff found that "With experience we (became) less preoccupied about trying to accurately assess client suitability for single sessions" (Young & Rycroft, 1997, p. 20). The experience of Bouverie, and later the ABI team, reflected those of Hoyt and Talmon (2014, p. 507) who argued that "severity of complaint and level of distress do not appear to be strong predictors of single-session success."

Before joining the Bouverie staff, I had already found that using a SST approach with child and adolescent clients who presented with long-term mental-health problems had led me and my colleagues towards more transparent, collaborative, and accountable practices. Moreover, we noticed that there was more fresh air and enthusiasm in the therapeutic space and a more strengths-based and client self-determined quality to the work (Diffey, et al., 2004). My own views were that the stress on families is persistent over time, but rather than requiring intensive services, long-term, *intermittent* services could be helpful to some families. The prevailing attitude to the difficulties associated with ABI was the expectation that there will be endemic problems. For example, Ponsford (2012, p. 8) commented:

> TBI (ABI) has a significant impact on caregivers, and on the family as a whole ... [who] provide most ongoing support of a practical, social and emotional nature to the TBI individual, and family interactions are an important determinant of the injured person's psychosocial adjustment. . . . It is vital that the family unit be involved in the rehabilitation process, and have access to supportive counseling and assistance . . . (and as) the adjustment process for families is likely to be lengthy . . . Access to family therapy services should be available to assist families who have difficulty in grieving, or in adjusting roles and expectations of the injured individual within the family following injury. All forms of family support should be available over the lifespan of the person with TBI.

Some practitioners (Cummings, 1990; Cummings and Sayama, 1995; also see Budman, 1990; and Hoyt, 1990, 2000a) were gradually becoming aware of the value of long-term intermittent work. They described "intermittent treatment across the life cycle." Within the context of SST, Battino (2014, p. 405) has referred to this as Sequential Single-Session Therapy (SSST).

Whilst the demands on families where a member has an ABI are likely to be lengthy, even life-long, there is a dilemma. Therapeutic support must be available to families that are already burdened with intense demands on their time and resources. Yes, it is necessary for therapists to acknowledge that there are on-going disability, grief, trauma, and often a lack of appropriate resources, yet the challenge is to be able to tune into the moment, not the chronicity. O'Neill (2017) summarized the history of the debate:

> Despite some debate in the literature about the suitability of SST for all clients, such as those with serious mental-health issues or neurological conditions (Cameron, 2007; Campbell, 2012), SST has been found to be effective with clients with a range of presenting issues such as post-traumatic stress disorder (Ollendick, et al., 2009), child and adolescent mental-health issues (Perkins, 2006, Perkins & Scarlett, 2008) and clients presenting with a range of mental-health and family issues at walk-in mental health clinics (Harper-Jacques et al., 2008). In fact some of the models of SST . . . such as the walk-in model developed in Canada by Arnie Slive and his colleagues (Harper-Jacques, et al., 2008; Slive, et al., 2008), have no formal assessment or exclusion criteria, but rather are focused on assisting any client or family that seeks help whatever their presenting issue.

By giving up tightly held allegiances to particular therapeutic conventions that link the length of therapy with diagnosis, and instead focusing on what the client is asking for, clinicians gain the freedom to be more responsive, effective, and energetic in therapeutic engagement and work. Hoyt (2000b, p. 56) cogently asked, "Whose therapy is it? Whose story is it? Whose life is it?" Families will tell us if we are willing to ask the questions and listen responsively to what they need from us in therapy. They will tell us how they wish to write their stories differently. When the therapist's focus is only on diagnosis and the recommended, clinically-indicated treatment, they can lose sight of what families are telling us they need in-the-moment. What families tell us is that they need help when they need it, but according to their needs and timing, and they are much more motivated when therapy occurs in this way. As Sue (Anderson) says:

> [I] cannot . . . explain adequately how fundamentally important it is that we come to Bouverie, *but also (that) we come on our own timetable.* It's crucial . . . I need to be able to pick up the phone when it's all going pear-shaped, and go, we need to come in for a spot, and then go OK we're good I'll call you ... *We call it at home, going in for a tune-up* . . . Yep, as you take your car in, oh its 50,000 km it's time to take it in for a tune-up . . . Bouverie is coming in for the tune-up. It's checking in with our, you know, our inside voices, are we doing OK, are we handling this OK, is this all still normal?

It is the therapist's challenge to assist families to trust the "inside voice" and respect their right to decide what they need and when they need it, while remaining clinically and ethically responsible.

The therapist's dilemma is often how to decide "Where to begin and what to ask" (the title of Lukas' [1993] assessment handbook), as well as "When is enough, enough?" The clinician may believe that more is needed or something other than what the client has requested is required. However, who should decide what is needed? There are many assessment tools, clinical suggestions, and frameworks (e.g., Lukas, 1993) that, in conjunction with the clinician's training and experience, can provide guidelines regarding focus, frameworks and direction—but in the end, shouldn't it be the family that decides? The emphasis, however, can often be at the discretion of the clinician: this is who provides the expertise and has to co-create, even sometimes drive, the therapeutic encounter. Apparently conflicting therapeutic frameworks, together with advice by colleagues and supervisors to be faithful to one or another therapeutic ideology, can seem to conflict with the differing needs of clients and client groups. In my previous work with very troubled clients, who presented with diverse and often apparently long-term problems, the constant challenge was to find a way to reconcile the immediate needs of the client with the strictures of theory—whether the framework was systemic, psychodynamic, CBT, group work, and so forth. Holding professional expertise alongside the demands of family and individual is both challenging and satisfying.

The SST approach—as applied with these families in a long-term engagement—consists of sessions being offered on an "as-needs," intermittent basis as required over time and as requested by the family or family members. As already suggested, these issues may occur in the context of normal developmental changes such as entry to secondary school or puberty, family crises such as deaths in the family, or individual challenges such as depression. For vulnerable families seen by the ABI team, these normal life challenges have the potential, if not responded to in a timely and appropriate fashion, to completely derail the family or individual. For families, the idea that they can "drop-in" on an as-needs basis, rather than undertaking either long-term therapy or having to re-engage with a service through the traditional intake service, is a relief. Clinical judgment and resources as well as collaboration with the family's request, determines what may be offered.

SST commonly falls into three types that Robert Rosenbaum (2006) has called the *Hops*, *Skips*, and *Jumps* varieties of SST. The hops (single step) involve symptom change resulting in differences in degree, not kind, with a return to "pre-morbid" functioning. Skips (phase of life) involve dealing with a phase-specific problem requiring aids in transition and may involve the client returning at different developmental phase points. Jumps (great steps forward), on the other hand, are transformative resulting in character change and are complete in itself. This concept is useful in helping the clinician and family to determine what is being requested or is required at any stage of therapy.

This idea of long-term therapeutic interventions may seem to beg the question of what is "long-term"? Our work with the Andersons, averaging a session every two months for five years, could be called "long (or continuous), but not intensive" therapy. However, it's "one-at-a-time" with an expectation that there will be more . . . and more . . . over time, as required or requested by families, and at times recommended by their therapists. Therapy may be continuous—weekly, quarterly, intermittent—but the SST focus ensures that each moment is complete in itself. The question can be asked, does this encounter relate to a hop, skip or a jump? In a similar vein, Hoyt (1995, p. 6) has written: "Patients can return for 'serial' or 'distributed' treatment as needed, often focused around developmental issues throughout the life cycle. The therapist–patient relationship may be long-term although frequently abeyant." Similarly, Hoyt (2009, p. 5) has described a component of brief treatment as "Time sensitivity, making the most of each session as well as the idea of intermittent treatment replacing the notion of a once-and-for-all 'cure.'" In our team, we have been fortunate to be able to be responsive to families' requests and needs for different types of interventions over time.

The Andersons' Journey and the Interventions Utilized

"The 'invisible' nature of the brain injury contributes to the sense of isolation, lack of understanding, and lack of validation the family . . . experiences" (Butera-Prinzi, Charles, & Story, 2014). With the Anderson family, this was certainly the case. Because the diagnosis was not made until about two years after the ABI episode, the trauma experienced by John and his family caused by the original injury was greater because they spent almost two years expecting that he would fully recover. An initial misdiagnosis of PTSD over the next two years further confused and distressed John and his family. The family's coming to terms with the permanent effects of an ABI was needlessly delayed by the misdiagnosis.

Each member of the family of five responded individually and differently to the trauma. Over the subsequent four years, Sue, John, Patrick (14 years old at referral), Abbey (12) and Rosie (9) have attended (and are still "dropping in") regularly but infrequently for what Sue has described as their "tune-ups." Sessions, five or six times per year on average after the initial more intense period of time, have been in response to a family or individual issue, or "hops" and "skips."

Different therapeutic theories, strategies and interventions have been appropriate at different points in the course of individual and family contact. The phases are described in text that follows. A team with diverse training and skills, but with a willingness to work together and with flexibility, has been essential to be able to provide the appropriate responses. Teamwork and resource-sharing with other professionals were highly useful, and at times with this family and others can include the need to refer out for specialist services such as psychiatry.

In the early stage post-referral, the team's task to respond to the trauma and distress was paramount. This included family and sibling sessions, ensuring that support networks at home (especially for Sue) and school were in place as well as some focused trauma work (EMDR) for one of the children, and later similarly for John. The next phase focused on addressing the sense of isolation and loss of identity as a result of the ABI, and the need to form a new sense of family and personal identities.

Rosie was a reluctant 9-year-old when she attended the initial SST. When interviewed at age 13, she described her response to three of the various SST-informed interventions with the family:

> I remember the [initial SST] family session was good because I was quite young and I don't think I was as confident talking by myself and we got the whole family problem sorted. The sibling ones was just to help us three with our problems [sibling family therapy sessions]. And then it was nice to meet other people who had gone through the same thing, so we can relate to some other people [F2f].

This last experience Rosie was describing was the Family-to-Family (F2f) Link-Up Program (Butera-Prinzi, et al., 2010) developed by the ABI team wherein families connected with other families having similar experiences for 3–4 hours. This affirming and normalizing experience involved Tree of Life work (Ncube, 2006; Denborough, 2008) with other children, and a concurrent session attended by partners of the person with the ABI. This was followed by a subsequent joint session for parents and the children and adolescents.

The Anderson's experience highlighted the need for agencies and therapists to be responsive to families and individuals at different developmental points in time ("Skips" such as commencing secondary school, adolescence, moving into adulthood):

Sue: We call, well I consider you to be sort of personal life savers actually, the therapy equivalent of the life buoy thrown over . . . and coming here has afforded me the luxury of getting on with it . . . and getting on with my life . . . in those moments where you think I cannot navigate these waters, I don't know what I'm doing, I don't know if I'm actively making it worse . . . [Bouverie sessions have] . . . literally been the lighthouse going, nope, you're going in the right direction, this is normal. It's OK, here's the support.

Karen: So you've actually been noticing your own resources, once you've . . . seen where the lighthouse is?

Sue: Yes . . . the other way I like to describe it is without Bouverie, our troubles are . . . they're on stage and a spotlight is on them and the whole theatre is dark and all I see is the troubles. Bouverie throws up the stage lights, it throws up the house lights, it illuminates the aisles. Yes, my problems are still there on stage, however, there's light everywhere else, there's other things going on. I can't get rid of those but there's not a spotlight on them. We call it at home, going in for a tune-up . . . Puberty happens, death in the family, personal changes and you . . . don't forget, it's still there, but you lose sight of it. You get the spotlight again because the houselights go down. So you need to come back in, get reminded, turn the light switch on . . . Ahhh . . . would you look at that, we've got the whole theatre, it's OK. Problem's still there [the ABI] because we can't get rid of it, but it's that reminder.

Therapists may find that helping families to navigate the waters (or to allow them to see the whole "theater" and not just the spotlighted area of crisis and on-going challenges) can take many forms, but determining what the difficulties of the current waters being navigated are, is essential for them to responsively and helpfully provide assistance. This may happen in a one-off consultation, a Family-to-Family session, or over a series of consultations. Continuing (long-term) therapy may not be wanted or welcomed by such families, as Sue described:

> The thought of on-going therapy, (a) makes my skin crawl and (b) I think would actively harm the process for us. It would be like constantly picking at a scab. And it would feel like we were in trauma all the time. Because you're just at it, and at it, and at it and that's not helpful at all . . . it's been a long-held belief that without Bouverie, we'd have gone under . . .

> *that ability to drop in and out as needed has been so important.* And I think the resilience it gives to myself and the family obviously, but mostly to me, is the ability that I can go, I'm struggling a little, I'll call Bouverie, I've made that choice. I've acknowledged I'm struggling. I've made the choice, I've made the call, I've come, I've tuned up, I can go . . . [to] keep us supporting John . . . that's the really important bit . . . over time, life gets in the way, things happen.

Sue's comment reinforced our belief that SST provides a timely, responsive, and flexible practice that ensured a continued focus on what the Anderson family and its individual members saw as their most pressing need *at a particular point in time*. Partnership and collaborative problem-solving with families was facilitated by this process without becoming problem-saturated. This approach was also inherently hopeful because it made use of family strengths and solutions that could make a difference at that moment. In addition, the team's built-in review mechanism (with the family an integral part of the team) ensured the work remained on track, and didn't drift.

Individuals are affected differently and therefore require different responses. Patrick had been traumatized by his father's ABI, both in terms of the actual physical event and bodily sequelae, along with the psychological trauma and major changes his family's circumstances and dynamics. Now at university and rarely attending therapy sessions, he reflected back on his experiences.

Karen: We haven't needed to touch base with you for some time now. . .

Patrick: Nah, it would be more than a year now . . . two years. I probably would have ended up dropping out of high school . . . if not willingly then just being kicked out for failing.

Karen: And what about the ideas you would have had about yourself and the problem?

Patrick: I would have been very full of self-hatred, this is me, why am I so rubbish, that sort of . . . real bad thoughts. My mental health at this point, we like to joke, around the family that it's just bulletproof and I'm the most functional one now. I've gone from being the least functional to the most functional . . . of all my friends and most of the people I know, I'm in the best mental health and I attribute it entirely to the stuff I've done here . . . and able to drop in whenever I need to is incredibly reassuring in that I know that if I'm doing poorly I can make an appointment, I can come in and work on it . . . and that's incredibly reassuring and comforting.

Sessions for Patrick, in addition to the initial family and sibling sessions, included EMDR for the trauma he had witnessed and experienced, and school liaison and professionals meetings to shore up support for him at school while he processed these issues. (Patrick had had frequent exposure to his father's injury—John's arm had exposed bones and flesh—as he visited hospital almost daily after school. Additionally Patrick had witnessed his father's frequent falls, psychotic episodes when medication changes were made and constantly worried whilst at school that his father would fall and either sustain another ABI or die.)

Sibling sessions helped move him back into the role of sibling, no longer needing to take his father's role (assumed after John's ABI) with his sisters.

Patrick: The main one that sticks out for me is that I've got to stop speaking for my sisters, to either of them when they are arguing . . .

Karen: You really keep an eye out for your sisters, don't you?

Patrick: Yep, someone's got to.

Patrick's comments highlighted firstly that for him this intervention was a "jump (transformative) resulting in character change, but also supports the contention that, if a family is supported, it is likely that the short and long outcomes for the family as well as the person with the ABI are significantly enhanced. This is not just at the acute, rehabilitation, and community stages, but remains relevant into the future when (as Sue puts it) "things get wobbly" or developmental issues (such as puberty or deaths) confront the family. Patrick had stepped into his father's role but it was not helpful to family relationships for him to maintain this permanently.

Whilst a considerable number of interventions were provided, Patrick shared some thoughts on whether he (and individuals and families) wanted or needed long-term therapy:

Karen: So what would the difference have been if you'd been required to commit to . . . regular on-going sessions compared to these more short-term, drop-in type . . . sessions?

Patrick: I would have been much more sour about the idea of showing up to . . . you've got to come for X number of sessions . . . I would've been quite despondent and grumpy about it (shakes head and shoulders). Just all a bit . . . Ahhh (*shakes head and throws hands up*) . . . Ah I just don't think it would have worked very well to be honest . . . Well like I was saying earlier, after coming here at the time that I was doing the single sessions, I was often physically and emotionally pretty wrecked and really fragile for a couple of days. It was like I would always have to have the day off school, be real "glass" [Aussie slang for "fragile/vulnerable"] for three or four days afterwards and if I had recurring weekly sessions I'd be spending most of my time in that state . . . And I don't think that's healthy.

SST enabled Patrick to be engaged fully in the therapy with powerful long-term effects because it was one session at a time. This underlines the effectiveness of SST as an engagement tool especially with adolescents.

A SST/OAAT ("single-session/one-at-a-time"; Slive & Bobele, 2011; Bobele & Slive, 2014) sensibility can also be useful when it comes to the question of the termination of therapy. If carefully elicited, family members have much to say about their own solutions to life's challenges:

Karen: So tell me about the times when you don't need us (*Patrick laughs*) when you are able to find your own solutions without outside assistance?

Patrick: At this point I mostly just sort of shrug and get on with it. You know, sort of, "this too will pass" type mind-frame.

Different family members require different things from us over time. Abbey was clear about why the family had come in the first place:

> It was like, all of us kids were not really coping but we didn't know that at the time. Mum kept going to different places, like we need help is there anywhere we can go, and that was how we found Bouverie . . . It was to help cope with Dad's brain injury and how we were just going to get through it because we were all quite lost, like none of our friends had ever had this happen, no one we really knew had had this happen. We had nothing to build off, we didn't know . . . [Bouverie] helped, like, to build up inner strength so I'm not constantly relying on my therapist, which is what you'd get if you did it weekly . . . without [Bouverie sessions] . . . I actually think I wouldn't be living at home, I would probably be doing very bad things towards my health, especially last year because it was really tough and I did slip into old really bad habits of self-hate and loathing, so yeah, I came here and had the courage to say yeah, "I'm not OK."

Abbey asserted here that being able to contact when she needed to built greater personal resilience in managing her daily challenges.

When Does SST Work and When Doesn't It Work?

It has been important to identify those times when on-going work is required and not "be captured either by the traditional therapeutic ideology that promotes the view that serious difficulties always require on-going work *or* by the idea that single sessions can always replace the role of on-going work" (Young & Rycroft, 1997, p. 20).

When a SST approach was introduced by the ABI team, the aim was to address many of the concerns facing clients, such as the need for timely and responsive support to time-pressured, heavily burdened families, and the ability to reach those rural and regional families unable to receive specialist support locally. Another aim was to "capture the moment"—approximately one-third of our families attend only once. Finally, we also chose to ensure a continued focus in the session on what the family and family members see as their most pressing need at that point in time and to offer a flexible practice that encourages partnership and collaborative problem-solving with families without being problem-*saturated.*

The ABI team discovered that working from moment-to-moment was congruent with the *episodic nature* of families adjusting to life following an ABI. Accordingly, there is a clear purpose in being responsive to the changing profile of needs that arise over the lifecycle and a material benefit in facilitating intermittent contact at critical points for people with ABI and their families.

Despite this, families and individual members struggle at times with this therapeutic work:

Karen: I know you don't really like coming in (*Rosie laughs*) although you really like seeing us . . . but it's not easy for you is it? It's not your favorite way of doing things.

Rosie: It's not my favorite way.

Karen: So is there anything that is not helpful about it?

Rosie: No, I just don't like to come, I know I need to, but I don't like to do it.

Karen: So how do you know you need to do it?

Rosie: Because I'm upset all the time, and then when I come here, I'm less upset.

Rosie indicated here her attendance at sessions was generally related to the "hop" variety. Clinicians often take this stated reluctance as a lack of willingness or readiness to engage; at times, this is interpreted as "resistance." Seen for what it is, there are—necessarily and understandably—mixed feelings. Contact around really tough issues is disturbingly hard work, an engagement that disrupts normal life even if it is judged helpful at a later point.

Just as it is important not to be rigidly wedded to particular therapeutic forms or practices, it is also important to be able to acknowledge when SST is *not* appropriate and to consider provision of on-going (continuous) long-term therapy in whatever form is required. Patrick alluded to his sister's (Abbey's) current difficulties when he said recently: "Although before they both started coming for their own personal sessions, they kinda had . . . hit rock bottom." "Rock bottom" meant a challenge to consider that more was required than could be provided using this framework. Despite Abbey's assertion that SST and Bouverie had "helped to build up inner strength" and her desire not to attend long-term therapy, there had been a return to previous difficulties she had spoken of in this interview, and she revealed that she had recently slipped into her old bad habits.

A SST/OAAT mindset has freed up our practice to be far more flexible, responsive, and effective with families with chronic long-term conditions (also see Rosenberg & McDaniel, 2014). Working moment-by-moment has enabled us to construct a life-long episodic model of care (which Hoyt, 1995, p. 6, refers to as an "intermittent treatment or a 'family practitioner' model") for families adjusting to life following an ABI without clinicians and families becoming overwhelmed and feeling excessively burdened. Equally important has been to know when the SST approach is not appropriate and to use professional judgment when continuous longer-term work may become necessary. By remaining responsive to changing needs over the lifecycle, the benefits of intermittent contact at critical points for people with ABI and their families has been welcomed by families as well as clinicians. As an old English proverb has it:

> One thing at a time and that done well
> Is a very good rule as many can tell.

Note

1 Special thanks to Mark Furlong for his editorial contribution and valuable assistance with this chapter.

References

Amundson, J. (1996). Why pragmatics is probably enough for now. *Family Process, 35*(4), 473–486.

Battino, R. (2014). Expectation: The essence of very brief therapy. In M.F. Hoyt & M. Talmon (Eds.), *Capturing the moment: Single session therapy and walk-in services* (pp. 393–406). Bethel, CT: Crown House.

Bobele, M. & Slive, A. (2014). One session at a time: When you have a whole hour. In M.F. Hoyt & M. Talmon (Eds.), *Capturing the moment: Single session therapy and walk-in services* (pp. 95–119). Bethel, CT: Crown House.

Bubenzer, D.L., West, J.D., & Boughner, S.R. (1994). Michael White and the narrative perspective in therapy. *The Family Journal, 2*(1), 71–83.

Budman, S.H. (1990). The myth of termination in brief therapy: Or, it ain't over till it's over. In J.K Zeig & S.G. Gilligan (Eds.), *Brief therapy: Myths, methods, and metaphors* (pp. 206–218). New York: Brunner/Mazel.

Butera-Prinzi, F., Charles, N., & Story, K. (2014). Narrative family therapy and group work for families living with acquired brain injury. *Australian and New Zealand Journal of Family Therapy, 35*(1), 81–99 (special edition). Also in *The International Journal of Narrative Therapy and Community Work*, 2014, *1*, 51–60.

Butera-Prinzi, F., Charles, N., Heine, K., Rutherford, B., & Lattin, D. (2010). Family to Family link up program: A community-based initiative supporting families caring for someone with an acquired brain injury. *NeuroRehabilitation, 27*(1): 31–47.

Cameron, C. (2007). Single session and walk-in psychotherapy: A descriptive account of the literature. *Counselling and Psychotherapy Research, 7*(4), 245–249.

Campbell, A. (2012). Single-session approaches to therapy: Time to review. *Australian & New Zealand Journal of Family Therapy, 33*(1), 15–26.

Charles, N. & Butera-Prinzi, F. (2008). Acquired brain injury: reconstructing meaning following traumatic grief. *Grief Matters: The Australian Journal of Grief and Bereavement, 11*(2), 64.

Charles, N., Butera-Prinzi, F., & Perlesz, A. (2007). Families living with acquired brain injury: A multiple family group experience. *NeuroRehabilitation, 22*, 61–76.

Cummings, N.A. (1990). Brief intermittent psychotherapy throughout the life cycle. In J.K. Zeig & S.G. Gilligan (Eds.), *Brief therapy: Myths, methods, and metaphors* (pp. 169–184). New York: Brunner/Mazel.

Cummings, N.A. & Sayama, M. (1995). *Focused psychotherapy: A casebook of brief, intermittent psychotherapy throughout the life cycle.* New York: Brunner/Mazel.

Denborough, D. (2008). *Collective narrative practice: Responding to individual, groups and communities who have experienced trauma.* Adelaide, Australia: Dulwich Centre Publications.

Diffey, C., Story, K., & Haslam, R. (2004, September). It's all in the phone call—Single session intervention in CAMHS. Paper presented at the *Australian Family Therapy Conference, QAFT (Queensland Association of Family Therapy. "Getting it Together: Family Therapy Practice for the Future."* Brisbane, Queensland, Australia.

Fisher, S. (1980). The use of time limits in brief psychotherapy: A comparison of six-session, twelve-session, and unlimited treatment with families. *Family Process. 19*(4), 377–392.

Fry, D. (2012). Implementing single session family consultation: A reflective team approach. *Australian and New Zealand Journal of Family Therapy, 33*(1), 1–97.

Furlong, M., Young, J., Perlesz, A., McLachlan, D., & Riess, C. (1991). For family therapists involved in the treatment of chronic and longer-term conditions. *Dulwich Centre Newsletter, 4*, 58–68.

Harper-Jaques, S., McElheran, N., Slive, A., & Leahey, M. (2008). A comparison of two approaches to the delivery of walk-in single session mental health therapy. *Journal of Systemic Therapies, 27*(4), 40–53.

Hoyt, M.F. (1985). Therapist resistances to short-term dynamic psychotherapy. *Journal of the American Academy of Psychoanalysis, 13*, 93–112.

Hoyt, M.F. (1990). On time in brief therapy. In R.A. Wells & V.J. Giannetti (Eds.), *Handbook of the brief psychotherapies* (pp. 115–143). New York: Plenum.

Hoyt, M.F. (1995). *Brief therapy and managed care.* San Francisco: Jossey-Bass.

Hoyt, M.F. (2000a). The last session in brief therapy: How and why to say "when." In *Some stories are better than others: Doing what works in brief therapy and managed care* (pp. 237–261). Philadelphia, PA: Brunner/Mazel.

Hoyt, M.F. (2000b). *Some stories are better than others. Doing what works in brief therapy and managed care.* Philadelphia, PA: Brunner/Mazel.

Hoyt, M.F. (2009). *Brief psychotherapies: Principles and practices.* Phoenix, AZ: Zeig, Tucker, & Theisen.

Hoyt, M.F, Rosenbaum, R., & Talmon, M. (1992). Planned single session psychotherapy. In S.H. Budman, M.F. Hoyt, & S. Friedman (Eds.), *The first session in brief therapy* (pp. 59–86). New York: Guildford Press.

Hoyt, M.F. & Talmon, M. (Eds.) (2014). *Capturing the moment. Single session therapy and walk-in services.* Bethel, CT: Crown House Publishing.

Keene, J. (2001). *Clients with complex needs: Interprofessional practice.* Oxford, England: Blackwell Science.

Luepnitz, D.A. (1988). *The family interpreted: Feminist theory in clinical practice.* New York: Basic Books.

Lukas, S. (1993). *Where to start and what to ask: An assessment handbook.* New York: Norton.

Maluccio, A. (1979). *Learning from clients.* New York: The Free Press.

Mayer, J.E. & Timms, N. (1969). Clash in perspective between worker and client. *Social Casework, 50*(1), 32–40.

Ncube, N. (2006). The Tree of Life project: Using narrative ideas in work with vulnerable children in Southern Africa. *International Journal of Narrative Therapy and Community Work, 1,* 3–16.

Ollendick, T.H., Oest, L.G., Reuterskiold, L., Costa, N., Cederlund, R., Sirbu, C., & Davis, T.E. (2009). One-session treatment of specific phobias in youth: A randomized clinical trial in the United States and Sweden. *Journal of Consulting and Clinical Psychology, 77*(3), 504–516.

O'Neill, I. (2017). What's in a name? Clients' experience of single session therapy. *Journal of Family Therapy, 39*: 63–79. doi:10.1111/1467-6427.12099.

Perkins, R. (2006). The effectiveness of one session of therapy using a single-session therapy approach for children and adolescents with mental health problems. *Psychology and Psychotherapy: Theory, Research and Practice, 79*(2), 215–227.

Perkins, R. & Scarlett, G. (2008). The effectiveness of single session therapy in child and adolescent mental health: Part 2: An 18-month follow-up study. *Psychology and Psychotherapy: Theory, Research and Practice, 81,* 143–156.

Perlesz, A., Furlong, M., & McLachlan, D. (1992). Family work and Acquired Brain Injury. *Australian and New Zealand Journal of Family Therapy, 13*(3), 145–153.

Ponsford, J. (2012, April). Understanding and managing traumatic brain injury. *InPsych, 34*(2), 1–11.

Rosenbaum, R. (2008). Psychotherapy is not short or long. *Monitor on Psychology, 39*(7), 4, 8.

Rosenbaum, R. (2006) Workshop at the Bouverie Centre, August 31. *Continuing Education Workbook, Single Session Work Manual.* The Bouverie Centre and Latrobe University Day 2, p. 6.

Rosenberg, T. & McDaniel, S.H. (2014). Single-session medical family therapy and the patient-centered medical home. In M.F. Hoyt & M. Talmon (Eds.), *Capturing the moment: Single session therapy and walk-in services* (pp. 349–362). Bethel, CT: Crown House Publishing.

Sanders, B. (1998). Why postmodern theory may be a problematic basis for therapeutic practice: a feminist perspective. *Australian and New Zealand Journal of Family Therapy, 19*(3), 111–119.

Slive, A. & Bobele, M. (Eds.) (2011). *When one hour is all you have: Effective therapy for walk-in clients.* Phoenix, AZ: Zeig, Tucker, & Theisen.

Slive, A., McElheran, N., & Lawson, A. (2008). How brief does it get? Walk-in single session therapy. *Journal of Systemic Therapies, 27,* 5–22.

Smiton, A. (2005). *Children's coping with parental brain injury*. Unpublished doctoral dissertation, University of Oxford, England.

Wolberg, L.M. (1965). Introduction, In L.R. Wolberg (Ed.), *Short-term psychotherapy*. New York: Grune & Stratton.

Young, J. & Rycroft, P. (1997). Single-session therapy: Capturing the moment. *Psychotherapy in Australia, 4*, 18–23.

15 Westside Stories

Walk-In and Single-Session Therapy in San Antonio

Monte Bobele, Chrystal Fullen, Brittany Houston, Ashlee M. Martinez, Lacey Moffat, and Jeanette Santos[1]

The following stories about walk-in/single-sessions and single-sessions by appointment are told by doctoral counseling psychology students who have received some of their clinical training in the Our Lady of the Lake University's Community Counseling Service (CCS). The CCS shares a building with a group of family practice physicians and is located about two miles from the university's main campus. The University and CCS are located in a neighborhood west of downtown San Antonio commonly referred to as "The Westside" that is predominantly Hispanic and lower-to-middle-income. The clients who come to the CCS reflect the Westside's demographics. The CCS offers services by appointment and by walk-in. The cases that follow illustrate our teams' application of the single-session mindset regardless of how the client arrived at the CCS.[2]

The CCS serves as the main clinical training facility for the psychology department's masters' and doctoral students. For over 30 years, Our Lady of the Lake University of San Antonio (OLLUSA) has used a training model that has been successful in preparing graduate students to do psychotherapy (Bobele, López, Scamardo, & Solórzano, 2008). Clients are seen by a team of therapists. The team ordinarily consists of six graduate students and a faculty supervisor. We have found the integration of beginning students with more experienced students, masters' students with doctoral students, all on the same team provides a rich training experience. Cases are usually seen by two students while the rest of the team and supervisor observe via closed circuit TV. At the CCS, Arnie Slive and Monte Bobele are the two supervisors who train students in our walk-in/single-session model[3] and have worked with the authors contributing to this chapter for at least two years. Our approach emphasizes strengths-based methods, and our basic principle is to be pragmatic and to do whatever helps clients reach their goals in a single-session.

The particular format for our sessions at the CCS has been described elsewhere (Bobele, et al., 2008; Slive & Bobele, 2011; pp. 207–208; 2012). In order to help us make the best use of the entire hour we have available to us, we try to adhere to the following agenda in each session:

Table 15.1 Agenda for a SST at the CCS

Segment	*Task*	*Time Allotted*
Pre-Session	Review intake form, choose therapists, preliminary plan for session.	5–10 minutes
Session: The Conversation	Joining/establishing a therapeutic alliance, consent, *ORS*[4], orientation to the CCS, problem definition, goal setting.	30–45 minutes
Consultation break	Review clients' strengths and resources, develop a plan for helping clients take a small step forward, construct homework if appropriate.	5–10 minutes
The Closing	Strengths-based feedback. "Did you get what you wanted?" Next steps? *SRS*	10–15 minutes
Debriefing	What went well, what did we learn, notes.	5–10 minutes

WESTSIDE STORIES

What follows are five case stories that illustrate how student-therapists conducted single sessions by walk-in or appointment at the CCS.[5] All of them were doctoral students at the time of this writing. We have endeavored to convey essential aspects of each case, but we also recognize that

> any attempt to describe clinical work is necessarily one-dimensional. Just as the map is not the territory and the description is not the thing described, the intervention reported is not the intervention delivered. The therapy that is described is always bereft of the context, the affect, and the subtleties that are a vital aspect of the process being described.
>
> (Bobele, 1988, p. 141)

Finding Hope

Ashlee M. Martinez

Hope, a 12-year-old girl, was referred by her school counselor following a "physical altercation" she had with a classmate that resulted in her suspension from school. Hope's counselor referred her to the CCS expecting that outside counseling would help her to make "better choices." The referral information indicated that Hope and her 34-year-old mother, Grace, would be coming to the appointment. They both identified as "half White" and "half Hispanic" when completing the intake form.

During our pre-session team consultation, my co-therapist, Wade Petree, and I wondered what Hope and her mother thought about the school counselor referring them to an outside therapist. The team wanted to obtain a clear understanding of what happened that led to the physical violence. We knew that establishing what Hope and her mother wanted to get out of this visit with us was critical. We wanted to know more about the family's home life, about the role Hope's father played and his thoughts about the current situation. We were curious about what Hope and her mother thought the school counselor was referring to when she wrote Hope needed to make "better choices." We were well aware that clients sent to us by schools are not always interested in counseling services, so we wanted to establish Hope and Grace's understanding of the referral.

Hope and her mother arrived on time for their appointment and were quietly chit-chatting with each other in the waiting room while they waited for the session to begin. Hope definitely did not look like a defiant or aggressive preteenager. We walked with them to the therapy room after they completed their paperwork. Wade and I worked from a strengths-based model and began the session assuming that this could be the first, and only, session we would have with the clients (Slive & Bobele, 2012). Therapists with this mindset are able to focus on the achievement of the beginning, middle, and end of a complete therapy session in one visit (Ray & Keeney, 1993). We began right away by developing a therapeutic alliance with Hope and Grace (Messer & Wampold, 2002). We asked about their daily activities, hobbies, and interests. Hope told us that she enjoyed art, music, and spending time with her friends. Grace added that they were very close, talked to each other frequently and spent lots of time together. Grace explained that, in some ways, all they had was each other. They were a single-parent household. Hope's father was not in the picture and had had no involvement with them for many years. Grace told us that they had moved to Texas from Chicago, Illinois a few years prior when Hope was in elementary school. Grace reported that they only had her extended family for support.

When we believed we had the beginnings of a working alliance with both Grace and Hope—they were both actively engaged in our conversation after only a few minutes into the session—we asked them to each complete the *Outcome Rating Scale* (*ORS*; Duncan & Sparks, 2010). Using this instrument allows for (1) a connection of scores with presenting problems, and (2) identifies changes over time. They completed the questionnaires and handed them back to us and we reviewed their scores, which were consistent with those obtained by the typical therapy-seeking clients. Wade then oriented them to our expectation that something helpful would happen in this session:

Wade: Oftentimes people find that one session here is enough to get them moving in the right direction. We'll see how that goes.

Ashlee: Yes, if we are helpful to you today, what would you like to get out of today's session?

Grace began to describe the event that had led to the referral. She told us that Hope's school counselor had referred them after some trouble Hope had gotten into at school. We asked Hope to elaborate on what her mom meant by "trouble."

Hope took a few moments, then very hesitantly began. She told us that she was being bullied and had enough of it. She was bullied by other children when she first moved to San Antonio because she was the "little white girl." She became best friends with Pita almost immediately because they found commonalities, and they had both been bullied. She recalled that they had been mutually supportive—Pita "stood up" for her against the other children.

She didn't know why she had snapped when she did. She knew it was wrong, and had never been in a physical fight before. Grace told us she was very worried because this behavior was out of character for Hope. Grace described her daughter as a rather quiet, sweet, and smart 12-year-old. She had always had a calm temperament and felt things very deeply.

As we began to unfold the layers of the event, Hope told us that she had been having a difficult time coping with the loss of her best friend, Pita, who had died four years earlier from cancer. This introduced the language of grief into our session. This allowed us to explore with Grace and Hope the possibility that Hope was not over grieving, or mourning, the death of Pita. I thought to myself that Hope may have been too young to fully comprehend the concept of death.

Grace and Hope both told us that Hope had been affected by recently aired fundraising commercials for a children's hospital on TV that featured children who had cancer. We asked Hope how the commercials had affected her, what she thought as she watched them? Hope said that one of the children in the commercials looked very much like her friend, Pita. Grace added that she thought that because Hope was getting older, Pita's death was becoming more real and affecting her more. Wade and I then began to explore with both Hope and Grace how they understood what people went through after losing a loved one. We asked both Grace and Hope what grief or mourning meant to them. What did they do to manage grief in their family? At this point, Grace recalled that her uncle, who was like a father to her, had passed away several years before. It turned out that Grace, too, was having difficulty dealing with a death, that of her uncle:

> The loss of my uncle still affects me, it hurts and I still miss him very much even to this day. I know it's not an easy thing to deal with, Hope, but I want you to feel like you can talk about these things and it's okay.

Having open dialogue, good communication and understanding were things they said were important for their family and felt would be useful when feeling sad about loss. Hope and Grace thought that thinking about Pita's death may have prompted Hope's response to the bullying she had experienced at school. Pita had stood up for Hope when girls teased Hope and called her names right after she moved to San Antonio. This was how they first became friends and then best friends. At this point in the interview, Hope opened up more about the problems she was having at school:

> The girl I got into a fight with had been bothering me, picking on me, calling me a "white girl," and making fun of me and, I don't know, I just snapped and stood up for myself. I was embarrassed because she was saying these things about me in front of the other kids. So, I took a swing at her.

The school's staff broke up the fight before either girl was seriously injured. Grace vouched for the problems Hope had been having, but did not know they had been a persistent issue for Hope. Grace said:

> The counselor and administrators were shocked when they found out she had been in a fight and told us they wished Hope had come forward sooner. If they had known about the bullying earlier, they wouldn't have suspended her. The school would have handled it differently.

Grace also disclosed that their transition from Chicago had been especially difficult for her daughter because of the racial and cultural differences Hope had experienced in San Antonio. Hope had experienced a "culture shock" because in Illinois, she had been living in an area that was not predominately Hispanic, and her lighter skin had not been unusual.

At this point, Wade and I decided it would be a good time to take a consultation break with the team. The team helped us focus on Hope and Grace's strengths.

When we got back from our consultation break, we couldn't help but notice that Hope and her mother were both grinning ear-to-ear. Although we were curious about this enormous change in mood, we decided to wait to ask about it. We told them that our team had a lot of ideas during the consultation break.

Ashlee: Would you like to hear what the team had to say?

Hope and Grace together: Sure! What did they say?

We shared the commendations, the assets and strengths the team had observed. We pointed out that Hope was lucky to have a mother who cared so much about her well-being, so much so that she dropped everything to make an appointment for them as soon as possible after the incident. We thanked Hope for being brave and for trusting us enough to open up to us and the team about something so painful and private. We commended Hope on her ability to think about what she could do to help reduce her sadness. We also reflected on how she had learned that talking, instead of fighting, helped to resolve situations. We also recognized the strength of their bond with each other and how truly remarkable it was. We conveyed that this was something the therapists and the team noticed right away about them. Hope and Grace were very pleased with the team's feedback.

Ashlee: What has been helpful about your session with us today?

Hope: The session has been helpful because I did not really understand what death was all about. It's really weird. I'm not a very spiritual person and want to know why bad things happen to good people.

Grace: I thought counseling would be helpful for Hope because I want her to feel special and have a supportive outlet to cry, if she needs to. I know she is a very talented girl.

Hope told us that she also found "putting my ear-buds in and listening to music" was helpful when she was feeling sad. It helped clear her mind. Grace agreed that Hope's mood improved when she was listening to music. These responses then led me to ask a follow-up question:

Ashlee: What will you be doing differently as a result of coming here today?

Hope told us that she would use music more often as a coping method. She found that when she listened to music, she focused on the words of the song and it helped the sadness go away. As a result of the session, Grace said she felt comfortable talking more openly to Hope about grief. She realized allowing them both to share their thoughts and feelings about this topic had been healthy for them.

Both Hope and Grace filled out individual *SRS*s upon completion of the session. They both rated the session as beneficial and said that it had allowed them to talk about the issues Hope was having along with her feelings and that was all they needed to get them on the right path. Although they did not think they would need to come in again, they said they would contact us if they needed to. We reminded them that they could call for an appointment or walk-in if they wanted to come back.

Moving Forward in the Right Direction (In One Session)

Jeanette C. Santos

Rodrigo was a Hispanic man, born and raised in San Antonio, Texas. His mother made the appointment for him to come to the CCS for individual counseling. He had a high school education and had been working odd jobs for several years, such as home improvement and landscaping. At the time of this session, he did not have a permanent job and was dissatisfied with his limited income. He was concerned about his loss of motivation and disengagement from daily social activities, poor interactions with others and dissatisfaction with his current job. He was also worried about how he had been using alcohol to cope with the emotional distress that resulted from a recent romantic break-up.

Rodrigo lived with his two sons, Joseph and Ernesto (ages 4 and 12 years) and was their primary caregiver. The children had different mothers, and neither were consistently involved in the children's lives. Joseph's mother, Rose, had made attempts to reconnect with Rodrigo and his children, but she struggled with substance use and abusive behaviors toward her family. Rodrigo told us that when Rose had left the family several times in the past, it had devastated him and his youngest son. Rodrigo admitted that he was still emotionally invested in his relationship with Rose, which made it difficult for him to move on with his life. His difficulties were exacerbated when she continued to return with the intention of rekindling the relationships with Rodrigo and the boys. Rodrigo also divulged that he had become "self-destructive" by "binge drinking" throughout the day. At the beginning of the session, Rodrigo was unable to clearly tell us what specific changes he wanted that would improve his situation. He also complained about experiencing a profound sadness and little motivation to socialize with his friends or to search for a new job.

Joining . . . It Is More Than Just Establishing Rapport

My co-therapist, Martha Guerra, and I began the session by establishing rapport with Rodrigo. This part of the session took between five and ten minutes. But we were not only establishing a therapeutic alliance; we were also learning important information about what resources and support systems he had available.

Jeanette: How did you get here [to the clinic], was it hard to find?

Rodrigo: No, I just used my GPS (*laughs*). [Making a client smile or laugh lightens the mood and helps put them at ease to talk about what they want to see different in their lives.]

Jeanette: How did you hear about the CCS?

Rodrigo: Well, I didn't. My mother actually made the call for me. [We now know that his mother is a possible ally and critical part of his support system.] I just kind of told her that I wasn't too happy, she said, "Well, do you want to talk to someone?" and I said "Yes." I could have put it off and said "No, I'm OK," you know, but my mom said, "You need to talk to someone."

Martha: It sounds like you have a mom that really cares.

Rodrigo: Oh, yes, she really cares.

At this point, we had clarified that not only did his mother care about him, but that she could potentially be a resource/support to help him make the changes he wanted. She had encouraged him to attend therapy, and he had followed her advice. Throughout the session he added other examples of the help he had received from his mother, not only as a caregiver for his children but also a source of encouragement for him. At one point, he explained, "I need to have an adult conversation, and I have friends, but they don't like to talk about these things [the breakup with his romantic partner]." His mother had been a tremendous cheerleader during his recent setbacks: "I have always been a momma's boy."

As Martha and I continued to identify other resources, we found out that both of his parents recently moved in with him to help care for Joseph and Ernesto. This reassured us that the children were being well-cared for. By now, we were two and half minutes into the session and we already had considerable information about Rodrigo's home life and some of the resources he could draw upon.

Why Now? What Prompted Rodrigo to Seek Counseling Services?

Martha and I began to learn about the "Why now?" of what prompted Rodrigo to seek counseling services. Rodrigo explained that two weeks earlier, Rose had abandoned the family for the fourth time. Rodrigo was finding that, this time, it was even harder for him and his son, Joseph, to cope with the abandonment.

Rodrigo: It was heartbreaking to tell my son that his mother has left.

Jeanette: It must be really hard to explain to a 4-year-old boy how mom is not in his life.

Later Rodrigo disclosed that it had been difficult to deal with the emotional aftermath of this situation and he had started to rely on alcohol to soothe "the hurt and the pain." He was concerned about overusing this unhealthy approach to coping with his heartbreak.

What was Working? Identifying Solutions that Rodrigo Already Had in Place

Throughout the session we never stopped "digging in" to search for solutions and resources that Rodrigo already had available. He proudly assured us that he had worked hard, as a father, to make sure his sons had a healthy and happy home environment. He was pleased that he made sure that his sons went to school and were receiving an education. He was animated when he described enjoying playing games with them.

Jeanette: You mentioned that playing with your kids is a way to get your mind off the hurt; what kind of games do you play with them? [My intention with this question was to get more details and spend more time helping Rodrigo identify all the coping strategies that he already had available to him.]

Rodrigo: We play ball, all kinds of sports. It makes me feel good, like a man, that I can still take care of them . . . My family is proud of me for still being there for the boys and caring for them.

Martha and I commended him (validating his perception of himself) for being a responsible father. We emphasized how unusual it was for a father to step in and be responsible after a mother had abandoned her family.

Was He Continuing the Same Unsuccessful Solutions? Searching for New Solutions

Martha: What do you do for a living?

This question opened a new set of potential solutions for some of Rodrigo's concerns. We found out that Rodrigo had not been permanently employed for several months. We understood that this had also contributed to his difficulties in coping with the broken relationship, which in turn triggered his drinking. From that point in the session, we focused on how he could get work as a way of helping him build confidence, become more physically active, and restore his financial security. We wanted to focus on concrete and measurable goals that would help Rodrigo to improve himself and relieve his "heartbroken" distress. Rodrigo remembered that he felt more "like a man" when he could fix things around the house, and that he used to be more inspired to do this when his "ex-girlfriend" was around. He elaborated that he usually worked as a home-repair contractor. Here we had an opportunity to encourage Rodrigo to re-engage in these activities to regain the "manhood" that was somewhat diminished after Rose left him. He agreed that finding more stable work would make him feel, as he put it, "like a man."

What Do You Expect to Get from Therapy? Identifying Goals and Setting the Stage for SST

I have learned to introduce the idea, within the first few minutes of a session, that one session may be enough for many people by saying, "Oftentimes people find that one session with us is enough to get them moving in the right direction. Maybe that will happen *today*." This has several purposes. Making this comment increases hope (Snyder, Rand, & Sigmon, 2002) for the client ("things are not as bad as I thought, I can get better with only one session"). This opening also sets the stage for identifying an achievable goal for the session. Rodrigo's session was an excellent example of how this opening SST statement and follow-up questions were both useful and effective.

Martha: Most people find that one session with us is enough to help them get moving in the right direction. So what would you be doing if you were starting to move in the right direction?

Rodrigo: Well, I don't have a steady job. I lost my driver's license because I had too many tickets. So, I can't drive, so I can't work. I feel self-conscious. Like I'm not a man, a good parent to my children. I think I drink too much and that is why I lost my self-confidence.

Jeanette: So, Rodrigo, if you were to begin to see some improvement in your situation—not having a job, not having a driver's license, not being a good parent—what would you be doing differently? What would be a small change you would see that would let you know that you were on your way?

We wanted to establish early in the session that something can happen that would make a difference in Rodrigo's life. Although Rodrigo did not answer in a very specific and concrete way, he provided the context for changes he wanted in his life. We were then able to get more details about where these changes could start. Rodrigo acknowledged that reducing his drinking would be a way to start these changes. He offered that, sometimes, he was able to avoid drinking, which then opened the door for eliciting and elaborating more exceptions.

Martha: You mentioned that sometimes you do [drink], but sometimes you don't. So those times when you don't, how do you do it?

Rodrigo: Keep myself busy.

Martha: Doing what?

Rodrigo: Fixing stuff around the house and cutting the grass, things like that.

What Can Rodrigo Do to Move in the Right Direction? Building a Concrete Goal

Martha and I had set the stage, with all these previous questions, to help Rodrigo identify clear goals for therapy and help him begin to move in the right direction and reverse his current setback. We knew that the time was right to ask a more precise question that would help us identify the specific behaviors that could move Rodrigo toward accomplishing his goals and making positive changes in his life.

Jeanette: What would be that one small thing that would move you in the right direction to get things moving?

Rodrigo: I think a big thing will be, I guess letting the past go and just moving forward, I mean, I guess getting a better paying job, and starting to pay my tickets off?

Jeanette: Getting a job that pays more and start paying your tickets would be something that would move you in the right direction?

Rodrigo: Yes . . . and it is going to happen again, my ex is going to show up or call . . .

Jeanette: It must be very frustrating that she does that, and it's not really under your control if she tries to come back again . . . but, getting another job and paying your tickets, that is something that is more under your control. I wonder, how would you make that happen? What would be *the first step* that you have to take towards either finding a job or paying the tickets? What would be *that first thing* that you have to do?

Rodrigo: Probably make some phone calls . . .

Jeanette: Who would be someone that you can call?

Rodrigo: Not just phone calls but also looking at job listings and some things like that.

Jeanette: You have the option to either call, I guess, people who you know about the jobs, or you can look in the newspaper. Which one do you think is easier for you?

Rodrigo: Well, recommendations from friends because they can get me in a lot easier.

Martha: When do you think you can make these phone calls?

What Has Been Helpful So Far? And, Taking a Consultation Break

Martha: Before we go talk to the team, tell us what has been helpful for you in talking with us so far today? [We always ask this before taking a consultation break. Frequently, it helps clarify whether or not we have a relevant goal. We think it also underscores for the client that something has been helpful for them.]

Rodrigo: Just talking and understanding. I think talking—that is a big step and you said that I have control on some things and others I don't.

Jeanette: [after a call from the team] The team would like for you to take a break to think about something that you could do, let's say tomorrow, to move you in the right direction. [We have been experimenting with this comment. It is a way of inviting the client to design their own homework assignment. We also think the client can make productive use of the break time (Sharry, et al., 2001).]

Rodrigo: OK.

Validations and Commendations

It is important to validate, validate, and validate even more. We commend clients for seeking help, being motivated to make changes, for being open to talk about uncomfortable topics, for sharing personal information, and for trusting the process of therapy.

At the CCS, when we come back from the break we ask the client whether they want to hear what the team had to say to them (so far I have never encountered a case where a client did not want to hear the feedback). We took this opportunity to convey the commendations, a summary of the resources, strengths and assets we had heard from Rodrigo and some of the team's ideas.

We then invited Rodrigo to consider what he thought the next step should be after coming to the session. Once again, he clarified that his next step was to find a job. He said that he had decided he would call a friend as soon as he left the CCS and ask about job opportunities.

Rodrigo: I already know what I have to do. I just need to push myself and do it.

At that point, Rodrigo agreed with our suggestion that it would be helpful to make a list of the friends he could call, along with the dates and times that he would make these calls. Rodrigo left that day with a concrete and reliable plan that he believed would help him move in the right direction.

When Rodrigo filled out the *Session Rating Scale* (*SRS*) (Duncan, Miller, Wampold, & Hubble, 2010) we were delighted that he gave the session perfect scores. Such scores are usually interpreted to mean that he felt understood and heard, that we had talked about what was relevant for him to talk about, that he had felt comfortable with our therapeutic style, and that overall he was satisfied with the session. We explored this by asking Rodrigo what had been most helpful about the session? His answer supported our understanding: he felt a strong therapeutic alliance and that he was able to see all the resources he has available and how to use them to move him in the right direction.

Would There Be Another Session? Clarifying Whether Rodrigo Got What He Wanted

Martha: Earlier, we talked about how some people, when they come, in one session they get what they need to get them moving in the right direction How do you feel, do you think you got what you needed?

Rodrigo: Yes, I guess the only thing that I think will be difficult for me, I guess, is not drinking.

Jeanette: What do you think our next step should be? Yours and ours?

Rodrigo: I think I know what I want to do. This was helpful.

Jeanette [after a telephone suggestion from the team]: The team was wondering if we could call you in about a week, just to check how everything is going.

Rodrigo: Yes, and I might come back next week if I need to.

Martha: You are welcome to come make another appointment with us, or take advantage of the walk-in services here.

We tried to get in touch with Rodrigo a couple of times, but we were not able to reach him. He never came back nor scheduled another appointment. Although we cannot tell whether this session was effective for the long term, Rodrigo's *SRS* scores and expression of high hopes and his motivation to make changes supported the team's impression that he found what he was looking for from this session. In this particular case, we identified early on that Rodrigo had many of the resources he needed to be successful. He was motivated to start making changes right away, saying toward the end of the session that he knew what he should do but just needed "a little push." We hope that he is moving forward. If he returns for another session, we will help him identify goals and how he can take his next steps towards where he wants to go.

Single-Session on Repeat

Lacey Moffat

Charlie was referred to the CCS by his case manager following his discharge from a local hospital for a brief psychiatric inpatient hospitalization. The intake worker had written at the bottom of the CCS intake form that the referring mental-health professional had reported that Charlie had been previously diagnosed with "Schizoaffective Disorder." The note also let us know that the case manger's expectation was that Charlie would be coming in for counseling to continue to "work with his diagnosis." The intake form also indicated that Charlie had been seen at the CCS before, and that he had asked to try a new combination of therapists. Because of my previous experiences working with clients with serious mental illness (SMI), I asked to be assigned to the case. Ashlee Martinez agreed to be my co-therapist to work with Charlie. Ashlee and I both knew that developing and maintaining rapport with Charlie would be important if we wanted him to feel heard, acknowledged, and ultimately trust the therapeutic process.

Our team frequently used a brief, single-session approach. We were intrigued by the idea of getting as much done as we could within an hour. In keeping with this approach, we had found that establishing a therapeutic alliance helped us to avoid becoming focused on problems and diagnoses. Instead, we frequently thought about what strengths and resources the clients have available outside of therapy . For example, with Charlie, a man with a long history of mental-health treatment, what had been helpful to him so far? The team briefly brainstormed about working with this idea, but ultimately we knew that we would cooperate with Charlie and work with whatever he gave us.

One Session at a Time

After our first session we knew that we would not be working from a traditional therapeutic model and would have to take each interaction with Charlie as if it was our last. It was evident from the first meeting that Charlie struggled with paranoid and persecutory delusions and grandiose ideations, and that he was actively hallucinating. We watched as he would track visual hallucinations throughout the therapy room and at times would speak in response or as an aside to someone who was not present in the room. These symptoms confirmed that Ashlee and I would have to take a different approach to therapy if we were going to help Charlie. Charlie, who verbalized an understanding of a medical model of therapy, was expecting Ashlee and I to identify him only as his diagnosis. Instead we endeavored to support him to be the expert of his own life and therapy. As therapists, and as a team, we choose to see what is going well with a client rather than what is not. Furthermore, we strive to do so in a way that allows for the client to be an active participant in the process. Simon and Nelson (2007, p. 91) elaborated this idea: "a collaborative relationship stands a better chance of including discussions around what can be different than one that focuses on what the individual is doing wrong. The difference is working *with* rather than *on* the client." For Charlie, having therapists who worked collaboratively with him as the expert in his own life was a completely new experience for him. With Charlie, we were sensitive to the unique language, experiences, and contexts that had shaped his life experiences.

The first session was difficult, to say the least. Charlie spoke at a low volume and it was difficult for the team in the next room to hear him over the monitor. We co-therapists had to relay to the team at the session break the specifics of what was going on in the room and clarify many of his statements. Additionally, although our program advocates a less diagnostic stance, it did not take long for each team member to recognize that we would have to approach Charlie differently and work with his active symptomology—but not make it the focus of each session. As a team we decided to use a "serial-single-session" model with Charlie and treat each session as if we might not see him again. Implementing a serial-single-session approach with Charlie allowed the co-therapists the flexibility needed when working with Serious Mental Illness (SMI) patients. Even though he scheduled appointments week to week we worked with whatever issue Charlie brought into session by viewing each meeting as if it were the last. When we met each week, we would join with him and allow him, as the expert in the session, to guide where he would like to go in therapy that day; it was up to Ashlee and me to maintain rapport and help him to work on his established goals. Through the use of the SST model, we were able to work with Charlie in a way that took his therapeutic needs and wants into consideration while helping establish coping strategies that were tailored to him. Ashlee and I eventually met with Charlie for a total of nine sessions throughout the semester. Each week we would focus on a goal that had been established in his "playbook" (see the following section), discussing and exploring different options that were viable for him to accomplish this goal.

"The Playbook"

In our first session Charlie told us that he had a love of sports. Accordingly, we devised a "playbook" for him to use to help navigate his goals for therapy. We gave him a notebook, or playbook, that he kept throughout treatment and brought to each session to record collaboratively set goals. The playbook also served as a tangible way for Ashlee and me to help Charlie focus on the concrete goals that he had set for himself. At first the goals were global, such as help with money, family, and his diagnosis. Each week we would ask him to pick a goal that he would like to work on during the session and we would tease apart the broad goal until we all reached an understanding of a specific problem he was trying to tackle. For example, he wanted to work on family, and specifically his relationship with his mother. He verbalized what appeared to us to be a persecutory and paranoid delusion that his mother wanted to hurt him. In the past, he had made threats against his mother and had even become violent with her within the home. Knowing that he had been violent in the past, Ashlee and I made sure to assess for any current risk of harm to self or others with Charlie. Through careful questioning we were able to establish that there was no immediate risk of harm to his mother and further explored safety factors, such as his religion, to reassure us that he was not dangerous at that time. After many sessions and consultations with the team and coming from a systemic approach, we decided to ask Charlie if he would like his mother to join us for a session. This idea served dual purposes: first, because of our established rapport with Charlie we thought he might feel more at ease speaking with his mother with us present and be more likely to accept an alternative view of her; second, Ashlee and I would be able to see a different facet of the family dynamic, which could allow us to better work with Charlie by seeing them through a relational lens.

Ashlee and I recognized early in treatment that we had been successful in establishing a strong rapport and continuity of care with Charlie because of the sustained use of his playbook and his meeting with us each week. Through respect, understanding, and technique Ashlee and I were able to help Charlie negotiate paranoid delusions concerning his mother, active auditory and visual hallucinations he experienced during sessions, grief of losing close family members and custody of his son, and ultimately help him to build self-esteem and the belief in himself that he was not just a diagnosis.

At the end of the semester we began to prepare Charlie for the possibilities of treatment after Ashlee and I were no longer at the CCS. We were able to discuss with him concrete evidence of the positive changes he had made throughout the semester. At the beginning of each session we have our clients use a self-report measure that allows us to chart therapeutic change called the *Outcome Rating Scale* (*ORS*). Through the utilization of the *ORS*, we were able to monitor Charlie's improvement from initial intake to termination, and it was ultimately seen that he was scoring himself well above the therapeutic cut-off at our last meeting. These results quantitatively showed us as a team that therapeutic growth was not only possible for some with chronic mental illness, but that implementing a single-session therapy approach with these clients is a good way to work efficiently to meet their needs.

SST and SMI

In my past experience working with clients with diagnoses of SMI, I felt stymied by the problem-driven treatment approaches used to "help" the clients. To me, it seemed to be a never-ending cycle for the client to try harder to be better but seldom achieving what was defined by others as better—an idea that conflicts with my values as a counseling psychologist who wants to help support client autonomy and self-determination. The hope for a positive therapeutic change for all clients is why I continue to work with SMI clients using a strength-based perspective. With Charlie we were able to implement a different way to approach therapy, one that could also be beneficial for others with SMI.

When You Have a Whole 30 Minutes

Chrystal Fullen

On a Thursday morning, my co-therapist, Brittany Houston, and I were assigned a couple, Gerry and Sarah, who had made an appointment. The CCS's telephone intake form provided some basic information about them: a household size of four, below-average income, and a goal to "improve communication."

Before sessions began, our clinical team routinely discussed cases to create a working plan of action for the therapists. The team was curious about a number of things about Gerry and Sarah. The team speculated as to what "communication" might signify for the couple. Suggestions such as trust, intimacy, and infidelity were themes other team members had experienced with couples who had indicated "communication" on their intake form—in the clinic we had found that often the reported problem on the intake form is not always the problem clients end up talking about in the session. Another discussion point was that the appointment was scheduled by the husband and not the wife. In our experience it was more common for wives to make the appointment call. The supervisor encouraged Brittany and me to share our own curiosities about what might have caused a breakdown in marital communication. Some of the ideas we came up with were based on differences that seemed challenging such as culture, religion, age, parenting styles, and financial stressors. Of course, as with many other pre-session discussions, what we discussed is frequently not what the clients bring to the session. However, the process is useful in building an easy rapport within the team, engaging the therapists in thinking outside the box, and stimulating professional creativity. Our plan of action also included how we would like to begin building rapport and joining with the clients, which therapeutic approach we would use, and how we would endeavor to incorporate the couple's strengths and resources in the session.

A Change to the Plan

About 15 minutes after the scheduled time for the couple's session, we were informed that the couple had called and would be late, but would still like to speak with someone. At 30 minutes after the appointment time, the couple arrived.

Usually, when a scheduled client is more than 15 minutes late, because of the allotted appointment times, limited space, and the overall training environment, the latecomers are referred to a walk-in team or rescheduled, depending on client need. However, in this case the supervisor asked Brittany and I how we would like proceed. Brittany and I both work from a single-session mindset. I had often pondered the rule-of-thumb regarding the 50-minute therapy hour. Why couldn't a session last 90 minutes, 30 minutes, or 15 minutes depending on the client and the process of change in the session? So, we both decided that we would like to use the 30 minutes the same way we would have originally used the therapy hour.

Our supervisor asked us what we would like to accomplish in the limited time, and we said that at minimum we would try to clarify the problem statement and hopefully get to a place in the session where we could collaborate with the couple to reach an agreed-upon goal. Others on the team thought this was a bit of a stretch, because of the limited time available, but we had confidence in the process. With a single-session mindset, we wanted to leave the couple after 30 minutes with the motivation necessary to reach their goals.

Meeting Gerry and Sarah

When we entered the therapy room, we introduced ourselves to the couple, sat down, and began the session as we do any other: by taking a few minutes to get to know our clients, putting them at ease, and building the therapeutic alliance through joining. Of course, we did explain to the clients that we had limited time in the session, but that we were happy to meet with them and accomplish what they felt most important in the small amount of time we had together. Gerry and Sarah agreed and were exceptionally friendly and gracious.

Chrystal: Usually we have about an hour in a session. Today, we have 30 minutes, but we understand that you wanted to see someone even if it was just for 30 minutes?

Sarah: Yes. We're so sorry we are late, but it doesn't matter how much time we have, we really need some help.

Chrystal: OK, well, Brittany and I are happy to speak to you guys. Besides, 30 minutes is still plenty of time.

The joining process is one that we use not only as a way to build the therapeutic alliance, but also as an assessment of the clients' strengths and resources. What we learned in a slow, deliberate, and unrushed conversation was that Gerry and Sarah were newlyweds, in their first year of marriage. The couple had met through church, Gerry a new member, Sarah an existing member and volunteer. Sarah had two children from a previous marriage, now living with the couple. Gerry had four children: one child from a previous relationship that he was working toward reconnecting with after a Child Protective Services

(CPS) case was opened, and three that he did not have contact with due to a tumultuous relationship with their mother. The therapists asked about the names and ages of all the children and remarked at the pride in the voices of the couple when speaking about their family. We find it helpful to talk about the important people who come up in session by their first name instead of unnaturally referring to people as "cousin," "brother," "oldest daughter," and so on. I noted in my mind to come back to the CPS case later in the session.

Gerry and Sarah were respectful in the conversation, pausing and allowing one another opportunities to talk without interruption. The therapists made that observation to the clients, who expressed that since the start of their relationship both were touched by the other's innate strength.

Chrystal: You guys are so respectful of one another, right Brittany?

Brittany: Yes, you guys give each other a lot of room to talk. You can tell there is a lot of love in the room.

Gerry: Yeah, well she's my best friend.

Sarah: Gerry is amazing. That's why we are here. We love each other; that's not the problem.

Rather than immediately asking about "the problem," we asked the couple to tell us how they met and fell in love. Sarah did most of the talking, while Gerry provided some well-timed blushing:

Sarah: Well, I was volunteering at the church and that's how I met him. We became friends because Gerry and I have a similar past. So, that's why I was kinda matched with him, you know, to help Gerry during a difficult time in his life. I guess that like pretty quickly we were attracted to each other. We felt it was right because we both are a big part of the church and it's important to us, so yeah. We got married.

Brittany: Wow! That's quick. So, you guys really knew, right away.

Chrystal: Yeah, sounds like love at first sight! How awesome that the church kind of brought you guys together.

Gerry: Yeah!

Sarah: Yes!

We asked about work and learned that both had multiple interests and two jobs each. Gerry worked in construction and for a soda machine company. Sarah had her own food truck and was also a home healthcare provider.

Introducing a Single-Session Mindset

Brittany and I paused the session to allow the couple to complete some necessary paperwork (informed consent forms and the *ORS*) and to share how therapy is not always a long process:

Chrystal: For many, one session of therapy can be enough to get the ball rolling in the right direction. Even with just a short session, let's see how we can be helpful?

My co-therapist and I, using a strengths-based, solution-focused approach, began to ask the clients more about what made them agree that therapy was necessary in their lives, specifically, at this time.

Brittany: OK, so what made you decide to make the appointment now?

Gerry: Well, OK. So, I'm an addict. There's a lot going on, with money, and trying to get my kid back.

Chrystal: With the CPS case?

Gerry: Yes, that's why I have to be clean. I can't get my rights back until I do.

Brittany: Sounds like a lot is going on.

Gerry: Yeah, and with Sarah I just want to be a good husband. I guess, like I've slipped up, and when that happens it's like we lose trust. And, I know I'm to blame. So yeah, we thought it was time to get help.

Chrystal: OK, so when was the last time you slipped up?

Gerry: That was like over the weekend.

Chrystal: Well, you know it takes a lot to come to therapy, it takes a lot to say to yourself, it's time. So, you say you are an addict; what do you use?

Gerry: Like drugs, you know, I use a few of them.

Chrystal: And you said you slipped up, so how long were you sober before the weekend?

Gerry: Like it was going to be a month.

Sarah: I'm proud of him. I know that we need help and it's not easy to ask for it.

Brittany: So, you both agree it's time. What would have to happen later today for you to feel like this session was helpful?

We have found that when we are working from a SST mindset, it is often helpful to ask measurable and behavioral questions to define a goal. Both partners explained how "communication" was a goal because they believed it would create trust at a time when both Gerry and Sarah needed it most.

Scaling Commitment and Searching for Exceptions

To get more information about the commitment the couple had to both the relationship and working towards their stated goal of improving communication, we asked them how committed they were to making the relationship work. Gerry pledged that he was 100% committed to the relationship and willing to do whatever was necessary to keep the marriage a happy one. Sarah agreed that she, too, was 100% committed. I also found it thought-provoking for the couple to hear how much faith they each had that they would be able to achieve their goals: Both were hopeful that they could overcome their difficulties, especially if they could learn to communicate better with one another.

We asked about times that the couple believed their communication was already positive and helpful in building trust. They described how, early on as friends, communication was much easier. We explored these instances that solution-focused therapists would call "exceptions."

Brittany: So, you say "communication." What does it sound like when you guys are communicating in a way that makes you feel "This is good, I trust him. I trust her"?

Sarah: I think when we first met, when we were friends, he told me everything. I didn't feel like I had to ask, or wonder. You know, I never had to like ask him every day if he was OK, if he was managing, if I should worry. He just told me.

Gerry: Yeah, it was easier then. It's different now because, like I don't want to disappoint her. I don't want to worry her.

Throughout the session, Brittany and I continued to talk to one another and to the couple about the immense barriers the couple had already overcome simply to be together, as well as the couple's dedication, not only to one another, but also to one another's children. Both were motivated, respectful, and spoke about the other with love in spite of hurt feelings and dark doubt created by growing distrust. We highlighted the foundation of respect in the relationship as well as the multitude of strengths each of them brought to the union.

Around the 25-minute mark, the couple had agreed upon a shared goal of gaining trust in the relationship. One of the ways that we helped to operationalize this vague goal into a smaller, more manageable goal was to enquire how the couple would notice the other partner could be trusted.

Chrystal: OK. So, communication is one thing. But trust is different. Sarah, what is one thing you need to hear from Gerry—to feel like you can trust him—when you are talking to each other throughout the day?

Talking about Trust

Sarah, around this time, made a major revelation in the conversation, acknowledging that she, too, was a recovered addict. As with Gerry, Sarah used illegal street drugs, and often used whatever she could get at the time. For both, most often methamphetamines were the drugs of choice. In this way, she was a mentor of sorts at the church to her then-friend, and now-husband. Of course, since then the relationship had changed. Although she was able to understand the darkness and struggle in recovery, she could not put aside the needs of her new family. Gerry shared his experience of losing parental rights to his daughter, and how this and his previous success at sobriety motivated him to "be accountable" to Sarah and his new family. This sparked a moving story:

Sarah: I get it, I understand (*crying*), I lost my kids, too. I didn't have my kids for a few years. That's what I had to overcome. I had to fight for them. I got sober. I did it for them. That's why I am here. I can't let that happen again. I know that Gerry is trying. I know he can do it. He's done it before. But, I will not risk my children. I love him, but I will not go through it again. If he keeps slipping up—I can't do this.

Chrystal: I understand. It sounds like you are afraid for Gerry and the kids. Gerry, what do you think after hearing what Sarah just said?

Gerry: I know she's scared. I know. I would never do that to her. I would never be around the kids messed up. I would never be around her like that. I would take myself out of this relationship first. I would rather do that if I feel like I'm coming to a point of no return. I will never let that happen to her again.

The therapists commended the clients for their honesty and shared their surprise at this missing piece of the couple's story, and how motivated and motivating both were in their very similar journeys. As both parents and friends, the couple inspired one another, and seemed to put their own needs on the back-burner for those of their family. As many supervisors at OLLUSA have explained to us, when providing services to couples, the trick is not to make both partners the identified clients, but to make the relationship the identified client. In this case, the couple also expressed the same idea, that their goal was the relationship.

30 Minutes and Counting

Brittany and I encouraged the couple to use themes of accountability and making their family the number one priority as motivators to encourage more open communication. We also discussed how they could communicate while aligned in shared goals as a husband and wife in the same way they could speak openly with shared histories when they were just friends. Brittany and I informed the couple that we were just about out of time (we had been meeting for about 32 minutes). We asked them what they thought their next step with us should be. We told them that they could schedule another appointment, call in, or walk-in in the future. They scheduled another appointment before they left the CCS. But, they then did not appear for their scheduled appointment and did not call to cancel. The couple did decide to schedule a second appointment. However, the couple did not return for their appointment. They rescheduled, but again did not return. After three weeks, I was curious, because of the several cancellations, about what was happening with them. I called them up and asked, "What was better?"

Both Gerry and Sarah, on speakerphone, responded that things were much better right now and that they were "doing more together." They expected bad times, expected Gerry's recovery to be bumpy, but also expected that they could communicate well when needed and share the difficult things people don't like to say out loud to the person they loved because they felt safe, non-judgmental support from one another. They assured me that the session helped them to remember what was most important in a relationship and about how much they loved one another.

I have spoken often about this session with my co-therapist. The couple were very much in love and that was evident in their session. But it was also a session that could have raised warning bells for other therapists: major themes such as past drug use, an open CPS case, and substance-abuse relapse usually come with recommendations of ten sessions or more. However, ten sessions or more are not always effective nor are they doable for a couple working two jobs each and raising a family. Here, Brittany and I provided an outside perspective, genuinely expressed hope for the relationship, and in 30 minutes worked with the couple to encourage motivation at a time when they said it was needed, not a week later, but on the day they scheduled the appointment. The couple could return to CCS when they wanted—and still can. If we had waited, we might have missed the opportunity to provide therapy when the couple was most ready for change. In Stone (2002), a psychologist details a session lasting a surprising and valuable 30 minutes. For most therapists the idea of time can become limiting. For clients, time in session is as unique as the client. This session also inspired me to think about time. It's not only 30 minutes, or only an hour; instead, it's a *full* 30 minutes, one *entire* hour.

Breaking Up Isn't Hard to Do—After a Good SST

Brittany Houston

This session particularly stands out for me because it embodied the idea of a single-session, as well as what we have come to call a "break-up session." At the CCS, it is not unusual for a client to return for a brief follow-up meeting not because they are seeking more services but rather to express their appreciation and to let the therapist(s) know that they are improving to the point that they can put future therapy sessions on hold (Bobele, et al., 2008). Anna's story resonated with me because she rejoiced in the fact that one session had been enough to move her in the right direction after years of feeling stuck and unmotivated. In what follows, I will describe the details of Anna's changes and what factors encouraged her to begin moving in the right direction.

When Anna, a 19-year-old Hispanic woman, and her mother initially walked into the CCS, no therapists were available that day, so she completed the walk-in intake form (reflecting her high motivation to change) and returned with her mother a week later during the walk-in hours. Her mother had come to the CCS for counseling years before and had encouraged her daughter to come for a visit—her mother's previous positive experience may have contributed to her and Anna expecting benefit from their visit. Anna appeared fatigued, as evidenced by the dark circles under her eyes and her disheveled appearance. Anna told us that she was coming to counseling to reduce her symptoms of "anxiety and depression."

When Anna arrived for her session with me and my co-therapist, Alyssa Arredondo, the following week she was as disheveled as she had been the previous week. Her mother, who had accompanied her, preferred to wait in the lobby for her. Anna's physician referred her to us to help her "manage panic attacks" after she experienced such an attack during a friend's memorial candlelight service. Anna had never talked to counselors or therapists before. Anna's goals for therapy were to "get rid of a lot of baggage," and become more motivated and less anxious. Her *ORS* score was a 10, which reflected her reported distress. An *ORS* score below a 25 indicates the individual is in the range of people we typically see in therapy.

Anna attributed her anxiety to her rushing to move into adulthood too quickly. After transferring to a new district at the end of middle school and being bullied, she and her family decided to homeschool her. Consequently, she graduated earlier than her peers from high school, at age 16. By then she was skilled on six different musical instruments. Anna recalled that she had "big goals" for her future and would jump ahead to achieve them. Anna was so worried about achieving her goals that she missed out on her childhood. She regretted missing countless coming-of-age experiences (e.g. prom, homecoming, high-school friends, etc.). Anna's preoccupation with her regrets had impaired her ability to keep up with her daily functioning such as hygiene, eating, and socializing. Others in her family noticed she often isolated herself from them. Anna explained that she did this out of fear of "inflicting her negative energy on them." Surprisingly, Anna's demeanor brightened when recalling the times she spent with her niece and nephew. She detailed numerous activities she participated in with them and the enjoyment she felt from their company.

Alyssa and I were using solution-focused (Molnar & de Shazer, 1987) ideas to guide our single-session therapy mindset. We commended Anna on the outstanding motivation that propelled her to excellence throughout her life.

We normalized her body wanting to rest after using excessive amounts of energy, and admired her dedication in pursuit of her childhood goals. We commented that we were nearly exhausted from hearing about all of the work she put in. We told her that we were astounded by the successes she had already achieved. We went on to highlight the fact (solution-focused therapists would call it an *exception*) that Anna remained active with her family despite her difficulties with everyday functioning. Much to our amazement, she reported being able to keep up with active toddlers and seemed to easily handle their rambunctious natures. I reflected that on most days I struggled to keep up with my own niece.

Alyssa: We are impressed with the consistent motivation during your life to be able to finish high school two years early and with 16 college credits hours. On top of that you learned how to play six instruments.

Anna: Yeah. I had a goal in mind, and I just pushed forward.

Brittany: We are not surprised your body is telling you that you need a break or vacation. You have spent all your motivation achieving these grand things and now your body is telling you to slow down.

Anna: That's true. I never really thought of it like that.

Brittany: However, now we are here to say your vacation is over.

We elaborated that it was time for her "vacation" to end, but also acknowledged that she needed to ease back into daily life after her vacation. Alyssa and I began by emphasizing the idea of small changes leading to big changes. We recommended that Anna slow things down and try not to do too much too fast. We reflected that her body might be letting her know she needed a rest, and she should take advantage of the rest by doing one small thing at a time. We asked her what the smallest change she would notice when she took one small step toward her goal; Anna simply offered, "If I could remember to eat." I have to say I was a little thrown back by an actual answer that was so specific and concrete. Often, I encounter clients' first response to be quite grand and vague (e.g., "I would be working out every day for three hours a day" or "I would be happy"). Together, we developed a plan defining the steps she would take to remember to eat (Zeig, 1997).

Brittany: Now that your vacation is over, you have to ease your body out of it. So, what would be the smallest step for you to do to begin moving toward where you want to be?

Anna: To remember to eat. I used to love to eat.

Alyssa: What is your favorite thing to eat?

Anna: I love meat. Any type of meat. YUUMMM!

Brittany: Me, too! How do you think you might remember to do what you loved, EAT?

Anna: I don't know, maybe write a song.

Brittany: Wow! Yeah, maybe you could like have a ceremony to open the event of eating and then close it.

Anna: Yeah, I could do that. Cool!

Alyssa: Using your six different instruments and all. I bet it's gonna be a pretty awesome song.

Brittany: So, how long do you think you will need to finish this song of yours?

Anna: Maybe about a week.

Alyssa: WOW! A week, that's fast.

Anna: I'm pretty good at it.

Brittany: Well, you know, some people find that one session is enough to get them going in the right direction. What do you think is best for you?

Anna: Let's just schedule an appointment for next week, just in case. I like therapy; I think it is part of keeping myself healthy.

A week later Anna returned to the CCS casually dressed, wearing makeup and her hair curled in a side ponytail. At the beginning of the session, it was evident that Anna had returned to give us a report of how well she had been doing. Her scores on the *ORS* had improved by 10 points (from a 10 to a 20) and she smiled throughout the session. The ten-point improvement placed her five points below the cutoff, indicating that she was still in the range of people that seek therapy. However, more than a 6-point improvement indicates significant change.

Brittany: What have you been doing to cause that 10-point jump?

Anna: Yes, I wanted to come back and tell you me and my fiancé have decided to take life to the next step. He convinced me to register for business classes.

Alyssa: What are you going for?

Anna: Double majoring in business and music.

Alyssa and Brittany: WOW!

Anna: Yeah. The business part helps because me and my fiancé started this business to cut peoples' phone bills in half.

Alyssa: So, not only are y'all in business together, but you are helping people as well. That's so awesome.

Anna: Yes, it has been super encouraging to me, you know seeing him do something. I was like, I wanna do that, too.

Brittany: Yeah, you're like, I can be on your level.

In addition to the time Anna, Alyssa, and I spent together brainstorming solutions in the first session, Anna's family and friends motivated her to look toward the future and leave the past troubles behind. Her family and friends acknowledged her progress and supported her decisions for her future.

Anna brought to therapy inner strengths of determination, faith, goal-directedness, social support, and a motivation to get better, among many others. These are qualities that have been identified as extra-therapeutic factors, one of the *common factors* that account for change in therapy (Lambert, 1992; Messer & Wampold, 2002; Duncan, et al., 2010) that contributed to her success. After she had established a day-to-day habit for functioning, the future was not clouded as much by the past.

Alyssa: What have others noticed about the change you have made?

Anna: My mom says I smile more.

Brittany: Who else has noticed a change in you?

Anna: Miles, my fiancé noticed that I'M EATING!

Brittany and Alyssa: Really?!

Anna: The eating progress got a lot better. I went from eating half a meal a day to two to three meals a day, which is really awesome.

Brittany: How did you do that?

Anna: In the beginning it was really hard. The first couple of days were like a force-feeding but it eventually became a habit and knowing when I was hungry.

Alyssa: What meat did you eat over the week?

Anna: Chicken.

Brittany: There is no bad way to cook chicken.

Anna: Grill it, fry it, tacos . . .!!!!

Anna continued to shift toward a positive future and how she would continue to live today and plan for her preferred future. She expressed her expectations for the future differently. At the end of the session, we amplified the first session's goal of taking small steps towards Anna's future and how she could take mini vacations when needed so her body would not get too tired. Anna did not schedule another session, saying she would return to counseling when needed.

The single-session mindset promoted the hope and expectancy that her life could and would get better after our brief meeting (Snyder, Rand, & Sigmon, 2002). This mindset challenges the idea that problems are an overbearing force in someone's life that requires months or even years of work. Creating a space where problems are expected to get better with small changes allows the clients to choose to immediately begin solving their problem. The small steps and the support of Anna's family, her fiancé, and the therapy team opened a space for Anna to become hopeful and excited about her future.

One of the important things I learned from this experience was to remember that each session is a single-session, and it has the potential to help solve the problem. By narrowing the focus to Anna's eating, it gave her momentum to move forward and not be held back by the regrets of her past. When Anna successfully took her first small step, she became motivated to continue stepping into other areas of her life. Finally, it was one of the most pleasant "It's me. I'm better without you, I don't need you" break-ups I have ever heard.

SOME REFLECTIONS ON THE CASES

Ashlee's case nicely illustrates how adopting a single-session mindset with a mother and daughter ("Hope") enabled her and her co-therapist, Wade, to be helpful in a situation many people would identify as unresolved grief. Labeling the problem as such without focusing on Hope's strengths would have led to an entirely different, and probably lengthier but less successful, therapy. The therapists capitalized on the resources and relationships present to help their clients find a more hopeful view of their losses.

Jeanette presented a very complex case with a number of concerns. Although the session ended with a plan to follow-up by telephone with their client ("Rodrigo"), Jeanette and her co-therapist, Martha, were not able to reach him. They had also offered him an invitation to return if he needed to, either by walk-in or scheduling an appointment. It is not unusual for clients at the CCS to be unavailable for follow-up phone calls. The role of follow-ups in clinics such as the CCS is elaborated in Chapter 2 of this book. The fact that he did not return within several months could be because he got what he wanted from the session, and did not need to be in touch with us anymore. The outcome was unclear, but we thought it important to respect his autonomy and let him decide if, and if so when, he might want to re-contact us. One of the goals of a single-session, even if it does not entirely resolve the presenting problem for the client, is that the client has a positive experience. We are hopeful that a positive experience will lead the client to consider another session with us or some other mental-health provider, if needed.

Lacey and Ashlee struggled with their client ("Charlie") before the team decided to treat each session with him as if it were the last; in other words, they took a "serial-single-session" approach with him. The supervisor encouraged this as a way of helping the team to overcome their frustration with trying to apply brief therapy with a client who had a history of chronic problems. When the therapists took this serial single-sessions approach[6] the client began making progress and the team's self-confidence and spirits rose. Even though the client and therapists had multiple meetings, it was one-session-at-a-time, each one a complete stand-alone with a specific focus, with the next session being set at the end of the previous one.

Chrystal and Brittany had an abbreviated session that ended with their clients ("Gerry and Sarah") saying that they had gotten what they had wanted but wished to return for another session. They then did not show up. This is not unusual in our clinic. Sometimes when we ask clients when they think a next appointment should be, they pick a remote time in the future, or we will suggest a month or two hiatus saying, "Well, let's schedule an appointment for a month from now. If you decide you are doing OK and don't need to see us, just call and cancel. You can always walk-in or reschedule. It's like that spare tire in your trunk; you like knowing it is there but hope you don't need it." Sometimes clients have a second session that is simply an opportunity for them to come in to report on their progress. A number of years ago, we had a client return for a second appointment saying, as she paused in the hallway on the way back to the therapy room, "I don't really need to meet with you today. I am doing really, really well [and she looked much better], and I just started this new job and this is my lunch hour, but I knew you would be here waiting for me and I didn't want to stand you up." She then left, never making it to the therapy room. Over time we have sometimes referred to this as a "*break-up session.*" Other, more conventional therapists might call it a "termination session."

CONCLUSION

Even though the cases reported here all used a team format, with doctoral students being the therapists, the walk-in/single-session and single-session by-appointment formats can be adapted to any practice. Several other practitioners in this book have described their work with walk-in and single-session therapies in settings that do not rely on volunteers and students for staffing. All the therapists have some time for reflection about an upcoming case, they establish or reestablish a therapeutic alliance, conduct a purposeful interview, close the session and reflect on the session after the client leaves. The only feature that might be different from many agency practices is the intersession break. We frequently recommend to therapists working without the benefit of a team, that they include a break in their sessions—a time when, for a few minutes, the therapist leaves the room to think (and perhaps, to consult). Why should a therapist, or a client, be expected to always be able to be thoughtful and creative while sitting across from the client? In a case demonstration by Insoo Kim Berg (2008), for example, she takes a break while working with a family—not to consult with a team, but simply to reflect and plan on closing the session.

The cases presented here all share several common features. In each case, the therapists' mindset, at the beginning of each encounter with their clients, was that the present, face-to-face contact with the client would likely be the last time that they would have to be helpful. So, even in the cases where clients returned, the first and subsequent sessions were always treated as the last session, not the first session, second session, and so on. We think that this is one of the most important features of our SST work; the assumption, at the outset, that this was going to be the only session. Some of these cases were scheduled appointments; others were walk-in sessions. Regardless, they were all treated as single-sessions. Sometimes the sessions lasted about an hour, sometimes a bit longer, and one was only 30 minutes. In every case there were two therapists and a team of four or five of their peers in an observation room with the supervisor. Finally, all of the vignettes describe work with Hispanic clients. We point this out because frequently, at workshops and other teaching venues, we are asked, "Does this model or approach work with [insert population/ cultural group]?" We have found that our walk-in/single-session model has been a particularly good fit in our community where walking in for services is commonplace, and the idea that multiple visits for help is uncommon. Other contributors to this volume, however, describe applications of SST with other populations in the United States as well as in Canada, Israel, Mexico, Cambodia, and Sweden—convincingly demonstrating the appropriateness of the model across cultures.

Notes

1 The authors want to acknowledge team members and co-therapists who participated in these cases: Alyssa Arredondo, Martha Guerra, Gabriela López, and Wade Petree. Monte Bobele was the supervisor for all of these cases.

2 Not all cases are seen using a SST model at the CCS. Some supervisors offer training in multisession models.

3 The CCS also trains masters' and doctoral students in other long- and short-term individual, couple, and family therapy models. OLLUSA's Counseling Psychology program has been accredited by the American Psychological Association for over 20 years, and the Masters' program is accredited by the American Association for Marriage and Family Therapy.

4 The *Outcome Rating Scale* is a short instrument administered at the beginning of the session as a way of assessing current levels of distress. The *SRS* is a short instrument administered at the end of the session as a way of assessing the therapeutic alliance (Duncan, Miller, Wampold, & Hubble, 2010; Duncan & Sparks, 2010).

5 See Green (2011) for an earlier collection of single-session stories from the CCS.

6 Battino (2014) has used the term *sequential single-session*. We have come to refer to this phenomenon as *serial single-sessions*.

References

Battino, R. (2014). Expectation: The essence of very brief therapy. In M. F. Hoyt & M. Talmon (Eds.), *Capturing the moment: Single session therapy and walk-in services* (pp. 393–406.) Bethel, CT: Crown House Publishing.

Berg, I.K. (2008). *"I'd hear laughter": Finding solutions for the family* (streaming video). Psychotherapy.net.

Bobele, M. (1988). Reply to "Public policy in life-threatening situations." *Journal of Marital and Family Therapy, 14*(2), 139–141.

Bobele, M., López, Scamardo, M., & Solórzano, B. (2008). Single-session/walk-in therapy with Mexican-American clients. *Journal of Systemic Therapies, 27*(4), 75–89.

Duncan, B.L. & Sparks, J. A. (2010). *Heroic clients, heroic agencies: Partners for change.* Jensen Beach, FL: HSCP Press.

Duncan, B.L., Miller, S.D., Wampold, B.E., & Hubble, M.A. (Eds.) (2010). *The heart and soul of change: Delivering what works in therapy* (2nd ed.). Washington, DC: American Psychological Association.

Green, K. (2011). Single-session stories. In A. Slive & M. Bobele (Eds.), *When one hour is all you have: Effective therapy for walk-in clients* (pp. 65–92). Phoenix, AZ: Zeig, Tucker, & Theisen.

Lambert, M.J. (1992). Psychotherapy outcome research: Implications for integrative and eclectic therapists. In J.C. Norcross & M.R. Goldfried (Eds.), *Handbook of psychology integration* (pp. 94–129). New York: Basic Books.

Messer, S.B. & Wampold, B. E. (2002). Let's face facts: Common factors are more potent than specific therapy ingredients. *Clinical Psychology: Science and Practice, 9*(1), 21--25.

Molnar, A. & de Shazer, S. (1987). Solution focused therapy: Toward the identification of therapeutic tasks. *Journal of Marital and Family Therapy, 13*(4), 349–358.

Ray, W. & Keeney, B. (1993). *Resource focused therapy.* London: Karnac.

Ripley, J.S. & Worthington, E.L. (2002). Hope-focused and forgiveness-based group interventions to promote marital enrichment. *Journal of Counseling & Development, 80*, 452–463. doi:10.1002/j.1556-6678.2002.tb00212.x.

Sharry, J., Madden, B., Darmody, M., & Miller, S. (2001). Giving our clients the break: Applications of client-directed, outcome-informed clinical work. *Journal of Systemic Therapies, 20*(3), 68–76.

Simon, J.K. & Nelson, T.S. (2007). *I am more than my label: Solution-focused brief practice with long-term users of mental health services.* New York: Haworth Press.

Slive, A.B. & Bobele, M. (Eds.) (2011). *When one hour is all you have: Effective therapy with walk-in clients.* Phoenix, AZ: Zeig, Tucker & Theisen.

Slive, A. & Bobele, M. (2012). Walk-in counselling services: Making the most of one hour. *Australian and New Zealand Journal of Family Therapy, 33*(1), 27–38.

Snyder, C.R., Rand, K.L., & Sigmon, D.R. (2002). Hope theory. In C. R. Snyder & S. J. Lopez (Eds.), *Handbook of positive psychology* (pp. 257–276). New York: Oxford University Press.

Stone, H. (2002). The thirty minute counseling case. *Journal of Pastoral Counseling, 6*(1), 71–76. doi: 10.1300/J062v6n01_06.

Zeig, J.K. (1997). Experiential approaches to clinician development. In J.K. Zeig (Ed.), *The evolution of psychotherapy: The third conference* (pp. 166–177). New York: Brunner/Mazel.

16 Single-Session Walk-Ins as a Collaborative Learning Community at the Houston Galveston Institute

Susan B. Levin, Adriana Gil-Wilkerson, and Sylvia Rapini De Yatim

At the Houston Galveston Institute (HGI) the way we practice walk-in counseling is informed by Collaborative Therapy. We use the same collaborative and dialogical practices as we do in all our work with clients. As Harlene Anderson (1997, p. 71, emphasis in original) stated, "Such a collaborative therapy system is like a *conversational partnership* in which therapist and client mutually define membership, determine boundaries, and select the target of treatment." When receiving clients on a walk-in basis we begin with the intention of creating a relationship with clients where they are as much a part of deciding how long or how often they want to attend therapy as well as in indicating what topics they want to discuss in therapy.

We practice with the tenets of Collaborative Therapy as developed by Anderson and Goolishian (1992) and embrace the idea that "the client is the expert" in his or her life. We create "treatment" while engaged in a process of mutual inquiry with the client and in a conversational partnership that begins when the client calls us or walks through the door (Anderson, 1997). One of the key concepts of Collaborative Therapy is "not knowing" (Anderson & Goolishian, 1992; Anderson, 1997), which emphasizes the constructed nature of knowledge and that we are always on the way to understanding rather than being able to find objective truth. Anderson (2007, p. 39) argued that "although silent thoughts are generative, it is the expression of thought whether through articulation or gesture into the relational space" that fosters a meaning-generating process. Anderson called this philosophical practice "being public." In each conversation, one's beliefs, values, and life experiences are undoubtedly involved and challenged. Articulating those inner thoughts and being aware of making them public may influence one to consider their potential impact and whether they may be relevant for the client served during a single session (Anderson, 2007; Paul & Ommeren, 2013). Making one's thoughts and values public becomes a very present thought or practice that we do with each of our clients when they walk-in for services; we may not be seeing them more than once. We acknowledge that each client has a choice and the ability to decide how often and how long they need to come to therapy.

Our Walk-in Program is built around the notion that clients decide how and when to access therapy. We promote the program alongside our other therapy and consultation services so that clients can identify and choose their own way in; the way they want to include us in their search for possibilities. We also promote our Walk-in Program as a training opportunity for therapists or student-therapists who are curious to learn more about Collaborative Practices as well as walk-in counseling services. After starting our Walk-In Program in 2013, it quickly became a part of our training tradition. We have created and engaged in a live Collaborative Learning Community, an approach to learning and training that is founded upon postmodern ideas (Anderson, 1997 2000; Anderson & Swim, 1993, 1995; Anderson, 2013). Anderson and Swim (1993) described Collaborative Learning as a tradition that "entails a partnership in which the wisdom, knowledge and customs of the members of a local learning community ... are acknowledged, accessed and utilized." This practice allows us to continue to use one of our long-standing collaborative practices—the reflecting team (Andersen, 1987). Many of our Walk-In clients are seen with a reflecting team, in the room, to work with them and generate possibilities and ideas with the client.

Another major influence on the development of HGI's Walk-In Program is Slive and Bobele's work (Slive, 2008; Slive & Bobele, 2011, 2012) and their generous consultations with us. They inspired and supported our thoughts about developing this program, as did the work of Hoyt and Talmon (2014), Hoyt (2011), and Young (2011).

Welcoming and Accessible Services

One of the most important concepts of our Walk-In Program is that it offers a welcoming and accessible environment to our guests. We consider our clients to be guests, and that their visit is a special opportunity to invite them into a conversation that will be helpful to them. Harlene Anderson talks about a host/guest metaphor (Anderson, 2007) wherein the therapist acts as both a host and a guest at the same time. As hosts, we are responsible for offering a therapeutic climate that is comfortable, respectful, inviting, and attentive. As guests in the lives of our clients, we must respect that they are sharing their lives with us as *they wish* to do so, and not poke around opening doors and cabinets without permission.

The Walk-In Program at HGI meets the demands of one of the most racially and ethnically diverse metropolitan areas in the U.S. (Emerson, Bratter, Howell, Jeanty, & Cline, 2014). The program opens possibilities for those who typically do not access therapy because potential clients do not have to call and answer a list of intake questions over the phone. There are no long waiting lists. Clients just arrive and a therapist welcomes them, providing them with intake forms and inviting them to join a counseling session. Having a brief intake process handled by therapists, not by reception staff, helps to reduce barriers and create a welcoming environment. On Saturdays, there is always a bilingual English-Spanish therapist, and often volunteer therapists who speak other languages. The possibility of offering face-to-face counseling services in languages other than English minimizes the stresses associated with language barriers such as speaking English with an accent, or not speaking English at all. Many immigrants describe hating to make medical/counseling appointments over the phone because they are concerned whether the person on the other side will understand what they are saying, including something as basic as how to spell their first and last names.

We have already mentioned a number of ways that we make services accessible to our community. We think of *access* in its broadest way, not just physical accessibility but also relational, cultural, and financial. We try to remove as many barriers as possible to make services optimally accessible. Walk-in clients meet a therapist in the waiting area and are given a brief welcome and a two-page information sheet. We do not screen clients ahead of time for diagnosis, nor financial status. All who show up are invited to participate, including family and non-family members. We assume that the people who come in the door have a reason for being there and we learn about them and why they are there as part of our introductions and in our session. The session does not involve screening, either. It is our practice to work with the client on the issues that *they decide* are important. Our motto for the Walk-In Program is "You Decide," meaning that the client decides when to come in, whether to come back, what they want to talk about, and what was meaningful for them in the conversation.

This atmosphere of our Collaborative Learning Community is isomorphic with the experience of our volunteers and learners who come to work in our Walk-In Program. Most of the time, our Walk-In therapists work in a team. These team members are welcomed as valued guests and hosts as part of a community that is supportive, and supporting, of each other and of our clients. This approach fosters a strong and connected experience as clients *decide* how, when, and whether they are interested in continuing their relationship with HGI.

Walk-In allows us to serve clients who, for various reasons, do not want to enter "traditional therapy." Some are not sure they are ready for therapy, and use the Walk-In to "try therapy out." They may be afraid of being diagnosed or judged, and this is an opportunity for us to offer them an alternative experience. Others are concerned that they do not have the money or the time to engage in "typical or traditional therapy." Many think that if they go to therapy it will take them months or years to complete. Some people have a very specific question or issue that they want to focus on, and know that it will be helpful for them to have a single session. Knowing that they won't be pressured or expected to "sign on" for long-term services may be important for people. Some people are in crisis and do not want, or need, to go to a hospital, where they may get more than they are expecting in terms of medication, hospitalization, etc. Some clients already have a therapist, but for some reason cannot get in to see their therapist when they want to (e.g., therapist is on vacation, or has a busy schedule, or something has come up between appointments). Some people live too far away to get to therapy regularly.

Program Operations

The Walk-In program operates six days a week, Monday through Friday from 3:00–7:00 p.m. and all day on Saturday. Sessions with clients are typically one hour, though occasional situations demand longer sessions. When clients come in for the first time they are informed at the beginning of the session that they will be able to choose whether they would like to come back or tell us that they have gotten what they need. Clients are told that they can make this decision while they are here, or they can call or come in for another single session. People find out about HGI's Walk-In Program through word-of-mouth, referrals from community agencies and professionals, and HGI brochures and website. HGI has many partners in the community for other services who also refer to the Walk-In Program.

Reflecting Team at HGI's Walk-In Program

At the HGI Walk-In Program, most of the time, single-session therapy is conducted using live reflecting teams, enriching the counseling process. This way of working is possible because there is a large room available that could easily hold a family of six members, two leading therapists and up to five reflecting team members. Chair arrangements occur easily and quickly to adjust to an individual, couple, or family session.

The reflecting teams at HGI consist of graduate students in counseling, marriage and family therapy, trainee therapists, intern or fully licensed professional counselors, licensed or associate marriage and family therapists. At the Walk-In Program, team members vary weekly and the coordinator of the Walk-In Program manages an online calendar that shows volunteers' schedule/availability. The Walk-In Program coordinators interview each volunteer and provide an orientation to the practices at HGI. Each volunteer must commit to being a part of the team for at least eight hours a month. HGI's volunteer therapists come from many different levels of experience and training backgrounds; the majority come from the field of family therapy, counseling, and social work. They are only allowed to be part of the reflecting team after they receive training in Walk-In and SST at HGI.

Clients served at the Walk-In Program at HGI are informed about the SST process and reflecting team live modality while filling out the required paperwork. At the beginning of the session, reflecting team members introduce themselves to the clients. Two lead therapists conduct the session for about 30–35 minutes, and then the client and the therapists listen to the conversation between reflecting team members, which lasts about ten minutes. Then the client and the therapists reflect on what struck them the most as reflecting team members listen to them. Many clients find this experience to be very helpful, and appreciate the attention and perspective of multiple therapists. This process provides support and ideas for the therapists, as well. However, though not a common experience, some clients are not interested or uncomfortable having a team, and they are welcome to turn down the invitation to have a reflecting team.

The reflecting process is transparent, favoring less secrecy; everything is public, so clients have access to the team's ideas and reflections first-hand; and clients decide what to take away, and are invited to share what reflections struck them the most. Therapists learn different communication styles and ways to pose strengths-based and empathic reflections. Clients observe respectful communication interactions. Several clients have shared that they like listening to different ideas from different therapists in just one session. In financial terms it appears to have a high investment return for clients. As a client once said, "I am paying only for one session but receiving feedback like if I would have attended several sessions."

HGI finds using reflecting teams to be an integral part of collaborative practice. During reflections the "not knowing" stance is used to offer multiple ideas rather than a single or consensual opinion or intervention from the team. The client is encouraged to take or leave the comments, ideas and suggestions from the team based on how they fit; the client is the expert on what is helpful for them; *they decide.*

Using and Collecting Client Feedback

Clients provide feedback on each session, using the *Partners for Change Outcome Measurement* system (PCOMS; Duncan, 2012). This system includes two simple but reliable feedback tools measuring client wellness (the *Outcome Rating Scale*) and the therapeutic alliance (the *Session Rating Scale*). The *Session Rating Scale* (*SRS*) provides a check-in with the client regarding the degree to which they feel "heard," understood, respected, and are getting to talk about what they want to talk about. PCOMS is listed as an assessment instrument in the Substance Abuse and Mental Health Services Administration's (SAMHSA) National Registry of Evidence-Based Practices and Programs (http://nrepp.samhsa.gov/ViewIntervention.aspx?id=250).

HGI decided to use this feedback system in the Walk-In Program as it is very compatible with Collaborative Therapy and the philosophy that the client is the expert, in this case evaluating their progress and the outcome of therapy. In addition to using the written feedback form, the therapist continues to check-in with the client during the session; however, the PCOMS offers a written documentation that is useful for larger scale data analysis. The PCOMS is (1) used to guide the therapeutic conversation, especially important if this is the only session; (2) gives feedback on the therapist–client relationship, a critical common factor in predicting change (Duncan, 2012); (3) gives us ideas of the level of wellness/distress people are in when they come to our Walk-In Program; and (4) can be used, if clients decide to come back, to view changes in these levels over time. Current data analysis of the clients (N = 32) who completed an *ORS* and *SRS* at walk-in sessions yielded a mean *ORS* score of 21.2. This is an interesting score to note, as it is only slightly lower than the average *ORS* score of 24 for clients (N = 112) who attend regular ongoing counseling at HGI. The mean *SRS* scores are almost the same for clients in the Walk-In Program (35.4), and in the regular counseling programs at HGI (36). This indicates a good level of satisfaction with the therapy services, with scores below 35 leading to conversations with clients about how to improve the therapeutic relationship.

The success of this program has recently resulted in our decision to offer walk-in services daily (except Sundays). Going from two days per week to six days per week takes some logistical and staff time; however, we are confident that these efforts will be met with positive response and better meet the needs of the community at large.

Clinical Example: From Desperation to Relief in Just One Hour

Mayte came to the Walk-In Program on a Saturday late afternoon. After Mayte filled out all the standard forms, the therapists invited her into the therapy room. She was informed about the SST format and that two therapists would be facilitating the collaborative conversation. She was offered a reflecting team in the room and she agreed. During the initial process she shared that she found out about HGI Walk-In services on the Internet and reported no previous experience in counseling. This young woman shared being of Hispanic background and evangelic faith; she reported being married and a stay-at-home mother of two children. Mayte expressed that she came to therapy due to feelings of despair and inadequacy. As the conversation evolved she shared having thoughts of harming her little one. She became emotional and expressed feelings of inadequacy and shame for having those thoughts. She denied ever doing anything to harm her children. When asked what prevented her from coming to therapy sooner, she stated she was ashamed and afraid she would be reported to the authorities and that they would remove her children. She also stated a fear that if she went to therapy she would be found to be "insane." She became emotional and repeatedly expressed feelings of inadequacy as a mother and said that she was living "in sin." She denied any form of abuse to her children. What initially appeared to be an emergency situation evolved into a dialogue in which Mayte felt more comfortable and elaborated on the specific times when the problem feelings emerged. She also identified times when those thoughts were not present and what she was doing in those times. Initially, praying and going for strolls were the coping skills identified.

After 30 minutes the reflecting team dialogued about her bravery in coming in for counseling, her ability to be able to control her thoughts of harming her children, and that other clients have similar problems. Mayte got struck by the last reflection and expressed that she thought she was the only one with intrusive thoughts. She further added that it was great listening to different therapists. Mayte's demeanor changed and her mood appeared to lift. "That means I am not crazy," she said. Then the therapists began to work with her on a plan to manage her thoughts in case they would arise again. Mayte said she would get out of the house more often and go for strolls twice or three times per day, she would attend religious services twice per week, and would seek to spend some time with a friend. At the end of the session she rated her ability to control those intrusive thoughts as 10 out of 10.

Community resources were provided, and Mayte was reminded that the Walk-In service was available during weekdays as well. A follow-up call was conducted a week later during which she reported doing well and feeling no need to come to therapy at that time.

The therapists working with this client were very tuned in to her story. Viewing her as the expert in her situation, utilizing a non-judgmental stance, and focusing on her story allowed the therapists to conduct a risk assessment in a non-obtrusive and non-threatening way. From the very beginning of the session she denied any desire, attempts, or gestures of harming her children. She voiced many times her love and devotion to them. Undoubtedly, if Mayte would have reported a gesture or attempt, or rated her ability to control intrusive thoughts below 10, further assessment would have been conducted. Our work with this client is an example of using collaborative practices such as listening with an intention of learning about her and her situation, using a reflecting team, having a not-knowing and non-judgmental stance and being with her. This conversation allowed the client to shift her beliefs about being crazy in just one hour.

Summary

The creation and growth of the HGI Walk-In Counseling Program has been very exciting. There were many unknowns that unfolded in positive ways, and others that we learned that we needed to modify. We were surprised to learn that so many volunteer therapists, more than 30 over the past three years, were interested in giving their time and services to this program. We learned that there were many, including some who could not end up joining the program, who wanted to learn how to work with Walk-Ins, and how to work in a reflecting team format. Working at HGI was something that many had been interested in, and this gave people a way to do so. In fact, several of our volunteers have ended up as employees. Another surprise was the recognition by the community that this was a needed service, and in addition to sending us referrals, having radio and newspaper media attention, one of the psychiatric hospitals in our area opened a Walk-In Program for psychiatric crises, to cut down on the high demand for psychiatric services in emergency rooms.

Another lesson we learned is that when people learned we had a Walk-In Program, they assumed that it was available during all of our working time. Since we started with only one day a week for Walk-In, and had people come in on other days, we had to scramble to accommodate them. This led to us needing to expand our Walk-In days to six days per week, though we still limit Walk-In hours to evenings Monday through Friday. We still have clients come in at other times, but the frequency of this has greatly reduced. Finally, due to the expansion to six days per week we had to add volunteers and coordinators who could cover the additional hours. We do have fewer volunteers during the week, as opposed to Saturdays; however, our staff therapists are more likely to be in the office and are available as backup, when needed.

The success of the HGI program is due to a combination of our collaborative and dialogical therapeutic approach, the use of reflecting teams, the resourcefulness of our clients, the enthusiasm and good will of volunteer therapists, and the enormous need for accessible services in the community.

References

Andersen, T. (1987). The reflecting team: Dialogue and meta-dialogue in clinical work. *Family Process, 26*, 415–428.

Anderson, H. (1997). *Conversation, language, and possibilities: A postmodern therapy*. New York: Basic Books.

Anderson, H. (2000, Fall). Supervision as a collaborative learning community. *American Association for Marriage and Family Therapy Supervision Bulletin*, pp. 7–10.

Anderson, H. (2007). The heart and spirit of collaborative therapy: The philosophical stance—"A way of being" in relationship and conversation. In H. Anderson & D. Gehart (Eds.), *Collaborative therapy: Relationships and conversations that make a difference* (pp. 43–59). New York: Routledge.

Anderson, H. (2013). Collaborative learning communities: A postmodern perspective on teaching and learning. In B. Irby, G. Brown, R. Lara-Alecio, & S. Jackson (Eds.), *The handbook of educational theories* (pp. 515–527). Charlotte, NC: Information Age Publishing.

Anderson, H. & Goolishian, H. (1992). The client is the expert: A not-knowing approach to therapy. In S. McNamee & K.J. Gergen (Eds.), *Therapy as social construction* (pp. 25–39). Newbury Park, CA: Sage.

Anderson, H. & Swim, S. (1993). Learning as collaborative conversation: Combining the student's and teacher's expertise. *Human Systems: The Journal of Systemic Consultation & Management, 4*, 145–160.

Anderson, H. & Swim, S. (1995). Supervision as collaborative conversation: Connecting the voices of supervisor and supervisee. *Journal of Systemic Therapies, 14*(2), 1–13.

Duncan, B. (2012). The partners for change outcome management system (PCOMS): The heart and soul of change project. *Canadian Psychology, 53*(2), 93–91.

Emerson, M., Bratter, J., Howell, J. Jeanty, P., & Cline, M. (2014). *Houston region grows more racially/ethnically diverse, with small declines in segregation: A joint report analyzing census data from 1990, 2000, and 2010*. Houston, TX: Kinder Institute for Urban Research for the Hobby Center for the Study of Texas.

Hoyt, M.F. (2011). Foreword. In A. Slive & M. Bobele (Eds.) *When one hour is all you have: Effective therapy for walk-in clients* (pp. ix–xv). Phoenix, AZ: Zeig, Tucker, & Theisen.

Hoyt, M.F. & Talmon, M. (Eds.) (2014). *Capturing the moment: Single-session therapy and walk-in services.* Bethel, CT: Crown House Publishing.

Paul, K.E. & Ommeren, M. (2013). A primer on single session therapy and its potential application in humanitarian situations. *Intervention, 11*(1), 8–23.

Slive, A. (2008). Special section: Walk-in single session therapy. *Journal of Systemic Therapies, 27*(4), 1–4.

Slive, A. & Bobele, M. (Eds.) (2011). *When one hour is all you have: Effective therapy for walk-in clients.* Phoenix, AZ: Zeig, Tucker, & Theisen.

Slive, A. & Bobele, M. (2012). Walk-in counseling services: Making the most of one hour. *Australian and New Zealand Journal of Family Therapy, 33*, 27–38.

Young, K. (2011). Narrative practices at a walk-in therapy clinic. In A. Slive & M. Bobele (Eds.), *When one hour is all you have: Effective therapy for walk-in clients* (pp. 149–166). Phoenix, AZ: Zeig, Tucker, & Theisen.

17 Co-Crafting Take-Home Documents at the Walk-In

Scot Cooper and "Ariane"

As is the practice of a brief narrative therapist, I met Ariane (age 15) at the walk-in therapy clinic[1] through her "wonderfulnesses,"[2] learning about her love for art, which she learned from watching her mother paint. She explained how with art "you can turn whatever mood or thought into something cool." She further introduced herself to me as someone who is a considerate person who enjoys helping people and giving care to others. She explained how through her volunteer work she gained experience helping others where her belief that "you should treat people the way you want to be treated" shines through in how she is with people. This introduction put her reason for coming into the walk-in on this day into perspective. Ariane described that she had found herself with thoughts and feelings that were not usual for her. She linked this to troubles at home and a great deal of stress that she had to handle.

Her stepfather had been ill for some time. He had survived a heart attack and was in and out of hospital. He was diagnosed with diabetes and subsequently had a leg amputated. In his struggles with these developments, Ariane experienced him as stubborn in that he would balk at any assistance and medical help. His mood was unpredictable as at times he was mean-spirited towards her while other times nicer. She noted how often she could tell it was the disease talking, not him. It was still difficult to hear and experience though.

Ariane's mother worked out of the home fulltime, so some of the responsibility for care of her stepfather was on Ariane's young shoulders. While she accepted this role, increasingly she was experiencing greater stress and a sense that she was becoming backgrounded, neglected, and ignored. She shared that thoughts of suicide would come and go but she had no intention or plan to act on them. They were like warning bells to her that something had to change. She wanted to be free of the stress and had a sense that she needed more help from her mom.

Despite this circumstance, Ariane noted she had been able to carry on in several ways. She would tap into what she called a "stubbornness" to do what she prioritized as needing to happen. She found ways to keep herself busy to take her mind off of the situation. She thought about the future and times when it was and will be better.

Hearing Ariane's story evoked for me at the time many memories of my own grandmother's experience of caregivers while she lived in a long-term care facility due to frontal lobe temporal dementia. I shared with Ariane how the disease seemed to erase her manners, patience, and social graces to the point that she was often harsh, difficult, and mean. Many caregivers found her insulting and awful to work with yet some seemed to have a gift for the job. They struck me as the kind of people who could see the person aside from the illness, recognizing in my grandmothers' situation, that it was the dementia hurling insults not my grandmother. They could depersonalize these moods and worked in a way to maintain her dignity. I shared with Ariane how I was reminded of this when she described how she could tell when it was the diabetes talking for her stepfather and not his caring voice. After re-telling what I had heard, I wondered if Ariane was the kind of caregiver that was more the exception than the norm. She supposed she might be. I shared how it seemed to me that she was in a young caregivers' apprenticeship of sorts, and I wondered if she was learning from the situation the kinds of skills professional caregivers would need? She had thought so, and highlighted that she already had many skills others would not have at her age. I asked what difference it made to know this about herself—that she has this gift for the work and that she has many skills ahead of her time? Ariane commented how it helped her to know "she already has gotten something out of it." She has "something to lean back on if needed to and that these skills will one day take her somewhere in her career."

I mentioned that in my walk-in conversations I meet many "young caregiver apprentices." Some are caring for a parent with cancer while others share in the care for aging grandparents. I wondered if Ariane would be willing to share with them some of what she had learned in her apprenticeship to date? What advice or things to remember would she think they may benefit from? And would she be willing to craft with me a document that archives her know-how with the intention to display it in our waiting room so it could be consulted by them in the future? Generously she took up my proposal and together we began to co-craft *Ariane's Manual for Young Caregivers* with the following content.

> All young caregivers live an apprenticeship of sorts. We are growing important skills! This manual shares those skills and learnings as well as even the hazards along the way on this precious journey!
>
> - Good days can turn into bad days in seconds. Remember—bad days can turn into great days just as quickly.
> - Always try and think of the days when everything will be better, try to hold on to that hope that things will be better, looking forward to something makes for great motivation.
> - It's hard to be help to others if you are no help to yourself.
> - Always remember to consider yourself, put yourself forward as well as others. Balance yourself.
> - Keep in mind those little things that can cheer you up, whether it's a cat or playing soccer.

- Keeping yourself distracted is a great way to cope with things whether you draw, go for nature walks, play music, anything to get your mind off what's got you down!
- Tap into any stubbornness when needed.
- Always remember, no matter how rough or hard it is, it's a learning experience. You will get something out of it. It gives you something to lean on or something that will take you places even if you didn't know it!

Ariane's Manual for Young Caregivers is one of many such documents that can be co-crafted in single-session therapy encounters. She took a copy home with her[3] and generously provided one for our waiting room to share with other young caregivers that we meet at the walk-in clinic. They are invited to add their wisdom to the manual so that it continues to grow.

Kinds of Take-Home Documents

I refer to these documents as "take-home documents" as they are crafted within the single session with the intention of returning home with the person consulting to us and perhaps finding a wider circulation with a fitting audience. This practice is fully inspired by the work of Michael White and David Epston (1990; White, 1995), and Jennifer Freeman, Epston, and Dean Lobovits (1997) who introduced co-crafting therapeutic documents as part of narrative practice. In the time-constrained context of single-session therapy their usefulness finds even greater importance. Many kinds of take-home documents can be co-authored within a single session as we are only limited by our imagination. Some documents I often turn to include those listed in the following text.

Letters

White and Epston (1990) introduced several kinds of therapeutic letters informed by narrative practice. The written word in letters does not fade in the same way conversations do and as such is very relevant to single-session therapy. At the walk-in the letter I most often invite people to co-craft within the single session is written to an externalized Problem[4] that we have been discussing. Together we put that problem on notice of a change in the person's relationship with It. The theme of these letters could involve a "break up" with the Problem, or serve the purpose to educate the Problem about changes to come (see "Letter to Depression" in Cooper, 2014). These letters seem most relevant to teenagers and adults who plan to circulate and consult the letters as needed.

Lists

The practice of listing provides a very brief and useful take-home document especially for young children. I take the opportunity to list counter thoughts and/or counter talk that young people employ in the face of problems. That material can be contrasted to the Problem's talk and tactics, bringing them into juxtaposition and providing an opportunity to examine their relevance. Other times a list may serve as a means to collect up the traces of know-how that could be put to further use. Many young people have come to discount or forget their own ideas about what they have done that has made a difference in the past or their ideas about how to proceed. Listing this knowledge collects it together and often informs plans and next steps to employ when they leave. Freedman and Combs (2002, pp. 167–182) speak to the many benefits of the co-development of lists with children and youths. Among these benefits I appreciate that lists can be continually revisited and added to. Given this, I am sure to leave space for prospective discoveries that can be added once the youth returns home.

Handbooks

Handbooks[5] go hand in hand with co-created lists. Alongside Ariane's manual another handbook that sits in the waiting room at my office is *The Big Book of Taming & Training Worry Critters, Creatures, and Varmints.* The inside cover reads as follows:

> Welcome to The Big Book of Taming & Training Worry Critters, Creatures, and Varmints. This book is a growing collection of the ways children and youth handle "Worry" when it becomes unruly, too big, or just takes up too much of their time.

The book is full of lists of ideas children have generated with me at the walk-in to assist with taming or training their experience of worry. The children and youths take a copy of their ideas and/or plan with them but are also thrilled to contribute to the book in the hope that their ideas will be given to other children facing similar circumstances.[6] Other additions to the handbook include pictures of these Worry Creatures rendered visible by the children. From Worry Bats, to Two-Headed Worry Critters, to more obscure monsterish looking animals, I have a diverse and useful collection of ideas and species.

Conversation Summaries

A co-developed document created most often at our walk-in is the Conversation Summary.[7] This is a form on which I will, with the client's permission, make notes in the moment of what I have heard during the session including parts of the problem story, particular skills and abilities or values and stated intentions, initiatives, and exceptions to the problem, counter thoughts, as well as the agreed-upon plan or next steps. I photocopy this document, and one copy becomes the filed record and the other is offered to the person(s) consulting to me to keep with them.

Poems

I meet many youths who have researched the Internet collecting poems and sayings relevant to their circumstances. Together poems can be co-crafted, drawing from their own words, meaningful phrases or expressions recorded on the conversation summary. Often youth are very generous in allowing these poems to be circulated to others.

Statements of Position

Periodically walk-in conversations assist people to revise their position towards a problem. Especially relevant to youth who often may not have had the opportunity to explore and make visible the influence of a problem in their life, these conversations invite them to reflect, revise their understanding, and form commitments to new action.[8] This shift can be archived in a "statement of position document" (White 1995, p. 205) that articulates the revision. For instance, youths arriving via others concerned about their "drug life" may initially arrive with little or no concern about that drug life. However, after conversation making visible the effects of the drug life on their relationships, education, and future they may come to a very different position about the drug life and perhaps step further into a commitment to shift their use of drugs. Recording this revised position and the benefits of it in a co-crafted take-home document keeps it visible and proves useful in "extending the conversation" (Epston, 1994) beyond the moment. They can be read for inspiration or as a reminder of a commitment to a course of action and its benefits.

Certificates/Diplomas

Specific certificates or diplomas can be crafted on the spot as markers of new or revised meanings. For instance, I may craft a certificate awarded for taking a new position on a problem or to mark a renewed commitment to action. I may co-craft a diploma highlighting a youth's knowledge as a means to elevate it and bring it to the foreground. In some situations, I may induct a youth into various clubs such as the Secret Society of Young Protesters or the Young Caregivers Club and award a certificate of membership. This serves to break the isolation that problems often benefit from.

Benefits of Co-crafting Take Home Documents

All these take-home documents serve common purposes. In co-crafting the document we are creating a context favorable to the experience of personal agency. That is, the youths in that very moment of co-authorship are taking action and intervening in their life. The experience of personal agency fosters a sense of hope and possibility of change.

These documents also archive a youth's and family's own knowledge as opposed to solely professional knowledge. As you can see from Ariane's manual, her recorded know-how is very nuanced. It reflects what she has learned, her skills, and ideas that she draws upon each day. As a brief narrative therapist, it is my responsibility to invite her to mentor me in that know-how and to collect it up with her so it may be put to more use. Capturing that know-how in a take-home document keeps it in the foreground so it is more accessible when needed. Keeping their ideas and skills present in this concrete way, the ideas and skills are less likely to be forgotten or overshadowed by the problem as people return to the context of their lives.

Take-home documents may also highlight sparkling moments, initiatives, and exceptions that can be drawn together into "stories in the making." They serve to elevate a developing counter-story[9] out of the panorama of lived experience and problem-dominant accounts of life. As these documents return home with people they serve to extend the range of influence of the conversation beyond the face-to-face contact. They provide a receiving context for new information and ideas congruent with their focus creating a favorable context for the story in the making to grow.

When take-home documents are shared they help to circulate the know-how or emerging story with a meaningful audience. That audience can be invited to respond and play a greater part in assisting with the project, whatever that might be. Furthermore, when that audience includes other youths and families who are experiencing similar circumstances the documents provide useful ideas and let them know they are not alone in their experiences. Very often youths and families offer a copy of their document to display in our waiting room so they can be easily accessed by other families arriving at the walk-in clinic.

Co-crafting Documents

In co-crafting these documents there is an etiquette that serves to structure safety, foster transparency, and provide guidance. It is common practice in brief narrative therapy to take notes as the discussion is occurring (Epston & White 1990; Freedman & Combs 2002; Young, Dick, Herring, & Lee, 2008). However, we ask permission to do this recording. Our notes strive to archive people's own words and phrases or the agreed-upon language we share in. Often the take-home document is drawn from these notes.

I first prefer the possible creation of a document in a preamble noting that perhaps it would be useful to craft a document collecting up the youth's/family's know-how. To act transparently I then share my thoughts about why I am suggesting this, noting that a document could be consulted later after our conversation or perhaps be shared with family members or help other people who might benefit from reading it. Once we have agreement, the process is one of co-creation in which I may begin taking the lead offering a phrase or partial sentence or pictorial idea but then gesture to my conversational partner to continue on to add their ideas and images. We weave back and forth as I provide structure and guidance often fitting with particular maps of narrative therapy and they provide the content specific to their lives. The process also involves summarizing back, editing and revising as we go.

Once the document is completed I ask if they would like to take a copy with them. It's important to ask, as in some contexts it may not be safe or private enough to store a take-home document depending on its content. I also ask if they would be interested in having their document shared with other people who may be facing similar circumstance and who may benefit from their ideas.[10] I have had many experiences in which these documents serve to inspire others and assure people that they are not alone in the experience of distress, but rather are part of a collective whose ideas can shoulder each other up when drawn upon. Copies of take-home documents such as poems or handbooks about the problem remain in our waiting room as material for people to browse or consult when they arrive at the walk-in clinic. Many times I will direct people to specific documents or invite them to add their contributions to a growing document such as *The Big Book of Taming & Training Worry Critters, Creatures, and Varmints.*

Consulting the Documents and Speculating

As a brief narrative therapist I am always looking for ways to foster the endurance of our conversations so that they become resistant to assimilation back into the problem story. White (1995) has proposed questions to foster endurance by eliciting from people their ideas about when to review their document as well as their predictions about the influence of the document in their life.

Following the completion of the take-home document, I invite people to identify the circumstances under which the document might be consulted. At times, they may articulate a schedule such as, "first thing when I wake up, before each class at school and then twice before bedtime." Other times children and families may decide to read their document together on a less formal schedule, perhaps whenever they sense a vulnerability to the problem. This practice serves to help people contextualize the document into their everyday living. I might ask:

- How many copies would you like to take with you?
- Where would it be useful to keep this document?
- When would be a useful time to read/review your document so that it has the most influence?

Next I invite people to speculate wildly about what difference consulting their document will make in their thoughts/feelings/actions throughout the most relevant domains of their life including to their sense of self:

- What difference will it make to have this with you when you leave?
- What might it make possible for you as you are continually reminded of this information?
- What will this remind you about who you are becoming that the Problem would want to blind you from?

- What will it be like to know your document is helping other youths and families who come to our walk-in service?

Thirdly, I invite the children/families to identify others with whom it would be important to share this document and how might those named respond.[11] This serves as a means to recruit an audience to the project who may witness and respond in meaningful ways. Inviting speculation about those responses paints a picture favorable to preferred outcomes. This serves as a way to further counter and eventually displace the problem story:

- Who would be most important person to share this document with when you leave here?
- How might they respond when you share this with them? Do you suppose they too would want to join you in this project?
- How will this shape how they are coming to know you?

Once the audience is identified, I then supply them with the appropriate number of copies for distribution of the document. As noted, people are often also very willing to leave a copy behind that can be displayed in our waiting room to assist others who may experience similar circumstances.

Further Thoughts from Ariane

It was very useful for me [Ariane] to co-develop the young caregiver guide. It made me realize the potential I really had and gave me a boost to see what I was really capable of. Taking the manual home with me gave me a chance to review it, which, like I said before, gave me confidence when I was at my worst. It gave me reminders on how to handle certain situations when everything was overwhelming and stressful. Knowing I've helped others going through what I went through is an amazing feeling. No one should have to go through those things alone. It's very hard and no one asks for those things to happen—it just does. It's very difficult to give someone proper care when you don't have any experience or any idea what you're doing. Having something to reference, too, is very helpful. I shared the manual with family and friends and they were very happy and supportive that Scot and I put this project together.

Closing

In the context of a walk-in therapy clinic finding ways to extend the influence of a single session remains a creative and important project. Take-home documents specifically co-crafted during the walk-in conversation with the people consulting to us provide a meaningful vehicle toward this effort. These documents informed by people's own know-how, skills, and preferences remain very relevant to their living context and serve as keepsakes foregrounding what they bring to the process. When shared more broadly, take-home documents can make a meaningful contribution to others who may be experiencing similar circumstances.

Notes

1 The Walk-in Clinic I work at is part of a diverse service menu at a Children's Mental Health Centre in rural Ontario, Canada. The Walk-in Clinic is open every Tuesday from noon to 6:30 p.m. We serve children, youth and families up to the age of 18 and it is free to access with no appointment needed.
2 This is a phrase often used by David Epston in training workshops referring to "getting to know the child apart from the problem" and meeting them through what they bring to the process—their interests, skills, wishes and values (see Freeman, Epston, & Lobovits 1997, p. 34–46).
3 Alongside her manual Ariane took home the contact for the local Young Carers Initiative—a non-profit organization that promotes the wellbeing of Young Carers and their families through social, recreational and educational programs. She and her mother were provided the 24-hour youth crisis service call number if needed. Her mother was provided with the contact information for the local Community Care Access Centre who could provide additional support to Ariane's stepfather with the intention to increase the circle of care.
4 The word "Problem" is capitalized to reflect the objectification of problems as an entity the person is in relationship with.
5 I was first introduced to handbooks in the chapter "Publishing the News" in Freeman, Epston, and Lobovits (1997, pp. 125–142) which provides a very useful account of the practice.
6 See Epston and White (1990; Epston, White, & "Ben," 1995) and Marsten, Epston, and Johnson (2011) for the practice of Consulting Your Consultants.
7 For a template of this document see the Field Notes at www.briefnarrative.com.
8 These conversations are informed by narrative therapy conversation maps 1 and 2. See White (2007) for a thorough account of the domains of inquiry.
9 A counter-story is a specific kind of story that is in juxtaposition to the problem story and sets out to rehabilitate an assigned spoiled identity (see Cooper, 2014; Nelson, 2001; and Freeman, Epston, & Lobovits, 1997, pp. 94–111).
10 This is drawn from Epston and White's (1990) practice of consulting your consultants.
11 White and Epston (1990) have shaped this category of inquiry for me in their discussion of "unique circulation questions." They note how "the scope of alternative stories can be further extended through the introduction of questions that invite persons to identify and recruit an audience to the performance of new meanings in their life" (p. 41).

References

Cooper, S. (2014). Brief narrative practice at the walk-in clinic: The rise of the counterstory (online). *International Journal of Narrative Therapy and Community Work*, *2*, 23–30.

Epston, D. (1994). Extending the conversation. *Family Therapy Networker*, *18*(6), 30–37, 62–63.

Epston, D. & White, M. (1990). Consulting your consultants: The documentation of alternative knowledges. *Dulwich Centre Newsletter*, 4, 25–35. Republished in D. Epston & M. White (1992), *Experience, contradiction, narrative and imagination: Selected papers of David Epston & Michael White, 1989–1991* (pp. 11–26). Adelaide, Australia: Dulwich Centre Publications.

Epston, D., White, M., & "Ben." (1995). Consulting your consultants: A means to the co-construction of alternative knowledges. In S. Friedman (Ed.), *The reflecting team in action: Collaborative practice in family therapy* (pp. 277–313). New York: Guilford Press.

Freeman, J., Epston, D., & Lobovits, D. (1997). *Playful approaches to serious problems: Narrative therapy with children and their families.* New York: Norton.

Freedman, J. & Combs, G. (2002). *Narrative therapy with couples . . . and a whole lot more! A collection of papers, essays and exercises.* Adelaide, Australia: Dulwich Centre Publications.

Marsten, D., Epston, D., & Johnson, L. (2011). Consulting your consultants, revisited. *International Journal of Narrative Therapy and Community Work, 3*, 57–71.

Nelson, N.H. (2001). *Damaged identities, narrative repair.* Ithaca, NY: Cornell University Press.

White, M. (1995) Therapeutic documents revisited. In *Re-authoring lives: Interviews and essays* (pp. 199–213). Adelaide, Australia: Dulwich Centre Publications.

White, M. (2007). *Maps of narrative practice.* New York: Norton.

White, M. & Epston, D. (1990). *Narrative means to therapeutic ends.* New York: Norton.

Young, K., Dick, M., Herring, K., & Lee, J. (2008). From waiting lists to walk-in: stories from a walk-in therapy clinic. *Journal of Systemic Therapies, 27*, 23–39.

18 Coincidence Favors the Prepared Mind

Single Sessions with Couples in Sweden

Martin Söderquist

It takes time to implement new models. New ideas are hard to introduce and old habits die hard. This is the story of what we[1] have learned introducing Single-Session Therapy (SST) in Malmö, Sweden and how this approach can be beneficial to the couples.

"Impossible—You're Nuts!"

When Moshe Talmon published *Single-Session Therapy* in 1990, I and many of my brief therapy colleagues were inspired and wanted to get going. We all met clients in different contexts, had many unplanned single sessions, and worked in brief and solution-focused ways. The idea of "every session could be the last" guided us.

For many reasons, we didn't get to the point of using the ideas in Talmon's book in a planned or structured way. It wasn't until 2006, after several years in private practice, when I began working in a Couple Counseling Team in Helsingborg, that Talmon's ideas popped up for real in my thinking. Together with my colleagues we telephone interviewed 68 couples who had attended one session and asked them how come they came just once. Fifty-eight percent of the couples said, "One session was enough" or "We planned for just one session" (interestingly, they didn't tell the counselor).

In 2009, my colleague Bertil Ekstedt and I visited Calgary and realized we had missed the opportunity to visit the Eastside Family Centre Walk-In. (In 2015, my colleagues Karin and Lars and I returned and greatly enjoyed our visit to EFC!) We decided to put extra effort into planning how to begin conducting SST in Sweden. Bertil Ekstedt and I finally (2011) began the pilot projects we had discussed and planned for so many years in Malmö. My colleagues and I started SST with couples, and Bertil and his therapist colleagues started Single-Session Therapy with alcohol and drug addicts and their relatives (mostly individual sessions).

The idea of seeing couples for just one session was hard to introduce and there were lots of discussions and debates about evidence-based models, the impossibility of one session with couples, and complexities of organizing anything like SST in our organization and team. We were accused of cheating couples, that by offering SST we were misleading and even promising couples they would be able to solve all kinds of problems very quickly. For us it wasn't so; all SST couples were invited to call us after a few weeks and schedule a new appointment with the same or another counselor if they needed it.

I had been in a similar situation before. In the 1980s Harry Korman and I introduced working with heroin addicts and their parents and relatives in an outpatient clinic. That was a crazy idea, everyone told us, but we ran that research and treatment project for several years. It was not only possible, it proved outpatient treatment was possible with drug addicts and helped many of them to start their way to a drug-free life (Korman & Söderquist, 1994). In a later project in the beginning of the 1990s I worked with sexually-abused children and their families. It was very hard work, involving legislative issues and being a witness in court besides the therapeutic work, but we found that it, too, was possible.

Context and Challenges

Sweden is probably unique in the sense that couple counseling for all kinds of client constellations is mandatory by law. All communities/local governments must offer access to affordable couple counseling to all citizens. This is quite well known in Sweden. Couple counselors have absolute confidentiality, can see couples anonymously, do not have to keep file records, and are not required to use protocols and diagnoses. This is a long and special tradition in Sweden and is liberating for couple counselors as well as for the couples.

Internationally, Malmö is a small city, the third biggest city in Sweden (330,000 people) and is unique in the sense that 177 nationalities live there. It places Malmö very high on world rankings of nationalities represented in a city. We do many of our sessions in English and we also offer free translators for clients preferring other languages in the sessions.

We also have a long tradition of individual therapy models dominating in Sweden. The Swedish Board of Health supports these models and is unsupportive of family therapy and some brief therapy models. Therapy and counseling are believed to require diagnoses, many sessions over time and, during the last years, manual- and evidenced-based models. The last decade you can even talk of an "Evidence Tsunami" in Sweden. This has over the years influenced the couple counseling field, too. This is one big challenge we had to face when introducing Single-Session Therapy for couples.

Another challenge is the couple work. I have met several therapists and counselors who say that they don't work with couples because it is too difficult—and to be honest, this was my experience, too, when I started doing couple counseling. In a couple session there are usually three people in the room and triangles are always hard to handle for all of us. As counselor you often see couples with different or antagonistic agendas and goals and it requires a lot to balance this; at the same time you must try to understand, match, and cooperate with both of them and their relationship. If you succeed with this

Figure 18.1 Couple counseling? (used by agreement with BizarroComics.com)

it is possible by the end of a session to reach the goal: the couple leaves with a sense of hope and direction about what to do together. A long waiting list also added to the challenges we faced when introducing Single-Session Therapy for couples. When we started in 2011 our waiting list was a few weeks. Contrary to the experience of other teams starting SST and despite our efforts, over the years of working with couples in a SST format we still have a prolonged waiting list for couples counseling. We prefer to believe this has to do with many couples and few counselors. In 2016 we shortened our waiting list in spite of more couples scheduling appointments. The throughput time is about the same. It is hard to draw conclusions on what has contributed to this, probably some kind of combination of one more colleague on the team and more one-at-a-time sessions per week than the single-session service offered previously.

We believed in the potential effectiveness of SST and wanted to try working with couples in that format. This belief made it possible for us to be persistent and continue our discussions and planning. The statistical fact that 30% of all the couples coming for one session year after year also was helpful. If we could offer the possibility of choosing SST when scheduling the appointment, it would be helpful for all involved, the counselor and the couple would know from the start that "one hour is all you have" (Slive & Bobele, 2011)—although more sessions could be scheduled in the future. SST with the possibility of more sessions could facilitate focusing and concentrating on small, important, and achievable goals and changes in the relationship.

From an SST Project to One Session at a Time

When a couple phones us to make an appointment we don't ask many questions, apart from their names, telephone number, their ages, and the ages of their children. No detailed questions at all about their problems. We just need to know that their issues are adult and relational. The only exception is that custody and access to children disputes are referred to another agency. We also see many IPV (Intimate Partner Violence) couples. If safety can't be guaranteed for couple sessions and if there are signs of Intimate Terror (Johnson, 2008, Lee, Sebold, & Uken, 2003, Söderquist, 2008) we refer them to another team working individually with one or both of the partners.

If they haven't seen it on our website (www.malmo.se/familjeradgivningen) the couples are informed about their choices for scheduling the session: (1) Single-Session Therapy (SST—one-off session with, if needed, the possibility to contact the counselor after a couple of weeks); or (2) Regular Couple Counseling (RCC—with the possibility to directly schedule more sessions after the first session).

Over the years we have followed up, evaluated, and continuously developed our ways of working with couples in a SST format. We are a small team with no administrative or research back-up and a long waiting list. In that sense we are restricted and are not able to do big studies, research and large-scale implementation work like the Bouverie Centre (Young, Weir, & Rycroft, 2012). Three phases can be distinguished in our work over the first five years:

2011–2013: From pilot project to regular service offer. Telephone follow-up. SST format.

2013–2015: Continued service offer. We name our service offer SSCC (Single-Session Couple Counseling) and RCC (Regular Couple Counseling). Evaluation scales before and immediately after the session with all couples (SSCC and RCC). No telephone follow-up.

2016–: Organizing our work in a more customer-friendly way: One-session-at-a-time/walk-in or by appointment. We will come back to this later.

We started as a pilot project in 2011 with Talmon's model: telephone interview before session, session, and telephone follow-up two months after the session. Encouraged by the results from the pilot study (30 couples), we were able to implement (2012) and offer SST as a regular service offer (2013). Follow-up interviews two months after the session with 88 couples gave the following results: 70% of the couples reported better or much better situation, 75% were satisfied with the session, and 60% reported reaching their goals at least partly. Before the pilot project and implementation of SST 30% of all couples attended one session. After implementing SST, the figures were about the same: 20% of SST couples returned for one or more sessions. These results were good enough and in line with follow-up results from other teams like Eastside Family Centre Walk-In (Calgary, Canada), The Bouverie Centre: Victoria's Family Institute (Melbourne, Australia), and others (Harper-Jaques, McElheran, Slive, & Leahey, 2008; Perkins, 2006; Hoyt & Talmon, 2014). We especially noticed that the results were less favorable for couples with separation problems/issues and better for couples with other problems. When couples are somewhere in the separation process they are never at the same place—e.g., one of them has already decided to separate and the other is in shock. We found SST seemed to be beneficial to four groups of couples: (1) "We don't have that big a problem—one session might be enough"; (2) "We want to start something together"; (3) "We want to see if a couple session is something for us—if it fits us"; and (4) "We are a little bit hesitant (or one of us is even reluctant)—can we schedule one session?"

Although the results were in line with other single-session teams, the telephone interviewing before and after the session was time consuming. It was time to organize our work differently. We knew from follow-up studies, our own experiences, and our reading of Scott Miller (Hubble, Duncan, & Miller, 1999), Michael Lambert (Lambert & Bergin, 1994; Hansen, Lambert, & Forman, 2002), and others that most changes will take place in the first sessions of therapy.

We stopped doing telephone interviews and introduced scales before and immediately after the session for both SSCC and RCC. We were inspired by Eastside and Bouverie and started using the same *Stress Scale* as Eastside (Harper-Jaques, McElheran, Slive, & Leahey, 2008) and the same *Confidence in Handling Problem Scale* that Bouverie uses as part of a post-session questionnaire (Jeff Young, 2105, personal communication). We also administered the *Session Rating Scale* (*SRS*; Duncan & Miller, 2000) after the session with both SSCC and RCC couples. The *SRS* is widely used all over the world but was not intended to be used in just one session. We still wanted to use it to see how we succeeded in Single-Session Couple Counseling and a first session of Regular Couple Counseling.

During the period of evaluation about 20% of all couples chose SSCC, and 80% chose Regular Couple Counseling. Forty-seven percent of the couples reported that the reason for choosing SSCC was to see "if counseling session is for us/fits us." Some of the couples reported that one of them was very reluctant or negative about attending the session. This was different from the years 2011—2013 when the SST couples more often reported that "One session might be enough" or "We don't have that huge a problem."

The total number of couples filling in the forms (scales and *SRS*) were 127 Single-Session Counseling couples and 239 Regular Couple Counseling couples.

Some of the SS Counseling couples (29) returned for one or more sessions (SSCC>1) and some of the RCC couples (42) attended just one session (RCC1; Unplanned Single-Session). That gave us four groups and the results for the different groups could be studied.

We had a lot of questions. What similarities and differences are there in just one session/first session of several between SSCC and RCC? How much stress reduction and increased confidence in handling relational problems occurs? Do the SSCC couples that come for more sessions and the RCC couples just attending one session differ in any way?

Immediate Effects

We have no baseline assessment and there are probably many factors and variables influencing outcomes and results. Caution is therefore important in looking at our results and we cannot draw too many conclusions from our evaluation. What we can do is to look at what we have found and discuss how we can use these findings in a helpful way for the couples.

"20"—A Magic Number?

As mentioned earlier, 20% of all couples chose SSCC, 20% of all sessions were cancelled, 20% of SSCC couples returned for more sessions (nearly always to the counselor they met in the first session), and 20% of all RCC couples attended just one session. This could be coincidence but it seems like these figures hold over time.

Similarities

All four groups report a pre-session stress level between 6 and 7 out of 10, somewhat lower than that at Eastside Family Centre (Harper-Jaques, McElheran, Slive, & Keahey, 2008). We see no differences in presented problems. All groups report the following as the most urgent problems: 60% communication problems; 20% conflict/fights; 15% separation issues; and 5% infidelity. The same with the confidence scale—all groups report a pre-session level between 3 and 4 out of 5 (on the Likert scale) where 0 stands for "not confident at all in handling the relational problem" and 10 stands for "very confident."

The *Session Rating Scale* is a brief alliance scale used to get information and feedback from clients about what they experienced in the sessions. The scale consists of four 0–10 scales measuring Relationship (client felt heard and respected), Goals and Topics (worked and talked about what client wanted), Approach and Method (good fit for client), and Overall (session was right for client). The maximum is 40 and the cutting point is 36. Numbers below 36 indicate the need to discuss with clients what can be done next session to better fit the client.

In general, *SRS* numbers are between 31 and 35 for all groups and that corresponds to other Couple Counseling teams using SRS in Sweden. Our experience is that it is harder to get higher scores on *SRS* with couples than individuals, at least in the first session. *SRS* for individual Single Sessions (32 of 366 = 9%) in our evaluation are all higher than 36.

The SSCC counselors also met RCC couples but some of our team members only met RCC couples. This made it possible to see if the results were the same or not for RCC couples seeing a SSCC counselor or a RCC counselor. The results were similar.

Differences

Topics for our evaluation are Stress Reduction and Increased Confidence in Handling Relational Problem. The goals of therapeutic/counseling sessions are to reduce stress and increase confidence in handling the problem amongst other possible goals. How much of this can be seen in the first session and what differences are there between the four groups previously mentioned?

As seen in Table 18.1, couples in all groups report stress reduction. In the SSCC group the stress reduction is more than 30% and in line with the results from Eastside (Harper-Jaques, et al., 2008). We consider this to be a good result considering the fact that there are two people coming to the session with often conflicting agendas/goals and blaming each other for the problems. They are not in the same position and they experience the session differently. One of them is perhaps very stressed and the other is not and still the stress reduction in the group as a whole is more the 30%.

As seen in Table 18.2, two of the groups report over 50% confidence increase in handling the problem and that is quite a lot in one session. RCC1 were

Table 18.1 Stress Reduction Comparisons

Stress Reduction	*Female*	*Male*
Single Session Couple Counseling	38%	32%
Single Session Couple Counseling > 1	27%	29%
Regular Couple Counseling	22%	23%
Regular Couple Counseling 1	20%	20%

Table 18.2 Increased Confidence Comparisons

Increased Confidence	*Female*	*Male*
Single Session Couple Counseling	55%	40%
Single Session Couple Counseling > 1	37%	47%
Regular Couple Counseling	27%	34%
Regular Couple Counseling 1	56%	46%

lower in stress reduction but were higher in confidence increase and these couples chose to attend one session (unplanned Single-Session). SSCC>1 and RCC-groups reported increased confidence. They seem to have had a good start with couple counseling and continued for more sessions. Interesting are the numbers for females: higher levels of increased confidence seem to help determine the percentage having one session.

As mentioned earlier, we can see no difference between groups in reported problems and the pre-session stress and confidence levels. We can't see any indication of more severe problems reported in any of the groups. When the session contributes to enough stress reduction and a higher confidence increase, the couples attend one session. They find their way about.

What We Have Learned So Far

These are some of the questions we put to ourselves and received from others:

- Is anything special with Single-Session Therapy?
- Is the therapy/counseling different in any way?
- Do you as a Single-Session couple counselor use different interventions than in other settings?
- How can we use the findings so far to improve our Single-Session Couple Counseling?

Special or Not That Special?

After many discussions, supervision, and looking through videotaped sessions, we couldn't really say there was much of a difference between Single-Session Couple Counseling and Regular Couple Counseling first sessions. Outpatient Team Gustav did the same and did more videotape reviewing than we did. We all concluded that Single-Session Therapy isn't that special. Sometimes it is hard to notice differences between Single-Sessions and other sessions, but what we can see is more of an immediate focus on detailed descriptions of hopes, goals, and next steps in Single-Session Therapy and Single-Session Couple Counseling. It makes it different but not special.

Our mindset in all sessions is focused on: (1) the idea that the client is in the lead (we are "the caddies and not the players," to use Hoyt's [2000] golf metaphor); (2) agreeing on couples' hopes and realistic/achievable goals and focusing on small steps; and (3) doing one-session-at-a-time and one-hour-at-a-time can be useful and enough for many couples. This leads to an agreement: "Let us all do our best this hour."

Format

SST is not a special therapy model. All therapists do single-sessions, at least unplanned SST (which they may call consultation). A Planned Single-Session is about format: a choice and agreement from the start to have one session. The SS mindset is possible and usable for all therapists, but you can't go in the other direction. It is not possible to squeeze all kinds of therapy models into the frame of Single-Session. You can't do a whole, several-session therapy (for example, psychodynamic therapy, emotionally-focused therapy, or different family therapies) in one session; but you can do a one-session consultation.

Our experience is that it is important for clients to be able to participate on equal terms and having a choice in sessions. Having a say and being allowed to decide means they are important and respected. When couples schedule the appointment with us they can choose the format of SSCC or RCC and we leave the question of theoretical therapy models out of the picture. Most people don't bother about therapy/counseling models; more important seems to be the counselor's training, experience, respectfulness, and the chance to have the session when most needed.

Custom Fit

We meet couples with all kinds of problems and all kinds of family constellations. Everything we do as counselors must fit specific couples and they are very different in many aspects. The questions and interventions have to be tailored to fit the couples so they feel "at home" and recognize what is being said and done in the session. The questions and interventions also have to be different enough from the usual to be something of a challenge to give the couple a new perspective (Andersen, 1991).

This is why it is very important to listen carefully to the goals of the couples, and to invite the couples to lead the session and follow their lead. With questions and interventions, the counselor can both validate and invite the couples to new perspectives. This gives the couples a chance to reduce their stress, increase their confidence and find their way. Our studies show the importance of focusing on and enhancing confidence in handling problems. This can be done by emphasizing what the couple successfully has tried previously, their resources and strengths, and possible actions in the immediate future. We are all trained in solution-focused brief therapy (de Shazer, et al., 2007), emotionally-focused therapy (Johnson, 2008), and the Gottman model (Schwartz-Gottman

& Gottman, 2015). It is up to us to use all this in a way that the questions and interventions are modified and tailored to be custom fit.

Multiple Goals: Higher Level, Lower Level, No Level

Couple relational problems are of many kinds and multiple and/or conflicting goals are often the case when couples present their hopes, problems and goals at the beginning of the session. In a Single-Session format you have a whole hour but you can't wait too long to come to an agreement about what to focus on in the session. Briefly put, the couple and the therapist can have three different foci for the session:

- Increasing closeness and intimacy—seeking a higher level
- Reducing conflicts, breaking patterns—seeking a lower level
- No commitment, no readiness—no level.

The couple and the therapist in collaboration need to figure out what is most helpful for the couple to deal with and focus on in the session. Sometimes all three aspects need to be covered to decide; sometimes it is obvious to all where to focus.

From the Session Room

Using some case examples, we want to describe our way of working with couples in the One-Session-at-a-Time format.

Case #1: High, Low, or No Level[2]

Like most couples, Ingrid and Mats were a bit nervous. We chatted some minutes regarding information, statistical questions, and a bit about the weather. It was pouring rain outside and Couple Counselor Lars Dannerup had a couple in the room looking like wet cats. Lars asked: "What could happen here in this session that would make it worthwhile coming here today?" They both looked at each other and then Mats said, "You start."

Ingrid: Actually, when we called we had had a real bad autumn. We could hardly see each other without getting irritated. There was lots of frustration and a little thing could just blow up to a big fight that could go on for hours. But strangely enough, the time after Christmas has been quite good.

Mats: Yes. It's true that the last weeks have been better than in many months. Then, this weekend it just exploded again. We were on the brink of breaking up. We need some guidance to make this work.

Ingrid: Yes. We have to change. We can't go on hurting each other this way. We need some tools that could help us get out of this messy situation.

Lars: (*counselor*) So, if we had seen each other last week, you had had nearly only good things to say about what direction you had taken in your relationship?

Ingrid: (*looking at Mats*) That's right. But this weekend was awful. You said you could not stay in this relationship. You were crying and crying. It felt like you really were going to leave me.

Lars: What I'm hearing is that you had a really hard experience this weekend. Is it OK if we come back to that? I would like to hear a bit more of the good experience you've had after the holidays.

Comment: *In a Single-Session, like in any other session, we are constantly making decisions of which way to go. Following this short dialogue, we have all of the three levels: things had been going in the right direction for some weeks, there was a hard fight, and one of them said, "I might not be able to stay in the relationship." If unsure of which way to go we usually start out to explore the higher level.*

Following the idea of starting out with what works and looking for pivot points, Lars continued:

Lars: Could you tell me if there was any occasion during the good weeks that had some more value to you?

Mats: I think it was more like an overall feeling, more harmony.

Lars: What if you were to say something about how you think Ingrid contributed to that?

Mats: Well, there was one occasion when we were out walking. The weather was nice. We were relaxed and you started talking about everything that needed to be done when we came home, kind of winding it up and me trying to back off. It was beginning to spoil the moment, making me feel afraid of you getting angry again. Then suddenly (*looks at Ingrid*) you stopped walking, took my arm, looked me in the eye and said: "Sorry, now I'm just spoiling the moment, starting to getting stressed instead of enjoying this nice moment. I guess I'm sometimes not so easy to live with."

Lars: Tell me a bit more of what made that so special to you?

Mats: To be honest, I think it was the first time I heard Ingrid apologize. But mostly I felt she cared for me, like she liked to be with me.

Lars: It sounds like that was very important to you. How do you think Ingrid noticed that you really appreciated that?

Mats: I don't know. (*Looks at Ingrid.*) Did you notice?

Ingrid: Yes, I did. I think you said it was OK and smiled. You didn't fuss about it. Usually when I get stressed I get angry fast. I've been thinking of that. I mean, that I get easily angry and I know that scares you a lot.

Lars: Wow, you have really done some self-reflecting. How did you come up with the idea of saying that to Mats during the walk?

Ingrid: I don't know . . . It just came out that way . . . Well, one thing that might have helped is that lately Mats has been asking me much more frequently what I want or what I like. You know, there has been so much struggle about my way or your way.

Comment: *Trying to build on that situation, Lars continued to ask more about it and what they learned from the occasion. The couple came up with some ideas: before arguing to show more interest in the other person's view, when things happen that you appreciate it's very important to show it in a way that is noticed by the other. Lars then got back to the fight they had the weekend before they came to see us. This can be seen as an example of exploring the low level. That level had been articulated by the couple as something that really had to change. The conflict climate was too bad. One way of looking at it could be how the high level and the low level interact. The better things are on the high level. The couple connecting in a way that is good for them in everyday life, the more they are likely not to have destructive conflicts. This means that dialogues regarding what works in the relationship could be an indirect way of improving the low level. At the same time it's usually also very helpful to have dialogue around couples' experiences of what is helpful to not end up in destructive conflicts.*

Lars: Talking about the conflict last weekend. Was there anything different this time compared with other times?

Mats: I don't think so. I was really sad and you were really angry. I felt really hopeless about the situation. I totally shut down.

Ingrid: I don't think I've ever seen you so sad . . . (*starts to cry*)

Lars: Is it OK if you say something about what is in those tears?

Ingrid: I get so angry when you shut down (*crying more and looking at Mats*). It's like you don't care, like you have given up. I feel so alone and all that comes out is anger.

Lars: So you are feeling alone, left out, and you express that in anger. It's like a conflict pattern where one of you is expressing anger and the other one withdraws and that kind of triggers the anger even more and that triggers the other to withdraw even further.

Ingrid: Yes. But I am also so afraid of losing you (*looking down and crying more*).

Lars: Mats, what are you hearing Ingrid saying here?

Mats: She's angry and she also feels alone. But she also is afraid of losing me.

Lars: How does that make you feel?

Mats: Glad. (*He starts to giggle and Ingrid stops crying and looks at him.*)

Lars: Glad?

Mats: Yes. Anger might not be so dangerous after all.

Lars: How's that?

Mats: If she's afraid of losing me I must mean something to her. I am not all that bad.

Lars: Would that be the voice of the anger, just telling you how bad you are?

Mats: Yes. Exactly. That's when I shut down.

Lars: But anger might not be so dangerous after all?

Comment: *Lars continued talking about the conflict pattern, what it looked like and what feelings and thoughts might trigger the response of anger and shutting down. When asked about what they thought they might do differently next time when they enter a conflict, Mats spontaneously said, "Anger might not be so dangerous after all." Ingrid then said, "I think it was so important for me to understand how glad Mats was when he understood that I'm afraid of losing him. I guess all the anger sometimes makes it hard for him to see how much he means to me."*

Start, Middle, and End

All sessions, whatever format, have a start, middle, and end. The Single-Session format is focused on collaboration for an hour with a narrow and immediate focus on the couple's concerns and aiming to help the couple know their way about after they leave the session.

Start: A Single-Session Couple Counseling session often starts with an immediate focus on NOW:

- "What is your main concern today?"
- "What are your best hopes for today?"
- "What can we do here today to . . .?"
- "What is the smallest sign of the right direction for you later today or tomorrow?"
- "If you get what you want from this session, how will you know when you leave in an hour?" and questions like this (Slive & Bobele, 2011).

This follows from the agreement between couple and counselor of meeting for one session and focusing on small steps. Sometimes I start the session with asking the partners to introduce each other to me and asking them to focus on what they appreciate. I follow this up with asking them to describe their strengths as a couple.

In SSCC you can't cover all aspects of the couple's lives. To use the session in the most effective way for the couple, the session needs to be focused on what is most important to the couple and what they can do in the nearest future. In SSCC you narrow the focus to what is most important and achievable for the couples and go deep into (or thicken) the descriptions of goals and signs of moving in the direction of the couple's goals. The importance of getting detailed and concrete descriptions of peoples' goals to be able to reach the goals have been pointed out by many different therapists (de Shazer, 2007; Lee, Sebold, & Uken, 2003, 2007; White & Epston, 1990).

Case #2: Tendency for Something New[3]

Sometimes it is hard for the couple to answer questions like, "What do we need to talk about today?" or "What is most important to talk about today?" The stress level is high and confidence in handling the problem is low for the couple. It is then urgent to catch the first small sign of the start of a positive change.

Malena Cronholm-Nouicer: (*counselor*)	What is the single most important thing to talk about in the session today?
Anna:	I don't know . . . It's so complicated. So many things . . . I don't know where to start.
Malena:	OK. Many things . . . But imagine we have this session today and after you leave . . . What will tell you tonight or tomorrow that: YES—it was worth having the couple's session today? . . . What will be the first thing in your everyday life that tells you . . . Maybe something has started to change for the better? What do you say, Anna?
Anna:	That we communicate better.
Malena:	OK, you would communicate better—how would you notice?
Anna:	I think we would criticize each other less . . . at the moment we are complaining all the time . . . it is extremely hard and taking my energy from me.
Malena:	Sounds really hard! If you communicated better—what do you think you and Erika would do instead of complaining?
Anna:	Well . . . I don't know . . . More of cheering up and pep-talk . . . and it would have been nice to hear that I am beautiful and do something good.

Malena: OK, instead of complaints—cheering up pep talk words like "You are beautiful" and "You are good."

Anna: Exactly!

Malena: If I ask you, Erika, the same . . . let us imagine this session will be of help for you . . . what would you notice at home with Anna?

Erika: Hmmm . . . we would listen more carefully to each other.

Malena: OK . . .

Erika: I have a feeling of us living parallel . . . that we don't connect (*tears in her eyes*).

Malena: I see you being moved to tears when talking about this.

Erika: Mmmm . . .

Malena: So . . . what would be the first sign for you listening to each other and connecting?

Erika: Anna wouldn't look away and pretend I am not there! ... Yes ... She would look me in the eyes.

Malena: OK. If I understand this correctly, Erika, you would notice a difference in how you listen to each other, connecting, looking each other in your eyes (*Erika nods*) . . . and you, Anna, would notice a better communication and pep talk?

Anna: Yes, absolutely.

Malena: So . . . if it was more like this at home what difference would it make?

Erika: We would fight less (*looking at Anna*).

Anna: Yes, I think so, too; less fights and negative feelings (*looking at Erika*).

Comment: *Anna and Erika continued to express and describe what these first small signs of change will mean to them and how they will lead to more connection, teamwork, feelings of being important for each other, and more presence with the children.*

Case #3: Smallest Signs[4]

Earlier in the session, Martin (the counselor) had talked about Maria's and Robert's wish lists, what they wanted from themselves and each other. Scaling was introduced and the couple was asked in which direction they imagine progress (up, forward, or . . .?). Both said "diagonal" (both upwards and forward) and Martin drew two diagonal lines on the whiteboard where 10 stands for "www" ("what we want—and strive for").

They said they were on 3 and 4 and we talked for a while about what makes them put themselves on 3 and 4. The session continued:

Martin: What are the small signs of 3,3 and 4,4?

Robert: Something from my wish list. Feeling we are on the same team, same side and we have open communication. Also, getting freedom in our lives.

Martin: What is the smallest thing next week?

Robert: Removal of frustration and starting talking together.

Martin: What is the smallest thing for you?

Maria: (*silent for a moment*) I am not so concerned about freedom in our lives. I think we have it. (*Silent again.*) He will listen to me.

Robert: That I what?

Maria: Listen . . . (*both laugh*) . . . and responding!

Comment: ***The session continued with detailing of their descriptions of removal of frustration and starting talking and listening and responding. How will they notice, what will it mean for them when this happens and what is most important for them?***

Whole Stories

What do you do when the couple may have chosen Single-Session Couple Counseling but they still want to tell their story, the whole story? You run the risk of time expiring and this situation can be hard to handle in the session. If you too directly stop their story or interfere too much it might be perceived as rude or having no interest. If counselors try to push their model on the couple, the clients might feel pressed in the wrong direction and have a feeling of not being listened to. Instead of a "solution-focused" session you can end up in a "solution-forced" session (see Nylund & Corsiglia, 1994). One way I have found to be constructive is to ask the couple, before they have told me too much, to give me a brief clue what they want me to especially listen for when they tell their story. Another option is to ask the client–couple what it will mean to them and what will be different after they have told their story.

Endings

Taking a break (or not) before giving a final intervention message is often part of the Single-Session format (see Hoyt [2015] for a discussion about breaks). Two of us prefer breaks, the other two don't. Before the break (I call it "reflection time on my own") I often ask the couple what they would like me to especially reflect on. If they say anything about ideas or suggestions from me, I ask them a little bit more about that. Sometimes it is better to reflect with all three together, clients and counselor, at the end of session.

Pause Button and Cards[5] (From a Session With a Couple with Two Children and Pregnant With the Third Child)

In the session the couple have described their relationship as rich in several ways but with lots of arguing and conflicts. Their energy is taken away by this and causes them to feel annoyed, defensive, and close to the edge of separation. They both want to communicate better, especially when they are in conflict. The counselor (Martin Söderquist) returns to the session room after some minutes of reflection on his own:

Martin: I'll try to summarize my reflections. I want to start with: You have a nice and rich relation when you talk to each other. I hear and see a nice feeling and there is warmth and love between you. I liked your description of watching *Homeland* and having tea together. That was very nice. Also when you express what you want—you want normal talk, to take away the dark side, you want energy, you want calm, and you want togetherness—more of the up part of togetherness. You also want to break this pattern of a negative conflictual style of talking that you get stuck in—Leave or Talk, Push or Withdraw, Talk or Silence—which you have described in many ways in the session. It's not good for either of you and you want to break this pattern. You have already done a lot to break that pattern. When you, Sara, put the ultimatum, Sam understood and that was important. You two decided to not let things go further, not to let that bad habit continue, and you agreed on "Let's do something else." Very important! I have two ideas to suggest. First idea: You, Sara, proposed the idea of having a "pause button" to stop or deescalate conflicts. I suggest that you invent or find a concrete symbol of a "pause button."

Sara: Maybe a picture of you? (*All laugh.*)

Martin: Maybe something of your own.

Sam: Works for me with a card.

Martin: Yeah—something like that. Reminds you and can be of help to pull yourself together. Not a pause for a long time, because you, Sara, don't want to be silent for a long time—just some time to think so you can talk. The other idea is (*Martin takes two blank small cards from his pocket*): This is not an expensive gift, just one blank card each. I suggest you write on one of the sides three small things you would appreciate your partner doing the next coming two weeks. On the other side write three small things you can do yourself that you know your partner would appreciate. (*Martin repeats what he just has said once more.*) Is that clear?

Sam: It was but now I am confused.

Martin: You heard what I said the first time?

Sam: (*tells what he heard Martin say*) Was that so?

Martin: Yes. And you can do it individually and talk to each other about what you have written or you can do it as a secret game—not telling each other but just observe.

Sam: Could be fun, too.

Sara: If I get a foot tickle from you suddenly!

Martin: "What good things are going on here?" (*All laugh again.*) I wish you good luck.

Sam: It was nice meeting you. Thank you for listening to me.

Sara: Thank you.

Comment: *Endings are often important. How you start and how you end things are often what is best remembered. A SSCC session ends with "Good Luck" instead of "To be continued . . ."*

"What's Next?"

So far we are satisfied with initiating and implementing Single-Session Therapy and Single-Session Couple Counseling in Malmö and Sweden. Benevolent persistence was our way to do this.

The follow-ups and evaluation have been important. Single-Session Counseling seems to be a good alternative for many couples. Hesitant couples wanting to try couple counseling, and couples in which one of the partners is very reluctant about counseling, have the chance to try a session without further obligations. The results seem to be at least at the same level as other formats and models of therapy and counseling (Bloom, 2001).

But! We are not satisfied with the poor accessibility. It is counterproductive to have such a waiting list, not just for Single-Session Counseling Couples but for most couples. Seeing the couples when they are ready for action is offering a more customer-friendly service. Another consequence of poor accessibility is that we get many canceled and missed sessions and that creates holes in our schedules—it is not efficient.

We wanted to change this and still keep our Single-Session mindset. In 2016, we organized (inspired by Eastside Family Centre Walk-In—see McElheran, et al., 2014) our Single-Session Couple Counseling service to offer couples a more customer-friendly way (Nancy McElheran, 2015, personal communication). When couples phone us to schedule an appointment they are scheduled for a first session of Regular Couple Counseling if they want to be able to have several session with the same counselor. We also inform couples that they can phone us on a special number Monday and Tuesday morning to schedule "One-Session-at-a-Time" (Single-Session Couple Counseling) for the same Tuesday or the week after. "One-Session-at-a-Time" is an offer to see a counselor within a week. The couples can return for one or several sessions more by phoning us again on a Monday or Tuesday. If they return for another session they aren't guaranteed to see the same counselor.

We believe that the One-Session-at-a-Time option has several benefits for couples, such as:

- increased accessibility
- the couples can by their own actions schedule an appointment when they need the session
- when there is a long waiting list for Couple Counseling, couples can schedule One-Session-at-a-Time in the meantime, and
- hesitant or reluctant couples can "Try if couples counseling is for us" when the "iron is hot." If they want another session they can schedule another One-Session-at-a-Time or they can be put on the waiting list for Regular Couple Counseling.

There are several benefits/advantages for the counselors, too, such as:

- relief from the burden of long waiting lists for all couples
- One-Session-at-a-Time makes us more free—we do the session and if the couple returns we might meet them again or one of our colleagues will
- fewer cancelled sessions, and
- a better chance to organize teamwork. Previously the combination of a heavy caseload and individual scheduling of appointments made teamwork and reflecting team hard to organize. One-Session-at-a-Time on Tuesdays make this much easier.

To Be Continued . . .

Beginning in January 2016 for half a year, we have been offering One-Session-at-a-Time and so far, our new service offer has been successful. Being able to have a session within a week maximum gives couples the chance to have the session when they need it, to take a first step or just give it a try. They can return for another One-Session-at-a-Time later or be put on the waiting list for regular couple counseling. This combines increased accessibility with guaranteed continued sessions if needed.

The results are somewhat lower (based on 114 sessions so far)—stress reduction 25% and confidence increase 35%. What we have noticed is that we meet couples in more urgent situations, many of those in separation crisis. There is also a small tendency for more individual sessions. A different condition now is that a couple can schedule both One-Session-at-a-Time and Regular Couple Counseling. This might have an effect on the couple's expectations of possible change in the session.

Our strictly structured teamwork on Tuesday mornings has given us the possibility to organize and develop teamwork in a much better way than before. It also makes it easier to introduce new couple counselors to the practice of One-Session-at-a-Time.

As mentioned earlier, we are a small team with no research resources and no administrative back-up. We cannot do strict research but we will continue asking the couples about their most urgent problem, their hopes, and the scaling questions (stress and confidence) before and after the session.

Notes

1 This chapter and the keynote on which it is based are the results of teamwork and I use both "I" and "we" in the text. I want to thank my couple counselor colleagues Karin Wulff, Kristina Engman, Malena Cronholm-Nouicer and Lars Dannerup for their efforts, contributions, and constructive ideas. Special thanks to Bertil Ekstedt, Outpatient Team Gustav, and Nancy McElheran for her important and valuable support.
2 Lars Dannerup is the author of this case example.
3 Malena Cronholm-Nouicer is the author of this case example.
4 Martin Söderquist is the author of this case example.
5 Martin Söderquist is the author of this case example.

References

Andersen, T. (Ed.). (1991). *The reflecting team: Dialogues and dialogues about the dialogues.* New York: Norton.

Bloom, B.L. (2001). Focused single-session psychotherapy: A review of the clinical and research literature. *Brief Treatment and Crisis Intervention*, *1*(1), 75–86.

de Shazer, S., Dolan, Y., Korman, H., Trepper, T., McCollum, E., & Berg, I.K. (2007). *More than miracles: The state of the art of solution-focused brief therapy.* New York: Haworth Press.

Duncan, B.L. & Miller, S. D. (2000). *The heroic client: Doing client-directed, outcome-informed therapy.* San Francisco: Jossey-Bass.

Hansen, N.B., Lambert, M.J., & Forman, E.M. (2002). The psychotherapy dose-response effect and its implications for treatment delivery services. *Clinical Psychology: Science and Practice*, *9*, 329–343.

Harper-Jaques, S., McElheran, N., Slive, A., & Leahey, M. (2008). A comparison of two approaches to the delivery of walk-in Single-Session mental health therapy. *Journal of Systemic Therapies*, *27*(4), 40–53.

Hoyt, M.F. (2000). A golfer's guide to brief therapy (with footnotes for baseball fans). In *Some stories are better than others* (pp. 5–15). Philadelphia, PA: Brunner/Mazel.

Hoyt, M.F. (2015). Solution-focused couple therapy. In A.S. Gurman, J.L. Lebow, & D.K. Snyder (Eds.) *Clinical handbook of couple therapy* (5th ed., pp. 300–332). New York: Guilford Press.

Hoyt, M.F. & Talmon, M. (Eds.) (2014). *Capturing the moment. Single-Session therapy and walk-in services.* Bethel, CT: Crown House Publishing

Hubble, M., Duncan, B., & Miller, S. (Eds.) (1999). *The heart and soul of change. What works in therapy.* Washington, DC: American Psychological Association.

Johnson, M.P. (2008). *A typology of domestic violence: Intimate terrorism, violent resistance and situational couple violence.* Lebanon, NH: Northeastern University Press.

Korman, H. & Söderquist, M. (1994). *Talk about a miracle! A book on cooperation with addicts and their network* (free download on www.sikt.nu).

Lambert, M.J. & Bergin, A.E. (1994). The effectiveness of psychotherapy. In A.E. Bergin & S.L. Garfield, (Eds.) *Handbook of psychotherapy and behavior change* (4th ed.). New York: Wiley.

Lee, M.Y, Sebold, J., & Uken, A. (2003). *Solution-focused treatment of domestic violence offenders: Accountability for change.* Oxford, England: Oxford University Press.

Lee, M.Y., Uken, A., & Sebold, J. (2007). Role of self-determined goals in predicting recidivism in domestic violence offenders. *Research on Social Work Practice, 17*(1), 30–41.

McElheran, N., Stewart, J., Soenen, D., Newman, J., & MacLaurin, B. (2014). Walk-in single-session therapy at the Eastside Family Centre. In M.F. Hoyt & M. Talmon (Eds.), *Capturing the moment: Single-session therapy and walk-in services* (pp. 177–194). Bethel, CT: Crown House Publishing.

Nylund, D. & Corsiglia, V. (1994). Becoming solution-focused/forced in brief therapy: Remembering something important we already knew. *Journal of Systemic Therapies, 13*(5), 5–12.

Perkins, R. (2006). The effectiveness of one session of therapy using a single-session therapy approach for children and adolescents with mental health problems. *Psychology and Psychotherapy: Theory, Research and Practice, 79*, 215–227.

Slive, A. & Bobele, M. (Eds.) (2011). *When one hour is all you have. Effective therapy for walk-in clients.* Phoenix, AZ: Zeig, Tucker & Theisen.

Schwartz-Gottman, J. & Gottman, J. (2015). *Ten principles for doing effective couples therapy.* New York: Norton.

Söderquist, M. & Gunnehill, B. (2008). I learned to think for myself: A solution-focused approach to domestic violence therapy. In J. Hamel (Ed.) *Intimate partner and family abuse. A casebook of gender-inclusive therapy* (pp. 323–344). New York: Springer.

Talmon, M. (1990). *Single-Session therapy: Maximizing the effect of the first (and often only) therapeutic encounter.* San Francisco: Jossey-Bass.

White, M. & Epston, D. (1990). *Narrative means to therapeutic ends.* New York: Norton.

Young, J., Weir, S., & Rycroft, P. (2012). Implementing single-session therapy. *Australian and New Zealand Journal of Family Therapy, 33*(1), 84–97.

19 *Terapia Breve Sin Cita*

Collaboration with a Marginalized Community in Mexico City

Irma J. Rodriguez[1]

In this chapter I will describe how from a Collaborative Therapy stance (Anderson, 1998; Anderson & Gehart, 2007) we have incorporated the ideas of single-session therapy (Talmon, 1990) and walk-in services (Slive & Bobele, 2011) at Centro de Atención a la Comunidad (CAC)[2] a community-based counseling center in the Palo Solo neighborhood in Mexico City.

Context

As a response to social inequality in Mexico, many citizens have developed a sense of social responsibility by creating projects to open opportunities for the underprivileged. These not-for-profit organizations provide opportunities for citizens to volunteer in a variety of projects to serve the community. This is the case of the Casa de los Niños de Palo Solo IAP,[3] a not-for-profit organization in the outskirts of Mexico City. Julie Rivera-Río, the founder of this organization, while studying to become a Montessori teacher, realized that this kind of education was popular in the higher socio-economical sector of society and decided to bring it to the children of this underdeveloped area. Her hopes were that a Montessori education would provide new opportunities for this community to develop a sense of belonging and responsibility to create a society where people are aware of their environment and are prepared to act upon it by understanding their role as part of the universe. Grupo Campos Elíseos (GCE),[4] an independent training institute in Mexico City, is committed to the development of postmodern and social constructionist ideas in psychotherapy, education, consultation, and coaching. It offers an International Certification in Collaborative Practices in Mexico City, Leon (Guanajuato, Mexico), and Tucuman (Argentina); and is affiliated with the Houston Galveston Institute (HGI) and the Taos Institute.

GCE has international affiliations and connections; one of them is with Our Lady of the Lake University in San Antonio, Texas (OLLUSA). This academic relationship resulted from the mutual connection to HGI and Collaborative Practices. Since the late 1990s students and faculty from OLLUSA, Universidad de las Americas, and GCE in Mexico City have been involved in multiple academic exchanges and collaborations in a variety of projects.

History

The idea of creating the Centro de Atención a la Comunidad (CAC), a center to serve the members of the underdeveloped Community of Palo Solo, began as a dream shared by Julie Rivera Rio and myself. It was many years before I was ready to proceed. In order to make it happen, I decided to enroll in a Master of Arts in Family Counseling and Therapy program. In the late 1980s this was centered in the systemic, strategic, and structural family therapy models, along with psychodynamic approaches for couple therapy. Now I can say that I found these approaches too rigid and hierarchical and therefore, without knowing, I started looking for something different. I was captured by postmodern constructive ideas and collaborative practices that invite more inclusive, respectful, relational, and dialogical ways of thinking and being with others (Shotter, 2005).

This change of paradigm became a milestone in my life. It started in 1996 when Sylvia London introduced me to Collaborative Therapy ideas, and in 1998 I went for a four-month intensive visitor study program at HGI. I was privileged to have Harlene Anderson as my mentor, and I had the opportunity to participate in all of HGI's programs and activities such as therapy sessions, individual and group supervision, OLLUSA's masters' program practica and consultations. After this experience, when I came back to Mexico City I was invited to become part of the newly created GCE.

In 2001 the conditions were set to open Centro de Atención a la Comunidad as a clinical and training site for GCE. CAC's mission is to offer high-quality and low-cost psychotherapy to the members of the community of Palo Solo; and to be a learning and training site for students at GCE and other institutions. The intention of GCE's trainings is to create collaborative learning communities (Anderson, 1999), spaces where participants and facilitators together create knowledge and experiences that are relevant for them in their own professional contexts. Operating from a "postmodern critique" (Lyotard, 1984), participants learn and analyze a range of theoretical frameworks and family therapy models, and use them to inform their practice, always connecting to the context and to the needs of the clients.

After ten years of hard work the waiting list was growing and we were not able to meet our clients' needs. As already mentioned, during the years I have been a frequent visitor to the practicum and walk-in service at OLLUSA's clinic.[5] These visits gave me the opportunity to keep learning and sharing ideas with supervisors and students regarding the possibilities of opening a walk-in service at CAC.

Once we decided to open the service we invited Monte Bobele[6] to kick off the training program with an intensive workshop at GCE (2012) followed by six months of weekly meetings with a group of students that became the core group to open the service in January 2013.

The Philosophical Stance

The work at CAC is inspired by Anderson's (2013) Philosophical Stance, which is not a technique but a posture, an attitude that reflects a way of being in relationship and conversation with people, including a way of thinking, talking, acting, and being responsive with them. This philosophical stance becomes a philosophy of life – a worldview that does not separate professional and personal.

Anderson's work is based on the seven Action-Orienting Sensitivities:

- shared inquiry
- relational expertise
- not-knowing
- being public
- mutually transforming
- uncertainty, and
- everyday ordinary life.

It is also based on seven Postmodern Perspective-Orienting Assumptions:

- maintain skepticism
- avoid generalizations
- privilege local knowledge
- knowledge as interactive social process
- language as creative social process
- knowledge and language as transforming, and
- everyday ordinary life.

Under this postmodern umbrella, our program includes a variety of frameworks such as Talmon, Hoyt, and Rosenbaum's (Talmon, 1990) Single-Session Therapy; Slive and Bobele's (2011) Walk-In; O'Hanlon and Weiner-Davis's (1989) Solution-Oriented Therapy; White and Epston's (1990) Narrative Therapy; and Andersen's (1987, 1990) Reflecting Teams, to mention some.

Naming the Service

How we came to call our service "*Terapia breve, sin cita*" ("Brief therapy, no appointment") is an interesting story. In the beginning, we used "Single-session, no appointment needed" but a few weeks after opening, many clients did not show up and we were wondering what was going on. A client we did have (a young woman who worked at the school) came for a second session and told us about a conversation she overheard between Lulu, the receptionist, and a gentleman who was enquiring about the service. The receptionist had offered him the option of having a "single-session," to which the gentleman responded: "and what if I need more sessions? One won't be enough, so thank you, I am not interested. I'd rather make an appointment." Talking with Lulu we learned how using *single-session* was confusing for her – she didn't know how to explain it to clients and "single-session" was not familiar for the clients. As a team, we realized that the best fitting name for our service was *"Terapia breve, sin cita"* – "Brief therapy, no appointment needed." This name emphasizes the three ideas we want to clarify to our clients and our staff: (1) this therapy is not a long-term treatment; (2) clients can just walk-in without making an appointment on Wednesday morning from 8 to 11 a.m.; and (3) they can come for one session at a time.

How We Advertise the Service

In order to spread the word, the team visited the public schools and talked with the principals, as well as with the business owners in the neighborhood and the public health clinic next door to CAC. We designed a flyer with the basic information and an invitation to "take the first step . . . to transform your life" (see Figure 19.1). The same flyer was displayed in the back window of the Casa de los Niños schoolbus to make the service available to the whole community.

Figure 19.1 CAC advertising poster

Principles that Guide Our Work at CAC

Using the metaphor of "host and guest" (Anderson, 2012) has been a way to bring into action our philosophical stance, and to describe our relationships with our clients. Being a host or guest is not a static role. The therapist is the host and the client the guest when the therapist welcomes the client and acts to make the client/guest comfortable and confident; the client is the host and the therapist a guest in that the therapist is a respectful visitor in the life of the client/host. The therapist should not open doors if they are closed nor ask what is behind them. A therapist/guest starts from a "not-knowing" position – not knowing anything about the client's/host's situation, beliefs, values, and local understandings – and so is curious to learn from the host. This creates an opportunity for a shared inquiry, a dialogic process of speaking, listening, and hearing, a collaboration of learning and trying to understand.

It is a way of inviting a polyphony of voices that allows the client to hear as many ideas as possible; toward this goal, we sometimes use a variety of reflecting processes (Andersen, 1987, 1990).

At CAC, the therapists, the clients and the team work in the same room; this format provides a very enriching experience for all (Fernandez, London, & Tarragona, 2002). The trainees learn to listen in a more respectful way, to be aware of their body language, to be in a reflective position, to take the time to think about the ideas and connect them with the client's story. On the other hand, the client has the opportunity to get to know the team and listen to them in a free and spontaneous fashion.

Following the Fernandez, London and Tarragona (2002) guidelines for reflections, we invite the reflecting team to:

- be tentative, brief, and conversational
- offer the ideas with the same care you wish somebody would talk with you or about you, and
- offer the ideas you think would be the most useful for the person and the situation.

The session is organized in the following way: two therapists will have a conversation with the client; meanwhile the other part of the group will be listening silently; at a certain point the two therapists and client will then listen while the reflecting team will have a conversation among themselves and share what they have been thinking. The members of the team won't be looking directly at the client, so that the client can be in a listening position and take in any ideas that might be useful.

We have learned to be *flexible* in the process and to respond to what our clients ask us to do. If a client chooses to participate with the members of the reflecting team, we continue the conversation all together. When we have only one therapist we open a space to have a "solo reflection" during the session. Being a training program, we offer our students many opportunities to practice.

The students participate as co-therapists and members of the reflecting team. In each session, we offer the students the opportunity to supervise and reflect on the process; this is what we call live supervision/intervision.[7] Sometimes I ask the students/therapists to think about their work, and identify if there is something in particular they would want me to pay attention to or to comment on; we also talk about the challenges of participating in a reflective team, how to express ideas in a more tentative, diverse, and dialogical way. We also discuss our personal styles and the challenges each one is facing.

Since we started, the following numbers of persons have attended our clinic:

Table 19.1 Numbers attending the clinic

	Male	*Female*
Adults	35	70
Teenagers	18	27
Children	18	14

Glancing at Our Work: Some Examples

Case #1: Maria and Her Grandma from the Sky

A teacher in pre-kindergarten saw how sad Maria was: the 6-year-old girl cried, wanted to sleep, and was not interested in participating in the classroom. Maria's mother had shared her concerns with the teacher, and together they decided to visit CAC. A reflecting team that included me and four students received Maria's mother at the clinic. The mother told us the story about her own mother, who was very close to Maria and had passed away a month earlier. While talking to the mother, I realized that Maria was not engaging in the conversation; so I invited Maria to participate. We slid to the floor, and I took some paper and colored pencils and asked her if she would like to draw her grandmother; she agreed. I looked to my co-therapist and briefly asked her to go on talking with the mother. While I was drawing with Maria, she was telling me her grandma's story. I realized that in the reflecting team there was a therapist experienced in working with children, and I invited her to join us. At this point we were having two simultaneous sessions: two therapists working on the floor with one client, and the rest of the therapists engaged in a conversation with the mother. The therapists and Maria were externalizing (White & Epston, 1990) her story with her grandma, and she drew the sky, the clouds, and the sun. The therapists asked Maria "How is grandma doing?":

Maria: Well, she is with God and she is happy.

Therapist: Is grandma looking at you?

Maria: Yes, she sits in a cloud and looks at me and after me, and she can hear me.

Therapist: So you can talk with her?

Maria: Yes.

Therapist: What do you talk about?

Maria: That I miss her.

Therapist: What does she say?

Maria: She misses me, too. She loves me a lot.

Therapist: Does she say anything when she watches you crying?

Maria: She wants me to remember about how we played together, the things we enjoyed doing.

Therapist: Even if you cannot see her, is she close to you?

Maria: Yes, she is with me all the time.

Therapist: Where in your body do you feel her?

Maria: In my heart.

Therapist: Would you like to draw your heart with Grandma inside? Can you talk with her?

Maria: Every night before going to sleep.

Therapist: What does your heart say?

Maria: I love her, she loves me.

Therapist: Can you choose when to talk with her?

Maria: Yes.

Therapist: Is she watching what we are doing?

Maria: Yes.

Therapist: Is there anything she would like to say?

Maria: She likes what we are doing.

Therapist: Anything you would like to tell her?

Maria: That I love her.

Therapist: So, this means you can contact her whenever you want?

Maria said "Yes" with her hand on her heart and a smile on her face. We asked her whether she would like to share her story and the drawing with her mother and she agreed. Together the therapists and Maria showed the drawing and told the story to the mother. We all ended up with tears in our eyes. Maria took the drawing with her as they left.

One week later, when I was coming to CAC, a man approached me and said, "I am Maria's father and I want you to know how thankful we are. I do not know what happened the other day, but from then on Maria is back to herself, she is in connection with her grandma, she plays, laughs and smiles." This case is an example of ways to listen to your client, tolerate uncertainty, and together do what the occasion calls for.

Case #2: Juan in Search of Himself

Juan, a 16-year-old, came with his mother and brother to a walk-in session for the second time. That first time, the mother wanted her sons to have a place to talk about their father's illness and death. Juan had been very close to his father; he admired and respected him. Juan had quit school to take his father's place in a family business. He had been a good student and he was now organizing himself to go back to school.

Weeks later, one Wednesday morning, Juan was standing by the door waiting to come in. We greeted him, and he said: "Here I am, my mother sent me here."

Therapist: Did you want to come?

Juan: No. My mother sent me.

Therapist: Is there anything you would like to talk about?

Juan: No.

Therapist: How can we make this session meaningful for you?

Juan: I don't know.

Therapist: Would you rather leave or stay?

Juan: I don't know.

I was wondering what were the things he liked, and his cellphone caught my attention. I started wondering about the music he liked and asked him if he would like to share with us the music he liked. He said "Yes." I moved to the same sofa and he started talking about his favorite groups and we heard and saw video clips (I was not familiar with the music, but the other therapists were), and they started talking about the groups and the music, what he liked, and what he didn't. At this point, we were all engaged in the conversation; we were part of it even though we were in different positions. If I were to try to describe the process of what was happening, I would say that there was space for the "experts" about this music, and there was also a space for people like me who did not know anything about it; and there was a safe place for me to ask questions and for them to give respectful answers.

The conversation visited many places until he said that enjoying music was a shared activity with his father, and he started to talk about the sexually-transmitted illness that his father got while living in another country. Juan said he was disappointed that his father had had an affair but at the same time he loved and admired him; he referred to him as a strong and a good man, a model for him to follow. Finally we were invited into his life, and visited the way he saw his sexuality, his fears, hopes, and dreams. The session moved to a close and intimate relationship where you could not tell who the client was – there were just four people engaged in a conversation.

There were moments where we forgot we were talking with a 16-year-old teenager. At some point during the conversation, Juan said: "You know, therapy is the place where I can give life to my questions."

Case #3: Luis, On Becoming a "Father/Man"

Luis was a 30-year-old man who walked-in for a session. He wanted to talk about his relationship with his wife, Diana (they were not living together) and Mario, his 7-year-old son that he takes care of. One of the situations he wanted to discuss was that when Diana had to pick up Mario, she was often late or she did not show up. Another situation was that Luis was still in love with Diana and was wishing she would come back. And another was that the school Mario attended asked the parents to bring lunch for the group once a month, and when Mario stayed at Diana's house she forgot to bring it, so that Luis had to solve it in a hurry. We talked about these situations and Luis decided to talk about Diana's lack of commitment.

Therapist: So, you would like to talk about the impact that has on you and on Mario when Diana does not fulfill her agreements – tell me more.

Luis: I am very worried about Mario because each time Diana doesn't show up he is very sad and cries. He asked, "Do you think you [the therapist] can talk with Mario?"

Therapist: Yes, maybe we can have a session, the three of us. Can we go back and talk about what is going on between Diana and you?

Luis: I still love her and want her to come back, so I ask her to do things for Mario, but she doesn't deliver and I get angry and Mario gets hurt.

Therapist: Have you tried anything different to try to bring her back?

Luis: To invite her out for dinner, or to the movie.

Therapist: . . . and?

Luis: Some times she comes, but most of the times she says she is busy . . .

Therapist: What do you understand from her behavior?

Luis: That *she doesn't want to be with me.*

Therapist: Is this the Diana you want to be with?

Luis: No.

Therapist: So?

Luis: I have to accept she is gone, that my family is Mario and I . . .

Therapist: What kind of family is this?

Luis: A loving and caring one.

Therapist: What have you done so far to show your love and care in your new family?

Luis: I have been there for Mario, taking care of his food, clothing, making sure he gets to school on time, talking with him . . .

Therapist: What does it say about the kind of father you are?

Luis: That I love him and that I am responsible.

Therapist: If you would have dreamed of the kind of father you would like to become, how would he look?

Luis: A strong, responsible, and loving one.

Therapist: Seems you have already done part of it.

Luis: Yes, it looks like it.

Therapist: In the way of becoming this Father – I would say, this Father/Man – are there other things you would dream about?

Luis: I have to take care of myself, be stronger and proud of myself to become the Father/Man we were talking about.

Therapist: Do you think we can take a pause here? So you'll have time to think about our conversation.

Luis: OK.

Therapist: I want you to know that this space will always be open for you, if would like to come back.

At this time, I was by myself in the session. Luis came back for other sessions to talk about how to close his relationship with Diana and how to go ahead in life. We had three more sessions with Mario and Luis. This was more of a solution-focused therapy.

New Projects

In 2014, we were invited to the Mental Health Department of the Pediatric Hospital at the Mexican Institute of Social Security by a group of psychiatrists, psychologists, and neurologists. This is a traditional medical-model institution; the challenge was how to invite the participants to be open to a postmodern paradigm. I presented a 14-session theoretical and clinical training. In September 2016, we began a new training in *Terapia Breve sin Cita* at Casa Tonalá[8] and opened a new walk-in service for the community in that area in Mexico City.

Some Final Remarks about Language

I would like to make some remarks about some of the different meanings of the word "single." First, in Spanish:

solo – "single," alone, one;
unico – only, unique.

When we tried to use "*sesion unica*" to translate "single session," our clients responded more to the concept of "one session" and said: "What if I need more sessions?" So, as we mentioned earlier, we decided to call our service "*terapia breve*" – "brief therapy."

A second distinction is between what for Talmon (1990) "*single-session*" meant when saying "when people have the opportunity, they can make significant changes in one session" and what Anderson (2012) meant when saying "each encounter is unique." Reflecting on writing this chapter, I would like to emphasize the difference that the words *unique* and *single* have for me. *Single* invites me to think of each encounter as the only opportunity to meet with a person and the responsibility to foster a meaningful conversation that opens possibilities. *Unique* invites me to appreciate, value, and recognize what is unique, special, and different in each person and situation. Whether we meet for one session, or more, each encounter brings out the uniqueness of each conversation and relationship. In this process, we have the privilege of becoming the therapist/team that the client needs and that the occasion calls for.

Notes

1 To Tamara and Sylvia: thanks for editing and thinking together.
2 Founded by Irma Rodriguez in 2001.
3 Founded by Julie Rivera Rio in 1979.
4 Founded by Elena Fernandez, Sylvia London, and Margarita Tarragona in 1998.
5 Special thanks to Glenn Gardner, Joan Biever, Monte Bobele, and Ezequiel Peña.
6 To Monte Bobele and Arnie Slive, thanks!

7 Matz Spearman, a Swedish colleague, coined the phrase "supervision – intervision."
8 Casa Tonalá was founded by Marina González in 2012.

References

Andersen, T. (1987). The reflecting team: Dialogue and meta-dialogue in clinical work. *Family Process*, *26*, 415–428.

Andersen, T. (1990). *The reflecting team: Dialogues and dialogues about dialogues.* Broadstairs, Kent: Borgmann.

Anderson, H. (1998). *Conversation, language and possibilities: A postmodern approach to therapy.* New York: Basic Books.

Anderson, H. (1999). Collaborative learning communities. In S. McNamee & K. Gergen (Eds.), *Relational responsibility: Resources for sustainable dialogue* (pp. 65–70). Newbury Park, CA: Sage.

Anderson, H. (2012). Collaborative relationships and dialogic conversations: Ideas for a relationally responsive practice. *Family Process*, *51*, 8–24.

Anderson, H., & Gehart, D. (Eds.) (2007). *Collaborative therapy: Relationships and conversations that make a difference.* New York: Routledge.

Fernández, E., London, S., & Tarragona, M. (2002). Las conversaciones reflexivas en el trabajo clínico, el entrenamiento y la supervisión. In G. Licea, I. Paquentin & H. Selicoff, *Voces y mas voces: El equipo reflexivo en México.* México D.F.: Alinde Instituto de Psicoterapia.

Lyotard, J.F. (1984). *The post-modern condition: A report on knowledge.* Minneapolis, MN: University of Minnesota Press.

O'Hanlon, W.H. & Weiner-Davis, M. (1989). *In search of solutions: A new direction in psychotherapy.* New York: Norton.

Shotter, J. (2005). Goethe and refiguring of intellectual inquiry: from "aboutness" thinking to "withness" thinking in everyday life. *Janus Head: Journal of Interdisciplinary Studies in Literature, Continental Philosophy, Phenomenological Psychology and Arts*, *8*(1), 132–158.

Slive, A. & Bobele, M. (Eds.) (2011). *When one hour is all you have: Effective therapy for walk-in clients.* Phoenix, AZ: Zeig, Tucker, & Theisen.

Talmon, M. (1990). *Single session therapy: Maximizing the effect of the first (and often only) therapeutic encounter.* San Francisco: Jossey-Bass.

White, M. & Epston, D. (1990). *Narrative means to therapeutic ends.* New York: Norton.

20 Reflections on Providing Single-Session Therapy in Post-Disaster Haiti

Brian Guthrie

This chapter continues the on-going discussion of the adaptation of single-session therapy (SST) to acute emergency settings (Miller, 2011; WHO, et al., 2012; Paul & van Ommeren, 2013; Akerele & Yuryev, 2017). Paul and van Ommeren suggested that the "framework behind SST's intervention and service potentially allows for flexible, creative and dynamic responses to mental health and psychosocial needs" (p. 17). They recommended that attention should be given to SST's potential for adaptation to fit the service needs in emergency settings in low and middle-income countries (LMIC). In addition, this chapter proposes that SST could be a viable treatment response post-disaster in LMIC to balance limited resources with the fact that psychological distress for some individuals continues long after the acute emergency stage.

The editors of the *Lancet* series on global mental health stated that "Mental health disorders represent a largely hidden, if not substantial proportion of the world's disease burden. They can often be neglected, especially in low and middle-income countries, many of which have no resources to tackle mental health concerns" (Executive Summary, 2007, p. 801). In a 2007 report on global mental health in LMIC, Saraceno, et al. (2007, p. 1171) identified a number of barriers that inhibited the development of sustainable mental health services. They included:

> [i]nsufficient funding for mental health services, mental health resources that are centralized in and near big cities and in large institutions, complexities of integrating mental health care effectively into primary-care services, low numbers and limited types of health workers trained and supervised in mental health care and mental health leaders often deficient in public-health skills and experiences.

These barriers pose significant challenges in responding to the increased demand for culturally sound mental health and psychosocial services post-disaster.

The process of providing SST in Haiti post-disaster will be discussed within the context of a detailed case study based on the my experience as a mental-health trauma therapist on a medical mission team in Cite-Soliel, Haiti, in February 2012, two years after the January 12, 2010 earthquake. I volunteered to join a local group of physicians, nurses, and paramedics on a two-week mission sponsored by Haiti Outreach Ministries. This Haiti-based Christian organization operated the medical clinic that the team worked out of; in addition, they provided information and training on the Haitian culture, accommodation, and translators. Although I am semi-fluent in French, 95% of the population only speaks Haitian French-based Creole. Translators were an important component in ensuring culturally congruent, clear, and accurate communication between myself and my clients. Although I had volunteered in LMIC countries in the past, this was my first trip to Haiti and my first trip as a designated mental-health professional. In addition, I will discuss how providing SST post-disaster can provide a framework for practice when it is not possible to plan continuity in case management, follow-up, and referral to mental-health treatment services.

Disasters

According to Leaning and Guha-Sapir (2013), the scale of disasters has expanded, owing to increased rates of urbanization, deforestation, environmental degradation, and intensifying climate variables such as higher temperatures, extreme precipitation, and more violent wind/water storms. Leaning and Guha-Sapir went on to say that:

> Natural disasters, particularly floods and storms, will become more frequent and severe because of climate change. Organized deadly onslaughts against civilian populations will continue, fuelled by the availability of small arms, persistent social and political inequities, and, increasingly, by a struggle for natural resources. These events affect the mortality, morbidity, and well-being of large populations. Humanitarian relief will always be required, and there is a demonstrable need, as in other areas of global health, to place greater emphasis on prevention and mitigation.
>
> (p. 1842)

Researchers of the mental-health effects of disasters (Galea, Nandi, & Vlahov, 2005; Green, 1998; North, 2007a, b; North, Oliver, & Pandya, 2012; and Rubonis & Bickman, 1991) have emphasized that the psychological impact on a survivor's mental-health may range from mild and transient to severe and chronic, increasing primary health care use for 12 months, or more, after the event. The long-term psychological effects may result in some individuals experiencing serious mental-health problems ranging from post-traumatic stress disorder (PTSD) to depression and anxiety.

PTSD is the most commonly identified disorder that occurs after exposure to a traumatic event. PTSD is characterized by re-experiencing of the traumatic event, avoidance, numbing, and hyperarousal. Symptoms need to be present for at least one month and cause clinically significant distress or impairment in functioning to fulfill diagnostic criteria for PTSD (American Psychiatric Association, 2013). It is important to note, however, that other disorders also commonly occur both with PTSD and independently of PTSD. Depression was the second most commonly observed psychological disorder in survivors of disasters followed by various forms of anxiety (Norris, Friedman, Watson, Byrne, Diaz, & Kaniasty, 2002).

The Haiti Earthquake

On January 12, 2010, an earthquake struck Haiti causing widespread damage to an already fragile infrastructure. It was estimated that more than 300,000 people died as a result of the 7.0 magnitude earthquake and some 300,000 were injured. The Haitian government estimated that 250,000 residences, 30,000 commercial buildings and 80% of the schools were destroyed or severely damaged by the earthquake. Approximately 1.5 million people found themselves living in 1,555 temporary camps (Disaster Emergency Committee, 2014). Cerdá, et al. (2013) documented earthquake-related experiences associated with risk for PTSD two to four months following the 2010 Haiti earthquake. They reported that 90.5% of survey respondents had a least one relative or close friend who was injured or killed. Haiti's health workforce was under-prepared to provide the physical care the population needed and much less the psychological and mental-health services (Pan-American Health Organization/WHO, 2003 Caribbean Country Management Unit, 2006).

Culturally, in Haiti mental-health problems are often attributed to supernatural forces, with problems in daily functioning often viewed as the consequence of a spell, a hex, or a curse cast by a jealous person. Mental illness is also attributed to the failure to please spirits, including those of deceased family members. Shame may be associated with the decline of functioning with severe mental illness, and family members may be reluctant to acknowledge that a member is ill (Nicolas, Jean-Jacques, & Wheatley, 2012; World Health Organization, 2010). In the face of tragedy and disaster, Haitians often rely on their inner spiritual and religious conviction to deal with mental-health problems. As the poorest nation in the global community, the Haitian community has a long history of tragedy that extends over two centuries. Haitians have endured slavery (1550–1795), revolution (1795–1803), the HIV epidemic (1983–2008), and numerous natural disasters. For Haitians, the Creole words *kenbe fem*, roughly translated as "to hold firm," represent the resilience of the Haitian people.

Single-Session Therapy Post-Disaster

SST is an established mental-health intervention and has been used by mental-health professionals for more than 40 years (Johnson, Whitaker & Porter, 1980; Walk-in Counseling Center, Minneapolis, MN, 1977) as a treatment of choice when the understanding between the therapist and the client is that a single-session may be the only response feasible (Cox & Campbell, 2003). Although mental-health treatment for trauma is mainstream in high-income countries, there are few references in the literature to the treatment of trauma post-disaster using single-session therapy (SST) in either high-income countries or LMIC. There are references to single-session behavioral therapy post-trauma (Başoğlu, Şalcıoğlu, Livanou, Kalender, & Acar, 2005), a single session of emotional freedom techniques following trauma (Church, 2014; Church, Piña, Reategui, & Brooks, 2012), and single-session psychological debriefing (Bisson, 2003). Each of these approaches is a specific model of therapy. SST is not considered a therapeutic model in itself (Talmon, 1990) and has been adapted by therapists from different theoretical orientations to provide planned single-session intervention. Miller (2011) provided an anecdotal narrative of his experience providing SST as a mental-health professional responding to Hurricane Katrina, August 23, 2005; and Urrego, Abaakouk, Roman and Contreras (2009) reported on a study by Medicins Sans Frontieres utilizing SST in the provision of mental-health services during the on-going armed conflict in Columbia.

Reflections on Providing Single-Session Therapy in Haiti: Preparation and Practice

Driving away from the airport in Port-au–Prince, I was struck by the extent of damage that remained two years after the earthquake. Every street seemed to have a least one house that was collapsed and frozen in time. If this was the state of recovery two years after the earthquake, I wondered about the emotional and mental health of the survivors and what resources had been made available over the past two years. The medical team I was with worked out of an existing clinic in the Cite Soliel and provided a makeshift clinic in the tent camp of Cappva. On the first day the clinic opened its doors, 200 patients, most of whom began waiting in line at 4 a.m., began seeing the medical team. As the physicians began requesting mental-health consults, it became apparent that many individuals were presenting with deep psychological pain as a result of their experience of surviving the earthquake. None had any previous mental-health support or intervention.

As physicians began assessing and treating patients, they referred patients to me for mental-health treatment with two primary diagnoses, PTSD and Complicated Grief Reaction. I was faced with the ethical dilemma of engaging individuals who are experiencing deep psychological pain without resources to refer to for on-going mental health treatment, while at the same time I could not abandon those who needed assistance in coping with the emotional trauma. I could not ignore their physically and psychologically precarious life situations. I was instantly reminded of Slive and Bobele's (2011) book, *When One Hour is All You Have: Effective Therapy for Walk-in Clients.* The authors detail the process of one hour of therapy focused on the clients' stated wants and advocate for SST to be added to the continuum of mental health services. These Haitian clients would not see me again as this medical mission's mandate ended in two weeks. They could, of course, see a mental-health therapist on a future visiting team if that team had a mental health therapist. The reality was, as identified by Raviola, Eustache, Oswald, and Belkin (2012), Haiti does not have a mental-health system to sufficiently support their people. The Haitians referred to me for mental-health treatment, in one of the poorest slums in the Western hemisphere, would most likely not see a therapist for follow-up services.

As a therapist in a high-income country, I often have the luxury of time and my clients have the luxury of service choice and resources. It was not unusual for me to work with clients who requested one session, and for me to employ the principles and premises of SST to ensure that the client leaves the clinic with a specific plan of action to address the presenting problem. In my clinical practice I have a certain degree of confidence in SST bolstered by knowing that, in Canada as a high-income country, the client could choose to come back at any time for further sessions or access a number of other resources to assist them in coping with their life issues.

Standing in the yard of the medical clinic compound in Citie Soliel, barricaded by 12-foot walls, I sat with my first client in the open air shaded by the wall of the clinic. For the first time as a therapist, I was confronted with the stark reality of *one session is all I have.*

Confidence in the SST: What Do I Believe?

Congruent with the principles and premises of single-session therapy, I believe that change is an inevitable process in life and that clients often need the support and assistance of therapists only for brief periods to enable them to use their own resources to solve their problems (Watzlawick, Weakland and Fisch, 1974). I assume that clients know what they need, and I encourage them to focus on what they can take away from a session that is going to be most helpful. In short, I have a deep belief that clients have the capacity to solve their own problems. I agree with Campbell (2012) when he describes SST as reinforcing an individual's personal resources and skills and that this enhances resiliency and promotes problem-solving.

Applying the process of SST, I engaged clients in Haiti in identifying their specific problems, exploring their attempted solutions, identifying current barriers and hurdles to solutions, identifying resources available, and encouraging clients to develop a new approach. Often the intervention was simply offering advice to the client, reframing the problem, or normalizing what the patient perceived as abnormal or unusual. In almost every situation the acknowledgment and validation of the tremendous grief and loss of loved ones provided a cathartic experience.

As emphasized by Miller (2011), as a therapist conducting SST, I worked toward two main objectives. I provided clients with a specific reframing of their presenting problem with the goal of enabling clients to view the problem as more manageable. *Reframing* is a technique frequently employed by therapists in order to present clients with different ways of understanding their current situation, i.e., it provides clients with ideas about what is possible and potential paths to a solution. The second objective, following reframing the problem, was to assist clients in identifying existing resources that they could use to resolve the reframed view of their presenting problem. SST can be seen to have been effectively accomplished when the client is presented with observations that commend their existing strengths, restore autonomy and confidence, and offer solutions that they can immediately begin to implement (Miller & Slive, 2004; Slive & Bobele, 2011; Talmon, 1990).

The SST Approach to Post-Disaster Work in Haiti

During my two weeks on this medical mission team, Haitians were referred for mental-health treatment by the team physicians. The majority of the patients connected the onset of their symptoms to their experience of surviving the earthquake, and the persistence of their symptoms to the daily struggle for survival. The case presented here is anecdotal and not intended as definitive evidence of the effectiveness of SST. It serves the purpose of reporting on the process of implementing SST as a mental-health intervention in a LMIC post-disaster. In addition, the case example demonstrates the process of acknowledging and validating the client's lived experience in their cultural context. Specifically, as emphasized by Mocun-Aydin (2000), I attempted to engage clients in a therapeutic relationship that contained shared and appropriate goals. As the therapist, I believed that my responsibility was to elicit and understand my client's desired goals.

Single-Session Therapy Assessment

Each client's situation was assessed within the therapeutic lens of SST practice principles (Hoyt, Rosenbaum, & Talmon, 1992, pp. 61--62):

(1) View each session as a whole, potentially complete in itself. Expect change.
(2) The power is in the patient. Never underestimate your patient's strength.
(3) This is it. All you have is now.
(4) The therapeutic process starts before the first session and will continue long after it.
(5) The natural process of life is the main force of change.
(6) You do not have to know everything in order to be effective.
(7) You do not have to rush or reinvent the wheel.
(8) More is not necessarily better; better is better. A small step can make a difference.
(9) Helping people as quickly as possible is practical and ethical.

In order to acknowledge and validate the client's lived experience and assist in identifying next steps, I followed the three primary assessment questions of SST: (1) How is the client stuck?; (2) What does the client need to get unstuck?; and (3) How can I provide or facilitate what is needed? (Hoyt, 1990, 1994).

Single-Session Therapy Intervention: The Process of SST from Referral to Intervention to Termination

Within each session, I primarily focused on reframing the client's presenting problems offering a viable alternative perspective that might be perceived as less overwhelming and more manageable. The client was encouraged to identify small steps toward reaching their goals in order to promote a sense of progress and strengthen a sense of hope. I assisted clients in redefining problems as behavioral, observable, specific, and under their control. In all cases, I provided feedback to the client that clarified the nature of the problem, as well as what could be done to deal with the problem (Talmon, 1990).

Case Example

Rachelle, a 75-year-old female, was referred for a mental-health consultation following a medical evaluation where she presented as frail and malnourished, complaining of headaches, muscle pain, decreasing weight (now at 90 lbs from her usual 200 lbs) and problems sleeping. The physician reported that the symptoms, although exacerbated by malnutrition, might be associated with depression. She was accompanied by two female neighbors who had been looking out for her since she lost her family in the earthquake. They reported that her symptoms emerged shortly after the earthquake and that they were concerned that her symptoms were becoming more prevalent.

As we sat in the sweltering heat, I was struck by the image of this frail elderly woman sandwiched between her two robust neighbors. They waited patiently and respectfully as the translator relayed my greeting and an explanation of who I was. I told them I was a doctor with the medical team and that I helped people with their emotional stress. I told Rachelle that the clinic doctor wondered if her physical symptoms were becoming worse because her life was difficult on her own. Rachelle and her neighbors nodded as the translator explained that I agreed with the clinic doctor that the hard work of surviving after the earthquake can be overwhelming.

It is important to note that I was acutely aware of the stigma of mental problems and that in Haiti individuals who are seen as mentally ill can be ostracized by the community. I choose to use the term "stress," instead of "depression," as I experienced that most if not all the Haitians I met and interacted with understood the concept of stress and how it impacted their lives. They would openly discuss struggling with headaches, fatigue, and sleeplessness which often lead to expressing worry about the future and how to cope. SST is not intended to treat an individual's diagnosis; rather, it treats the problems the individual presents with. Therefore, my task was to discover Rachelle's unique lived experience of grief and to explore potential resources within her community and culture to assist her in navigating the grief process.

I asked her to tell me what she felt she needed. She said that she was worried as she could not sleep, could not eat and that her head ached. I was curious about why she thought she couldn't sleep and what made her head ache? She said she longed for her children and at night she was very lonely and sad, and that the pain of not having them with her hurt her head. She told me that her entire family had been killed in the earthquake.

She began to weep quietly as she recounted holding her son as he died from injuries sustained in the collapse of the family home. She emphasized the joy she felt in life before the earthquake and her sense of pride as a mother. She also spoke of being strong before the earthquake and emphasized her physical well-being, "I was 200 pounds. Now I'm nothing," referring to her current weight of 90 pounds. She described herself as being lonely and avoiding people and places in the community as they reminded her of her children.

I first commended her for the love she had for her children, and the importance of keeping their memories alive in the face of great physical and emotional hardships. I asked her how she had survived with such unbearable loss, and how she had remained alive living alone when there was limited food and shelter. Her explanation for having survived was that it was the will of God and that her neighbors were caring for her. I tried to normalize her symptoms in the context of the stress of survival post-earthquake and a mother's grief over the death of her children. This normalization is a standard intervention for individuals experiencing trauma as an outcome of a disaster. The physical and psychological issues experienced as a result of a disaster are explained as expected reactions to an abnormal event. I said that it made sense that she would be feeling the way she was feeling having survived the earthquake and that she was alone and grieving the loss of all her children. I wondered out loud about how difficult it would be to accept the loss of one child and said that I couldn't imagine how painful it would be to lose all of one's children. Lastly, I commended her on her strength in being a survivor of the earthquake and explained that the stress of being a survivor often shows up as physical symptoms of headaches and trouble sleeping and that these are expected symptoms for many people who have been through what she has experienced.

The next step was to help her get unstuck and begin a healthy grieving process. Since she described herself as overwhelmed by worries about her children no longer being with her, I focused the session on her beginning to experience how she might remember her children and not the loss of her children. I asked her to tell me about her children and what she loved about each. I asked her opinion about what her children would want her to do, and which memories they would hope she would keep close to her heart. She said her children would want her to be happy and to know that they are safe with God. At the end of our time together, she thanked me and said it was helpful to be heard and understood, and that she felt a burden had been lifted from her heart. As she prepared to leave she said she would talk to her (deceased) children during her prayers and tell them about what we had talked about and that she believed that God would provide and keep her strong.

In closing the session, I provided practical stress management techniques to address her initial problems of insomnia and anxiety. I taught her simple relaxation response exercises that she could use when she became anxious and fearful, or couldn't sleep.

Single-Session Therapy: Working within a Cultural Context

There is a significant amount of information to assist a helping professional from a high-income country to make a healthy and helpful transition into the host culture and increase their cultural sensitivity. For me the *World Health Organization Report on Culture and Mental Health in Haiti* provided information about gender, religion, Haitian Vodou, mental-health issues, and service utilization (WHO, 2010).

Doing one's homework prior to being immersed in a LMIC culture enhances a mindfulness that many LMIC cultures view mental illness in primitive terms, that there are cultural norms of response to trauma, and that the concept of psychology is an emerging development. Watters (2010) noted that Western-trained psychologists offering psychological services in post-disaster areas have been observed implementing diagnostic categories and treatment that have little or no proven cross-cultural validity. For example, Nicolas and her colleagues emphasize that the Western criteria for depression are not valid when understanding or identifying the depression of Haitian women (Nicolas et al., 2007; WHO, 2010). They recommended that "by taking culture into consideration, mental health clinicians and health care providers will be able to treat and relate to their patients more effectively, ultimately leading to more successful interventions" (p. 96). Campbell and Alexander (2002) and Sue and Sue (1999) wrote that when treatment fails to integrate the cultural background of the client, it will not lead to positive behavior change by the client. Mocun-Aydin (2000, p. 292) cautioned Western counselors that:

> Helping clients achieve insight, self-awareness, and personal growth may be the counselor's goals; however, unless these goals are owned by the client, no positive outcome will be achieved. It is quite common that the client may want solutions to practical problems without any reference to internal change. In a situation such as this, it is important to recognize that the therapeutic relationship should contain shared and appropriate goals if it is to be effective. In practice, this means that the therapist will find out from the client what are his or her desired goals. The therapist, then, may explain the way counseling works and both parties may negotiate a common purpose.

In a study on single-session walk-in therapy with Mexican-American clients, Bobele, López, Scamardo and Solórzano (2008, p. 87) pointed out how SST is likely to be a "more comfortable fit" for persons whose cultural backgrounds might make them reluctant to engage in long-term therapy and who believe there is a stigma associated with being seen as someone with a mental illness. For example, with Rachelle, I ensured the therapeutic process was within an understanding of culturally constructed experiences and responses to trauma that are unique to Haitians. That is, given the stigma of mental illness and the possible consequences of being identified as having a mental illness, problems were discussed in the context of somatic symptoms and physiological complaints prior to the exploration of emotional reactions to stress. Additionally, it was important to keep in mind that religious beliefs are an important aspect of Haitian life, and that religious beliefs help Haitians see beyond tragedy and instill hope for improved circumstances. I observed that prayer and church are preferred coping strategies for many Haitian people, and I was constantly confronted with the prevalence of belief in God and God's will. As identified by Maltby, Lewis, and Day (1999), who wrote about the important role of prayer in psychological well-being, I came to understand how important validation of this belief is in mental-health service delivery in order to provide culturally sensitive services in Haiti.

SST as a framework of intervention is syntonic with the recommendations of integrating culture into the treatment process with the client. Techniques such as rapport building, assuming a one-down position, assuming a non-judgmental stance, focusing on being goal-oriented, and maintaining a genuine curiosity about each client's lived experience promoted the validation of the cultural experience of the client. In SST, therapists and clients formulate shared goals that enable their clients to find or create answers that work within their lived experience, while making the most of their innate abilities to heal themselves. SST focuses on problems as they are occurring in the present and resulting from aspects of human interaction (Slive, McElheran, & Lawson, 2008) in the context of the client's lived experience, relationships, and cultural community.

Potential Limitations of SST in LMIC Post-Disaster

The potential disadvantage of SST post-disaster is the adoption of the model as a solution to the limited availability of mental-health services in LMIC. SST should not become the default position in the face of limited resources in LMIC struggling to cope with overwhelming mental-health issues post-disaster. Additionally, it should not be seen as a panacea in the context of no alternative for on-going follow-up and treatment. SST should be, as it is in high-income countries, integrated into the existing mental-health delivery system. Suman Fernando (2012, p. 10), in discussing challenges for mental-health development in LMIC, stated that:

> Developing mental health systems in LMI countries is not a simple matter of transferring established strategies commonly used in high-income countries, irrespective of ground realities without taking on board what local people want. And mental health is not just a technical matter but is tied up with ways of life, values, and worldviews that vary significantly across cultures and societies. A basic principle of development is that we have to start by looking at what happens currently and work from there. This is important not just to ensure social and cultural relevance of services and ownership by the people responsible for sustaining them, but also for cost-effectiveness—using the least resources to achieve the greatest gain. In most LMI countries, a variety of services are accessed by people—but usually, only if they can afford to do so.

The major problem with mental-health in Haiti, in addition to the lack of services, is the lack of mental-health structure within the country's health delivery system. The goal of providing SST should be to add to the existing mental-health services within the community to contribute to enabling wellness.

Potential Benefits of SST in LMIC Post-Disaster

Many LMICs have underdeveloped mental-health care systems with limited capacities before the onset of a disaster. The potential benefit of SST as a planned time-limited intervention resource in LMICs is that therapeutic interventions are not contingent upon the number of sessions available, the number of therapists available, or access to follow-up services. The SST framework of providing a complete psychotherapy in one session with the intended outcome of ensuring that the client leaves the single-session with a specific plan of action to address the presenting problem has the potential to positively impact the availability of mental-health care. SST has the potential of providing mental-health intervention to more of the affected population, and in decreasing the demands on the existing mental-health systems for follow-up treatments. SST has the potential to be an adjunct to existing treatment resources available in LMICs in the same way that it is sanctioned as a valid mental-health intervention in high-income countries (Paul & van Ommeren, 2013).

My experience of implementing SST to provide mental-health intervention post-disaster in Haiti demonstrated significant promise from the perspective of being a therapist treating the mental-health needs of survivors of disasters when follow-up mental-health care was inaccessible. To further support the use of SST as an additional resource in limited capacity mental-health systems, and as an intervention service post-disaster, a concerted focus will be required by practitioners, researchers, and local mental-health professionals to conduct methodologically sound empirical studies that will advance the knowledge and practice of SST as a viable treatment option post-disaster.

Postscript

My experience of being a helping professional in Haiti was extremely stressful. Being a therapist for 30 years was not enough to shield me or to provide a buffer to protect me from the abject poverty and the intensity of the trauma that permeated every interaction. Although I have significant experience in the field of mental health and significant experience in the treatment of psychological trauma, I was not prepared for the sensory and emotional overload of very long and difficult days, forgoing nutrition and hydration to see more clients, only to be immersed deeper and deeper into too many stories of psychological trauma and death. It became important to be purposefully mindful and monitor my stress levels as the day progressed. I made it a priority to ensure that I had adequate nutrition and hydration and that, at the end of the day, I shared my experiences with my colleagues, listened to music, completed my journal, and promised myself that I would take my self-care seriously. Self-care in Haiti wasn't that easy; it was a chore but a necessary chore.

References

Akerele, E. & Yuryev, A. (2017). Single session psychotherapy for humanitarian missions. *International Journal of Mental Health, 46*(2), 133–138.

American Psychiatric Association (2013). *Diagnostic and statistical manual of mental disorders* (5th ed.). Washington, DC: Author.

Başoğlu, M., Şalcıoğlu, E., Livanou, M., Kalender, D., & Acar, G. (2005). Single-session behavioral treatment of earthquake-related posttraumatic stress disorder: A randomized waiting list controlled trial. *Journal of Traumatic Stress, 18*(1), 1–11.

Bobele, M., López, S. S., Scamardo, M., & Solórzano, B. (2008). Single-session/Walk-in therapy with Mexican-American clients. *Journal of Systemic Therapies, 27*(3), 75–89.

Bisson, J.I. (2003). Single-session early psychological interventions following traumatic events. *Clinical Psychology Review, 23*(3), 481–499.

Campbell, A. (2012). Single-Session approaches to therapy: Time to review. *Australian and New Zealand Journal of Family Therapy, 33*, 15–26.

Campbell, C.I. & Alexander, J.A. (2002). Culturally competent treatment practices and ancillary service use in outpatient substance abuse treatment. *Journal of Substance Abuse Treatment, 22*(3), 109–119.

Caribbean Country Management Unit (2006). *Social resilience and state fragility in Haiti: A country social analysis.* Port Au Prince. World Bank. Retrieved http://siteresources.worldbank.org/SOCIALANALYSIS/1104894-1115795935771/20938696/Haiti_CSA.pdf.

Cerdá, M., Paczkowski, M., Galea, S., Nemethy, K., Péan, C., & Desvarieux, M. (2013). Psychopathology in the aftermath of the Haiti earthquake: A population-based study of posttraumatic stress disorder and major depression. *Depression and Anxiety. 30*(5):413-24. doi: 10.1002/da.22007. Epub 2012 Nov 1.PMID: 23124841.

Church, D. (2014). Clinical EFT (emotional freedom techniques) as single session therapy: Cases, research, indications, and cautions. In M.F. Hoyt & M. Talmon

(Eds.), *Capturing the moment: Single-session therapy and walk-in services* (pp. 299–324). Bethel, CT: Crown House Publishing.

Church, D., Piña, O., Reategui, C., & Brooks, A. (2012). Single-session reduction of the intensity of traumatic memories in abused adolescents after EFT: A randomized controlled pilot study. *Traumatology*, *18*(3), 73.

Cox, L., & Campbell, A. (2003). Let's live, and see: Interview with Moshe Talmon. *Australian and New Zealand Journal of Family Therapy*, *24*(1), 38–40.

Disaster Emergency Committee. (2014). Haiti earthquake facts and figures. Retrieved from http://dec.org.uk/haiti-earthquake-facts-and-figures.

Executive Summary (2007). Global mental health 2007. *The Lancet*, *370*, 801–908.

Fernando, S. (2012). Challenges for mental health development in low and middle-income countries. Paper presented at the Advanced Studies Institute Conference. Global Mental Health: Bridging the Perspectives of Cultural Psychiatry and Public Health. Montreal, Canada, July 5–7.

Galea, S., Nandi, A., & Vlahov, D. (2005). The epidemiology of post-traumatic stress disorder after disasters. *Epidemiology Review*, *27*, 78–91.

Green, B.L. (1998). Psychological responses to disasters: Conceptualization and identification of high-risk survivors. *Psychiatry Clinical Neuroscience, 52*(suppl), S67–S73.

Hoyt, M.F. (1990). On time in brief therapy. In R.A. Wells & V.J. Giannetti (Eds.), *Handbook of the brief psychotherapies* (pp. 115–143). New York: Plenum Press.

Hoyt, M.F. (1994). Single session solutions. In M.F. Hoyt (Ed.), *Constructive therapies* (Vol. 2, pp. 140–159). New York: Guilford Press.

Hoyt, M.F., Rosenbaum, R., & Talmon, M. (1992). Planned single-session psychotherapy. In S.H. Budman, M.F. Hoyt, & S. Friedman (Eds.), *The first session in brief therapy* (pp. 59–86). New York: Guilford Press.

Johnson, N.J., Whitaker, L.C., & Porter, G. (1980). The development and efficacy of a university mental health service walk-in clinic. *Journal of the American College Health Association*, *28*(5), 269–271.

Leaning, J. & Guha-Sapir, D. (2013). Natural disasters, armed conflict, and public health. *The New England Journal of Medicine*, *369*, 1836–1842.

Maltby, J., Lewis, C.A., & Day, L. (1999). Religious orientation and psychological well-being: The role of the frequency of personal prayer. *British Journal of Health Psychology, 4:* 363–378.

Miller, J.K. (2011). Single-session intervention in the wake of hurricane Katrina: Strategies for disaster mental health counseling. In A. Slive & M. Bobele (Eds.), *When one hour is all you have: Effective therapy for walk-in clients* (pp. 185–202). Phoenix, AZ: Zeig, Tucker, & Theisen.

Miller, J.K. & Slive, A. (2004). Breaking down the barriers to clinical service delivery: Walk-in family therapy. *Journal of Marital and Family Therapy, 30*, 95–105.

Mocun-Aydin, G. (2000). Western models of counseling and psychotherapy within Turkey: Crossing cultural boundaries. *The Counseling Psychologist*, *28*, 281–298.

Nicolas, G., DeSilva, A.M., Subrebost, K.L., Breland-Noble, A., Gonzalez-Eastep, D., Manning, N., & Prater, K. (2007). Expression and treatment of depression among Haitian immigrant women in the United States: Clinical observations. *American Journal of Psychotherapy*, *61*(1), 83.

Nicolas, G., Jean-Jacques, R., & Wheatley, A. (2012). Status and plans for the future mental health counseling in Haiti: Historical overview. *Current Journal of Black Psychology, 38*, 509.

Norris, F.H., Friedman, M.J., Watson, P.J., Byrne, D. M., Diaz, E., & Kaniasty, K. (2002). 60,000 disaster victims speak Part I: An empirical review of the empirical literature, 1981–2001. *Psychiatry, 65*(3), 207–239.

North, C.S. (2007a). Epidemiology of disaster mental health response. In R.J. Ursano, C.S. Fullerton, L. Weisaeth, & B. Raphael, (Eds.). *Textbook of Disaster Psychiatry* (pp. 29–47). New York: Cambridge University Press.

North, C.S. (2007b). Addressing the psychiatric sequelae of catastrophic trauma. *US Psychiatry*, 35–37.

North, C.S., Oliver, J., & Pandya, A. (2012). Examining a comprehensive model of disaster-related posttraumatic stress disorder in systematically studied survivors of 10 disasters. *American Journal of Public Health,102*(10), e40–e48.

Pan American Health Organization. (2003). *Haiti: Profiles of the health services system* (2nd ed.). Retrieved http://new.paho.org/hq/dmdocuments/2010/Health_System_Profile-Haiti_2003.pdf

Paul, K.E. & van Ommeren, M. (2013). A primer on single session therapy and its potential application in humanitarian situations. *Intervention: Journal of Mental Health and Psychosocial Support in Conflict-Affected Areas, 11*(1), 8–23.

Raviola, G., Eustache, E., Oswald, C., & Belkin, G.S. (2012). Mental-health response in Haiti in the aftermath of the 2010 Earthquake: A case study for building long-term solutions. *Harvard Review of Psychiatry, 20*(1), 68–77. http://doi.org/10.3109/10673229.2012.652877.

Rubonis, A.V. & Bickman, L. (1991). Psychological impairment in the wake of disaster: The disaster-psychopathology relationship. *Psychological Bulletin, 109*(3), 384–399.

Saraceno, B., van Ommeren, M., Batniji, R., Cohen, A., Gureje, O., Mahoney, J., Sridhar, D., & Underhill, C. (2007). Global mental health 5: Barriers to the improvement of mental health services in low-income and middle-income countries. *The Lancet, 370* (9593), 1164–1174.

Slive, A. & Bobele, M. (2011). *When one hour is all you have: Effective therapy for walk-in clients.* Phoenix, AZ: Zeig, Tucker & Theisen.

Slive, A., McElheran, N., & Lawson, A. (2008). How brief does it get? Walk-in single session therapy. *Journal of Systemic Therapies, 27*, 5–22.

Sue, D.W. & Sue, E. (2012). *Counseling the culturally diverse: Theory and practice.* New York: Wiley.

Talmon, M. (1990). *Single-session therapy: Maximizing the effect of the first (and often only) therapeutic encounter.* San Francisco: Jossey-Bass.

Urrego, Z., Abaakouk, Z., Roman, C., & Contreras, R. (2009). *Evaluation of results of a single-session psychotherapy intervention in people affected by the Colombian internal armed conflict.* Medecins Sans Frontieres.

Walk-In Counseling Center, Minneapolis, MN. (1977). No-red-tape counseling for clients alienated from traditional services. *Hospital and Community Psychiatry, 28*(11), 843–845.

Watters, E. (2010). *Crazy like us: The globalization of the American psyche.* New York: Free Press.

Watzlawick, P., Weakland, J.H., & Fisch, R. (1974). *Change: Principles of problem formation and problem resolution.* New York: Norton.

WHO, UN ACTION, UNFPA, UNICEF. (2012). *Responding to the psychosocial and mental health needs of sexual violence survivors in conflict-affected settings, final report. Technical meeting on responding to the psychosocial and mental health needs of sexual violence survivors in conflict-affected settings*, Ferney-Voltaire, November 28–30, 2011. Retrieved from http://resourcecentre.savethechildren.se/library/responding-psychosocial-and-mental-health-needs-sexual-violence-survivors-conflict-affected

World Health Organization. (2010). *Culture and mental health in Haiti: A literature review. Geneva: World Health Organization*. Retrieved from www.iawg.net/Mental%20Health%20in%20Haiti%20%20A%20Literature%20Review%20_WHO_.pdf.

21 Some Ways to End an SST

Michael F. Hoyt and Robert Rosenbaum

Fifty Ways Not to Leave Your Client
You just insist they come back, Jack
Make a new treatment plan, Stan
Avoid the topic of ending—be coy, Roy
Tell them they're not ready, Freddie
If they try to cancel, make a big fuss, Gus
They still need to discuss much
Before they can leave, Steve
("How could you do this to me?")
And don't forget your fee, Lee.

(M.F. Hoyt, *The Last Session in Brief Therapy: How and Why to Say "When"*, 2000a, p. 239)

Ending is never far off when doing a one-at-a-time single-session therapy. Given the importance of finishing well for enhancing potential therapy benefits, it may be helpful to review some of the issues that often need to be addressed in terminating a single session (or other brief) therapy. Two thousand years ago, verse 64 of the *Tao Te Ching* (Rosenbaum, 2013, p. 257) warned:

Busy people often launch a great project
But just near the point of completion
Spoil the work and it fails.

Golfers have their own version of this. They say, "You drive for show, but you putt for dough," which we take as meaning: ending well is what really counts. (Astute golfers also know that good form at the finish is a reflection of good form at the beginning—vague goals make for vague therapy, and clear goals make for a more purposeful, efficient therapy: "It's a long day on the course if you don't know where the hole is. Have a specific goal and be purposeful on every stroke"—Hoyt, 2000b, p. 6.) All of this is to say that a good golfer—and therapist—knows the wisdom of paying attention to beginnings and endings.

In Hoyt (1995, 2000a, 2009) and Hoyt and Talmon (2014, pp. 517–522) a schema was presented for organizing the tasks and skills associated with

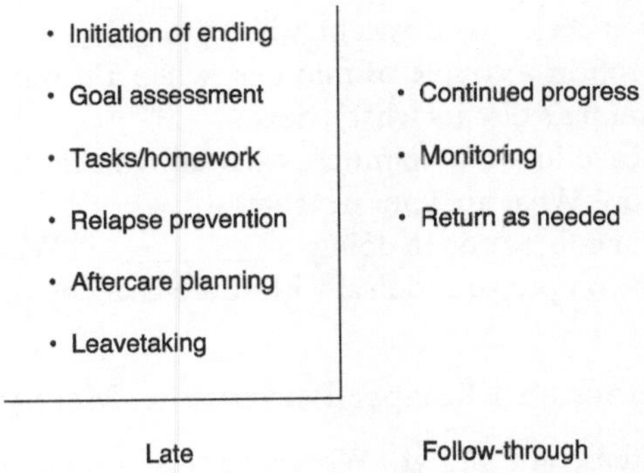

Figure 21.1 The ending (termination) phases of a session (and treatment): subtracting the therapist from the successful equation (adapted from Hoyt, 2000a, p. 246. ©M.F. Hoyt, 2000. Used by agreement)

the different phases of treatment and sessions: pre-, early, middle, late, and follow-through (see Figure 11.2, Chapter 11 in this volume). There is often a microcosm-macrocosm parallelism—the structure of each session resembling the overall structure of the therapy—and it all comes together when one session (at a time) comprises the entire treatment. The beginning (pre- and early) of each session and each therapy involves the client and therapist forming an alliance, identifying goals, and determining what positive movement may have already occurred since the client originally sought contact. The middle of each session and treatment involves refocusing and the application of various change processes. The later phases (late and follow-through) of a session and a treatment—the topic of this communication—involve "subtracting the therapist from the equation of the successful relationship" (Gustafson, 1986, p. 279): ending and leave-taking, preventing relapse and promoting continued progress, and possible return to treatment (see Figure 21.1).

There are guideline questions that can structure discussions for each of the tasks involved in the Late and Follow-Through phases:

Late in Session/Treatment

Initiation of Ending/Goal Attainment/Homework/Post-Session Tasks

- Has this meeting been helpful to you? How so? Do you feel we've achieved what you wanted?
- Is there anything we should have talked about but haven't?
- Which of the helpful things you've been doing do you think you should continue to do? How can you do this?

- To keep things going in the right direction [or, between now and the next time we may meet], would you be willing to ____________?
- Before we stop in a couple of minutes, when I'll walk you back to the waiting room, let's discuss what's next . . .
- When you leave in a few minutes, what are you most likely to do with today's session? What are your next steps?
- Who can be helpful to you in doing ____________? What might interfere, and how can you prepare to deal with those challenges?

Goal Maintenance and Relapse Prevention/Management

- Problems often come and go. What would be a signal that the problems you were having might be returning? How can you respond if you see that happening?
- We all have the capacity to be our best friend as well as our worst enemy. Suppose you wanted to go back to all of the problems you were having when you first came in—what would you need to do to make this happen, if you wanted to sabotage yourself?
- How might [the problem] try to trick you into letting it take over again? What can you do to resist that?
- What do you need to do to increase the odds that things will work out OK even if you were not to come in for a while?
- Who will be glad to hear about your progress? Who in your present or past [family, friends, colleagues] would support your efforts?

Leave-taking

- Would you like to make another appointment now, or wait and see how things go and call the clinic as needed?
- What is the longest you can imagine handling things on your own?

Follow-Through

Continued Progress and Monitoring/Return as Needed

- Would you please complete this brief questionnaire to let me know how helpful was this session?
- In the future, may we [the clinic] send you a follow-up questionnaire to see how you're doing?
- If you want, you can always come back to see someone here. Do you have the number/know the hours when we're here and you can come in?

Tailoring Termination

One size doesn't fit everyone; each therapy is individualized, based on the client's particular context and situation as well as the various skills and resources that the therapist and client can bring to bear. The same is true, of course, when finishing the session—one size doesn't fit all. In writing about how to use termination constructively, Rosenbaum, Hoyt, and Talmon (1990/1995, pp. 133–135) pointed out:

> Termination is about the structure of memory and the realization of implications. In order to make a single session of therapy complete in itself, it must contain a fitting ending . . . Memory is a key to our experience of time, and the structure of sequences of events influences how they will be remembered . . . The SST therapist, by highlighting certain events and deemphasizing others, attempts to help the client focus on what will be useful while letting go of whatever needs to be left behind. In terminating the session, the SST therapist may help a client remember to remember, forget to remember, remember to forget, or forget to forget . . . Saying something at the beginning and then again at the end of a session is very different from saying the same thing several times in the middle of the session; the former will be much more likely to be remembered than the latter. Termination, by creating an ending point, punctuates experience and so structures how we remember and interpret what has occurred, both within the therapy session and in the passage of our lives. When concluding an SST, we may first ask the client if he or she feels that enough has been accomplished in the session to help him or her move on. If the answer is yes, we may ask for a description of what it was, to encourage lexical encoding, storage, and recall of a useful lesson. At other times, we may prefer to have the client leave with a more diffuse sense that "something" changed or will change soon.

We may conclude an SST with a mutual sense of the work being finished and completed; at other times, we may stop after an important piece of work has been partially accomplished but before all of its ramifications are spelled out. The appropriate degree of closure is influenced by whether the client was primarily seeking resolution of some issue or attempting to open up new possibilities. Since some SST clients will in the future seek further therapy, it is important to end the session in such a way that a decision for more treatment will be seen as an opportunity for further growth rather than as an indicator of failure.

The conclusion of an SST will likely not put an end to all of a client's problems, but can form a point of departure from the same old problems recurring again and again. SST has faith in the client's ability to use the end of the therapy as the start of a new way of approaching their situation. When the session wraps up, it may not be the end of their ills; it may not even be the beginning of the end of their ills. It may not be (with apologizes to Shakespeare) that "all's well that ends well," but without a good ending, the chances of maximal benefit are less than they should be.

Endings give meaning both to what has gone before and to what follows. A client might start a session with abrasive bluster; in the course of the meeting we may learn that he is struggling with constant corrosive internal self-condemnation, perhaps mirroring some on-going abuse he hears from those closest to him; any irritation the therapist experienced at the initial denigration may be replaced with compassion now that the insult is seen as a desperate attempt to keep the internal critic at bay; by the end of the session the client may express gratitude for the therapist's support and be more willing to engage constructively with others to solve the problems he is facing. Another client's weak farewell handshake, which we might have initially interpreted as timidity, may give way to the understanding that the person is suffering from a degenerative neurological illness; this awareness may lead us to better understand what the client has been through and may also effect the types of solutions the client and therapist realistically are able to consider. A couple finishes their session with some specific plans for how to communicate better; this also renews and reinforces their view of themselves as committed partners. A young woman struggling with alcohol abuse walks in for a session ostensibly "just to get information"—by the end of the session, reminded of her desires for health and hopes for a better life, she pledges to abstain from alcohol for 24 hours and subsequently uses the SST as a portal to more services. Another client, who seeks counseling for help extricating herself from an unsatisfying relationship, becomes tearful at the ending of our single session—and reports that our practicing saying goodbye is sufficient preparation for her to achieve her goal. One size doesn't fit all.

Sometimes things are fairly straightforward and the "light touch" of a single session avoids complications (Hoyt, 2000a, 2011); sometimes not. How does the client respond to the impending termination of treatment? How does the therapist respond?

Knowing that all endings are potential beginnings does not necessarily make them easier. There is something about endings which smells too much like loss and even death. So it helps to have a sense of good form, of being able to construct artful endings crafted to fit the needs of the moment. A piece of music can end with a dramatic cadence or fade away quietly; it can give a sense of conclusion by coming "home" to its starting key or have a sense of ambiguity by intentionally refusing to resolve its developments and conform to expectations. The former feels more satisfying; the latter, though, projects the process of the music past its stopping point so that any ending is left to the listener rather than imposed by the composer. These different musical endings (e.g., fade-out, slow-down, multi-path, sudden cessation, restatement, etc.—see Rosenbaum, 1989; Rosenbaum & Bohart, 2007), by structuring our subsequent recall of what we've heard, help ensure that how we end the therapy session will influence how well the client is able to use an SST.

We can often end therapy effectively by borrowing a musical technique. Many musical pieces end with a restatement of the beginning theme. Because there have been intervening musical developments, this is not a mere repetition but a return that provides and consolidates the different perspectives that have emerged. Often the restatement is followed with a coda that gives a satisfying sense of closure.

Coda

Ending is never far off when doing a one-at-a-time single-session therapy. Given the importance of finishing well for enhancing potential therapy benefits, it is helpful to heed the *Tao Te Ching*'s advice:

> Busy people often launch a great project
> But just near the point of completion
> Spoil the work and it fails.
> Take care at the end just like at the beginning:
> Continuous practice never knows failure.

References

Gustafson, J.P. (1986). *The complex secret of brief psychotherapy.* New York: Norton.

Hoyt, M.F. (1995). On time in brief therapy. In *Brief therapy and managed care: Readings for contemporary practice* (pp. 69–104). San Francisco: Jossey-Bass. (work originally published 1990).

Hoyt, M.F. (2000a) The last session in brief therapy: Why and how to say "when." In *Some stories are better than others: Doing what works in brief therapy and managed care* (pp. 237–261). Philadelphia, PA: Brunner/Mazel.

Hoyt, M.F. (2000b). A golfer's guide to brief therapy (with footnotes for baseball fans). In *Some stories are better than others: Doing what works in brief therapy and managed care* (pp. 5–15). Philadelphia, PA: Brunner/Mazel.

Hoyt, M.F. (2009). *Brief psychotherapies: Principles and practices.* Phoenix, AZ: Zeig, Tucker, & Theisen.

Hoyt, M.F. (2011, November). *Termination: Breaking up is (sometimes) hard to do.* One-day workshop for Avante Behavioral Health. Fresno, CA.

Hoyt, M.F., & Talmon, M. (2014). The temporal structure of brief therapy: Some questions often associated with different phases of sessions and treatment. In M.F. Hoyt & M. Talmon (Eds.), *Capturing the moment: Single session therapy and walk-in services* (pp. 517–522). Bethel, CT: Crown House Publishing.

Rosenbaum, R. (1989, April). *Music and mind: Forms of stability, change, and integration.* Paper presented at Fifth Annual Conference of the Society for the Exploration of Psychotherapy Integration, Berkeley, CA.

Rosenbaum, R. (2013). *Walking the way: 81 Zen encounters with the Tao Te Ching.* Boston: Wisdom Publications.

Rosenbaum, R., & Bohart, A.C. (2007). Psychotherapy: The art of experience. In S. Krippner, M. Bova, & L. Grey (Eds.), *Healing stories: The use of narrative in counseling and psychotherapy* (pp. 295–324). Charlottesville, VA: Puente Publications.

Rosenbaum, R., Hoyt, M.F., & Talmon, M. (1995). The challenge of single-session therapies: Creating pivotal moments. In M.F. Hoyt, *Brief therapy and managed care: Readings for contemporary practice* (pp. 105–139). San Francisco: Jossey-Bass (work originally published 1990).

Section 4
Supervisory

22 The First Time

Teaching Skills that Prepare Interns and New Therapists for Walk-In Counseling

Joanna Bedggood

For more than half a century KW Counselling Services has been offering training and hands-on experience to emerging therapists. Our Walk-In Counselling Clinic is a key part of this training and often a favorite part of their practicum for our graduate students. Our extensive involvement in training the next generation of therapists has created a situation that has often been described at our agency as "win-win-win": new therapists receive first-rate training, our agency receives the energy and new learning that learners bring, and the community gets added service because of the added capacity to our resources.

Background

KW Counselling Services (KWCS) is a multi-service, multi-funded, non-profit family counseling agency in Kitchener, Ontario, Canada. Since 2007, KWCS has been running a weekly Walk-In Counselling Clinic every Thursday from noon until 6 p.m. Originally created to address the needs of a waiting list of nearly 1,000 individuals seeking on-going counseling, the service has evolved to meet a variety of community needs.

Clients attending the Walk-In Clinic at KWCS first have a 15-minute meeting with an intake worker, who will perform a variety of functions:

- ensuring that the client understands what single-session counseling is and help them access another service if that is not what they are seeking
- determining the funding of counseling—many clients are eligible for fully funded counseling at no cost to them; those who are not pay on a sliding scale based on income
- reviewing and signing a service agreement, including the limits of confidentiality, and
- gathering demographic and clinical data.

Currently, in a typical week the clinic serves approximately 70 individuals. Fewer than 50 people is considered a very slow week. The busiest week to date saw 96 people served. Although the clinic stops taking new clients at 6 p.m., everyone who arrives before that time will be seen for an intake appointment and a 90-minute counseling session. Hence, therapists are scheduled to work until 8 p.m. All clients at the clinic are self-referred; however, they may learn of the service through family, friends, Internet searches, social media, walking by our office and seeing our electronic sign or from a social service, medical, or legal professional. There are several government funders and foundation funders that allow clients to be seen at no cost; the remainder of clients are assigned a fee based on a sliding scale from CAN$0 to $125 per hour. If people have insurance benefits they are encouraged to use them. No one is turned away based on an inability to pay.

To provide this level of service each week requires that we schedule five intake workers, 25 therapists, and one clinical director. Staffing is a mix of paid staff, interns, externs, and professionally qualified volunteers. Therapists must have graduate-level training.

The clients of our agency reflect the diversity of the Waterloo Region community. We see equal numbers of male and female clients; this is a contrast to our on-going counseling services in which we see disproportionately more female clients (Horton, et al., 2012). We also disproportionately see people who are living in poverty (Stalker, et al., 2015).

KW Counselling Services as a Training Facility

KWCS has a long history of providing training, internships, and externships to counseling professionals. In 1950, our founders expressed a fundamental and foundational direction for the newly established Family Service Bureau, which later would become KW Counselling Services. Our Letters Patent states KWCS' purpose is "To offer assistance to families disorganized by environmental or personality factors or other conditions for the purpose of creating or maintaining wholesome family life to promote a sound community life." In addition to a mandate to offer services to families, our founders also defined our purpose as "To encourage education and training for social work" (KWCS archival document, 1950).

In 1965, Alvis Stayt, the first executive director of the agency, was a key supporter in launching the area's first Master of Social Work (M.S.W.) program at an accredited Kitchener-Waterloo university (Bonesteel, 2000). KWCS's second executive director, Bernard Poirier, was one of the first graduates of this program (Bonesteel, 2000). For more than 50 years, the agency has offered graduate placements to students across Canada and is considered a preferred placement choice. Currently, KWCS provides approximately 50 placements a year. In addition to this, many new and qualifying professionals come to KWCS to gain additional experience and training through our externship program and/or through working at the Walk-In Counselling Clinic.

Methods of Training

Our interns typically come in cohorts starting at three different times of the year. They participate in six days of orientation which includes topics such as orientation to the agency, creating quality documentation, using an attachment theory-informed lens, working with depression and anxiety, woman abuse, anti-oppressive practice, suicidality, and making child protection reports. Before seeing their first clients, new interns shadow sessions and receive instruction in some of the key competencies and knowledge that KWCS considers to be base starting skills. Throughout their placements interns are encouraged to review their cases with the Walk-In Director during clinic hours, as well as during their scheduled supervision. Our interns can have ad hoc supervision at any time during the Walk-In Clinic. All interns have a scheduled hour of group supervision and one and a half hours of dyadic supervision every week. Additional supervision can be arranged if needed.

Key Knowledge and Competencies

KW Counselling Services Walk-In Counselling Clinic embodies a culture of learning. While many providing services are new to the profession, many others are "veterans" and the feeling about professional development at the clinic is that no one ever "arrives" at a place where they are done learning about single-session work. An exciting part of the learning every week is discussion between clinical staff members of cases, readings, and counseling techniques as they come and go from cases. Over time, we have found that there are certain skills and competencies new therapists should have a good understanding of before they can start to learn by doing. These key skills and competencies are:

- a non-anxious presence
- a single-session mindset
- a sense of comfort with the unknown
- unconditional positive regard
- tool kit items for common presenting issues
- brief solution-focused questioning
- understanding the importance of pacing, and
- understanding when to process and when to problem solve.

Generally speaking, these core competencies could be divided into three broad categories:

(1) *Philosophical stance.* A non-anxious presence, a single-session mindset, a sense of comfort with the unknown, and unconditional positive regard.
(2) *Specific clinical skills.* Tool kit items for common presenting issues and brief solution-focused questioning.
(3) *Practice wisdom.* Understanding the importance of pacing, and understanding when to process and when to problem solve.

Philosophical Stance

As an educator of new therapists, I try to engage in a parallel process that mirrors the counseling process itself (see Hoyt, 1991). While the downloading of specific knowledge is an important part of the learning process, more important and meaningful for our students tends to be a strengths-based and collaborative approach in which emerging clinicians are encouraged to be reflective of the transferrable experience they are bringing to the process. This is particularly so with respect to the philosophical stance that therapy uses. This conversation includes a talk about the importance of non-anxious presence, particularly noting that clients want a sense that they are not alarming or worrisome to their therapist. We have a discussion about how, for some clients, this is the single most clinically effective intervention we can offer. Students are encouraged to reflect deeply upon their self-talk – for example, the difference between the feelings and thoughts experienced telling oneself "I am just a student" versus "I am a student." Building on the discussions of non-anxious presence is a discussion about what it means to be comfortable walking into a session without knowing what is going to happen. I often speak with new therapists about the many times we have to simultaneously believe opposite truths to be good therapists; being prepared for given presenting issues while at the same time being prepared to throw the preparation out and follow the client's lead is one of these paradoxes. As one of our former students shared at the end of her placement: "Counseling at Walk-In means [to] pull out everything you know about a topic ... then hold it very loosely."

I always train new Walk-In therapists in having a single-session mindset. I share with them the words of one of our former interns regarding counseling at Walk-In: "You don't have to know where it's going. You just have to roll with it."

Other important training in how to prepare for walk-in single-session counseling comes from O'Hanlon and Weiner-Davis' (1989) list of elements of a single-session mindset which include items like normalizing rapid change as a part of the human experience, the lack of link between duration of concern and treatment length, the implicit messages we may be giving clients by our suggestion of how much therapy they need, and how therapists are more interested in therapy than are clients.

I also direct our trainees to Slive and Bobele's (2011) book, *When One Hour is All You Have*, and describe this as an excellent way to help prepare oneself for single-session work. In our training, we talk about Slive and Bobele's responses to the objection that single session is a "band aid." Similarly, *Capturing the Moment* (Hoyt & Talmon, 2014. p. 85) is a recommendation that gives an excellent foundation to the mindset required for single-session work.

Specific Clinical Skills

At KW Counselling Service's Walk-In Counselling Clinic the most common presenting problem is depression (Stalker, et al., 2012). We spend time talking specifically about single-session interventions for depression with our new therapists. One resource which I have found to be very useful in helping new practitioners feel equipped to talk about depression at Walk-In is Wehrenberg's (2010) *The 10 Best-Ever Depression Management Techniques.*

Other very common presenting problems include anxiety, relationships, stress, serious mental illness, work and school problems, parenting, conflict with the law, grief, abuse, coping with trauma, difficulty accessing community resources, poverty, anger, isolation, being new to Canada, addiction, and family and couples work. As part of the training for Walk-In, I encourage new therapists to develop a portfolio of worksheets, practice techniques, safety plans, psychoeducational material, and knowledge of community/online/written resources pertaining to our most common presenting problems. In our Walk-In hub room, we keep binders of these types of materials organized by topic and therapists are encouraged to spend time sharing resources with each other between sessions.

Although therapists at our clinic are diverse in the theoretical orientations with which they approach the work, Brief Solution-Focused Therapy is one of the more commonly practiced. For new therapists, it is easy to think of ways in which solution-focused questioning and practices can be applied to single-session work. Here are some questions I give as examples to therapists as often useful for SST:

- What will you notice if today's session is helpful?
- What have you tried so far?
- What have you tried that works sometimes?
- What would be the first sign that things are improving slightly?
- How have you coped with the burden of this problem?
- Why haven't things gotten worse?
- When is the problem less of a problem?
- What gives you hope that things can improve?
- On a scale of 1 to 10, where are you now with the problem?
- What would one point up the scale look like?
- The Miracle Question: Describe in detail a situation in which the problem has been totally resolved.
- What would be the first sign that the miracle had occurred? What would you notice?
- How have you been taking care of yourself while living with this problem?
- What have you learned about how to live with this problem?
- How did you have the strength/energy/resolve to cope with this problem?
- How did you do that? (after hearing about a positive action)
- What are some of the most clever/creative/unusual/brave things you've tried to deal with this problem?
- What works sometimes?
- When is the problem not a problem?
- (After "solution-oriented talk"): Tell me more about that . . .

Two books that I recommend to students as offering great overviews of SFBT are Ratner, George, and Iveson's (2013) *Solution Focused Brief Therapy: 100 Key Points and Techniques* and Bannink's (2010) *1001 Solution-Focused Questions*.

I also encourage therapists to listen for clues and do lots of check-ins about whether the client is looking to do problem solving or processing—or both. A helpful notion for discussing the difference is the question posed by Wilson and DuFrene (2009): "Is your client a math problem or a sunset?" The ways in which we interact with math problems and sunsets are practically and qualitatively very different.

Practice Wisdom

A quotation that I share with students on the day that they first see a client without a co-counselor present is: "Do not wait: the time will never be 'just right.' Start where you stand, and work with whatever tools you may have at your command and better tools will be found as you go along" (Hill, 2016).

Using the narrative therapy practice of honoring lived experience as insider knowledge, (Epston, 1999), I like to bring the learning of previous cohorts of new therapists into the training session. I often ask students at the end of their placements what advice they think would be most helpful for the next cohort of students and they learn how to practice SST, and ask their permission to share this advice. This is a list given by one such group:

- A lot of check-ins, before, during, and after
- Be comfortable with silence
- Just do it
- Language and posture matching
- Don't unpack everything
- Sincere, empathetic, curious, calm
- Rely on your basic counseling skills
- Validating
- Go slow but intentional
- Ask SFT questions
- Don't make assumptions
- Realistic expectations
- Talk with clients about daily planning and self-care
- Be comfortable leading and being led
- Ask after exceptions
- Have a tool kit

Summary

As an organization with a strong culture of learning and continuous quality improvement, our practices with training new single-session therapists are ever evolving, and each cohort of new therapists brings to the agency knowledge that both helps the agency grow and deliver more service to our community.

References

Bannink, F. (2010). 1001 *Solution-focused questions: Handbook for solution-focused interviewing.* New York: Norton.

Bonesteel, S. (2000). *The first hundred years ... halfway there.* C.E. McGee (Ed.). Waterloo, ON: Kitchener-Waterloo Counselling Services Inc.

Epston, D. (1999). The making of an alternative knowledge. In P. Moss & P. Butterworth (Eds.) *Narrative therapy and community work: a conference collection.* Adelaide, Australia: Dulwich Centre Publications.

Hill, N. (2016). Quoteland.com: Napoleon Hill quotes. Retrieved from www.quoteland.com/author/Napoleon-Hill-Quotes/641/.

Horton, S., Stalker, C.A., Cait, C., & Josling, L. (2012). Sustaining walk-in counselling services. *Healthcare Quarterly, 15*(3), 44–49.

Hoyt, M.F. (1991). Teaching and learning short-term psychotherapy within an HMO. In C.S. Austad & W.H. Berman (Eds.), *Psychotherapy in managed health care: The optimal use of time and resources* (pp. 98–107). Washington, DC: American Psychological Association.

Hoyt, M.F. & Talmon, M. (Eds.) (2014). *Capturing the moment: Single session therapy and walk-in services.* Bethel, CT: Crown House.

Letters Patent (1950). KW Counselling archival documents. Kitchener, ON: KW Counselling Services Inc.

O'Hanlon, B. & Weiner-Davis, M. (1989). *In search of solutions: A new direction in psychotherapy.* New York: Norton.

Ratner, H., George, E., & Iveson, C. (2012). *Solution-focused brief therapy: 100 key points and techniques.* New York: Routledge.

Slive, A. & Bobele, M. (Eds.) (2011). *When one hour is all you have: Effective therapy for walk-in clients.* Phoenix, AZ: Zeig, Tucker & Theisen.

Stalker, C.A., Horton, S., & Cait, C.A. (2012). Single-session therapy in a walk-in counselling clinic: a pilot study. *Journal of Systemic Therapies, 31*(1), 38–52.

Stalker, C.A., Riemer, M., Cait, C.A., Horton, S., Booton, J., Josling, L., Bedggood, J., & Zaczek, M. (2015). A comparison of walk-in counselling and the wait list model for delivering counselling services. *Journal of Mental Heal*th. Retrieved from http://scholars.wlu.ca/cgi/viewcontent.cgi?article=1015&context=scwk_faculty.

Wehrenberg, M. (2010). *The 10 best-ever depression management techniques: Understanding how your brain makes you depressed & what you can do to change it.* New York: Norton.

Wilson, K.G. & DuFrene, T. (2009). *Mindfulness for two: An acceptance and commitment therapy approach to mindfulness in psychotherapy.* Oakland, CA: New Harbinger.

23 Supervision and the Single-Session Therapist

Learnings from Ten Years of Practice

Sandy Harper-Jaques

In November 2004, the Mental Health Walk-In service (WI) at South Calgary Health Centre opened. At that time, people who lived on the south side of my city of Calgary, Canada traveled long distances to access mental-health care. This program was designed to improve access. I was the clinical supervisor of this walk-in single-session program from 2004 to 2014. Since it opened, it has been operated by Alberta Health Services, a publicly-funded healthcare organization. Clients do not pay a fee and there are no exclusion criteria. Therapists (nurses, psychologists, and social workers) are employed by the health service. This was an exciting opportunity. Implementation involved the "nuts and bolts" of service delivery and creation of ways to support therapists' skill development in the practice of walk-in single-session therapy.

In this chapter, I will offer a road map for supervision with single-session therapists. Ideas from the literature, my perspective on supervision relationships, examples of supervision activities in a single-session walk-in service, and examples of the experiential activities used during group supervision meetings with walk-in single-session therapists will be included. The emotional reactions of the therapist who works in a walk-in therapy service is simultaneously excitement and anxiety. These emotions arise from the unknown regarding "the whom," "the what," and "the why now" of the individuals, couples or families who choose to attend a walk-in session on a particular day. Added to that is the unknown pairing of the therapist with the client[1] and the unknown quality of the relationship that evolves during the session. And, like any therapeutic encounter, the therapist sometimes experiences clinical puzzles, ethical dilemmas, and situations that require social control. This type of work requires a clinician with knowledge about a variety of interventions, an understanding about a range of mental-health concerns, and therapeutic skills to guide the interview. Therapists who are successful in working in a single-session program also need a mindset that differs from the mindset when one is meeting a client for a course of therapy. The single-session mindset includes: viewing the session as a complete course of therapy, placing greater priority on the client's agenda, moving quickly to engage the client in a meaningful conversation, and seeking feedback from the client to insure the correct focus (Rycroft & Young, 2014; Slive & Bobele, 2011).

Supervision

Supervision is a crucial component of a therapist's journey from initial training through seasoned practice. At its best, supervision conversations invite clinicians to reflect on practice, promote skill development, and foster positive outcomes for clients (American Association for Marriage and Family Therapy, 2014). There are two main categories of supervisory activities. *Administrative supervision* involves review and discussion of productivity benchmarks and documentation. *Clinical supervision* "is a working alliance and on-going process between practitioners intended to enhance knowledge, skills and judgment; provide professional support and clinical development and improve client/patient outcomes" (Addiction and Mental Health Clinical Supervision Reference Group, 2013). Throughout this new venture, I was aware that the combined roles of administrative and clinical supervision might constrain my ability to create a process designed to enhance reflection and growth (Chang & Gaete, 2014).

Consultations were undertaken with the program manager and therapists in the program and over time we evolved a process intended to promote skill development and to enhance client care.

Like the client–therapist relationship, supervision is influenced by the context in which it occurs and the multiple roles of the supervisor and therapist. This program is situated in a publicly-funded health service; it is strengths-based and focused on working with clients to discover solutions. A major challenge in the role that I assumed was striking a balance between the needs of the organization to insure the provision of ethically sensitive therapy, the requirements of the therapists' licensing bodies, and the needs of the individual therapists in developing and enhancing skills (Storm, 1997). Hierarchy is an inescapable aspect of supervision; I needed to strike a balance between hierarchy and collaboration. Typically, supervisors are viewed as clinical experts. They are assigned responsibility, by the employing agency, to ensure quality client care and they are asked to provide feedback about a therapist's performance. Supervisors who are employed by agencies are generally expected to engage in supervision conversations with clinicians who are trained in a variety of treatment models. This situation challenges the supervisor to be multi-lingual (i.e., to be conversant with the basic premises of a variety of models) and very curious about the way a particular therapist thinks about his or her model. Karam, Blow, Sprenkle, and Davis (2015) suggested that it may be more useful for a supervisor to be enthusiastic about a variety of theories as they relate to practice rather than focusing on *a* theory. They also posited that is equally important to attend to common factors. Common factors are the techniques and therapeutic activities that promote change versus the ideas or techniques related to a particular model. Empirical evidence (Lambert & Bergin, 1994; Hubble, Duncan, & Miller, 1999; Sprenkle, Davis, & Lebow, 2009) suggests that positive client improvement is more likely to be associated with the common factors than with the use of a particular therapy model. The common factors include: the client–therapist alliance, helping clients to think differently in order to experience hope, the ability of the therapist to invite the client's trust and confidence in the therapist, and the client's readiness for change.

In many practice jurisdictions, therapists' licensing bodies and/or their employer require that the practitioner provide evidence-based treatment and many disciplines highlight the importance of self-reflection on the part of clinician. Supervision processes can enrich practice in both of these areas. When supervision is sanctioned and time set aside for reflection and discussion, one hopes that client outcomes are improved and therapist knowledge and skill are enhanced (Harper-Jaques & Houger-Limacher, 2009). "Good supervisors encourage their trainees [therapists] to take risks, try new ideas and techniques and learn by making mistakes" (Emerson, 1999, p. 21). As a supervisor, my goal is to create a safe environment where a new therapist is encouraged to take the risk of developing conceptual, perceptual, and executive skills and where a seasoned therapist can enhance and challenge his/her skills. I am also cognizant of the therapist's discipline and the codes of conduct and ethical guidelines for each discipline. My preferred outcome of this relationship is a therapist who has success in engaging with an individual, couple or family in a change-oriented process.

Assumptions

Supervisors, like therapists, need to reflect on their practice. Part of the self-reflection is awareness of the assumptions one makes about supervision. These assumptions will be informed by their education and training, life experience and worldview. There is a myriad of possible assumptions. Some of mine are:

- The therapist views supervision as helpful. In settings where clinical supervision is mandated, further discussions are necessary when the therapist does not agree with the requirement for supervision.
- Supervision is relational. The dialogue that takes place between the supervisor and the therapist provides opportunities to explore multiple realities; there is the potential to generate new ideas and understandings (Chang & Gaete, 2014).
- The supervisor assumes a stance of curiosity regarding the clinician's perspective. Each therapeutic encounter can evolve in a number of directions. A not-knowing stance on the part of the supervisor can be helpful in inviting the clinician to reflect on the choices to be made during a therapy session (Flemons, Green, & Rambo, 1996).
- The therapist–supervisor relationship is a collaborative, respectful endeavor guided by goals and expectations (Lee, 1999). The conversation should be a place where the clinicians feel safe to talk about both successes and dilemmas.
- Clinicians who feel safe are more likely to create a safe therapeutic environment for their clients (Harper-Jaques, 2002).

- The hierarchy is overt (Cook, 1997). It is talked about at the outset of the relationship and from time to time over the course of the relationship.
- Both the therapist and supervisor bring expertise to the supervisory relationship (Harper-Jaques & Houger-Limacher, 2009).
- It is useful to attend to the therapist's learning style (Carroll, 2010).
- The supervisor's role is to support the clinician's work with the client. In essence the supervisor's client is the therapist.

In addition to the assumptions listed above, clinical work in a single-session context requires the supervisor to attend to parameters that are a unique aspect of this work. In single-session work the entire course of therapy occurs in one session. The session is time limited. In the case of WI, the goal is to compete the course of therapy in an hour. The therapist and client engage quickly to focus on the most salient concern. The approach endeavors to determine the client's ideas about the problem and possible solutions and to determine the client's resources (Slive, McElheran, & Lawson, 2008; Campbell, 1999). The therapist matches the intervention to the client's readiness for change (Prochaska & DiClemente, 1982). The structure of the walk-in program (described in the following text) lent itself to the evolution of regular clinical discussions that incorporated both peer consultation and supervision.

Program Goals and Structure

When the WI program at South Calgary Health Centre opened, I was invested in ensuring its success. In each therapy session, I wanted the client to receive a response to his/her request. I also wanted the service to meet the goals that were set out by the organization in the business case (Calgary Health Region, 2004). The goals included: reducing the client's distress, diverting demand away from emergency rooms and physician offices, and delivering the service in a time-efficient manner. It was also important that there was consistent response to clients during each of the walk-in shifts. This included similar processes, length of session, client satisfaction, and clinical outcomes. The process and outcomes of the service were evaluated (Syverson, 2006; Harper-Jaques, McElheran, Slive, & Leahey, 2008; Harper-Jaques & Foucault, 2014). It is outside of the scope of this chapter to write about the outcomes—suffice to say that the outcome data pointed to distress reduction, client satisfaction, and sustained improvement.

The program structure at WI that was established in 2004 has remained the same throughout the time that the service has been open. Three therapists work each of the four-hour daily shifts; each week there are five shifts. Therapists use a variety of treatment models. These include solution-focused, narrative, cognitive-behavioral, and emotionally focused. Each of the therapists has a graduate degree in nursing, psychology, or social work. At times, graduate students join the team as part of a practicum placement. One of the three therapists is designated as the shift coordinator (SC) or the clinical lead. The other two therapists see clients who present while the SC provides clinical support through pre-session, intersession, and post-session consultation. The role of the SC rotates between the three therapists during subsequent shifts.

When clients arrive for service, they are asked to complete a brief set of questions in the waiting room. The questions are solution-oriented and strengths-based. The client's answers to the questions inform the SC and therapist about the presenting concern and the client's goal for the session. This assists in generating ideas about the possible directions that could be undertaken during the dialogue between the therapist and client. The session follows the Milan (Selvini-Palazzoli, Boscolo, Cecchin, & Prata, 1978) five-part interview format. The five parts are: pre-session; session; intersession; intervention; and post-session. The therapist always meets with the SC to consult after 30–45 minutes with the client. The physical environment of the WI provides opportunities for live observation, clinical consultation, and when clients provide consent, recording of sessions. The session structure and the physical environment foster a rich learning environment, multi-disciplinary dialogue and open space for multiple perspectives about clinical ideas. At the outset the clinicians and I established guidelines for interactions in the observation room. These guidelines were designed to promote an emotionally safe context for the therapists and students who worked in the program.

- The observer's job is to support the therapist meeting with the clients.
- Discussions among the observers are respectful of both the client and the therapist.
- Critical comments or judgments are discouraged.
- Questions asked about the therapeutic encounter are done in a manner that supports the therapist, that may question clinical decisions but do not question the therapist's personhood.

A Road Map for Supervision of Single-Session Walk-In Therapists

Single-session work is not every therapist's "cup of tea." Some therapists cannot move away from the need for an in-depth discussion of the client's past or a substantive identification of symptoms in order to arrive at a *DSM* (American Psychiatric Association, 2013) formulation. Still others struggle with a change in practice to quickly engage and intervene with a client; and some do not like the requirement, in this particular program, of consultation with another clinician before, during, and at the end of the session. For those who do survive and thrive in a single-session walk-in, there are a number of supervision activities that can support them. I will provide an in-depth discussion of group supervision; but first, I will offer a brief description of the other activities.

Therapist Engagement with Single-Session Work

Therapist engagement begins with recruitment. This stage must focus on the scope of practice for the single-session therapist. The posting is written to invite therapists who are interested in providing solution-oriented, strengths-based, and systems-leaning treatment to a variety of clients in an hour to apply. The recruitment interview includes a discussion of the practice. Some of the areas I am curious to learn about are:

- What are the therapist's ideas about the amount of client data that is required before an intervention can be offered?
- What are the therapist's beliefs about peer consultation and working with a team?
- How would the therapist balance the need for quick engagement with the need to attend to nuance and risk?

Orientation

During my years of practice, I have discovered that orientation is very important in fostering successful practice and promoting good client outcomes. I developed an orientation process that included theory and practical guidelines; and it was offered in various formats to accommodate the learning style of the new therapist. The components of the orientation are: a three-hour seminar about the theory and practice of single-session therapy in this program; required reading of two articles from a selected list of current literature; practice in completing the required documentation for the client's health record; and two observation shifts in WI. I also followed the formal orientation process with regular review of the therapist's documentation, informal discussions with the new therapist, and a check-in discussion with the therapist after he/she worked six shifts.

Ad-Hoc Individual Supervision Discussions

I have always had an open-door practice regarding my availability to the therapists I supervise, including while supervising WI. A therapist or a WI team member from one of the shifts could seek me out to discuss a particular presentation, a theme or trend that was occurring, or to problem-solve regarding the dynamics of a particular team.

Shift Coordinator Orientation

Therapists who worked on a regular basis[2] in WI were asked to train as a SC after working six to eight months. This role provides opportunity for the therapist to develop leadership skills in the areas of service coordination and in leading peer consultation discussions. The orientation includes completion of a learning module, participation in a three-hour seminar, and two shifts of supported training in WI.

Group Supervision

This rich clinical environment of collaboration and dialogue lent itself to establishing group supervision meetings. Group supervision is described as a process in which a group of clinicians and a supervisor meet to participate in the professional development of the clinicians (Addiction & Mental Health Clinical Supervision Reference Group, 2013). With the input from the program manager and the WI therapists, two-hour group supervision meetings co-evolved into a forum for the generation of new ideas and meanings through dialogue (Philp, Guy, & Lowe, 2007). Therapists offered their ideas and experience to co-create new ideas about clinical dilemmas and ethical puzzles. Scheduled four times per year, these meetings were a combination of supervision and peer consultation.[3]

The initial portion of each meeting provided time for updates about staff changes, new initiatives, or policy/procedure changes. Clinical practice was the focus of 60 to 90 minutes of the meeting. The clinical practice discussions mirrored the single-session practice setting. Like the pre-session or intersession consultations during the walk-in shift, clinical questions were posed and therapists were asked to discuss the questions and make recommendations. In each of the meetings, three or four questions/topics were discussed. Prior to these meetings, the program manager and therapists were invited to offer questions or ideas for discussion. Topics (discussed in the next section) were also selected to focus on themes that emerged from recent client presentations or specific complex situations. The topics were presented to the clinicians and they would self-select into small group "think tanks" to debate and discuss the topic or respond to a specific set of questions. The small group was expected to jot down ideas from the discussion and to share the summary with all of the therapists when the group reconvened. As the supervisor, I tried to foster a group dynamic in which all of the therapists had a voice and where generative dialogues could occur. The guidelines that were established for observation in WI were also a fundamental component of these meetings. I endeavored to flatten the hierarchy by maintaining a stance of curiosity, inviting and asking questions, and insuring that everyone who wanted to speak was able to do so. The notes from each of the peer consultation groups were collected, transcribed and distributed electronically to all of the WI therapists, students and the manager. Therapists' informal feedback indicated appreciation for the time to reflect on practice and to consult with peers. One survey on multidisciplinary cooperation was completed (Harper-Jaques, Foucault, & Leahey, 2008). The respondents reported a work environment where all disciplines were respected and had an equal voice. I offer some examples of the topics discussed in the next section.

Group Supervision and Clinical Development: Promoting Evidenced-Based Practice

In 2011 an unfunded longitudinal research project was undertaken with 126 adult clients who presented to WI and consented to participate in the study. Of those who consented, 98 completed all of the measures (49% male, 51% female). The researchers wanted to determine if the reduced distress previously reported by clients at the conclusion of the 60-minute single-session of therapy was maintained one month later. In addition, there was interest in adding to outcome studies about single-session walk-in services (see Hoyt & Talmon, 2014) and to obtain additional information in order to improve practice. As reported in Harper-Jaques and Foucault (2014), the findings included: high satisfaction with the service, lowered distress, and increased hope. A sub-set of the respondents was asked, “Is one session enough?” and 44% said “Yes.” This study was undertaken within the WI program; therapists were consulted about the least intrusive manner for collecting data and how the instruments might assist them with interactions with clients. Preliminary and final findings were shared with the therapists in both written and spoken formats; therapists discussed the findings during the group supervision meetings in 2013 and explored ways of modifying practice.

Some of the topics discussed were instilling hope, planning to meet goals, attending to the context of the service when meeting clients, promoting family involvement in walk-in, responding to clinical challenges and inviting reflection.

Instilling Hope

During the initial development of the research proposal my co-investigator (Darlene Foucault, 2012, personal communication) completed secondary data analysis on quantitative data that had been collected during previous evaluation projects. A subset of the data was pre-and post-session measures of distress and post measures of client satisfaction. Multivariate analyses of variance were performed on the subset to determine if there were differences in pre- and post-session levels of distress among clients with high versus low hope. Individuals with less hope reported higher distress levels before and after the session than individuals with more hope. In addition, the two groups differed on 15 of the 16 items on the pre-session questions. Low-hope individuals reported more negative symptoms such as suicidal ideation, less enjoyment, social isolation, more worries, and less personal agency. These findings are consistent with Snyder (2002), who found that individuals with low hope do not do as well in therapy, are more pessimistic, and have trouble pursuing goals and problem solving. The analysis provided rationale for our decision to include an instrument that would measure hope. We chose the *Snyder State Hope Scale* (Snyder, Sympson, Ybasco, Borders, Babyak, & Higgins, 1996). The scale is a self-report measure: respondents are asked about their current life events. Our research findings indicated that hope is an important element for clients to take with them when they leave single-session/walk-in. One peer consultation group was asked to "think outside of the box" about interventions, comments, and questions that have been offered or could be offered to walk-in clients that may instill hope. They reported the following ideas back to the team: highlighting strengths, talking about the "ripple effect" of taking small steps, offering commendations, telling the client that the problem they have is "treatable," and offering information about other people getting better.

Planning to Meet Goals

Campbell (1999) developed and used the *Problem Evaluation Summary* in a study of clients who presented for single-session therapy. This seven-item self-report instrument was used in the study at the WI program. Our results suggested that a therapeutic conversation in which the client and therapist were able to open space to consider new ideas was influential in the person's improvement one month after the session. The second peer consultation group was asked to focus on the construct of pathways (planning to meet goals). The same stem of questions as those for the discussion about hope was provided. One suggestion was the use of a series of questions that invited the client to "examine the evidence" about a certain way of thinking and to follow these questions with inquiry about options. Another suggestion was drawing from the client's own resources and asking them to talk about a time when they faced a big challenge and how they solved the problem. A third suggestion was to inquire what the client would say if a friend asked for advice about solving the problem.

Attending to the Context of the Service When Meeting Clients

Therapeutic conversations with clients take place in space and time and are influenced by the policies of the agency, the requirements of the therapist's licensing body, and the legislation in existence in the jurisdiction where the conversation takes place. The presentation of unaccompanied minors[4] to WI is a situation when all of these factors must be considered. During a meeting one of the peer consultations groups was asked to consider the following situation:

> A 13-year-old presented to Walk-In alone. Her school counselor told her about Walk-In and suggested she talk with someone. The teen's answers to questions about her own safety on the pre-session forms were worrisome to the therapist and SC. The group was asked to discuss how to proceed with this type of presentation. They were presented with two options; namely, the therapist sees the 13-year-old, explains the limits of confidentiality, determines the girl's ability to consent, and decides about parental involvement during the intersession break. Alternatively, the SC tells the teen that she cannot be seen alone and invites her to return with a parent or guardian.

This case example fostered an in-depth discussion among the therapists regarding minors' ability to provide consent for treatment. The practice in WI was guided by the Alberta Health Services' guidelines and Canadian case law. The discussion included the teen's ability to understand both the nature of and the consequence of providing consent. The therapists recommended asking the teen to explain what she was agreeing to and exploring other areas of her life where she made decisions. The conclusion to the question "What would you do?" like the conclusion of many clinically-focused questions, was, "It depends" because each presentation must be assessed on its own merit.

Promoting Family Involvement in Walk-in

Syverson's (2006) evaluation of WI had indicated low client satisfaction ratings regarding family involvement, despite the service being designed as a family-centered program. A follow-up evaluation (Foucault, Leahey, Harper-Jaques, & Southern, 2008) was completed to understand how clients wanted their family/friends involved in care. The implications of the findings were that clients placed great importance on family/friends actively participating in their care; family/friends likely require more information on the client's presenting problem and ways they can be supportive. The findings also supported the need for training for therapists and process changes to promote family-centered care.

Once again, group supervision was used as a forum to promote evidence-based practice and to invite the therapists to provide input to shape clinical practice. One of the outcomes of the discussions by the peer consultation groups was the addition of a question on the pre-session questionnaire. This question asked whether the identified client was accompanied to the healthcare center and, if so, whether that accompanying person would be involved in the session. By asking the question on the pre-session questionnaire, the client and his/her supports were informed that others could attend the session and they were given a few minutes to think about the options. When the therapist came to the crowded waiting room to meet the client, the client's privacy was protected in that the decision about who would attend the session was already made—the therapist did not have to jeopardize the client's privacy by discussing the options in front of strangers in the waiting room. A second change was increased training in family-focused interviews. A third effect of the group supervision was therapists' greater awareness of asking clients who were seen alone if they wanted written information about the presenting concern for a family member.

Responding to Clinical Challenges

It is not unusual for clients who are seeking help to respond, when ideas are offered, with "Yes . . . but." In a time-limited single-session walk-in this is a particularly challenging presentation. A small group was asked the following questions: (1) What interventions have worked with walk-in clients like this?; (2) What can the SC do to help?; and (3) How can the team support the therapist with this type of presentation? In response to the questions, the group wondered: (1) Was the client's goal clearly stated and was it heard by the therapist?; (2) Could the therapist comment on the interaction pattern that was occurring with the client and could the two of them explore the meaning of the pattern?; and (3) Is it possible that there is a mismatch between the therapist's readiness for the client to change and the client's readiness?

Inviting Reflection

One of the major challenges as a supervisor in providing supervision to a group of experienced, talented clinicians is creating opportunities or asking questions that create "ah-ha" moments where the individual or the clinical team stop to reflect on practice, where they ask questions about the "usual" processes, and where they look at the clinical work from a different angle. Practice in a busy walk-in single-session service with high client volumes can promote stereotyping of clients and move practice away from the unique story presented by each client. In some group supervision meetings, I created a different format and used role-play conversations to explore practice dilemmas; or, I found video examples of client–therapist interactions on a particular theme and used those as a starting point for discussion. Another time, I asked each of the therapists to come to the meeting and to be prepared to demonstrate a technique or strategy they would offer a client who presented with concerns about anxiety (at the time, anxiety was a frequent presenting concern). The technique was discussed along with indications and contraindications for its use. This fostered discussion about the conceptual framework of the clinician who presented the idea; and it fostered opportunities for others to talk about an alternative and equally valid framework.

Conclusion

In this chapter I have offered one way of structuring supervision for and with a group of skilled therapists. It was designed to promote review and reflection by the therapist, and to provide the funding organization some assurances about the quality of the services. Supervision is a vital component of single-session practice. In the past 25 years, single-session therapy and walk-in services have grown and expanded, and there have been a number of outcome studies suggesting that this is a useful component of mental-health treatment. An important next step is further dialogue and research about the practice of supervision and how it promotes therapist skill development and client outcomes in single-session therapy.

Notes

1 The term *client* refers to an individual, couple, or family.

2 Staffing of WI included therapists hired to work in the program as a regular part of their job; there were also therapists who were on-call and worked in WI to

replace someone on vacation, at an education event, or unable to work due to illness or family emergency.

3 Peer consultation is "an arrangement in which two or more practitioners come together to share information, discuss cases, seek feedback and receive support in a non-hierarchical format" (Addiction and Mental Health Clinical Supervision Reference Group, 2013, pp. 12–13).

4 In this context, an unaccompanied minor is a person under the age of 18 who presents seeking health services and is not accompanied by a parent or other legal guardian.

References

Addiction and Mental Health Clinical Supervision Reference Group. (2013). *Clinical supervision and practice supports for an integrated service delivery system: A guidance framework*. Edmonton, Alberta, Canada: Alberta Health Services.

American Association for Marriage and Family Therapy. (2014). *Approved supervisor designation: Standards handbook*. Washington, DC: Author.

American Psychiatric Association. (2013). *Diagnostic and statistical manual of psychiatric disorders* (4th ed., rev.). Arlington, VA: Author..

Calgary Health Region. (2004). *Business case—South Link Mental Health Growth*. Unpublished report. Calgary, Alberta, Canada: Calgary Health Region.

Campbell, A. (1999). Single session interventions: An example of clinical research in practice. *Australia and New Zealand Journal of Family Therapy, 20*(4), 183–194.

Carroll, M. (2010). Supervision: Critical reflection for transformational learning. *The Clinical Supervisor, 29*(1), 1–19.

Chang, J. & Gaete, J. (2014). IPS supervision as relationally responsive practice. In K. Tomm, K.S. St. George, D. Wulff, & T. Strong (Eds.), *Patterns in interpersonal interactions: Inviting relational understandings for therapeutic change* (pp. 187–209). New York: Routledge.

Cook, M. (1997). Systems-oriented supervision in an agency setting. In T.C. Todd & C.L. Storm (Eds.), *The complete systemic supervisor: Context, philosophy and pragmatics*. (pp. 112–124). Boston, MA: Allyn & Bacon.

Emerson, S. (1999). Power and pain: Unavoidable aspects of supervision? In R.E. Lee & S. Emerson. (Eds.), *The eclectic trainer* (pp. 13–21). Galena, IL: Geist & Russell.

Flemons, D.G., Green, S.K., & Rambo, A.H. (1996). Evaluating therapists' practices in a post-modern world: A discussion and a scheme. *Family Process, 35*, 43–56.

Foucault, D., Leahey, M., Harper-Jaques, S., & Southern, L. (2008). *Perceptions of family involvement in mental health care: Through the lens of clients and their families*. Presentation at Institute for Family-Centered Care Annual Conference, Calgary, Alberta, Canada.

Harper-Jaques, S. (2002). Supervision philosophy statement. Unpublished manuscript. Calgary, Alberta, Canada.

Harper-Jaques, S. & Foucault, D. (2014). Walk-in single session therapy: Client satisfaction and clinical outcomes. *Journal of Systemic Therapies, 33*(3), 29–49.

Harper-Jaques, S. & Houger-Limacher, L. (2009). Providing marriage and family therapy supervision in a multidisciplinary psychiatric setting: Contextual sensitivity as a cornerstone of supervision. *Journal of Systemic Therapies, 28*(3), 49–58.

Harper-Jaques, S., Foucault, D., & Leahey, M. (2008). *Collaboration and mutual respect: Key ingredients in delivering walk-in single session mental health therapy*. Poster presented at Collaborating for Patient-Centred Care-Moving it into Practice. Calgary, Alberta, Canada: Alberta Health Services-Calgary Region.

Harper-Jaques, S., McElheran, N., Slive, A., & Leahey, M. (2008). A comparison of two approaches to the delivery of walk-in single session mental health therapy. *Journal of Systemic Therapies, 27*(4), 40–53.

Hoyt, M.F. & Talmon, M. (2014). What the literature says: An annotated bibliography. In M.F. Hoyt & M. Talmon (Eds.), *Capturing the moment: Single session therapy and walk-in services* (pp. 487–516). Bethel, CT: Crown House.

Hubble, M.A., Duncan, B.L., & Miller, S. (1999). Directing attention that works. In M.A. Hubble, B.L. Duncan, & S. Miller (Eds.), *The heart and soul of change: What works in therapy* (pp. 407–447). Washington, DC: American Psychological Association.

Karam, E.A., Blow, A.J., Sprenkle, D.H., & Davis, S.D. (2015). Strengthening the systemic ties that bind: Integrating common factors into marriage and family therapy curricula. *Journal of Marital and Family Therapy, 41*(2), 136–149.

Lambert, M.J. & Bergin, A.E. (1994). The effectiveness of psychotherapy. In A.E. Bergin & S.L. Garfield (Eds.), *Handbook of psychotherapy and behavioral* change (4th ed.; pp. 143–189). New York: Wiley.

Lee, R.E. (1999). Getting started. In R.E. Lee & S. Emerson. (Eds.), *The eclectic trainer* (pp. 33–44). Galena, IL: Geist & Russell.

Philp, K., Guy, G. & Lowe, R. (2007). Social constructionist supervision or supervision as social construction? Some dilemmas. *Journal of Systemic Therapies, 26*(1), 51–62.

Prochaska, J.O. & DiClemente, C.C. (1982). *The transtheorectical approach: Towards a systemic eclectic framework.* Homewood, IL: Dow Jones Irwin.

Rycroft, P. & Young, J. (2014). Single session therapy in Australia: Learning from teaching. In M.F. Hoyt & M. Talmon (Eds.), *Capturing the moment: Single session therapy and walk-in services* (pp. 141–156.). Bethel, CT: Crown House Publishing.

Selvini-Palazzoli, M., Boscolo, L., Cecchin, G., & Prata, G. (1978). *Paradox and counterparadox: A new model in the therapy of the family in schizophrenic transaction.* New York. Jason Aronson.

Slive, A., & Bobele, M. (2011). Making a difference in fifty minutes: A framework for walk-in counseling. In A. Slive & M. Bobele (Eds.), *When one hour is all you have: Effective therapy for walk-in clients* (pp. 37–54). Phoenix, AZ: Zeig, Tucker, & Theisen.

Slive, A., McElheran, N., & Lawson, A. (2008). How brief does it get? Walk-in single session therapy. *Journal of Systemic Therapies, 27*(4), 5–22.

Snyder, C.R. (2002). Hope theory: Rainbows of the mind. *Psychological Inquiry, 13*, 249–275.

Snyder, C.R., Sympson, S.C., Ybasco, F.C., Borders, T.F., Babyak, M.A., & Higgins, R.L. (1996). Development and validation of the State Hope Scale. *Journal of Personality and Social Psychology, 70*(2), 321–335. Doi:10.1037/0022-3514.70.2.321.

Sprenkle, D.H., Davis, S., & Lebow, J. (2009). *Common factors in couple and family therapy: The overlooked foundation for effective practice.* New York. Guildford Press.

Storm, C.L. (1997). The blueprint for supervision relationship contracts. In T.C. Todd & C. L. Storm (Eds.), *The complete systemic supervisor* (pp. 272–282). Boston, MA: Allyn & Bacon.

Syverson, A. (2006). *Final report: South Calgary Health Centre—New mental health services evaluation.* Unpublished report. Calgary, Alberta, Canada: Calgary Health Region.

24 Capturing the Moment in Supervision

Pam Rycroft

> Supervision interrupts practice. It wakes us up to what we are doing. When we are alive to what is happening now, we wake up to *what is*, instead of falling asleep in the comfort stories of our clinical routines and daily practices.
>
> (Sheila Ryan, *Vital Practice*, 2004, p. 49)

There are many descriptions of supervision (with the above being a personal favorite), but no one universally accepted definition. What's more, it can look like a very different enterprise in different contexts. There are, however, many frameworks outlining the various functions and roles within supervision, with one of the most oft-quoted being Brigid Proctor's (2011) "normative, formative, and restorative" functions. These represent, respectively, accountability, professional development, and support, all of which are generally agreed to be essential to good clinical supervision. More recently, the process of experiential learning and reflection have been held as central to the provision of such functions. In this way, the work itself becomes the teacher, with the supervisor facilitating a process of reflecting on the past, in the present, in order to learn for the future. For this reason, I prefer to use a list of four functions: accountability, reflection, support, and education. That supervision is both a complex and a wondrous enterprise is reflected by Michael Carroll (2011, p. 27):

> Supervision is artistry and science, a way of being and a way of doing. It's about techniques and strategies, and relationships. It involves both development and evaluation, is about supporting and challenging, about fact and imagination, about truth and opinion, about symbol and sentence. It's a relationship, a learning partnership. It supports learning and unlearning. It meditates on the past in the present to prepare the future. It makes meaning and new meaning using reflection, curiosity and imagination. It involves dialogue and conversations about conversations. It deals with work and with the person doing the work. It thinks personally, relationally, systemically, internally and beyond. It banishes fear and shame and anything that threatens the fragile flower of learning. It takes stands

and can be dogmatic. It opens up and is flexible. It's an oasis, a valet service, a large mirror and a retreat. Now, tell me you can't get passionate about that?

Capturing Moments in Supervision

As Carroll (2011) said, supervision reflects on the past, in the present, for the future. Even though supervision is most often sequential and on-going, and will have a broad contractual agreement, every supervision session needs its own negotiated "contract" or shared agenda, so that both supervisor and supervisee can be attuned to the learning possibilities in the present moment. Otherwise supervision itself is in danger of falling asleep in its own "comfort stories."

And if supervision is to be anything more than "incidental," the more formative (or educational) function will require the supervisor to be alert to on-going learning edges or "pivot chord" moments (Rosenbaum, Hoyt, & Talmon, 1990; also see Talmon, 1990, pp. 38–41) in the on-going "story" of that particular supervisee's work that is brought to supervision. In other words, issues brought along to supervision will be both in-the-moment issues and on-going developmental learning opportunities and cornerstones. This presents a challenge to the supervisor, who needs to be alert and present to both current issues and on-going learning opportunities.

Of the many models of supervision, it is a rare find when an author takes a "close-up lens" and considers what constitutes the best use of the supervision "hour." Certainly there are some shared understandings of the qualities of good supervisors and good supervision, but little analysis (if any) of the within-session process that highlights what is likely to be most helpful. It is understandable (and desirable) that good supervision shouldn't necessarily be "prescribed" or manualized. Nevertheless, in the absence of a discussion of good process and relevant skills, trainee supervisors are left to learn their craft in the way most of us have had to do so up until recently: by modeling ourselves on our own experience as a supervisee—good, bad, or indifferent.

By negotiating what is important in the here-and-now in each supervision session, the supervisor can also be keeping an ear and an eye on repeating themes/issues over time. A risk inherent in on-going, regular supervision (as with our work with longer-term clients), is that we feel as though we have come to know our supervisees, their strengths, weaknesses, and foibles. The relationship is established—we love them; they love us. And we stop being fully present in the moment. We can become too comfortable in our knowledge of the "dance" between us, and cease to be surprised, challenged, disrupted, perturbed, uncomfortable, awake to possibilities that we hadn't seen before.

Of course, as soon as we try to "capture" a moment, it is gone. But if we are awake to the endless possibilities in the present accounting of our supervisees' "stories of their work," we have the privilege of witnessing the present and being part of the reflection process such that both supervisee and supervisor are actively learning for the future. I marvel at and feel very grateful for being paid to continue learning in this way: from—not only our own but from—our supervisees' work. This brings to mind a quote from the Phil Collins song "Son of Man," mentioned in an earlier chapter on SST training (Rycroft & Young, 2014, p. 140): "In learning you will teach, and in teaching you will learn."

At this point, it must be said that participants in the Bouverie Centre's Clinical Supervision Training course should be credited with pushing for a more particular outline or form to guide them through their early practice exercises in providing supervision to each other. It was a welcome challenge to be asked to articulate what is considered to be a productive and useful supervision hour, and to capture what can be generalized from this to guide those new to supervision. We began to talk to trainee supervisors about structuring conversations that are collaborative, invite reflection, that embrace both challenges and strengths, and that have a clear beginning, middle, and end.

The arts, as they so often do, provide us with some great analogies. Some have seen the three-act play providing a model for each therapy session (Ray & Keeney, 1993; Keeney & Keeney, 2014; Duvall, King, Mishna, & Chambon, n.d.) wherein the first act involves the backstory, the problem, the crisis; followed by space to reflect and discover things, hold the event up to the light, develop ideas, open to "aha" moments, turning points, looking at it in different ways. The third act then witnesses some summary and resolution, bringing it into the present, holding the new and considering ways to sustain it. As Keeney and Keeney (2014, p. 442) put it: "This orientation provides a 'single session mindset' which can be applied to any session, independent of whether the therapeutic offering is reified as single session therapy, long-term therapy, multiple single session therapy, or indeterminate-duration therapy."

There is also a musical analogy in the three-part sonata form. While the details of such a form may not be familiar, the music itself will be. You just have to think of Beethoven's Moonlight Sonata as a well-known example (easily available on YouTube). In the opening section, the "Exposition," the central theme in the work's main key is introduced. The second section, the "Development," "plays with" the theme, exploring harmonic and textural possibilities and developing variations; until the last section, the "Recapitulation," returns the thematic material to its original key and "resolves" any material from different keys by bringing that into the original key also. Some sonatas will also include a brief Introduction and/or a coda (a brief, connected but separate ending—see Rosenbaum & Bohart, 2007; Hoyt & Rosenbaum, Chapter 21 this volume).

The significance of both these analogies lies in the apparently simple idea of facilitating conversations (be they therapeutic or supervisory) with a clear beginning, a middle, and an end. What is implicit in the direction of the play, the conducting of the sonata, or the facilitating of the conversation is the dramatic development of themes leading to some resolution, which is both a return to the original, and new. In the case of supervision, it is particularly useful in its emphasis on a return to the central theme, and a bringing together and resolution of other themes or variations. The outcome of each "performance," of course, is a combination of the material, the performer, the audience, and the context in which the performance takes place.

Now, Back to SST . . .

While such three-part forms allow for a sense of the broad movement across time, more guidance and direction about the skills involved in "conducting" a good supervision interview were needed, so we looked back at the template that we had developed in our SST training (Rycroft & Young, 2014) to coach people through a single-session therapy. We had, like Moshe Talmon (personal communication, 1997; Talmon, 2014) resisted the idea of developing SST as a particular therapeutic model, and opted to see it instead as a service delivery framework (see Chapter 10). Training participants, however, had challenged us to articulate the way in which we applied the single-session principles to an actual therapy session. A broad process framework was developed, which brought particular skills, useful in (but not particular to) this approach, to the forefront. In training groups, we agree when we often hear, "but isn't this just good practice?"

The format we developed (see Figure 24.1) includes nine different sections, divided broadly into the three-part sonata-like form comprising three sections: (1) Exposition (context-setting; finding a focus or main theme; staying on track); (2) Development (where curiosity guides a growing understanding of the issues, of attempted solutions, of constraints and resources); and (3) Recapitulation (in which the therapist reflects her or his thoughts, ideas, possibilities, and hears back from the client, before considering "where from here").

While it is seen not as a model, but as a process outline, this had been generally welcomed by participants as providing broad guidelines for the conducting of a session, while allowing for (in fact encouraging!) their own particular therapeutic model and style. Translating this to the supervision context was not difficult, and proved to be just as useful in that particular training context. (Also see Hoyt [1991] for a discussion of parallel processes between therapy and supervision.) Many of the skills involved in conducting clinical SST are applicable in good supervision: developing a clear, shared agenda for here and now; listening for what is likely to be most helpful; interrupting respectfully as needed in order to stay on track; checking in with the client (or supervisee); moving between content and process, reflecting one's thoughts in ways that can be heard and integrated usefully.

And Now, to SSS . . .

Translating this to the supervision context was not difficult, and proved to be just as useful. Many of the skills involved in conducting clinical SST are just as applicable here: developing a clear, shared agenda for here-and-now; listening

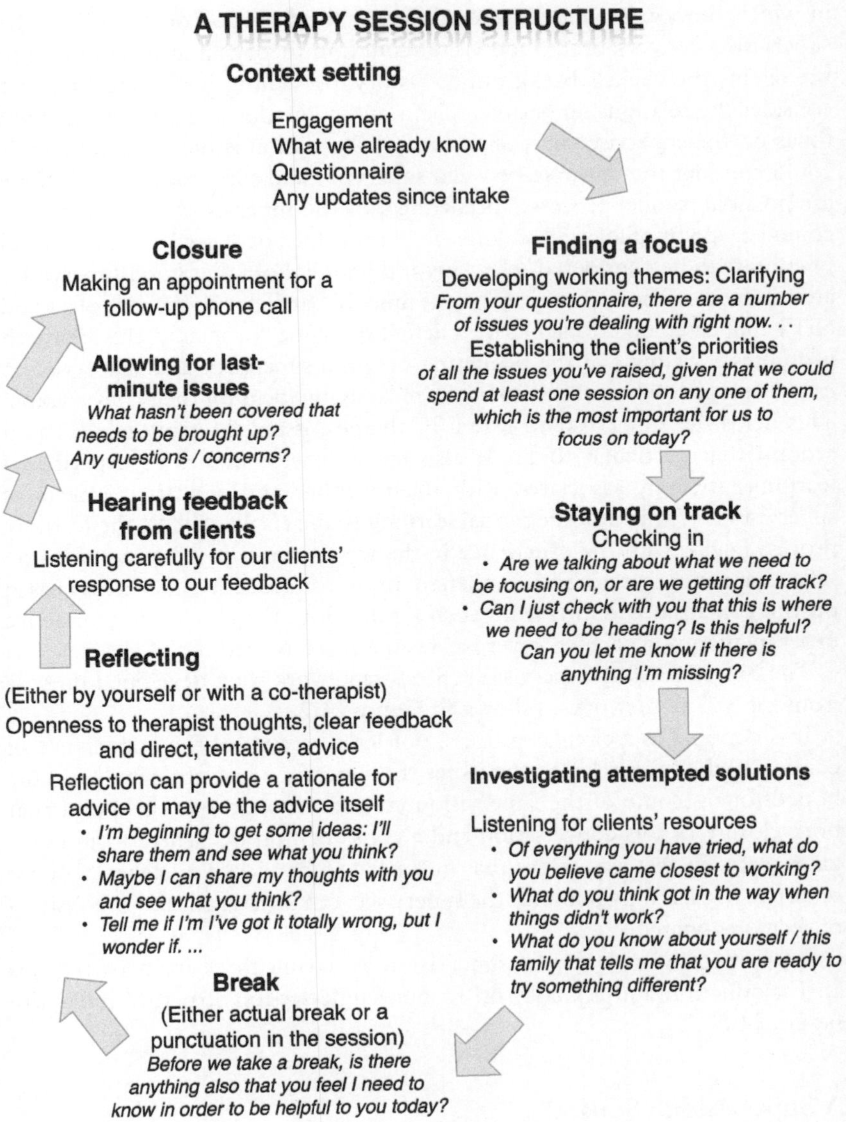

Figure 24.1 Therapy session structure

for what is likely to be most helpful; interrupting respectfully if needed, staying on track; checking in with the client (or supervisee); moving between content and process, reflecting one's thoughts in ways that can be heard and integrated usefully.

Such a process guideline also fitted well with the model of supervision which is included in the training: the Double Matrix (or Seven-Eyed) Model (Hawkins & Shohet, 2006). This model holds both the client/supervisee and the supervisee/supervisor matrices in its gaze, as well as the broader system in which both exist, allowing for different focal points (or "eyes") in the supervision conversation. Supervision could, in theory, limit its attention to the client, the client's background, history, presenting issues, etc. It could consider the relationship between client and counselor (supervisee); it could focus on the supervisee her- or himself, if the clinical issues resided there; it could consider the dynamic between supervisor and supervisee (e.g., if there are possible parallel processes occurring), or the supervisor's own responses could be a point of focus. And for each of these foci, or "eyes," there are issues of context to be considered. Hawkins and Shohet hold that good supervision attends to all of these possible foci over time. In parallel with the idea of a good SST being based on the client's own definition of the "problem," this approach promotes a dialogue at the beginning between supervisor and supervisee to establish exactly what is likely to be the most useful focus for their conversation. This helps the supervisor to listen for themes, issues, learning edges based around that particular focus. It also fits well with frames of experiential learning, strongly associated with the reflective and educative aspects of supervision. Within an experiential learning frame (Kolb, 1984), the learning process begins with the experience in the work, moves to a review based on reflection about that experience, then to more abstract conceptualization based on the conclusions drawn from such a reflection, then to a phase of active experimentation where whatever has been learned is tried out.

The Single-Session Supervision (SSS) framework then developed directly from the SST framework, as shown in Figure 24.2.

It is denoted as a circular process, not least because of the importance of coming back "full circle" to the issues the supervisee had presented, and the hoped-for outcome of the supervision conversation. It is at this point that both closure of this conversation and a consideration of "where from here" takes place. In this way, issues that may need to be picked up again, that are reflective of a learning point for the supervisee, can be flagged, and a re-visiting of them negotiated.

Superimposing the idea of supervision as having three main parts (plus an Introduction and a Coda) on to our single-session structure looks like Figure 24.3.

A Supervision "Sonata"

Below are some extracts from a single-session supervision. Vivian, the supervisor, had not met Melina, the supervisee, before. She had to establish an "in-the-moment'" contract in order to work with the issues that Melina brought along from her work in a multicultural counselling and support service, where she was working with an older man from the same cultural background as her own family. Melina had become angry with this client in a way that was out-of-character for her; he had walked out, and she was anticipating ringing him, fearing that he may not come back to counselling or may lodge a complaint.

Figure 24.2 A supervision session structure

Exposition

In this first meeting, the supervisor connects with the supervisee by hearing about her work, and what is important to her in her work. Then Vivian invites Melina to tell the "story" of the incident that is worrying her. The main issues are unraveled, and working themes are identified. At this point, Vivian consults

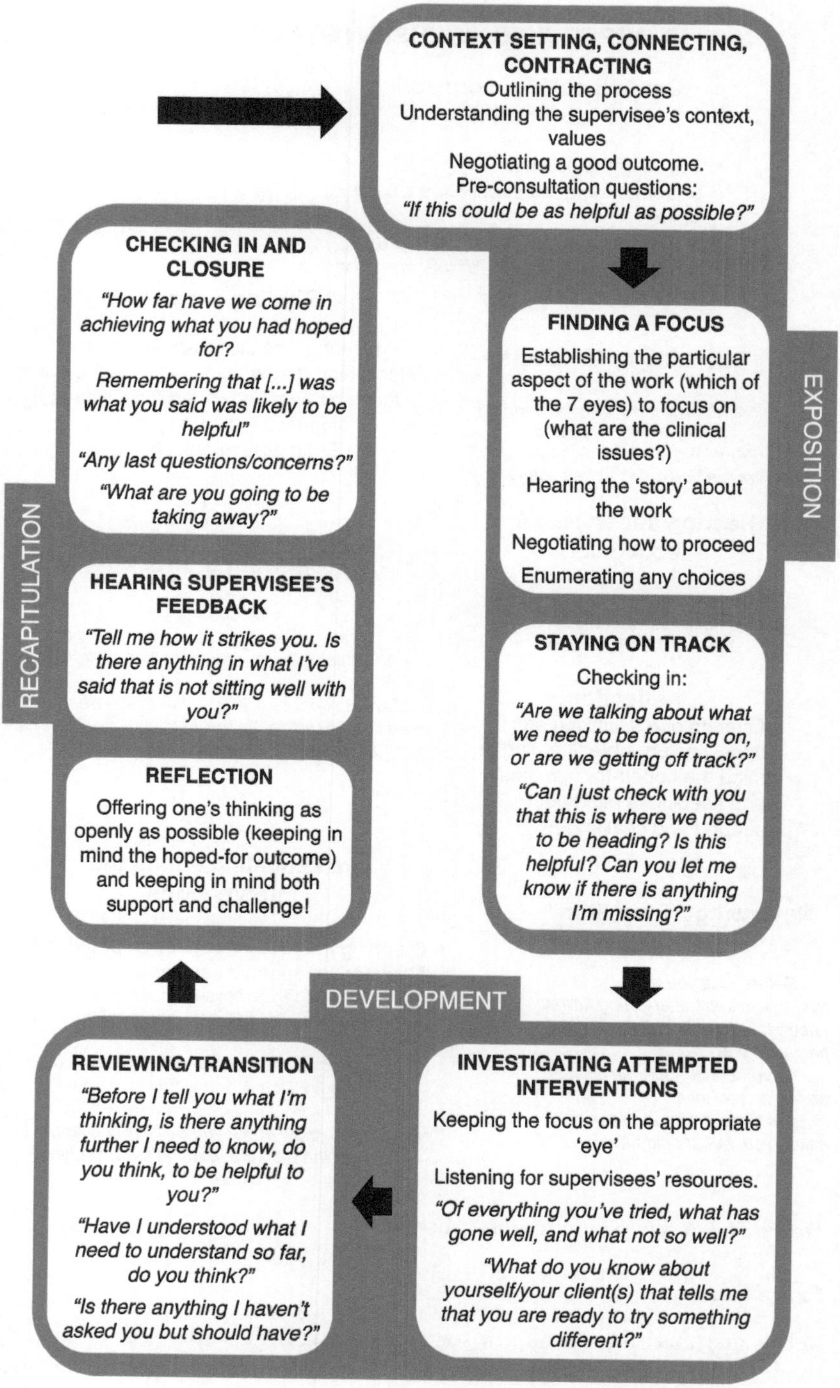

Figure 24.3 A supervision session structure: Including introduction and coda

her supervisee about what is most likely to be helpful in the here-and-now, and outlines some choices about how to proceed. It is here that supervisees might have a clear idea of which of the seven "eyes" or foci they want to concentrate on. They may also have ideas about particular processes that they have found useful. For example, if they work with families and/or complex systems, they may want to use figurines or draw diagrams to help make sense of their position and role in the work. This forms part of the here-and-now contracting process.

With our supervisor and supervisee, in what follows notice how:

- the "story" of the work is told, and the main theme and focus named
- an idea of what is likely to be helpful (the agenda) is developed
- the conversation moves between content and process (with the supervisor "checking-in"), and
- a joint decision is made about what to focus on and how to proceed.

Vivian: Melina, maybe we should start by your telling me what you know about this case, and then if you . . . can tell me what bothers you. Perhaps if you start by telling me what you think I should know.

Melina explains that she has a few "emotional dilemmas" in relation to her work with an elderly gentleman who had lost his wife to a heart attack some six months ago and was feeling anxious and displaced. Melina was helping him deal with his grief, and he disclosed to her that, as an outlet not long ago, he had gone on a holiday to a third-world country. He had met a young woman there, whom he was now interested in bringing into the country to become his partner. Then Melina heard that the woman was 20 years old (decades younger than her client).

Melina: For some reason I changed my whole perspective in working with him [when I heard this] . . . something got triggered in me emotionally.

Melina explained that she had begun to feel concern about her client's intentions. She explained that what she was grappling with was how to keep him engaged in working on issues of grief and loss, and not be so judgmental about his choice of partner. In addition to this, Melina was questioning whether she even wanted to work with this man. Again, she said: "When I heard this, it just triggered something in me."

Vivian: You mentioned an emotional dilemma. What was the dilemma?

Melina: The dilemma was that I felt that there was a very big age difference . . . almost 50 years age difference, and I felt that . . . that just did something for me in terms of the content of the relationship and, you know, issues around their sexual relationship and him being much older and . . . he has grandchildren, and I was wondering if they were close to her age . . .

Vivian: This might be hard for you so tell me if it feels like it's too difficult to talk about. Can you tell me what got triggered for you in the age difference? What was it about it that troubled you?

Melina: I think a part of it might be that in other areas of my work I've worked with young women who've been sexually abused, and . . . I don't know . . . I just had this image of this older man, and he was quite tall and quite big in physical size, and I just imagined in my mind that if she was a young woman, 20, and from an underdeveloped country, she might be smaller and thin-framed, and in terms of power and size . . . I just questioned the whole appropriateness: it could be his daughter, it could be his granddaughter, and . . .

Vivian: All of that makes sense, but now that you're looking back on it, and it seems like your concerns about checking out whether there was abuse, and whether there was exploitation—all of that seems like they are normal anxieties for anyone to have. Thinking back on it now, how would you approach those anxieties differently? How would you deal with it differently?

Melina: I think I'd deal with it differently in that I'd have to check in with my emotions about it's not my place to judge him, in terms of looking at whether their age is appropriate or not—that she is 20 years old and that's a legal age—it could be her free will. I know I shouldn't be looking at the whole context of where she came from and her reasons to come out here. I'd have to try to leave that aside and not be so judgmental and try to engage the client in just working with the original issues. So probably exploring a bit more about why he originally came to see me and not, you know, lead the session with my emotions.

Vivian: I've got a couple of ideas in my mind, Melina, and I want to run it past you to see what might be more helpful to you here, today. One is—we can look at the emotional issues for you and what that's about, and the other one is—we could look at strategies for how you might be aware of these issues and how you can bring these into the therapy session. Which one do you think would be more helpful for you?

Melina: Ummm . . . I think the idea of working more with the emotional issues fits better with me, and I was thinking that if I can become aware of some of those issues myself, as a person, as a therapist . . . then hopefully that won't get in the way of work with other clients with similar presenting issues.

Vivian: This might mean exploring you a bit more, and we've only recently kind of met as supervisor/supervisee. Do you feel confident that we can go to that place?

Melina: Can give it a try . . .

Vivian: You can give it a try . . . and you'll tell me, if it feels . . .

Melina: Yes.

Note that choices in terms of focus are outlined. Some supervisors, like some therapists, believe that the more time spent gathering information about the client's (or supervisee's) story, the more helpful we can be. But if we consult our supervisees, we can get to the "main themes" without needing lots of historical information. Here Vivian invites Melina to say "what you think I should know," and works with that. A main theme emerges: Melina's "emotional dilemma," which is deconstructed through the supervisor's questions. Note that the supervisor is conscious that Melina has raised an issue that is going to require some personal exploration (the "eye" is the supervisee herself), and she is careful to get informed consent to proceed ("This might mean exploring you a bit more, and we've only recently kind of met as supervisor/supervisee. Do you feel confident that we can go to that place?"). In terms of the SSS frame, Vivian has heard what is important to hear about the issues troubling the supervisee, established a main theme, offered some choices about how to proceed and what to focus on, and through that, developed a shared agenda.

Development

In this section of the conversation, the supervisor invites her supervisee to consider what may be evoking strong feelings for her, such that she had become angry with her client to the point where she worried that he may not return to counselling. This is where the initial presenting issue may develop into a number of themes, or a main theme with variations, and together supervisor and supervisee need to decide which is most important for now to pursue.

Notice how:

- the main themes are developed/opened up, to be better understood, via reflexive questioning
- other things that arise may be taken up and choices made about whether these constitute separate themes or just "variations"
- the supervisor continues to check in with the supervisee about process as well as about content, and
- the supervisee's resources are explored.

Vivian: Just coming back to your client . . . any of your personal relationships . . . in terms of your father, grandfather . . . do you think that any of that got triggered while you were working with him?

Melina: I suppose I . . . Yes . . . thinking a little bit about it, I put my father in his shoes, and thought: "How would I feel about it if my father had done something like that with a younger woman . . ."

Melina goes on to reflect on a number of parallels with her client: her mother had recently passed away and her father also went away to an underdeveloped country with some friends.

Melina: I suppose it's a bit close to home, and I got into thinking that: what if my father was to bring a young woman home and how would that feel for me, and I suppose it was very close to home . . .

Vivian: . . . pressing some buttons . . .

Melina: Yes . . . the idea of another woman taking the place of my mother, and particularly of that age, and I put myself in her shoes (and I'm not 20 by any means) but—yeah—I kind of put myself in their position and that triggered a lot of emotions.

Vivian: Now that you're making those connections, what do you think would help you to keep that separate?

Melina seems to be struggling to answer this.

Vivian: Let me help you a bit more . . . How do you take care of yourself . . . when you go through some grief and loss issues? Do you have some strategies for supports?

Melina speaks of a close network of good friends.

Vivian: So there were a few parallels for you between your client and your own situation . . .

Melina: Yeah . . .

Vivian: Did you know that before talking about it now?

Melina: No—to be honest—it just dawned on me . . .

Vivian: What's that like, making that connection?

Melina: (*thoughtful*) A little bit more . . . I can't say liberating, but I've been able to get a bit more insight . . . that I was probably projecting my own stuff with the client, and that's probably what I have to be aware of . . . issues that might be going on in my mind . . . not bringing them into the session with me.

Vivian: Okay. I want to come back to your nerve-wracking part. Just say what would help you not to . . . having done this once . . . what would you do next time to . . .

Melina: I think I'd still be cautious, Vivian . . .

Vivian: I'm thinking about the phone call . . .

Melina: Yes—the phone call still . . . I have this expectation on myself that I have to get it right, for some reason.

Vivian: Yep.

Melina pauses, and looks a little teary suddenly.

Vivian: Something's got triggered for you in getting it right . . . okay—let's stop there a moment, so you can breathe . . . take your time . . . (*after some moments*) . . . that obviously touched a painful spot for you, Melina.

Melina: Yes, a bit of a sensitive spot.

Vivian: I'm just wondering . . . because it happened at the point where you were talking about needing to get it right, Melina . . .

Melina: (*slight laugh*) You observed correctly . . .

Vivian: So . . . do you want to say a little bit—I'm emphasizing "a little bit"—about what that means for you?

Melina: Yeah, just a little bit . . .

Melina talks about her experience growing up in which, no matter what she did, it didn't feel good enough.

Melina: It was about getting it right, and that's probably why I felt so nervous, approaching the client again . . .

Vivian: Yeah.

Melina: . . . it's about getting it right . . .

In this section, a number of related themes are developed from Melina's original description of her "emotional dilemma": the connection between this client's story and her own family story (which emerges in answer to the question: "your personal relationships . . . in terms of your father, grandfather . . . do you think that any of that got triggered while you were working with him?"). Melina hadn't made the connection prior to this conversation, but it opened up for her an important reflection: "I was probably projecting my own stuff with the client, and that's probably what I have to be aware of . . . issues that might be going on in my mind . . . not bringing them into the session with me." As the conversation moves back to the client, and the need to make a follow-up phone call, a pivot chord moment arises when the supervisor becomes aware of the emotion behind her supervisee's comment that she puts an expectation on herself to always "get it right." Because this supervision session was being filmed (with Melina's consent, of course) for the purposes of a teaching demonstration, the supervisor requested that filming stop, to give Melina a moment to feel her feelings, and to make the choice that was right for herself—to take a break; to continue the conversation without filming; or to proceed. Melina made a clear decision that this seemed significant, and she was happy to proceed. (This constituted a sort of re-contracting, in light of the context and the supervisee's best interests.) Notice how Vivian is careful not to blur the boundary between supervision and therapy, by asking Melina: "Do you want to say a little bit—I'm emphasizing 'a little bit'—about what that means for you?" This encourages the supervisee to say what is important to say in order to make sense of her feelings, at the same time as keeping the focus clearly on the impact on her work: "It was about getting it right, and that's probably why I felt so nervous, approaching the client again . . ."

Recapitulation

In this final part of the supervision conversation, the supervisor may take some time to "think aloud" and reflect in front of her supervisee. Here, Vivian continues to use reflexive questions instead, because her supervisee is doing her own reflective work. Together they have made some progress in understanding the parallels between Melina's client and her own family, and why her client's relationship "pushed buttons" for her. The theme of "getting it right" was present in Melina's worrying about the phone call, but it was also likely to be an on-going theme in her work more generally. This is a good example of a single-session supervision which deals with the here-and-now while leaving the door open for further work.

Notice how:

- the supervisor comes back to the themes and reflects her thinking in relation to these and to the desired outcome for the conversation
- the supervisee responds to the supervisor's reflections
- the "contracting" around their relationship and the process of supervision continues throughout the conversation, and
- together, supervisor and supervisee consider where from here.

Vivian: When you leave this session and become your own supervisor, what will help you to say: "It's okay to make a mistake!"?

Melina: When I become my own supervisor?

Vivian: Yes—like when you're with a client, and you're thinking . . . you're supervising your own work . . . what will help you to say to yourself that it's okay to make a mistake?

Melina: Probably a similar process as what you're making me think about . . . that—I'm in a particular role, and I have particular duties I have to fulfill, and there will be gaps in between and I don't need to know everything. And I don't work alone; I work as part of a team . . . so I can use my other colleagues to talk things out with, get support from, and other resources inside my agency . . . or outside my agency if need be . . .

Vivian: One of the key issues in ethical practice is to do no harm. What do you know about yourself that will give you confidence that you won't do any harm?

Melina: . . . what I do know about myself is that I really love my work, and I'm very conscious of the ethics of duty of care; I like supporting my clients; I want to be there . . . I want to be in that process . . . just making sure they feel safe, that they feel trusting. I suppose that comes with time, but just checking in with them . . . and I'm very conscious of creating a positive environment where a positive process can begin.

Melina goes on to say that she doesn't know if she answered that correctly [!] *and Vivian picks up again on the theme of "getting it right." Melina becomes very thoughtful.*

Melina: I think I'm probably harsh on myself—I'm probably a worse critic than the reality of the situation is. But sometimes I find it hard to distinguish the line between my personal self and my professional self.

Vivian: Do you know when you step over from being kind of thoughtful and responsible and when you become too harsh on yourself? Can you tell the difference?

Melina: Yes—that's interesting—something I've noticed over the past few years . . . I've noticed a difference because I tend to disengage very quickly . . . I allow my emotions to flow a lot more easily . . . my negative emotions, that is . . . to become more transparent. And I'm aware when I do that. And I think the client or other people that I might be working with . . . I probably pose a dilemma for them . . .. "This is not like you—what's going on?" . . . and I am aware of that, and I have been trying to keep it contained . . .

Vivian: So can I ask your permission . . . whether that would be okay to come back to touch on that theme for you of "Getting Things Right"?

Melina: Yep . . .

Vivian: Has it felt all right today, talking about this?

Melina: Yes—I actually feel comfortable . . . it's been okay.

Vivian: So tell me—are you going away with some ideas about how you can support yourself better about not giving yourself such a hard time for not getting it right?

Melina: Um . . . Yeah—my ideas would probably be to not slog myself so much and share my experience and externalize my experiences of what I might be doing on the job. Or in a session or even just as part of my overall role in the agency. I think externalizing—not being so afraid of being criticized . . . Yeah, and that too is part of learning, and it's okay to get some feedback that maybe doesn't sit nicely with me, but—if it's true, I'm ready to hear that.

Vivian: . . . and if it doesn't feel comfortable, the feedback, would you let me know that it doesn't feel comfortable?

Melina: Yeah, I would. But I'd probably be more inclined again to try and explore that, as well. But I think I'm really confident in saying "this doesn't feel okay" or "it does feel okay."

Vivian: Good . . . because I also want to not have to be perfect—to sometimes get it wrong by you, and for me to learn from you.

Briefly, Melina worries again that she has got something a little wrong.

Vivian: No, no . . . I mean, in my supervising of you, I'd like to be able to sometimes get it wrong and for me to learn from you by you telling me "Hey—that wasn't so helpful!"

Melina: (*smiling*) Okay—that sounds nice.

Vivian: Okay?

Melina: Yep—thanks, Vivian.

Vivian has reflected on Melina's theme of "getting it right," which is a development of her original "emotional dilemma" in such a way that she has normalized the idea of sometimes getting it wrong, making a mistake. (In a part of the conversation not transcribed, they had together explored the difference between a mistake and an ethical breach.) Vivian is aware that Melina's understanding of this particular emotional trigger is quite new, and that she will probably need to keep processing this. The question: "When you leave this session and become your own supervisor, what will help you to say, 'It's okay to make a mistake!'?" initially throws Melina. Vivian is keen, though, for Melina to develop her skills in reflecting not only "in-the-moment" in supervision, but also "in-the-moment" in sessions with clients, so that she can exercise new choices when such a trigger occurs again. In this way, Vivian is replaying Melina's original theme about her emotional dilemma, her own critique of her judgmental attitude toward her client, at the same time as inviting her to hold that within a different frame—the idea that it is okay to sometimes get things wrong. She is also keeping in mind that this is likely to be an enduring challenge for Melina in her work, and she seeks permission to return to this theme. Notice how she continues to develop the contract with her supervisee by inviting reciprocal feedback: "in my supervising of you, I'd like to be able to sometimes get it wrong and for me to learn from you by you telling me 'Hey—that wasn't so helpful!'"—in this way, further normalizing the idea that we sometimes get it wrong, and need others' feedback.

Conclusion

Clinical supervision has only a recent history of "coming into its own" as a field of endeavor, of theorizing and research. While many different models of supervision have arisen, most highlight overarching tasks and functions within supervision, with very few offering the new supervisor clear guidelines on how to provide useful supervision conversations. Further, there is a common pressure that new supervisors exert upon themselves to "be the expert" and come up with answers to complex clinical questions. This can be particularly challenging when supervising practitioners who may be more experienced, or who were former peers.

This chapter attempts to convey that it is not clever solutions that supervisors need, but a clear process to help work together with supervisees to discover what is important for them to do their best work. So often in supervision there will be a particular challenge in the here-and-now as well as on-going themes that get played out in various ways in our work. For Melina, the immediate challenge was to understand what had evoked such a strong emotional response to her client, to understand and confront her reticence in making the follow-up phone call, and the broader theme for her about "getting it right."

The example in this chapter shows that, even in such brief encounters, on-going themes may be identified and explored; but a single-session framework is seen as useful in supervision not only in "incidental supervision" where there may only be one opportunity. In the case of regular, on-going supervision, it is also important to avoid getting too comfortable in our practice routines and our knowledge of our supervisees, such that we become deaf to the possibilities in the here-and-now of new and important discoveries.

The idea of each supervision session being complete in itself does not preclude the holding of on-going themes in the work, but it invites collaboration and ensures that the supervisee works toward whatever is important here and now. Just as every therapy should aim at being a new and a whole therapy (Yalom, 2002), so supervision should aim to be a new supervision every session, with the door left open. Given the range of possible tasks and functions within supervision, we need to consult our supervisees about what is most important for them and for their learning. Checking in throughout the supervision, and moving between content and process (talking about the talking; wondering about thoughts, etc.) helps us, as in single-session therapy, to evaluate the process as we go, and to share any dilemmas and choice points.

In fact, the same principles and skills used in SST are useful within supervision:

- establishing a clear, negotiated agenda (what is likely to be most useful here and now)
- hearing the "story" of the work
- checking in with the process, and moving between content and process
- using questions that invite reflection, and being transparent about our own thinking where helpful

- optimizing empowerment (being clear about choices, making them overt), and
- finishing well, while keeping the door open.

In its capacity to negotiate with clients what is likely to be most helpful here and now, in its need for the practitioner to be fully present to the possibilities that unfold in the conversation, in its openness to being the first and possibly the only contact, and in the skills which optimize those possibilities, SST provides a very useful framework for clinical supervision. Just as SST considers each therapy session a whole therapy, SSS is a microcosm of supervision, with a beginning (Exposition) which includes a contracted agreement about what to focus on and how; a middle (Development) section, where the main theme is further developed, and new themes and variations explored; and the final (Recapitulation) section, with a return to the main theme, progress reviewed and future steps anticipated.

References

Carroll, M. (2011). Supervision: A journey of lifelong learning. In R. Shohet (Ed.), *Supervision as transformation: A passion for learning* (pp. 14–28). London: Jessica Kingsley Publishers.

Duvall, J., King, E., Mishna, F., & Chambon, A. (n.d.). Research as re-telling: Capturing pivotal moments in therapy and training. The Brief & Narrative Therapy Network: www.brieftherapynetwork.com/articles.htm. Retrieved June 9, 2016.

Hawkins, P. & Shohet, R. (2006). *Supervision in the helping professions.* London: Open University Press/McGraw-Hill.

Hoyt, M.F. (1991). Teaching and learning short-term psychotherapy within an HMO. In C.S. Austad & W.H. Berman (Eds.), *Psychotherapy in managed health care: The optimal use of time and resources* (pp. 98–108). Washington, DC: American Psychological Association.

Keeney, H. & Keeney, B. (2014). Deconstructing therapy: Case study of a single session crisis intervention. In M.F. Hoyt & M. Talmon, (Eds.), *Capturing the moment: Single session therapy and walk-in services* (pp. 441–461). Bethel, CT: Crown House Publishing.

Kolb, D.A. (1984). *Experiential learning: Experience as the source of learning and development.* Englewood Cliffs, NJ: Prentice Hall.

Proctor, B. (2011). Training for the supervision alliance: attitude, skills and intention. In J.R. Cutcliffe, K. Hyrkäs, & J. Fowler (Eds.), *Routledge handbook of clinical supervision: Fundamental international themes.* Abingdon, Oxon: Routledge.

Ray, W.A. & Keeney, B. (1993). *Resource-focused therapy*. London: Karnac Books.

Rosenbaum, R. & Bohart, A.C. (2007). Psychotherapy: The art of experience. In S. Krippner, M. Bova, & L. Grey (Eds.), *Healing stories: The use of narrative in counseling and psychotherapy* (pp. 295–324). Charlottesville, VA: Puente Publications.

Rosenbaum, R., Hoyt, M.F., & Talmon, M. (1990). The challenge of single-session therapies: Creating pivotal moments. In R.A. Wells & V.J. Giannetti (Eds.), *The handbook of brief psychotherapies* (pp. 165–189). New York: Plenum Press.

Ryan, S. (2004). *Vital practice*. Portland, Dorset, UK: Sea Change UK.

Rycroft, P. & Young, J. (2014). Single session therapy in Australia: Learning from teaching. In M.F. Hoyt & M. Talmon (Eds.), *Capturing the moment: Single session therapy and walk-in services* (pp. 140–156). Bethel, CT: Crown House Publishing.

Talmon, M. (1990). *Single session therapy: Maximizing the effect of the first (and often only) therapeutic encounter*. San Francisco: Jossey-Bass.

Talmon, M. (2014). When less is more: Maximizing the effect of the first (and often only) therapeutic encounter. In M.F. Hoyt & M. Talmon (Eds.), *Capturing the moment: Single session therapy and walk-in services* (pp. 27–40). Bethel, CT: Crown House Publishing.

Yalom, I.D. (2002). *The gift of therapy: An open letter to a new generation of therapists and their patients*. New York: HarperCollins.

Section 5

Editors' Conclusion

25 Walk-In and By-Appointment Single-Sessions Now and In the Future

Michael F. Hoyt, Monte Bobele, Arnold Slive, Jeff Young, and Moshe Talmon

The contributors to this volume have provided a veritable cornucopia of information about the theory and practice, development and implementation, training and supervision, and utility and cost-effectiveness of walk-in and by-appointment single-session/one-at-a-time therapies with diverse populations. Clinical methods and administrative arrangements are described, research data are presented, and many touching human stories of hope and help are told.

We would first like to highlight a few themes; then consider some other issues; and then offer some ideas of what the future may hold.

Some SST/OAAT Themes

While each chapter is valuable for its unique perspectives and insights, there are a number of overarching themes that emerge.

Single-session therapy (SST) is distinguished by an intention to approach each therapeutic encounter as a complete-unto-itself, stand alone, "this is it" experience.

It is a way of maximizing the value for clients, many of whom decide not to return even if further sessions are available. SST is a "one-at-a-time" (OAAT) approach to providing services. The basic idea (or "mindset") is that the client and clinician, from the beginning, operate with the understanding/assumption that they may be having only one meeting, and that the one meeting may be sufficient. The contributors describe different service contexts and ways to follow up the session, but all agree SST is a transparent and deliberate agreement for the clinician and client to approach the session as if it may be the last—SST is not open-ended, could-have-been-more-but-stopped-after-only-one.

SST/OAAT is thus a service delivery model rather than a particular theoretical orientation.

An opportunity is provided for a person to have a meeting, visit, interview, or encounter with a mental-health professional. Different approaches, theories, and methods can be employed (e.g., solution-focused, cognitive-behavioral,

EMDR, family therapy, narrative, strategic-interactional, hypnotic, psychodynamic, many traditional healing practices); the "client" could be one person, a couple or family, or a group; the session could occur in a private-practice office, a clinic, or in an alternative setting (e.g., at someone's house or even in the street). SST/OAAT is a format or modality, not a specific method or theoretical orientation.

SST/OAAT is effective, efficient and responsive to client help seeking.

In addition to many qualitative, anecdotal reports, several chapters in this volume also present quantitative research evidence supporting the frequency and effectiveness of SST/OAAT approaches in responding to client help seeking:

In Chapter 1 (Editors' Introduction), we note that in the original Kaiser study (Talmon, 1990), a retrospective review of 200 patients who had de facto attended therapy for only one visit found that many of the patients had been very satisfied with their one-session experience and did not feel the need for continuing therapy. Talmon, et al. then prospectively saw a series of 58 outpatients, ages 8 to 80, with a wide range of diagnoses. Their basic findings were that (a) 34 of 58 (58.6%) of the patients elected to complete their therapy in one session even when more sessions were available; (b) more than 88% reported significant improvement in their original "presenting complaint" and more than 65% also reported "ripple" improvements in related areas of functioning; and (c) while not experimentally assigned to one session or longer, on follow-up there was no difference in satisfaction and outcome scores between those who chose to stop after one visit versus those who continued for more sessions;

In Chapter 2, Slive and Bobele summarize evidence demonstrating that the largest gains happen in the earliest sessions of therapy and that walk-in visits are consistently rated by clients as being very helpful, and go on to make the case that WI/SST is an efficient and desirable way of delivering mental-health services;

In Chapter 3, Jeff Young from the Bouverie Centre in Melbourne presents contact data that provided community health counselors with a compelling rationale for embracing a single-session approach. Forty-two percent of more than 115,000 clients attending community health counseling services over a three-year period, prior to SST implementation, attended only one session;

In Chapter 4, Karen Young reviews evaluation data that her Reach Out Centre for Kids (ROCK) organization accumulated on 352 SST clients across Ontario, Canada, and reports consistently positive results on a variety of outcome measures. Noting that a high level of therapeutic alliance was achieved in many SSTs, she calls for future research to examine the possible connection between alliance and positive outcomes in SSTs;

In Chapter 5, Janet Stewart, Nancy McElheran, and their colleagues at the Eastside Family Centre (EFC) in Calgary report that since 2012 they have aggregated data on more than 2600 unique clients, and they have found that 86.7% had reduced distress after a single session; they also report that 30% of their clients indicated they would have gone to a hospital emergency room had the EFC walk-in service not been available. They document a high level of patient satisfaction and note that it was those people with higher initial levels of distress and those who showed the most change that were most satisfied by their SST experiences;

In Chapter 18, Martin Söderquist provides an account of a SST pilot study of 88 Swedish couples in which 70% reported a better or much better situation and 75% reported satisfaction with the one session. Follow-up studies are underway;

In Chapter 6, Leslie Josling and Cheryl-Anne Cait at the KW Counseling Center in Kitchener-Waterloo, Ontario, Canada, report that in a study of walk-in clients, 79% of those who sought help for problems that made them unable to work communicated at four-month SST follow-up that they had been able to return to work; improvements were also found in ability to participate in usual family and community activities, and in fewer visits to the Emergency Room. In a second study, walk-in clients improved more rapidly and were subsequently less distressed compared to traditional service delivery clients. The authors highlight the value of such data when advocating for funding;

In Chapter 23, Sandy Harper-Jaques reviews her study with Darlene Foucault (2014) of 126 adult walk-in clients one month after they were seen at the South Calgary Health Centre. The main findings were high client satisfaction with the service, decreased distress, and increased hope. A sub-set of respondents were asked, "Is one session enough?" and 44% said "Yes";

In Chapter 7, Rachel Barbara-May, Paul Denborough, and Tess McGrane tell us about a study of 174 walk-in sessions conducted at Headspace, a youth mental-health service in Southern Melbourne, Australia. They found that 70% of clients had one visit, 20% two visits, and 10% had 3-plus visits. (Recent Australia-wide Headspace data indicated that about 50% of clients attended one to two sessions only—see Rickwood, Telford, Mazzer, Parker, Tanti, & McGorry, 2015.) The authors found that SST sessions were consistently rated highly by the participants in terms of client satisfaction and improved functioning;

In Chapter 16, Susan Levin, Adriana Gil-Wilkerson, and Sylvia Rapini De Yatim at the Houston Galveston Institute report that questionnaire responses from on-going and walk-in clients are highly favorable and essentially equivalent;

In Chapter 2, Bobele and Slive contrast walk-in services that provide an immediate response with traditional make-an-appointment-and-wait services that typically have several levels of bureaucracy before treatment actually begins, and ask:

> If you were a client, which of the above processes would you prefer? If you were an administrator of a mental-health service, would you be asking yourself about the comparative cost of these two forms of service delivery as well as the accessibility of your services and satisfaction of your clients? What if you learned that one session is the modal length of psychotherapy and that most single-session clients report high satisfaction and significant

improvement? Would you then begin to consider walk-in services as one element of your agency's offerings?

SST by walk-in is especially "user friendly." It is accessible and available when the client is ready.

According to Slive and Bobele in Chapter 2, "They seize the moment. They work. They are efficient." In Chapter 6, Josling and Cait quote one client's remarks about how important is was to "have someone there that day" and another saying, "if I couldn't have gotten in when I needed help I would have been overwhelmed and probably at the point of self-harm." In Chapter 14, Karen Story at the Bouverie Centre reports that approximately one-third of their Traumatic Brain Injury patients are seen for a single session; she also gives an account of the case of a family who, over several years, came for a total of 32 single sessions! They knew the "door was open" for more meetings, but they would only seek sessions one-at-a-time when they felt the need and were more willing to access services this way because they did not feel that attending a session would obligate them to continue on a regular basis.[1] Research indicates that perhaps 50% of clients will eventually return for another session. Battino [2014] refers to this as *Sequential Single Session Therapy*; and in Chapter 15 Bobele, et al. refer to this as *Serial Single-Session Therapy—SSST* in either usage.

SST/OAAT focuses on client hopes, goals, skills, competencies, and resources.

Due respect is given to the situation that troubles the client, but the therapeutic effort is toward highlighting whatever the client can do to cope and improve the situation. Consistent with well-known *common factors* theories (Lambert, 1992; Hubble, et al., 1999; Sprenkle, Davis, & Lebow, 2009; Wampold, 2001) that client contributions plus a positive therapeutic alliance, empathy, hope, and expectation (rather than specific therapist techniques and procedures) do the most to produce good outcomes, emphasis is given when possible to "solution talk" rather than "problem talk" (Furman & Ahola, 1992). For example, in Chapter 20, Brian Guthrie recounts having to face the terrible realities of post-earthquake Haiti with the realization that most of the accoutrements of his usual professional office-based practice were not available, and that humanity, love, and prayer (as well as normalization, reframing, and teaching stress-management techniques) were all tools to be used in his one-time meetings with disaster victims. Similarly, in Chapter 8, John Miller, Jason Platt, and Kevin Conroy portray incorporating Khmer (Cambodian) folkways into their SST fieldwork. In Chapter 10, Moshe Talmon (one of the originators of the SST approach) relates his personal journey from approaches that favor therapist knowledge, mastery, and power to ones that allow for more humbleness, flexibility, and trust.

SST is facilitated by having some guidelines to organize what occurs in the meeting.

Each case is considered unique: "We have always resisted the idea of developing 'one size fits all' solutions or any attempt to create a universal formula or protocol" (Talmon, 2014, p. 34). Nevertheless, some orienting principles can be helpful. In general, an alliance with the client is formed, an achievable goal for the session is co-negotiated and identified, various change strategies may be used, and discussion often helps clients figure out what their next practical steps may be vis-à-vis the problem that led them to seek consultation. In Chapter 11, Hoyt enumerates many questions that may be helpful at different phases of a session; in Chapter 4, Karen Young provides guidelines for walk-in sessions influenced by brief narrative therapy; in Chapter 5, Stewart and her colleagues outline a five-part sequential organization for walk-in therapy sessions at the EFC consistent with the Milan model for conducting a session (Boscolo, Cecchin, Hoffman, & Penn, 1987; also see McElheran, et al., 2014); in Chapter 24, Pam Rycroft delineates a SST and single-session supervision (SSS) structure that flows from Exposition to Development to Recapitulation; in Chapter 21, Hoyt and Bob Rosenbaum discuss ways to end sessions that can increase the likelihood of enduring positive results; in Chapter 17, Scot Cooper and his client "Ariane" illustrate the use of take-home documents intended to help reinforce and extend the work done during the session; and in Chapter 15, Bobele and his supervisees at Our Lake of the Lake University explicate an overall session structure that guides their WI/SST work.

SST is more likely to be effective when the therapist works in a culturally congruent way with the client.

Terry Soo-Hoo demonstrates, in Chapter 13, how attending to cultural sensitivities allows a quicker positive alliance to form, and draws upon the specific strengths and resources of particular cultural groups; it also helps to avoid asking the client to do something that would go against his or her personal-cultural values. One of the features of this volume is the portrayal of SST/OAAT work done in various cultural contexts, including in Canada (Chapters 4, 5, 6, 12, 17, 22, and 23), Australia (Chapters 3, 7, 14, and 24), Israel (Chapter 10), Haiti (Chapter 20), Sweden (Chapter 18), Cambodia (Chapter 8), and Mexico (Chapter 19), as well as in the United States (Chapters 2, 9, 11, 13, 15, 16, and 21). A previous volume (Hoyt & Talmon, 2014) also featured reports from the United States, Canada, Israel, Australia, England, Mexico, and China.

SST training and supervision involves teaching general good practice skills as well as the specifics of SST.

In Chapter 22, Joanna Bedggood outlines the training program for interns and new therapists at KW Counselling Services, highlighting the teaching of basic skills and core competencies. In Chapter 23, Sandy Harper-Jacques presents various supervision exercises, with case examples, developed over ten years at the South Calgary Health Centre. In Chapter 24, Pam Rycroft (also see Rycroft & Young, 2014) illustrates that there can occur in supervision a parallel process in which therapist–trainer, like client–therapist, rapidly form a working alliance, develop goals for the meeting, and discuss ways client-therapist skills can be applied meaningfully in a planned single session. Clinics that offer SST/OAAT often use a combination of individual and team/group formats for training and supervision—"collective wisdom" (to borrow the term Mary Weeks and Lori Zook-Stanley use in Chapter 9) allows for better teaching/modeling, discussion and support, and more clinical coverage.

SST/OAAT implementation takes time and a concerted effort.

While SST/OAAT makes great sense and has clear scientific evidence, several authors note difficulties in getting adequate clinical and administrative support. In Chapter 10, Talmon acknowledges some of the challenges facing a clinician wanting to shift perspectives toward greater client empowerment. In Chapter 2, Slive and Bobele observe that the mental-heath field is still in the process of catching up with the fact that "no appointment necessary" walk-in services have become a part of everyday life; in Slive and Bobele (2014) they provide a veritable primer of practical strategies for implementing such services. In Chapter 3, Jeff Young (also see Young, et al., 2014) recalls that his center had to do their SST implementation twice and remarks on the need to keep SST alive with on-going activities such as evaluation, research and supervision as well as policy and core practices, especially if key supporters of the SST approach leave the organization. His implementation strategies (as well as those described in Slive and Bobele, 2011, 2014) would be useful for both walk-in and by-appointment SSTs. In Chapter 7, Rachel Barbara-May, et al. also explain that their initial attempt at setting up SST practice did not work; two years later they tried again, with success, by directly involving clinicians and dedicating time. Martin Söderquist in Chapter 18 and Mary Weeks and Lori Zook-Stanley in Chapter 9 lament that monies for formal research unfortunately are still often lacking. In Chapter 6, Leslie Josling and Cheryl-Anne Cait assert that further research can both improve clinical practices and provide evidence of SST/OAAT effectiveness and cost-savings to help advocates seeking appropriate funding for these valuable services.

Some Other Issues to Consider

Is SST/OAAT only for the poor and disadvantaged?

While there are obvious economic (and other) temptations for therapists to do long-term rather than brief (including single-session) therapy (see Hoyt, 2009a, pp. 6–7), it is important to remember that our primary duty is to serve clients, including those who are traditionally disadvantaged and underserved. SST is not a panacea, but when included as part of a range of services, walk-in (and by-appointment) SSTs can meet immediate needs and also help make more resources available for clients truly needing them. SST is essentially "good practice" (Rycroft & Young, 2014, p. 156) that is client-driven—it "captures the moment" as it acknowledges and works with clients' natural seeking-help-when-I'm-ready behavior. This may be especially helpful in oversubscribed public clinics, but many people of all socioeconomic strata would prefer effective and efficient help if they knew it was available (Huffington Post, 2016).

Deciding when to support clients' views and when to offer other perspectives. The various authors in this volume have emphasized, in different ways, the importance of identifying and supporting clients' own problem-solving abilities and resources. There are strong resonances with the Collaborative Therapy idea that "the client is the expert" (Anderson and Goolishian, 1992), the Ericksonian concepts of "the answer within" (Lankton and Lankton, 1983) and "utilization" (Short, Erickson, & Klein, 2005); as well as with the narrative therapy ethic that "The person is not the problem; the problem is the problem" (White & Epston, 1990) and the solution-focused therapy (de Shazer, 1988) assumption that clients have the resources, sometimes with skillful facilitation, to solve their problems. There are times, however, when a clinician may have some special expertise based on his or her training and experience that would benefit the client (e.g., knowledge of effective treatments). This can be a fine line.[2] The authors contributing to this volume largely challenge the traditional hierarchy of "expert professional/supplicant patient." There is no automatic assumption that there will be more therapy later, so SST/OAAT thinking invites clinicians to ask themselves: "What would I want to say and do with this person if we never meet again?" Approaches are primarily based on a presupposition of client competence, with the therapist endeavoring to create a context or process that elicits the client's positive contribution. Learning from the client and the need for clinical-cultural sensitivity is also emphasized: "The world of therapy and the clients we serve globally will greatly benefit from our efforts to promote genuine two-way exchanges of knowledge and healing traditions" (Miller, 2014, p. 212).

SST/OAAT: Likely Future Trends

More Research

Which clients most benefit from SST/OAAT? Who may not benefit? What are the advantages of treating each session as one-at-a-time versus planning multiple sessions? What is the role of the therapeutic alliance? What adjustments should be made to nurture it mid-session? More documentation of cost-benefit (as well as reduced human suffering); the potential savings from early interventions and more accessible services will help funding for both research and additional services.

Although research follow-ups were part of the study reported by Talmon (1990), and have also been used regularly at the Bouverie Centre (see Boyhan, 1996; Young, Rycroft, & Weir, 2014), routine post-therapy data collection is not part of most WI/SST clinical work—just as follow-ups generally are not part of other clinical approaches. Slive and Bobele detail in Chapter 2 several factors that inhibit routine follow-up evaluations with WI/SST clients:

the high volume of clients, difficulties contacting people and getting replies, avoiding dilution of the focus of the one session, not wanting to convey a message that the therapists missed something important, or that there were special liabilities (e.g., that something was "missed" because of the brevity of therapy). It is important for us to recognize that "Sometimes a process will be set in motion or amplified, but not completely resolved, during a session or course of treatment – both the therapist and the patient may need to live with a certain amount of suspense" (Hoyt, 2000, p. 248). Research follow-ups are of primary interest to administrators and researchers, not the clients, although some clients also may like hearing from "the clinic" and some clinicians may find it heartening to receive reports of all the good that has resulted from one therapeutic encounter. (As Talmon [1990] reported, pulling the charts and contacting 200 clinic patients who had been seen only once was a step that led toward their prospective SST study.) Josling and Cait propose in Chapter 6 that research data might be helpful in advocating for more much-needed funding, but some support will need to be already available to do the research, and care will have to be exercised to make sure that any follow-ups are done in a way that does not disrupt the integrity of SST/OAAT approaches.

More Services

Responding to natural help-seeking patterns and supportive research data, clinicians, program administrators, policy makers, and consumers should all want, and strongly advocate for, more SST/OAAT availability. Places that are doing walk-in and by-appointment SST/OAAT work sometimes employ paid staff; some universities and training centers use students and interns; some places use mental-health professionals who volunteer their time; some use a combination of some or all of these staffing options. While there is usually not much "down" time, when they are waiting for clients they can be doing group supervision, discussing cases, catching up with charting, etc. Walk-in services are expanding rapidly and we expect that they will continue to do so.

WI/SST in primary-care clinics is another emerging opportunity (see Collaborative Family Healthcare Association, www.cfha.net; Hoyt, 2009b; McDaniel, Doherty, & Hepworth, 2014; Rosenberg & McDaniel, 2014; Ruddy, Borrensen, & Gunn, 2008). Co-location of physical and mental-health services at medical stations is a natural fit, puts therapists where the action is, and patients will often avail themselves of such convenient services (Cummings & O'Donohue, 2008).

More Use of Modern Technology

Consistent with our "instant society" ethos and the popularity of social media and the Internet, we anticipate the development of more "click-ins" (computer-based) and "call-ins" (telephone-based) as well as more "walk-ins" (bricks-and-mortar clinics and offices, often placed in convenient locations such as shopping centers). Similarly, distance learning and clinical supervision over the Internet (e.g., using Skype or FaceTime) will continue to grow, for both SST/OAAT and other therapeutic approaches—along with concomitant issues of confidentiality and jurisdiction.

One at a Time: Until Next Time

Practitioners and researchers understand that when given a choice, many clients (and therapists) will elect to have a single session of therapy and will report that the one meeting was helpful and sufficient—and that clients can return for an additional session (or sessions) as needed. The basic idea of SST/OAAT is that we should endeavor to make the most of each session and that we should set out with the expectation that a single session could be a complete therapy.

A natural aspect of developing a field of knowledge and practice is to continue the discussion and embrace the debate over how to describe and implement the enterprise. We invite readers of this volume to use what they already knew and what they have discovered here to promote walk-in and by-appointment single-session/one-at-a-time therapy. We hope their explorations will lead them to contribute further ideas and inspirations.

Notes

1 This off-putting "once-you-start-you-can't-stop" concern is sometimes referred to as the "Flypaper Model": once you land, you're stuck!
2 As noted and illustrated in several chapters, there are also times when mental-health professionals' mandates regarding assessing and preventing possible abuse, violence, and suicidality/homocidality may require special attention and necessitate a change in the focus of a session.

References

Anderson, H. & Goolishian, H. (1992). The client is the expert: A not-knowing approach to therapy. In S. McNamee & K.J. Gergen (Eds.), *Therapy as social construction* (pp. 25–39). Newbury Park, CA: Sage.

Battino, R. (2014). Expectation: The essence of very brief therapy. In M.F. Hoyt & Talmon (Eds.), *Capturing the moment: Single session therapy and walk-in services* (pp. 393–406). Bethel, CT: Crown House Publishing.

Boscolo, L., Cecchin, G., Hoffman, L., & Penn, P. (1987). *Milan systemic family therapy: Conversations in theory and practice.* New York: Basic Books.

Boyhan, P. (1996). Clients' perceptions of single session consultations as an option to waiting for family therapy. *Australian and New Zealand Journal of Family Therapy*, *17*(2), 85–96.

Cummings, N.A. & O'Donohue, W.T. (2008). *Eleven blunders that cripple psychotherapy in America: A remedial unblundering.* New York: Routledge (Taylor & Francis).

de Shazer, S. (1988). *Clues: Investigating solutions in brief therapy.* New York: Norton.

Furman, B. & Ahola, T. (1992). *Solution talk: Hosting therapeutic conversations.* New York: Norton.

Harper-Jaques, S. & Foucault, D. (2014). Walk-in single session therapy: Client satisfaction and clinical outcomes. *Journal of Systemic Therapies, 33*(3), 29–49.

Hoyt, M.F. (2000). The last session in brief therapy: Why and how to say "when." In *Some stories are better than others: Doing what works in brief therapy and managed care* (pp. 237–261). Philadelphia, PA: Brunner-Mazel.

Hoyt, M.F. (2009a). *Brief psychotherapies: Principles and practices.* Phoenix, AZ: Zeig, Tucker, & Theisen.

Hoyt, M.F. (2009b) Psychotherapy in organized healthcare. In *Brief psychotherapies: Principles and practices* (pp. 97–107). Phoenix, AZ: Zeig, Tucker & Theisen.

Hoyt, M.F. & Talmon, M. (2014). The temporal structure of brief therapy: Some questions often associated with different phases of sessions and treatments. In M.F. Hoyt & M. Talmon (Eds.), *Capturing the moment: Single session therapy and walk-in services* (pp. 517–522). Bethel, CT: Crown House Publishing.

Hubble, M.A., Duncan, B.L., & Miller, S.D. (Eds.) (1999). *The heart and soul of change: What works in therapy.* Washington, DC: APA Books.

Huffington Post. (2016, August 30). Sometimes just one session of therapy can be enough. Retrieved online September 11, 2016.

Lambert, M.J. (1992). Psychotherapy outcome research: Implications for integrative and eclectic therapists. In J.C. Norcross & M.R. Goldfried (Eds.), *Handbook of psychotherapy integration* (pp. 94–129). New York: Basic Books.

Lankton, S.R. & Lankton, C. (1983). *The answer within: A clinical framework for Ericksonian hypnotherapy.* New York: Brunner/Mazel.

McDaniel, S.H., Doherty, W.J., & Hepworth, J. (2014). *Medical family therapy and integrated care* (2nd ed.). Washington, DC: APA Books.

McElheran, N., Stewart, J., Soenen, D., Newman, J., & MacLaurin B. (2014). Walk-in single session therapy at the Eastside Family Centre. In M.F. Hoyt & M. Talmon (Eds.), *Capturing the moment: Single session therapy and walk-in services* (pp. 177–194). Bethel, CT: Crown House Publishing.

Miller, J.K. (2014). Single session therapy in China. In M.F. Hoyt & M. Talmon (Eds.), *Capturing the moment: Single session therapy and walk-in services* (pp. 195–214). Bethel, CT: Crown House Publishing.

Rickwood, D., Telford, R., Mazzer, K., Parker, A., Tanti, C., & McGorry, P. (2015). The services provided to young people by Headspace centres in Australia. *Medical Journal of Australia, 202*(10), 533–537.

Rosenberg, T. & McDaniel, S.H. (2014). Single session medical family therapy and the patient-centered medical home. In M.F. Hoyt & M. Talmon (Eds.), *Capturing the moment: Single session therapy and walk-in services* (pp. 349–362). Bethel, CT: Crown House Publishing.

Ruddy, N.B., Borrensen, D.A., & Gunn, Jr., W.B. (2008). *The collaborative psychotherapist: Creating reciprocal relationships with medical professionals.* Washington, DC: APA Books.

Rycroft, P., & Young, J. (2014). SST in Australia: Learning from teaching. In M.F. Hoyt & M. Talmon (Eds.), *Capturing the moment: Single session therapy and walk-in services* (pp. 141–156). Bethel, CT: Crown House Publishing.

Short, D., Erickson, B.A., & Klein, R.E. (2005). *Hope and resiliency: Understanding the psychotherapeutic strategies of Milton H. Erickson, M.D.* Norwalk, CT: Crown House Publishing.

Slive, A. & Bobele, M. (Eds.) (2011). *When one hour is all you have: Effective therapy for walk-in clients.* Phoenix, AZ: Zeig, Tucker, & Theisen.

Slive, A. & Bobele, M. (2014). Walk-in single session therapy: Accessible mental health services. In M.F. Hoyt & M. Talmon (Eds.), *Capturing the moment: Single session therapy and walk-in services* (pp. 73–94). Bethel, CT: Crown House Publishing.

Sprenkle, D.H., Davis, S.D., & Lebow, J.L. (2009). *Common factors in couple and family therapy: The overlooked foundation for effective practice.* New York: Guilford Press.

Talmon, M. (1990). *Single-session therapy: Maximizing the effect of the first (and often only) therapeutic encounter.* San Francisco: Jossey-Bass.

Talmon, M. (2014). When less is more: Maximizing the effect of the first (and often only) therapeutic encounter. In M.F. Hoyt & M. Talmon (Eds.), *Capturing the moment: Single session therapy and walk-in services* (pp. 27–40). Bethel, CT: Crown House Publishing.

Wampold, B.E. (2001). *The great psychotherapy debate: Models, methods and findings.* Mahwah, NJ: Lawrence Erlbaum Associates.

White, M., & Epston, D. (1990). *Narrative means to therapeutic ends.* New York: Norton.

Young, J., Rycroft, P., & Weir, S. (2014). Implementing single session therapy: Practical wisdoms from Down Under. In M.F. Hoyt & M. Talmon (Eds.), *Capturing the moment: Single session therapy and walk-in services* (pp. 121–140). Bethel, CT: Crown House Publishing.

Index

Note: Page numbers in *italics* refer to figures.